THE RULE BOOK

"All things whatsoever ye would that men should do to you, do ye even so to them."—**Golden Rule**

THE RULE BOOK

Stephen M. Kirschner
Barry J. Pavelec
and
Jeffrey Feinman

Illustrations by
Ivor Parry

A Dolphin Book
Doubleday & Company, Inc.
Garden City, New York
1979

ACKNOWLEDGMENTS

For a period of about six months a very small army of researchers armed with a vacuum-like curiosity descended into the stacks of most of the libraries of the state of New Jersey from the small but treasure-laden county library in Mount Holly to Princeton University's giant Firestone (two-million-plus volumes). There in a scanning display that would warm the heart of Evelyn Wood herself, thousands of books, periodicals, and other documents were searched for those telltale enumerations that indicated an author was setting down rules for something or other. Then with the aid of those two most important inventions of man—money and the Xerox machine—these rules were gathered for review, editing, reorganization, and final inclusion in *The Rule Book*.

We would like to thank those researchers first:

        Annette Swerdel Van Deusen

        Leslie Spraker May

        Ida B. Hammond

        Karin Ava Weinraub

        Braxton Preston

Thanks too to Gayle Skorny, our main typist, who managed to complete the manuscript on time between her other full-time and part-time jobs, and remained socially active as only a newly engaged young woman can be. For assisting with the typing we thank as well Agnes Alexander, Annette Swerdel Van Deusen, and Beth Solow.

Also a special thanks to our good friend Milton Pierce, who helped the project come to be.

Thanks to Barbara Kirschner (organizer of our permission request operation) and Kathy Pavelec, who saw their husbands only rarely during that half year and are still at home. Finally, a loving thank you to Jared and Brian Kirschner and Jan, Audrey, Amanda, and Rebecca Pavelec, who are not yet old enough to understand what motivates grown men, but who are loving enough to tolerate it nonetheless.

And the most special thanks of all to our editor, Lindy Hess, who truly made this book a reality. The most important *rule* of being successfully published is to have an editor who can see a rose when it is still a seed. For the foresight, advice, and counsel, we thank Ms. Hess.

THE RULE BOOK

INTRODUCTION

It has long been held that the critical distinction between man and the lower forms of life on this planet is that man alone is possessed of a "free will"; that commonly being defined as having the ability to choose between alternative courses of action as he makes his way through life.

If that were the extent of its influence on man and the totality of its definition, it would seem a comfortable-enough concept. But history demonstrates that, left to his own devices, man, more often than not, chooses the wrong alternatives. Armed with nothing more than the *ability* to choose, man would long ago have gone the way of the dodo.

What man needed was a way of knowing what alternatives to choose. What man really needed was rules! Free will is really better defined as *that state which permits man to follow the rules if he so chooses*!

Man didn't have to wait long for the first rule. Indeed, the very first words heard by Adam were a simple exposition of the rules for living as delivered by his Creator: "Be fruitful, multiply, fill the earth and conquer it. Be masters of the fish of the sea, the birds of heaven and all living animals on the earth."

And, man didn't have to wait much longer to find out what happened when he broke the rules. Rule 2: "You may eat indeed of all the trees in the garden. Nevertheless of the tree of knowledge of good and evil you are not to eat, for on the day you eat of it you shall most surely die."

So man, flexing his free will, challenged the rules for the first time and immediately got his fingers burned. He had discovered rules were power, and because he now knew what was good and what was evil, he decided to make his own.

He could say, "Do this because it is good." "Don't do that because it is bad." Later (and not much later) he would say, "Do this," and secretly think, "because it is good *for me*." And, "Don't do that (because it is bad *for me*)." He had created the first unfair rules!

In short time man totally integrated rules into his life-style. He could create them, enforce them, live by them, and break them—all in the exercise of his free will; all because he rightly or wrongly believed that, at least in the short run, he would be happier because of his actions.

Over the centuries, as man obeyed the first rule (it was easy) and covered the earth with his offspring, civilizations rose and fell largely because of the quality of the rules that guided them. Reasonably fair and tolerable rules could gain everlasting fame and respect—Greece and Rome. Weak, nonexistent, or unfair rules could bring infamy—the Vandals, the Inquisition. And, where prevailing rules were unjust and too oppressive, mob rule often superseded, toppling governments and even entire civilizations—Sybaris.

Clearly, rules made to control or even guide large portions of mankind had to come from God or from someone else with both the wisdom to create them and the power to back them up. Unfortunately, that very requirement prevented the majority of men from enjoying the pleasures of rule making and rule enforcing.

If the common man couldn't create and enforce rules of morality or the rules governing his formal society, what was left to him? Everything else! He could create rules for eating, rules for dressing, rules for grammar, rules of honor, rules for sex, rules for dying. He could create rules for *everything* else. And he has.

Thoreau observed, "Any fool can make a rule, and every fool will mind it." Whether made by wise men or by fools, rules exist everywhere, covering almost every situation, real or imagined. In fact, it is quite likely more time has been spent by man in the creation of rules than in the actual pursuit of the activity governed by them.

The Rule Book is an unscientific survey of these rules in all their forms, which by definition are 1. "A prescribed guide for conduct," 2. "A legal precept or doctrine," 3. "An accepted procedure, custom, or habit," and 4. "A usually valid generalization."

We have attempted to include rules which have historical interest—Roman Rules for Divorce, Rules from the Magna Carta; rules which can have immediate and future practical benefit—Rules for Power Tool Safety, Rules for Delivering a Baby at Home, Rules for Cleaning Your House; rules which can be thought-provoking—Rules for Having an Affair, Rules for Recognizing an Alcoholism Problem; and rules which almost defy classification—Rules for Becoming Invisible, Rules for Cooking a Porcupine, Rules for Making Gold.

Although we hope *The Rule Book* will be primarily a source of entertainment, we have included many, many sets of rules which can help you deal with frustrating, challenging, and even life-threatening situations.

Most of our favorites are here, some are not (because they were thought by the editors to be unfit for family reading or too often broken to be considered valid).

One important fact we learned during the creation of this book: The world will never run short of rules. From the first man-created rule, which might have been "Don't draw on the cave roof," to the modern "Do not fold, spindle, or mutilate," there has never been a lack of good, bad, frustrating, confusing, and foolish rules by which to live. As long as there is a Washington, D.C., parents, lovers, stronger, weaker, bigger, smaller—there will be, if not a need, at least a constant source of new rules.

We learned that rules can be gems of simplicity, as in the Birkenhead Drill (rules derived from the unfortunate sinking of the ship *Birkenhead* on February 26, 1852):

"Women and children first";

and they can be horrors of verbosity, as in this single-sentence, 440-word rule from the Internal Revenue Service:

"(1) General Rule.—If contributions are paid by an employer to or under a stock bonus, pension, profit-sharing, or annuity plan, or if compensation is paid or accrued on account of any employee under a plan deferring the receipt of such compensation, such contributions or compensation shall not be deductible under subsection (a) but shall be deductible, if deductible under subsection (a) without regard to this subsection, under this subsection but only to the following extent:

(A) In the taxable year when paid if the contributions are paid into a pension trust, and if such taxable year ends within or with a taxable year of the trust is exempt under section 165(a), in an amount determined as follows:

(i) an amount not in excess of 5 per centum of the compensation otherwise paid or accrued during the taxable year to all the employees under the trust, but such amount may be reduced for future years if found by the Commissioner upon periodical examination at not less than five-year intervals to be more than the amount reasonably necessary to provide the remaining unfunded cost of past and current service credits of all employees under the plan plus

(ii) any excess over the amount allowable under clause (i) necessary to provide with respect to all of the employees under the trust the remaining unfunded cost of their past and current service credits distributed as a level amount, or a level percentage of compensation, over the remaining future service of each such employee, as determined under regulations prescribed by the Commissioner with the approval of the Secretary, but if such remaining unfunded cost with respect to any three individuals is more than 50 per centum of such remaining unfunded cost, the amount of such unfunded cost attributable to such individuals shall be distributed over a period of at least 5 taxable years, or

(iii) in lieu of the amounts allowable under (i) and (ii) above, an amount equal to the normal cost of the plan, as determined under regulations prescribed by the Commissioner with the approval of the Secretary, plus, if past service or other supplementary pension or annuity credits are provided by the plan, an amount not in excess of 10 per centum of the cost which would be required to completely fund or purchase such pension or annuity credits as of the date when they are included in the plan, as determined under regulations prescribed by the Commissioner with the approval of the Secretary, except that in no case shall deduction be allowed for any amount (other than the normal cost) paid in after such pension or annuity credits are completely funded or purchased.''

We learned, too, that man's need to amass data, to publish it for consumption of his fellow man, is never more evident than when it involves relaying his own or other's rules for more effective living. Consider that we have gathered something approaching two hundred thousand words designed to make you think twice about the current order of your life. And consider that the best-selling book of all time, the Bible, is really a rule book.

Now start your trip through *The Rule Book*. There is no pattern to follow, no step-by-step procedure to use, no guidelines to which to adhere, no rules for reading it.

We hope you will read all the rules, follow some and reject outright those which you feel are deserving of that fate. But, and this is, perhaps, a rule: Remember the rules you may choose to reject will be the very ones followed faithfully by the next purchaser of this volume.

Stephen M. Kirschner
Barry J. Pavelec
Jeffrey Feinman

RULES FOR BECOMING MORE ASSERTIVE

1. Don't slip back into compliance. This occurs when you make your assertion and then you get scared and take it right back, giving it a little compliant twist like, "Is that all right?" One example of this is: "I don't like your asking me to do that and I don't want to do that—but I'll do it this time."

2. Don't "overkill." One example of this is when a woman, compliant for years, suddenly announces that she won't be available to cook dinner Tuesday evenings because she wants to take a course. But other people have rights and problems too. They have a right to expect, in a family unit, that their problems of getting dinner will be solved.

3. Understand that as you assert your own rights, other people also have rights too. For example, it's an assertion when you say to your husband: "I'd like you to go to the party with me because I really don't enjoy going alone." But he has a right to answer: "I understand your feelings, but I don't want to go." It is not the assertive person, but rather the controlling person who will then try to manipulate her husband into going.

4. Don't forget the positive component of an assertion. If people had had a lifelong problem with compliance, the struggle to say no and to express their own feelings and act on their own beliefs is so difficult that they can't make the total assertion—they can only make the negative part.

5. Choose the right time to make your assertion. Many people think that any time of morning, noon, or night is the right time to hit somebody with their assertion. This is a major mistake. There are appropriate times.

6. Introduce your assertion slowly. For example, if you've decided you're not going to make coffee for your boss anymore, instead of suddenly coming out of the blue with the assertion: "I'm not going to do that," warm up to your assertion. For instance, tell him the time you spend making coffee can be put to better use.

7. Don't think that other people have to be different in order to respect your assertion. That's a common mistake. Just because people in your world or in your particular circle haven't had experience with your assertive nature is no reason to think that if they were more "reasonable," your assertion would work.

8. Stick with it. Some people muster up all their courage to make the assertion, but if it doesn't work out, they can't stay with it. The mistake there is in thinking that just because it was so hard for you it ought to work without you repeating it.

9. Join an assertiveness training group led by a trained, skilled person if you really want to learn it well. Study it seriously like anything else you want to learn. Becoming assertive does take work and time.

RULES FOR SAFE SKATEBOARDING

1. Do not skateboard on public streets or on driveways that incline into the street.
2. Use only paved surfaces free of large bumps and cracks that cause spills.
3. Wear sneakers or shoes with nonslip soles.
4. Emphasize control of the skateboard, not speed.
5. Be sure that the skateboard is not broken or cracked and that the wheel mechanisms are not loose.

RULES FOR SUCCESSFUL AUCTION BUYING

1. Beware of Auction Fever, with symptoms such as sweaty palms, pounding heart, and an inability to stop bidding.
2. Examine and evaluate every lot on which you are bidding, and bid only on what you have examined.
3. Utilize the catalog the auction house publishes, but read descriptions carefully.
4. Set a limit on each lot, write it down and stick to it.
5. However, if you are poorly placed in the bidding sequence and your next bid will place you only a small percentage above your limit, you may stretch *one* more bid.
6. Never waive a bid unless it is part of a planned strategy.
7. Know your auctioneer.
8. Do not hesitate to ask the auction house how long they've been in business, or for bank or other references.
9. Find out if there are "reserves" (minimums set by the consignors).
10. Avoid bidding against a collector.
11. Do bid against dealers, but make sure he is not a "shill," or bidding for a collector who has no monetary limit.
12. Stay alert, and be patient.
13. Remember, if you accidentally buy the wrong lot, call it to the auctioneer's attention *immediately*, and ask him to reopen the lot.

RULES OF THE TABLE — FIFTEENTH CENTURY

1. Learn these rules.
2. Take care to cut and clean your nails; dirt under the nails is dangerous when scratching.
3. Wash your hands when you get up and before every meal.
4. Do not be the first to take from the dish.
5. Do not put back on your plate what has been in your mouth.
6. Do not offer anyone a piece of food you have bitten into.
7. Do not chew anything you have to spit out again.
8. It is bad manners to dip food into the saltcellar.
9. Be peaceable, quiet, and courteous at table.
10. If you have crumbled bread into your wineglass, drink up the wine or throw it away.
11. Do not stuff too much into yourself, or you will be obliged to commit a breach of good manners.
12. Do not scratch at table, with your hands or with the tablecloth.

RULES OF PUNISHMENT FOR SPECIFIC BODILY INJURIES ISSUED BY ALFRED, KING OF THE WEST SAXONS (A.D. 871–899)

1. If the shooting (i.e., fore) finger is struck off, the fine is fifteen shillings; for its nail it is four shillings.
2. If a man's thigh be pierced, let thirty shillings be paid him as fine; if it be broken, the fine is likewise thirty shillings.
3. If the great toe be struck off, let twenty shillings be paid him as fine; if it be the second toe, let fifteen shillings be paid as fine; if the middlemost toe be struck off, there shall be nine shillings as fine; if the little toe be struck off, let five shillings be paid him.
4. If a man's arm, with the hand, be entirely cut off before the elbow, let fine be made for it with eighty shillings.
5. For every wound before the hair, and before the sleeve, and beneath the knee, the fine is two parts more.

RULES OF THE BED —1729

1. You ought neither to undress nor go to bed in the presence of any other person.
2. Above all, unless you are married, you should not go to bed in the presence of anyone of the other sex.
3. It is still less permissible for people of different sexes to sleep in the same bed, unless they are very young children.
4. If you are forced by unavoidable necessity to share a bed with another person of the same sex on a journey, it is not proper to lie so near him that you disturb or even touch him; and it is still less decent to put your legs between those of the other.
5. It is also very improper and impolite to amuse yourself with talk and chatter.
6. When you get up you should not leave the bed uncovered, nor put your nightcap on a chair or anywhere else where it can be seen.

RULES OF
PRESIDENTIAL SUCCESSION IN THE UNITED STATES

In case of individual deaths or national disaster, the following indicates who will succeed the President of the United States:

1. The Vice President.
2. Speaker of the House.
3. President pro tempore of the Senate.
4. Secretary of State.
5. Secretary of the Treasury.
6. Secretary of Defense.
7. Attorney General.
8. Secretary of the Interior.
9. Secretary of Agriculture.
10. Secretary of Commerce.
11. Secretary of Labor.
12. Secretary of Health, Education, and Welfare.
13. Secretary of Housing and Urban Development.
14. Secretary of Transportation.

Note: An official can only succeed to the Presidency if he or she meets constitutional requirements.

RULES FROM THE MAGNA CARTA—1215

1. No scutage or aid shall be raised, except in the case of the case of the king's captivity, the knighting of his eldest son, or the marriage of his eldest daughter, except by the general council of the kingdom.
2. No feeman shall be imprisoned or disseised, outlawed or proceeded against other than by the legal judgement of his peers, or by the law of the land.
3. Right or justice shall not be sold, delayed, or denied to any.
4. The civil court shall be stationary, and not follow the king's person.

THE RULES OF DUELING (1777)

1. The first offense requires the first apology, though the retort may have been more offensive than the insult. Example: A tells B he is impertinent, etc.; B retorts that he lies; yet A must make the first apology, because he gave the first offense, and then (after one fire) B may explain away the retort by subsequent apology.
2. But if the parties would rather fight on, then, after two shots each (but in no case before), B may explain first, and A apologizes afterward.
3. If a doubt exists who gave the first offense, the decision rests with the seconds; it they will not decide, or cannot agree, the matter must proceed to two shots, or to a hit if the challenger require it.
4. When the *lie direct* is the *first* offense, the aggressor must either beg pardon in express terms, exchange two shots previous to an apology, or three shots followed up by explanation, or fire on till a severe hit be received by one party or the other.
5. As a blow is strictly prohibited under any circumstances among gentlemen, no verbal apology can be received for such an insult. The alternatives, therefore, are: the offender handing a cane to the injured party, to be used on his own back, at the same time begging pardon; firing on until one or both are disabled; or exchanging three shots and then asking pardon *without* the proffer of the *cane*. If swords are used, the parties engage till one is well blooded, disabled, or disarmed; or until after receiving a wound, and blood being drawn, the aggressor asks pardon.
6. If A gives B the lie, and B retorts by a blow (being the two greatest offenses), no reconciliation *can* take place till after two discharges each, or a severe hit; *after* which B may ask A's pardon for the blow, and then A may explain simply for the lie, because a blow is *never* allowable, and the offense of the lie therefore merges in it. (See preceding rule.)

7. But no apology can be received, in any case, after the parties have actually taken their ground, withour exchange of fires.

8. In the above case, no challenger is obliged to divulge his cause of challenge (if private) unless required by the challenged so to do *before* the meeting.

9. All imputations of cheating at play, races, etc., to be considered equivalent to a blow, but may be reconciled after one shot, on admitting their falsehood and begging pardon publicly.

10. Any insult to a lady under a gentleman's care or protection to be considered as, by one degree, a greater offense than if given to the gentleman personally, and to be regulated accordingly.

11. Offenses originating or accruing from the support of ladies' reputations to be considered as less unjustifiable than any others of the same class, and as admitting of slighter apologies by the aggressor. This to be determined by the circumstances of the case, but *always* favorably to the lady.

12. In simple unpremeditated *rencontres* with the small-sword, or *couteau-de-chasse* the rule is, first draw, first sheathe, unless blood be drawn; then both sheathe and proceed to investigate.

13. No dumb-shooting or firing in the air admissible *in any case*. The challenger ought not to have challenged without receiving offense, and the challenged ought, if he gave offense, to have made an apology before he came on the ground; therefore *children's play* must be dishonorable on one side or the other, and is accordingly prohibited.

14. Seconds to be of equal rank in society with the principals they attend, inasmuch as a second may either choose or chance to become a principal, and equality is indispensable.

15. Challenges are never to be delivered at night, unless the party to be challenged intends leaving the place of offense before morning; for it is desirable to avoid all hotheaded proceedings.

16. The challenged has the right to choose his own weapon, unless the challenger gives his honor he is no swordsman; after which, however, he cannot decline any *second* species of weapons proposed by the challenged.

17. The challenged chooses the ground; the challenger chooses his distance; the seconds fix the time and terms of firing.

18. The seconds load in presence of each other, unless they give their matual honors that they have charged smooth and single, which should be held sufficient.

19. Firing may be regulated, first, by signal; secondly, by word of command; or thirdly, at pleasure—as may be agreeable to the parties. In the latter case, the parties may fire at their reasonable leisure, but *second presents* and *rests* are strictly prohibited.

20. In all cases a misfire is equivalent to a shot, and a *snap* or a *non-cock* is to be considered as a misfire.

21. Seconds are bound to attempt a reconciliation *before* the meeting takes place, or *after* sufficient firing or hits, as specified.

22. Any wound sufficient to agitate the nerves, and necessarily make the hand shake, must end the business for *that* day.

23. If the cause of meeting be of such a nuture that no apology or explanation can or will be received, the challenged takes his ground, and calls on the challenger to proceed as he chooses. In such cases, firing at pleasure is the usual practice but may be varied by agreement.

24. In slight cases, the second hands his principal but one pistol; but in gross cases two, holding another case ready charged in reserve.

25. Where seconds disagree, and resolve to exchange shots themselves, it must be at the same time and at right angles with their principals. If with swords, side by side, with five paces interval.

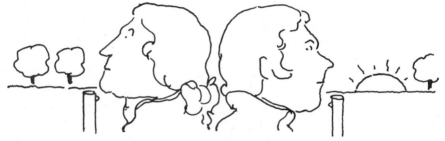

BIBLICAL RULES FOR CHARITY TO THE POOR

1. Water quenches blazing fire, almsgiving atones for sins.

2. Whoever gives favors in return is mindful of the future; at the moment of his fall he will find support.

3. My son, do not refuse the poor a livelihood; do not tantalize the needy.

4. Do not add to the sufferings of the hungry, do not bait a man in distress.

5. Do not aggravate a heart already angry, nor keep the destitute waiting for your alms.

6. Do not repulse a hard-pressed beggar, nor turn your face from a poor man.

7. Do not avert your eyes from the destitute, give no man occasion to curse you; for if a man curses you in the bitterness of his soul, his maker will hear his imprecation.

8. Gain the love of the community, bow your head to a man of authority.

9. To the poor man lend an ear, and return his greeting courteously.

10. Save the oppressed from the hand of the oppressor, and do not be mean-spirited in your judgments.

11. Be like a father to orphans, and as good as a husband to windows.

12. And you will be like a son to the Most High, whose love for you will surpass your mother's.

ST. ALBERT'S RULES FOR MONKS

1. The first thing I require is for you to have a Prior, one of yourselves, who is to be chosen for the office by common consent, or that of the greater and maturer part of you.

2. Each of the others must promise him obedience—of which, once promised, he must try to make his deeds the true reflection—and also chastity and the renunciation of ownership. If the Prior and brother see fit, you may have foundations in solitary places, or where you are given a site that is suitable and convenient for the observance proper to your Order.

3. Next, each one of you is to have a separate cell, situated as the lie of the land you propose to occupy may dictate, and allotted by disposition of the Prior with the agreement of the other brothers, or the most mature among them. However, you are to eat whatever may have been given you in a common refectory, listening together meanwhile to a reading from Holy Scripture where that can be done without difficulty.

4. None of the brothers is to occupy a cell other than that allotted to him, or to exchange cell with another, without leave of whoever is Prior at the time.

5. The Prior's cell should stand near the entrance to your property, so that he may be the first to meet those who approach, and whatever has to be done in consequence may all be carried out as he may decide and order.

6. Each one of you is to stay in his own cell or nearby, pondering the Lord's law day and night and keeping watch at his prayers unless attending to some other duty.

7. Those who know their letters, and how to read the psalms, should, for each of the hours, say those our holy forefathers laid down and the approved custom of the Church appoints for that hour. Those who do not know their letters must say twenty-five "Our Fathers" for the night office, except on Sundays and solemnities when that number is to be doubled so that the "Our Father" is said fifty times; the same prayer must be said seven times in the morning in place of Lauds, and seven times too for each of the other hours, except for Vespers, when it must be said fifteen times.

8. None of the brothers must lay claim to anything as his own, but your property is to be held in common; and of such things as the Lord may have given you each is to receive from the Prior—that is from the man he appoints for the purpose—wherever befits his age and needs. However, as I have said, each one of you is to stay in his allotted cell, and live, by himself, on what is given out to him. You may have as many asses and mules as you need, however, and may keep a certain amount of livestock or poultry.

9. On Sundays too, or other days if necessary, you should discuss matters of discipline and your spiritual welfare; and on this occasion the indiscretions and failings of the brothers, if any be found at fault, should be lovingly corrected.

10. An oratory should be built as conveniently as possible among the cells, where, if it can be done without difficulty, you are to gather each morning to hear Mass.

11. You are to fast every day, except Sundays, from the feast of the Exaltation of the Holy Cross until Easter Day, unless bodily sickness or feebleness, or some other good reason, demand a dispensation from the fast; for necessity overrides every law.

12. You are always to abstain from meat, unless it has to be eaten as remedy for sickness or great feebleness.

13. Since man's life on earth is a time of trial, and all who would live devotedly in Christ must undergo persecution, and the devil your foe is on the prowl like a roaring lion looking for prey to devour, you must use every care to clothe yourselves in God's armor so that you may be ready to withstand the enemy's ambush.

Your loins are to be girt with chastity, your breast fortified by holy meditations, for, as Scripture has it, holy meditation will save you. Put on holiness as your breastplate, and it will enable you to love the Lord your God with all your heart and soul and strength, and your neighbor as yourself. Faith must be your shield on all occasions, and with it you will be able to quench all the flaming missiles of the wicked one: there can be no pleasing God without faith (and the victory lies in this—your faith). On your head set the helmet of salvation, and so be sure of deliverance by our only Saviour, who sets His own free from their sins. The sword of the spirit, the sord of God, must abound in your mouths and hearts. Let all you do have the Lord's word for accompaniment.

14. You must give yourselves to work of some kind, so that the devil may always find you busy; no idleness on your part must give him a chance to pierce the defenses of your souls. In this respect you have both the teaching and the example of Saint Paul the Apostle, into whose mouth Christ put his own words. God made him preacher and teacher of faith and truth to the nations: with him as your leader you cannot go astray. We lived among you, he said, laboring and weary, toiling night and day so as not to be a burden to any of you; not because we had no power to do otherwise but so as to give you, in your own selves, an example you might imitate. For the Charge we gave you when we were with you was this: that whoever is not willing to work should not be allowed to eat either. For we have heard that there are certain restless idlers among you. We charge people of this kind, and implore them in the name of our Lord Jesus Christ, that they earn their own bread by silent toil. This is the way of holiness and goodness: see that you follow it.

15. The Apostle would have us keep silence, for in silence he tells us to work. As the Prophet also makes known to us: Silence is the way to foster holiness.

Elsewhere he says: Your strength will lie in silence and hope. For this reason I lay down that you are to keep silence from Vespers until Terce the next day, unless some necessary or good reason, or the Prior's permission, should break the silence. At other times, although you need not keep silence so strictly, be careful not to indulge in a great deal of talk, for, as Scripture has it—and experience teaches us no less—sin will not be wanting where there is much talk, and he who is careless in speech will come to harm; and elsewhere: The use of many words brings harm to the speaker's soul. And our Lord says in the Gospel: Every rash word uttered will have to be accounted for on Judgment Day. Make a balance then, each of you, to weigh his words in; keep a tight rein on your mouths, lest you should stumble and fall in speech, and your fall be irreparable and prove mortal. Like the Prophet, watch your step lest your tongue give offense, and employ every care in keeping silent, which is the way to foster holiness.

16. You, brother B., and whoever may succeed you as Prior, must always keep in mind and put into practice what our Lord said in the Gospel: Whoever has a mind to become a leader among you must make himself servant to the rest, and whichever of you would be first must become your bondsman.

17. You other brothers too, hold your Prior in humble reverence, your minds not on him but on Christ who has placed him over you, and who, to those who rule the Churches, addressed the words: Whoever pays you heed pays heed to me, and whoever treats you with dishonor dishonors me; if you remain so minded you will not be found guilty of contempt, but will merit life eternal as fit regard for your obedience.

18. Here then are the few points I have written down to provide you with a standard of conduct to live up to; but our Lord, at his second coming, will reward anyone who does more than he is obliged to do. See that the bounds of common sense are not exceeded, however, for common sense is the guide of the virtues.

BIBLICAL RULES FOR RELATIONS WITH MEN

1. Do not desert an old friend; the new one will not be his match.
2. New friend, new wine; when it grows old, you drink it with pleasure.
3. Do not envy the sinner his success; you do not know what turn his career will take.
4. Do not take pleasure in what pleases the godless; remember they will not go unpunished to their grave.
5. Keep your distance from the man who has the power to put to death and you will not be haunted by the fear of dying.
6. If you do approach him, make no false move, or he may take your life.

BIBLICAL RULES REGARDING SHAME AND HUMAN RESPECT

1.   My son, bide your time and be on your guard against evil, and have no cause to be ashamed of yourself; for there is a shame that leads to sin, as well as a shame that is honorable and gracious.

2.   Do not show partiality, to your own detriment, or deference, to your own downfall.

3.   Do not refrain from speech at an opportune time, and do not hide your wisdom; for wisdom shall be recognized in speech, and instruction by what the tongue utters.

4.   Do not contradict the truth, rather blush for your own ignorance.

5.   Do not be ashamed to confess your sins, do not strive against the current of a river.

6.   Do not grovel to a foolish man, do not show partiality to a man of influence.

7.   Fight to the death for truth, and the Lord God will war on your side.

8.   Do not be bold of tongue, yet idle and slack in deed; do not be like a lion at home, or a coward before your servants.

9.   Do not let your hands be outstretched to receive, yet closed when the time comes to give back.

BIBLICAL RULES FOR RELATIONS WITH WOMEN

1.   Do not be jealous of the wife you love, or teach her lessons in evil to your detriment.

2.   Do not give your soul to a woman, for her to trample on your strength.

3.   Do not keep company with a harlot, in case you get entangled in her snares.

4.   Do not dally with a singing girl, in case you get caught by her wiles.

5.   Do not stare at a virgin, in case you and she incur the same punishment.

6.   Do not give your soul to whores, or you will ruin your inheritance.

7.   Keep your eyes to yourself in the streets of a town, do not prowl about its unfrequented quarters.

8.   Turn your eyes away from a handsome woman, do not stare at the beauty that belongs to someone else.

9.   Woman's beauty has led many astray; it kindles desire like a flame.

10.   Never sit down with a married woman, or sit at table with her drinking wine, in case you succumb to her charms, and in your ardor you slide down to your ruin.

BIBLICAL RULES REGARDING WITNESSES

1.   A single witness cannot suffice to convict a man of a crime or offense of any kind; whatever the misdemeanor, the evidence of two witnesses or three is required to sustain the charge.

2.   If a malicious witness appears against a man to accuse him of rebellion, both parties to this dispute before Yahweh must be brought before the priests and judges then in office.

3.   The judges must make a careful inquiry, and if it turns out that the witness who accused his brother is a lying witness, you must deal with him as he would have dealt with his brother.

4.   You must banish this evil from your midst. Others will hear of it and be afraid and never again do such an evil thing among you. You are to show no pity.

RULES FOR HOLY LIVING AND DYING—1690

1.   Believe in and become baptized into all the articles of the Christian faith.

2.   Study to improve your knowledge in the matters of God, so as to best live a holy life.

3.   Worship God diligently, in obedience to Christ, frequently and constantly, with natural religion; that is, or prayer, praises, and thanksgiving.

4.   Take all opportunities to remember Christ's death by a frequent sacrament, (as it can be had), or else by inward acts of understanding, will, and memory (which is the spiritual communion).

5.   Live chastely.

6.   Be merciful.

7.   Despise the world, using it as a man, but never suffering it to rifle a duty.

8.   Be just in your dealing and deiligent in your calling.

9.   Be humble in your spirit.

10.   Be content in your fortune and employment.

11.   Do your duty because you love God.

12.   And especially, if after all this you be afflicted, be patient and prepared to suffer affliction for the cause of God.

RULES FOR CANONIZATION

1.   Once the process for beatification is completed, an investigation is conducted of the person's reputation for holiness, his writings, and (except in the

case of martyrs) miracles ascribed to his intercession after his death. (Miracles are not required for martyrs.)

2.   The Pope can dispense from some of the formalities ordinarily required in canonization precedures if he so chooses.

3.   Once declared a saint, the person is worthy of honor in liturgical worship throughout the Universal Church.

4.   The beatification pricedure and that of canonization is conducted under the auspices of the Congregation for the Causes of Saints under the Code of Canon Law.

5.   The official decree reads in its essential portion:

"For the honor of the holy and undivided Trinity; for the exaltation of the Catholic faith and the increase of Christian life; with the authority of our Lord Jesus Christ, of the blessed Apostles Peter and Paul, and with our own authority; after mature deliberation and with the divine assistance, often implored; with the counsel of many of our brother,

"We decree and define that (name) is a saint and we inscribe him (her) in the Catalog of Saints, stating that he (she) shall be venerated in the Universal Church with pious devotion.

"In the name of the Father and of the Son and of the Holy Spirit. Amen"

6.   The official listing of saints and blessed is contained in the Roman Martyrology and related decrees issued after its last publication.

7.   The Church regards all persons in heaven as saints, not just those who have been officially canonized.

RULES TO FOIL A WITCH

---

1.   If a witch should bewitch you, she will probably appear to you next time as an animal. Shoot the animal with a silver bullet if you desire to injure the witch.

2.   To keep off witches, lumbermen wrap themselves in fresh deerskin.

3.   Any witch or ghost may be destroyed by merely asking them what they want of you.

4.   To frighten witches away, sprinkle salt around the house.

5.   Your milk will be hard to churn if witches are in it. To get rid of them, set the churn in a chimney corner and whip the milk with a switch or drop a dime in the churn.

ST. BENEDICT'S RULES FOR ABBOTS

1. The Abbot who is worthy to rule over a monastery should always remember what he is called and suit his actions to his high calling. For he is believed to take the place of Christ in the monastery, and therefore is he called by His title, in accordance with the words of the Apostle: "Ye have received the spirit of the adoption of sons, whereby we cry: Abba, Father."

2. Therefore the Abbot ought not to teach, ordain, or command anything which is against the law of the Lord; but he should infuse the leaven of divine justice into the minds of his disciples through his commands and teaching.

3. Let the Abbot always remember that there will be an inquiry both as to his teachings and as to the obedience of his disciples at the dread Judgment of God.

4. Let the Abbot know that whatever lack of profit the Father of the family may find in His sheep will be accounted the fault of the shepherd. However, if the shepherd has used all his diligence on an unruly and disobedient flock, and has devoted all his care to amending their corrupt ways, he shall be acquitted at the Judgment of the Lord and may say to Him with the Prophet: "I have not hidden Your justice in my heart, I have declared Your truth and Your salvation; but they have scorned and despised me." And then at last, death itself shall be the penalty for the sheep who have not responded to his care.

5. When, therefore, anyone receives the name of Abbot, he ought to rule his disciples with a twofold doctrine—that is, he should display all that is good and holy by his deeds rather than by his words. To his intelligent disciples, let him expound the commands of the Lord in words, but to those of harder hearts and simpler minds, let him demonstrate the divine precepts by his example.

6. All things which he teaches his disciples to be contrary to God's law, let him show in his deeds that they are not to be done, lest while preaching to others he himself should become a castaway and God should someday say to him as he sins: "Why do you declare My justice and take My testament in your mouth? For you have hated My discipline and cast My words behind you"; and: "You saw the mote in your brother's eye and did not see the beam in your own."

7. Let him make no distinction of persons in the monastery. Let no one be loved more than another, unless it be him who is found better in good works or obedience. Let not the freeborn monk be put before the man who was born in slavery unless there is some good reason for it. For if the Abbot, for some reason, shall see fit to do so, he may fix anyone's rank as he will; otherwise let all keep their own places, because whether slave or freeman, we are all one in Christ and we must all alike bear the burden of service under the same Lord. "There is no respect of persons with God." In this regard alone are we distinguished in His sight, if we are found better than others in good works and humility. Therefore let him show equal love for all; and let one discipline be imposed on all in accordance with their deserts.

8. In his teaching, the Abbot should always observe the apostolic rule which says: "Reprove, entreat, rebuke." That is, he ought to adapt himself to the circumstances and mingle encouragements with his reproofs.

9. Let him show the sternness of a master and the devoted affection of a father. He ought to reprove the undisciplined and unruly severely, but should exhort the obedient, meek, and patient to advance in virtue. We warn him to rebuke and punish the negligent and scornful.

10. Let him not blind himself to the sins of offenders, but let him cut them out by the roots as soon as they begin to appear.

11. He should use words of warning to punish, for the first and second time, those who are of gentle disposition and good understanding; but he ought to use the lash and corporal punishment to check the bold, hard, proud, and disobedient even at the very beginning of their wrongdoing, in accordance with text: "The fool is not corrected by words"; and again: "Beat your son with a rod, and you will free his soul from death."

12. The Abbot should always remember what he is and what he is called, and he should know that from him to whom more is entrusted, more is also required.

13. Let him know how difficult and arduous a task he has taken upon himself, to govern the souls and cater to the different dispositions of many men. One must be encouraged, the second rebuked, the third one persuaded; in accordance with disposition and understanding of each. He must so adapt and accommodate himself to all that not only will he endure no loss in the flock entrusted to his care, but even rejoice in the increase of his sheep.

14. Above all else, let him not slight or undervalue the salvation of the souls entrusted to him by giving more attention to transitory, earthly, and perishable matter.

15. Let him always remember the souls he has undertaken to govern, for which he will also have to render an account.

16. Let him not complain of lack of means, but let him remember that it is written: "Seek first the Kingdom of God, and His justice, and all things shall be given unto you"; and again: "Nothing is lacking to those who fear Him."

17. Let him know that they who undertake to govern souls must prepare themselves to give answer for them.

18. Let him understand that, however great the number of brothers he has under his care, on the Day of Judgment he will have to answer to God for the souls of all of them, as well as for his own. And so, fearing always the inquiry which the shepherd must face for the sheep entrusted to him, and anxious about the answers which he must give for the others, he becomes solicitous for his own sake also. Thus, while his admonitions help others to amend, he himself is freed of all his faults.

RULES FOR INTERPRETING YOUR DREAMS

1. Clean or shiny objects or conditions in dreams are usually good omens, but dirty or dull ones forecast obstacles and/or difficulties.

2. A dream of going up indicates success or improvement, going down signifies reverses.

3. Successful efforts in a dream are a good omen, but unsuccessful efforts forecast difficulties.

4. If a dream involves an illness to the dreamer, it is advisable to have a medical checkup.

5. Dreams involving members of the dreamer's family with whom the dreamer is on pleasant terms generally pertain to business advancement, but if the relations are unpleasant, the reverse is forecast.

RULES FOR DEVELOPING ONES'S ESP

1. Remember and record your dreams; they may actually be instances of ESP.

2. Learn to recognize ideas that "just come to you." This is part of intuition.

3. Write down ideas that occur when you're not actively seeking them or thinking about them.

4. Pay attention to your feelings; they are another important part of your intuition and you must learn to recognize them.

5. Practice guessing what someone is thinking. This works much better with those people you know well, of course, but with a little bit of trial-and-error, it should work with strangers as well.

6. At the same time as you practice guessing what someone else is thinking, you should also practice sending silent messages and seeing if your respondent can correctly interpret them. This can be done with or without the other person's knowledge.

7. Learn to listen for unusual sounds and voices; often, people experience ESP through hearing voices of people who are not present or sounds of things that are not physically there.

8. Every time you have an experience that you believe to be ESP, relate the details to someone you can trust.

9. Find others who use ESP often and get together with them to discuss your common interest.

10. Keep a diary or record of your ESP experiences over a long period of time. (This will be especially helpful when sharing them with a friend or with an ESP group—and could also be invaluable research materials for investigators.)

11. Once you have developed your ESP to a certain point, consult specialists in the field for their suggestions.

12. Don't forget long-distance ESP; sometimes it works just as well as (or better than) local ESP. To practice, start by trying to communicate with (or see) someone you know who lives at least five hundred miles away. Then, try your skills on people and places that are not familiar to you.

13. A good deal of developing one's ESP depends also on developing one's powers of concentration. Obviously, if you can't stay with any one subject or project for more than five minutes you're going to have real problems when it comes to ESP. So now—today—practice sticking with whatever you're doing until it's done or until you've done all you can do for the present.

14. Don't give up! This may seem like a matter of common sense, but you'd be surprised how many prospective ESP experts quit before they develop their full potential. Sometimes ESP experiences are few and far between, but that is no reason for you to stop looking for them. After all, they're well worth the wait!

RULES FOR BECOMING A VAMPIRE

1. In Transylvania, criminals, bastards, witches, magicians, excommunicated people, those born with teeth or a caul, and unbaptized children can become vampires. The seventh son of a seventh son is doomed to become a vampire.

2. If a cat or other "evil" animal jumps or flies over someone's dead body before it is buried, or if the shadow of a man falls upon the corpse, the deceased may become a vampire.

3. If the dead body is reflected in a mirror, the reflection helps the spirit leave the body and become a vampire.

4. Any person who does not eat garlic or who expresses a distinct aversion to garlic could be a vampire.

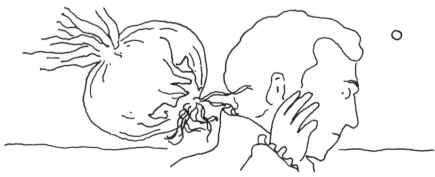

BIBLICAL RULES OF PRUDENCE AND COMMON SENSE

1. Do not try conclusions with an influential man, in case you later fall into his clutches.
2. Do not quarrel with a rich man, in case he turns the scales against you; for gold has destroyed many and has swayed the hearts of kings.
3. Do not quarrel with a man of quick tongue, do not pile logs on his fire.
4. Do not jest with an ill-mannered man, in case you hear you ancestry insulted.
5. Do not revile a repentant sinner; remember that we all are guilty.
6. Do not despise a man in his old age; after all, some of us too are growing old.
7. Do not gloat over a man's death; remember that we all must die.

MISCELLANEOUS BIBLICAL RULES

1. Do no evil, and evil will not befall you; shun wrong, and it will avoid you.
2. Son, do not sow in the furrows of wrongdoing, or you may reap it seven times over.
3. Do not ask the Lord for the highest place, or the king for a seat of honor.
4. Do not parade your virture before the Lord, or your wisdom before the king.
5. Do not scheme to be appointed judge, in case you are not strong enough to stamp out injustice, in case you let yourself be swayed by an influential man, and so risk the loss of your integrity.
6. Do not wrong the general body of citizens and so lower yourself in popular esteem.
7. Do not be drawn to sin twice over, for you will not go unpunished even once.
8. Do not say, "God will consider the great number of my gifts; when I make my offerings to the Most High God he will accept them."
9. Do not be impatient in prayer; do not neglect to give alms.
10. Do not laugh at a man when he is sad of heart, for he who brings him low can lift him high.
11. Do not draw up a lying indictment against your brother, do not do it against a friend either.
12. Mind you tell no lies, for no good can come of it.
13. Do not make long-winded speeches in the gathering of elders, and do not repeat yourself at your prayers.
14. Do not shirk wearisome labor, or farm work, which the Most High created.

15. Do not swell the ranks of the sinners, remember that the wrath will not delay.

16. Be very humble, since the punishment for the godless is fire and worms.

17. Do not barter a friend for profit, nor a real brother for the gold of Ophir.

18. Do not turn against a wise and good wife, for her charm is worth more than gold.

19. Do not ill-treat a slave who is an honest worker, or wage earner who does his best for you.

20. Love an intelligent slave like your own self, and do not deny him his freedom.

RULES FOR BECOMING A MONK IN AN AUGUSTINIAN MONASTERY

1. Monks are admonished to love their neighbor.

2. There must be perfect harmony in the monastery.

3. All property is to be held in common.

4. The Superior is to give particular consideration to the necessities of each individual.

5. All the monks are to enjoy a share in the common property, regardless of how much each contributed to it.

6. The poor are warned against greed for luxuries they had previously lacked.

7. Formerly rich monks should beware a sinful pride in their renunciation of the world.

8. Each brother is a temple of God, and should be revered as such by his brethren.

9. The church is to be used only as the house of prayer.

10. Nothing but that which is authorized may be sung.

11. Sensuality is to be overcome by fasting.

12. During meals, the reader must be listened to attentively and silently.

13. Jealousy between monks arising out of difference in their former possessions is condemned.

14. The habit must be a simple one.

15. It is recommended that the brothers avoid the presence of women, as far as possible.

16. They are to maintain a constant guard over their chastity, and assist their brethren in vanquishing temptation.

17. He who freely confesses having accepted gifts or letters without the permission of his Superior may be pardoned.

18. One common wardrobe will serve all.

19. The weekly reading of these rules and the obedience thereof are prescribed.

RULES FOR THWARTING VAMPIRES

1.   Vampires are frightened by light, so one must build a good fire to ward them off, and torches must be lit and placed outside the houses.
2.   Even if you lock yourself up in your home, you are not safe from the vampire, since he can enter through chimneys and keyholes. Therefore, one must rub the chimney and keyholes with garlic, and the windows and doors as well. The farm animals must also be rubbed with garlic to protect them.
3.   Crosses made from the thorns of wild roses are effective in keeping the vampire away.
4.   Spread thorns or poppy seeds on the paths leading to the village from the churchyard. Since vampires must stop to pick up every one of them, he may be so delayed that he cannot reach the village before sunrise, when he must return to his grave.
5.   If you take a large black dog and paint an extra set of eyes on his forehead with white paint you will alienate vampires. (Editors' Note: And large black dogs!)
6.   You may locate the grave of a vampire by choosing a boy or girl, young enough to be a virgin, and seat such a person on a horse of a solid color, all white, brown, or black, which is also a virgin and has never stumbled. The horse is led through the cemetery and over all the graves. If it refuses to pass over a grave, a vampire is likely to live there.
7.   To kill a vampire, drive a stake through his body into the earth in order to hold him securely in his grave. The stake should be made from a wild rosebush, or an ash or aspen tree. In some areas, red-hot iron rather than wood is used for the stake. The vampire's body should be burned or else reburied at the crossroads.
8.   If a vampire is not found and rendered harmless, it first kills all members of its immediate family, then starts on the other inhabitants of the village and its animals.
9.   If the vampire is allowed to go undetected for seven years, he can travel to another country or to a place where another language is spoken and become a human again. He or she can marry and have children, but they all become vampires when they die.

RULES FOR EXORCISTS

1.   After making the recommended confession and celebrating Mass, wearing a surplice and purple stole, begin the ceremony by sprinkling holy water and tracing the sign of the cross on yourself, the possessed person, and a very limited number of bystanders.

2. After the Litany of the Saints and several Scripture readings, pray: "I cast you out, unclean spirit. Tremble in fear, Satan, you enemy of Faith, you foe of the human race, you begetter of death. Why, then, do you stand and resist, knowing as you must that Christ the Lord brings your plans to nothing?"

3. Continue the prayers, if you see signs of progress, for two, three, four hours or longer if you can. Any words which especially torment the evil spirit should be repeated often.

4. Besides holy water, have a crucifix at hand and relics of the saints which must be encased. Prescribe no medication and do not bring the Holy Eucharist near the possessed person.

5. During the rite do not digress into senseless prattle with the demon or try to get the spirit to answer questions prompted by curiosity. But ask the number and name of the spirits, the time they entered, and the cause of the possession. Often the rite may have to be repeated for weeks, months, or years before the exorcism is successful.

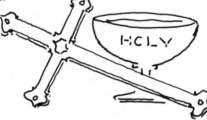

RULES FOR
DETERMINING POSSESSION BY THE DEVIL—1644

True Possession Is Indicated By Any Of These Manifestations:

1. To think oneself possessed.
2. To lead a wicked life.
3. To live outside the rules of society.
4. To be persistently ill, falling into heavy sleep and vomiting unusual objects (either natural objects: toads, serpents, worms, iron, stones, and so forth, or artificial objects: nail, pins, and so forth.)
5. To blaspheme.
6. To make a pact with the Devil.
7. To be troubled with spirits ("an absolute and inner possession and residence in the body of the person").
8. To show a frightening and horrible countenance.
9. To be tired of living.
10. To be uncontrollable and violent.
11. To make sounds and movements like an animal.

FOLK RULES FOR DETERMINING THE MEANING OF DREAMS

1. If a person dreams that a tooth is pulled without starting blood, it means that some member of his family is going to die. If it is a back tooth, the person will be an aged one; if a middle tooth, the person will be of medium age; if a front tooth, the person will be young.

2. If a person dreams that he is eating white grapes, it means that it will surely rain the next day.

3. To dream that a certain man, attired in his finest clothes, is in a company where the others are not so attired, mean that the man is going to die.

4. To dream of blood, means that nothing will happen.

5. If a person dreams that he sees his deceased father or mother talking angrily to him, it means that he or she wishes him to pray or make some atonement for him, or her.

6. If a person dreams that a large sore breaks and the matter is discharged, it means that he will be able to settle up all his debts.

7. If a married man dreams that he is being married, and sees himself attired in his wedding garments, it means that he is is going to die.

8. A man (A) has a certain number of troubles to pass through. If another man (B) dreams that he (A) is dead, he (A) has already passed the first trouble. If a second man (C) dreams that he (A) is dead, he (A) has passed the second trouble. This continues till all are passed.

9. To dream that the leaves fall to the ground yellow means that there will be an epidemic in the town.

10. If a person dreams that he sees a naked figure dancing in the air, it means that death will come and release a soul from its body.

11. If a person dreams that he sees a line of camels traveling single file, it means that angels from heaven are descending to inspire the little children.

12. If a person dreams of a river, it means that something stands between him and his wishes.

13. If a person dreams of a woman, it means that he will have happiness. If, however, her hair is disheveled, it means that some member of his family will die soon.

14. To dream of seeing a cloud in the shape of a camel means there will be no rain and consequently a poor harvest.

15. To dream of snakes brings bad luck.

16. If a person dreams of an old woman carrying a baby in her arms, it means that some man of the town will die.

17. If a person dreams that there are many priests in his house, he may be sure that on that same day a year hence some member of his household will die.

RULES FOR CURING DISEASE WITH WITCHCRAFT

1. To cure children of fever, put them on the roof or in the oven, or pass them through the earth of a crossroad.
2. To cure whooping cough, wear a live spider or caterpiller as an amulet.
3. To cure a person of insanity, bury a cock alive.
4. To cure warts, rub them iwth a snail and impail the creature on a thorn-bush.
5. To cure ague or whooping cough, enclose a live spider in a box or a hollowed-out nut.
6. To cure toothache, bite out the tooth of a corpse, or rub the infected gum with a dead finger.
7. To cure headache, scrape moss from a skull, pulverize it, and take it as snuff.
8. To cure a corn, cut it with a razor that has been used to shave a dead man.
9. To cure ringworm, warts, or piles, rub on grease from the church bells.
10. To ward off rheumatism, carry a silver coin from the church offertory in your pocket.

RULES FOR RIDING A BROOMSTICK AND FLYING

1. Make an ointment from the leaves of belladonna, stramonium, monkshood, and celery seeds.
2. Add to it one toad and boil until the toad's flesh has fallen off the bones.
3. Strain and rub the ointment on the body, under the armpits, on the forehead, and on your broom.
4. Eat celery seeds so that you won't get dizzy when flying.

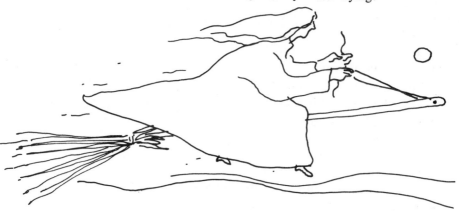

RULES FOR READING IRISH OMENS

1. **If the following happens, you'll have good luck:**
   - White button or horseshoe or pin (with point toward you) found lost
   - Plow team first seen facing toward you
   - Certain birds fly into the house
   - Two magpies seen together
   - Cuckoo first heard in right ear
   - A weasel met on the road
   - A goat accompanies the cattle
   - A garment put on inside-out
   - A sunny wedding day
   - West wind on New Year's Eve
   - Possession of an object stolen from a fisherman

2. **If the following happens you'll have a future marriage:**
   - Two knives or spoons set by mistake for a person at table
   - Girl's apron catches fire in front
   - Three magpies seen together
   - A frog comes to the door
   - Cuckoo heard at sunrise or before dawn

3. **If the following happens someone will die:**
   - Hearing cuckoo while in bent posture
   - Hen enters house with straw on tail
   - Four magpies seen in company
   - Cock crows at door or during the night
   - Crows desert a house
   - Crickets chirp at midnight
   - Cat looks at person after washing its face
   - Ass brays
   - Dog howls at night
   - Sound of drum or death carriage heard
   - Strange lights seen
   - Strange animal of funeral seen
   - Plank breaks in boat making
   - Knot occurs in thread
   - Chair falls as person rises
   - Noise heard in ear
   - Person sleeps late on May Morn
   - Person stumbles into hollow in graveyard
   - Blood seen in unexpected places

- Patient improves on Sunday
- Corpse remains limp during wake
- Funeral breaks apart
- Person dreams of meat or a falling tooth

4. **If the following happens you'll have bad luck:**
   - White foal or horse is seen
   - Black hare or dog seen at night
   - Neighbor's animal dies on land of another
   - You kill a cat
   - Cuckoo seen or heard on a leafless tree
   - Magpies seen alone
   - Cock crows by day
   - Hen crows
   - Moving residence on Monday
   - Being last in a funeral or leaving the graveyard
   - Striking animals with certain kinds of sticks
   - Seeing the new moon through glass
   - Breaking a mirror
   - Rain falls on a wedding day
   - Wedding meets funeral
   - Wedding ring drops to ground
   - East wind on New Year's Eve
   - You see a redheaded woman
   - You see a mermaid

RULES OF SUPERSTITION

1. Never walk under an open ladder.
2. Don't let a black cat cross your path.
3. Don't carry an open umbrella in the sunshine.
4. Stay away from anything with the number 13.
5. Don't step on cracks in the sidewalk.
6. To prevent warts, don't handle toads.
7. Don't eat pickles and drink milk at the same time.
8. For luck, carry a rabbit's foot, lucky penny, or four-leaf clover.
9. Don't break a mirror, unless you want seven years bad luck.
10. Don't prick your finger with a needle.
11. Don't let the wind blow out a lighted candle.
12. Don't walk in a forest after dark.
13. To ward off evil, throw a pinch of salt over your shoulder.

THE ELEVEN RULES FOR YIELDING TO THE DEVIL AS DERIVED FROM CONFESSIONS OF WITCHES ON THE RACK

Firstly, the Novices have to conclude with the Demon, or with some other Wizard or Magician acting in the Demon's place, an express compact by which, in the presence of witnesses, they enlist in the Demon's service, he giving them in exchange his promise that they shall enjoy honors, riches, and carnal pleasures.

Secondly, they abjure the Catholic Faith, withdraw from their obedience to God, renounce Christ and the protection of the most Blessed Virgin Mary, and all the sacraments or the Church.

Thirdly, they cast away the Crown, or Rosary of the most Blessed Virgin Mary, the girdle of Saint Francis, or the Cincture of Saint Augustine, or the Scapular of the Carmelites, should they belong to one of those Orders; the Cross, the Medals, the Agnus Dei, whatever other holy or consecrated object may have been about their person, and trample them underfoot.

Fourthly, into the hands of the Devil they vow obedience and subjection; they pay him homage and vassalage, laying their fingers on some foul black book. They bind themselves never to return to the faith of Christ, to observe none of the divine precepts, to do no good work, but to obey the Demon alone and to attend diligently the nightly conventicles.

Fifthly, they promise to strive with all their power, and to devote their utmost zeal and care to the enlistment of other males and females in the service of the Demon.

Sixthly, the Devil administers to them a certain sacrilegious baptism, and after abjuring their Christian Godfathers and Godmothers of the Baptism of Christ and Confirmation, they have assigned to them a new Godfather and a new Godmother, who are to instruct them in the arts of witchcraft; they drop their former name and exchange it for another, more frequently a scurrilous and absurd nickname.

Seventhly, they cut off a part of their own garments, and tender it as a token of homage to the Devil, who takes it away and retains it.

Eighthly, the Devil draws on the ground a circle wherein stand the Novices, Witches, and Wizards, and there they confirm by horrid oaths all their aforesaid promises.

Ninthly, they request the Devil to strike them out of the book of Christ and to inscribe them in his own book. Then is brought forth that foul black book on which, as has been explained above, they laid hands when doing homage, and they are inscribed therein with the Devil's claw.

Tenthly, they promise the Devil sacrifices and offerings at stated times:

once a fortnight or at least each month, the slaughter of some child, or a murderous act of sorcery, and week by week other vile misdeeds to the bitter hurt of mankind, such as hailstorms, tempests, fires, rinderpest, the destruction of sheep and kine, etc.

Eleventhly, the Demon imprints on them some mark, especially on those whose constancy he suspects. That mark, moreover, is not always of the same shape or figure: sometimes it is the likeness of a hare, sometimes a toad's foot, sometimes a spider, a puppy, a dormouse. It is imprinted on the most hidden parts of the body: with men, under the eyelids, or it may be under the armpits, or on the lips, on the shoulder, the fundament, or somewhere else; with women, it is usually on the breasts or the privy parts. Now, the stamp which imprints those marks is none other but the Devil's claw.

RULES FOR CAPTURING LOVE WITH VOODOO

1. **Simple—A lover:**
   a. Take a picture of someone you would like to have an affair with and hang it on the wall.

   b. Turn it upside down each evening at sunset, and right side up each morning at sunrise.

   c. Do this for nine consecutive days. This conjuring method is said to draw a desired lover to your bed.

   d. Note: It can also be used to force an unfaithful partner to return to your side.

2. **Harder—A married lover:**
   a. Simply write down the name of the man and his wife, or the woman and her husband, on a small piece of plain white paper.

   b. Slip the paper into a fresh chicken bladder and sew the end tightly up. Hang outside in the bright sun and allow to completely dry for seven days.

   c. On the seventh day, the desired lover will leave their mate and come to see you. This old voodoo method always works well.

RULES FOR USING VOODOO TO END AFFAIRS

1. **To stop a couple from getting married or to break up an affair between married individuals:**
   a. Use a combination of four pigeons and rum.

   b. Feed the liquor to the four birds while the couple's name is written on four separate pieces of paper. One scrap of paper is inserted in each bird's beak and it is then released, and allowed to fly away.

   c. This act will abruptly stop the affair.

2. **To rid yourself of your lover or mate:**
   a. Take an old black shoe that belongs to your lover or mate.

   b. Soak it in pure rainwater for a period of seven full days and nights.

   c. Then place in an oven and allow to completely dry out again. When thoroughly dried, get a dirt dauber's nest and crumble into dust. Add cayenne pepper and blend.

   d. Dump this mixture into the old shoe.

   e. Stretch a dirty sock over the entire shoe and carry it to the nearest river or lake. At exactly noon, begin to run as fast as possible near the water's edge.

   f. Toss the sock-encased shoe over your left shoulder and into the water. So not, under any circumstances, turn and watch it hit the water.

   g. Leave for home immediately. It is said a mate will leave within seven days and never bother you again

3. **To stop your daughter's affair with a married man:**
   a. Simply utilize the voodoo power of a John the Conqueror root. Mix equal amounts of goofer dust and red brick dust together and sprinkle all over the root.

   b. Within one week (seven days), the man will break the relationship. Your daughter will not grieve for more than seven days after the affair has ended.

RULES FOR CURING INSANITY WITH VOODOO

1. Comb the insane person's hair and collect any hairs that fall out, or pull them out of the comb or brush.

2. Purchase one pound of ground beef. Make a group of patties and insert one hair in each.

3. Roll each patty into a small ball. Take all of the meatballs and go for a walk.

4. Each time you see a dog, drop one ball. Continue until you have given all the meat away.

5. Never look back. That mad person is supposed to be back to normal by the time you have completed this task.

RULES FOR BECOMING INVISIBLE

1. Perform this on Wednesday before dawn.

2. Take seven black beans and the head of a dead man.

3. Turn the head face up.

4. Put two beans in the head's eyes, two in its ears, and one in its mouth.

5. Each day for nine days—before dawn—sprinkle brandy on the dead head.

6. When a spirit says, "What doest thou?" say, "I am watering my plant." (This will probably happen on the eighth day.)

7. If the spirit asks for the brandy bottle, don't give it until it shows you a figure drawn on the dead head.

8. By the ninth day, the beans will be ripe. Swallow one of them.

9. Look in a mirror. If you cannot see yourself, you know you are invisible.

10. If you see yourself . . . try the whole procedure again.

RULES ON TIPPING FOR SERVICES AROUND THE WORLD

United States
1. Generally, you should tip 15 to 20 percent of the bill, unless it is under $1.00, when you should tip 25 cents. This rule is good for beauticians, waiters and waitresses, bartenders, and taxi drivers.
2. Tip barbers 50 cents to $1.00, depending on their service and skill.
3. Tip skycaps and porters 25 to 35 cents per bag, and hotel bellmen 50 cents per bag, more if the baggage is heavy or cumbersome.

Great Britain
1. Tip 15 percent to the bill to waitresses and waiters, hairdressers, and taxi cab drivers with whom you have run up a fare of over 10 shillings. (If a cab fare is less than 5 shillings, tip 9 pence; between 5 and 10 shillings, tip 1 shilling.)
2. Tip 1 shilling to doormen who call you a cab, 1 shilling per bag to porters and bellhops (not less than 2 shillings total), and 1 shilling per day to chambermaids.
3. Tip ladies room attendants 6 pence.
4. Tip a concierge 3 to 7 shillings for special service.

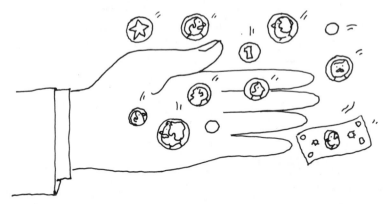

Switzerland
1. Tip 15 percent of the bill to waiters and waitresses (if there is a service charge, just leave small change in addition), taxi drivers, and hairdressers.
2. Tip 10 percent of the charge to a station porter, and 1 Swiss franc per day to bellhops.
3. Tip 50 centimes to doormen who call you a cab and to ladies room attendants.
4. Tip a concierge and a chambermaid 2 francs *only* if they have performed a special service.

Greece
1. Add 5 to 10 percent of the bill over the service charge for a waiter of waitress.
2. Tip 5 drachmas to a taxi driver, a doorman who calls you a cab, and a bellhop or porter who carries a load of luggage.
3. Tip 15 drachmas per day (100 per week) to a chambermaid, and 10 drachmas to a hairdresser.
4. Yip a concierge 50 drachmas for a special service.
5. Tip 2 drachmas to a ladies room attendant and a theater usher.

Germany
1. Tip 5 percent of the check over the service charge to waiters and waitresses.
2. Tip 15 percent of the meter reading to taxi drivers.
3. Tip 10 percent of the charge to station porters and 50 pfennige per bag to bellhops.
4. Tip 50 pfennige per day (up to 2 marks per week) to a chambermaid, 50 pfennige to a doorman for calling a cab, and 50 pfennige to a hairdresser.
5. Tip a concierge 1 to 2 marks for a special service.

Italy
1. Tip 5 percent of the check over the service charge to waiters and waitresses.
2. Tip 100 lire per day (up to 500 lire per week) to a chambermaid, 100 lire per bag to bellhops and porters, and 100 lire to a doorman who calls you a cab, or to a hairdresser.
3. Tip 50 lire to a ladies room attendant and a theater usher.
4. Tip 15 percent of the meter reading to taxi drivers.
5. Tip a concierge 10 percent of his bill for cables, phone calls, etc.

France
1. Tip 15 percent of the bill to waiters and waitresses, cab drivers, and hairdressers, if there is no service charge included. If there is a service charge, tip 2 francs extra to waiters and waitresses.
2. Tip 1 franc to doormen who call you a cab, 1 franc per day to chambermaids, and 1 franc per bag to bellhops and porters (up to 3 francs).
3. Tip the concierge 1 franc for special services, 5 to 6 francs a week, even if there are no special services performed.
4. Tip a ladies room attendant ½ franc.
5. Tip ½ franc to an usher at a cinema, up to 2 francs for orchestra seats at a play or concert.

Spain
1. Tip 5 pesetas to a doorman who calls you a cab, a taxi driver, a ladies room attendant, and a hairdresser.
2. Tip 5 pesetas minimum over a 15 percent serivce charge to a waiter and waitress. If no service charge, tip 5 percent over the check.
3. Tip 10 pesetas a day (50 pesetas per week) to a chambermaid, and 5 to 10 pesetas per bag to porters and bellhops.
4. Tip a concierge 25 pesetas a day or more, depending on service. Leave no tip if no serivce has been performed.

Portugal
1. Tip 5 to 10 percent of a check over the service charge to waiters and waitresses.
2. Tip 15 percent of the meter reading to taxi drivers.
3. Tip porters and bellhops 5 escudos per bag, chambermaids 20 escudos per week, and concierges and hairdressers 10 escudos per service.
4. Tip two $50 escudos to a doorman who calls you a cab or a bellhop who performs a special service.
5. Tip one $50 escudos to a ladies room attendant and a theater usher.

Egypt
1. Tip 5 percent of the check over a 10 percent cover charge to a waiter or waitress.
2. Tip 20 percent of the bill to a hairdresser, 10 percent to a taxi driver.
3. Tip 5 piastres per bag to a bellhop or porter, 5 piastres to a theater usher and to a doorman who calls you a cab.
4. Tip a chambermaid 35 piastres a week and a concierge 10 piastres at the end of your stay.
5. Tip a ladies room attendant 2 piastres.

RULES FOR SETTING THE TABLE

Breakfast:
1. For the breakfast table the centerpiece may be simple flowers, a green plant in a silver or copper urn or a convenient Lazy Susan. The table is usually bare except for place mats, but on a beautifully surfaced table or a breakfast nook where the table has a composition top, even these may be dispensed with.
2. The silver at each place consists of a small fork and knife, a dessert-size spoon for cereal, if needed, a butter knife on the butter plate and a teaspoon on the saucer beneath the coffee cup or to the right of the knife to the left of the cereal spoon.

3. Coffee cups may be before the hostess or at each place to the right of the knife.

4. Jam or marmalade is served on a small serving dish or silver-topped or other decorative jam jar on a small service plate, with a spoon on the right side of the plate or in the jar or dish.

5. Fruit or fruit juice is at each place on the breakfast plate.

6. Breakfast is the one meal at which it is permissible to read the paper, mail, or anything else that suits your fancy.

Informal Lunch:

1. The basic silver for lunch is always a fork and knife, whether or not both are actually needed. To this is added a spoon for soup or appetizer, if needed.

2. The table may be covered with a lunch cloth, elaborate or simple, depending on the degree of formality. But, as in the modern fashion, it is more likely to be set with place mats. Water is in the goblets at each place, or may be poured.

3. The centerpiece can be simple garden flowers or an arrangement of fruit.

4. There are ashtrays, cigarettes, and matches at each place, unless the hostess is unalterably opposed to smoking at any meal.

5. Butter plates are always used.

6. Luncheons are usually limited to three courses—which may be soup (in cream soup or bouillon cups rather than soup plates) or appetizer such as shrimp cocktail or paté, a main course often combining meat and vegetable, salad with cheese or simple dessert, often with a fruit base.

7. Dessert silver may be on the table above the place plate or on the dessert plates, passed by maid or hostess.

Informal Dinner:

1. The silver is placed one inch or so from the edge of the table at place settings that are equidistant from one another on a table laid with care and precision.

2. The napkin is placed on the place plate, unless the first course is in place, and then it is to the left of the forks, but it should not obscure them, nor should the silver be obscured by the plate.

3. Candles may be in any color but should be above eye level and, if they are on the table at all, lighted.

4. The silver is placed traditionally, that needed first, farthest right and left of the plate. The forks are usually two, for meat and salad, occasionally one more for an appetizer, but never more than three at once. The salad fork is inside the meat fork, unless the salad is served as a first course, in which case it is the first fork in the setting. An iced tea spoon may be placed to the right of the knives. Spoons for soup or fruit are on the table, to the right of the knives.

5. On the informal table, butter plates and knives are used with the butter knife placed in a variety of ways—across the top of the plate, blade toward the user, across the plate, tip toward the center of the plate, or occasionally parallel to the knives, blade to the left.

Formal Dinner:

1. The silver should not be obscured by the place plate. The large damask dinner napkin, folded, is on the place plate, no matter how decorative the latter may be. But the place plate, if it is pictorial, is carefully arranged so that the design is toward the diner.

2. No butter plates or butter knives appear on a really formal table, as breads that are passed are placed directly on the tablecloth.

3. There must be a foot or more between each guest, the space accurately measured. But there should never be so much space between guests that conversation becomes difficult.

4. At a long narrow table with few guests the seating is arranged so that the host and hostess sit opposite wach other at the center of the table with guests grouped right and left of each and with the ends of the table unset.

5. At a formal dinner all serving is from the kitchen or pantry, so no serving implements are on the table.

6. At each place, in addition to the plate, the roll, and the napkin, is the following silver: knives, to the right, never more than three, for appetizer, if necessary, fish, and meat, or for meat, fish, and salad. To the left are the forks, also never more than three at a time, one for the appetizer, if any, one for the fish, if needed, one for the meat, or the first for the fish, the second for the meat, and third for the salad. If a fourth fork is needed for salad, it it placed when the salad is served. With the exception of the spoons for soup or melon there are no spoons to the right of the knives, as at all settings, except buffet, silver is placed left and right so the diner works from the outside in toward the plate in choosing his implements. Dessert spoons with their forks are in place, spoon right, fork left, on the dessert plates when they are brought in.

7. Glasses are placed in order of their use above the knives, and each is removed with the course it accompanied with the exception of the dessert wine glass, which remains through the fruit and demitasse.

RULES FOR HOSTING A SUCCESSFUL PARTY

1. Take one final look—everything ready?

2. Check your appearance. How do you look? Calm, happy, completely dressed? If you didn't allow yourself enough time, your guests may find a picture-perfect table, but a frazzled, thrown-together hostess.

3. Double check: Is the fire going? Are the guest towels out? Is the entire production—with you as director, producer, and star—assembled?

4. Welcome each arriving guest with spirit and confidence. Let them know you're happy to see them. If you're not, it's either because you're unprepared or because you don't want to see them—in which case you shouldn't have invited them.

5. If the gathering is large, don't continue to introduce all guests to one another as you do the first few. It interrupts a blooming spirit of festivity and can even become annoying. Instead, hand around the door, introduce the new arrivals to a few people nearby and show them where to put their wraps. (Since many homes don't have a closet to spare, the next best place is the bed.)

6. Tend to the care and feeding of your guests, don't buzz around in an obvious attempt to be the perfect hostess. The only smooth performance is one that's prearranged.

7. If you have a scattered cocktail gathering, keep an eye on the well-being of your guests. If the heavy drinker is beginning to look glazed, whisper to the bartender to go slow on his drinks and water them down a bit.

8. If husband and wife are beginning to snap at each other, separate them tactfully before it hurts.

9. Watch for the wallflower—introduce him to someone. Or ask him to help you tend bar. He'll be happier with something to do.

10. If the women huddle separately from the men—start integrating before you have a scene reminiscent of your first high school dance. Induce a conversation between members of each group.

11. Don't urge your guests to overeat or overdrink. If it's a dinner party, keep the hors d'oeuvres light and keep your guests hungry for the meal you so carefully planned.

12. Threaten, insist, hiss, scream—but allow no one to jump up from the table to help. Guests are invited to have a good time, not to act as auxiliary maids. You can count on it—if one person pops up, another soon will, then another, and finally there's one person left, giving a monologue. Besides, "helpful" guests will plunk down a dirty platter just where you were counting on tossing the salad. Make a deal—if guests don't help in your house, you won't in their.

SPECIFIC RULES FOR HOTEL TIPPING IN THE UNITED STATES

1. The quality of the hotel, the amount of baggage one has, and the service expected, all have a bearing on the size of the tip dispensed to the doorman. The man who opens the door of the cab and sets bags on the curb usually does no more than call a bellhop to take over. If he performs no service, no tip is required. If he helps unload heavy and extensive baggage or assists anyone into the hotel itself, or at some other time summons a taxi, tipping is expected. For summoning a taxi from the stand in front of the hotel and merely opening its door for a passenger, a doorman usually gets a quarter. If he must fare forth in the rain and find one in the midst of traffic, the tip is gauged by the amount of trouble he has had—twenty-five cents or fifty cents or, perhaps in a bad storm late at night for guests in evening clothes, as much as a dollar.

2. The standard tip for a bellhop carrying up luggage for a newly registered guest or couple is a quarter if he does nothing but perhaps carry a light bag, or turn on the air conditioning and check the bath in one trip. If large amounts of luggage are involved the tip may be a dollar (about fifty cents a bag is expected but usually not more than a dollar).

3. Page boys usually receive a tip of a quarter from the person paged.

4. For a chambermaid, the guest staying two or three nights is certainly considerate to leave the once customary twenty-five cents per person for each night, and more for a suite, with the amount depending of course on the quality of the hotel.

5. Tipping in hotel beauty salons is the same as at home—15 to 20 percent, not less than fifty cents for a manicure and as much as a dollar, and seventy-five cents or one dollar for a shampoo and hair set or more depending on the operator. Shop owners are not tipped.

6. Thirty-five cents is a minimum tip for a haircut in large cities and fifty cents is nore common in a good shop. For services in addition to the haircut such as sunlamp, shampoo, or shave, as much as two dollars is customary.

7. A hotel porter receives fifty cents per trunk carried up to a room. If there is other heavy baggage as well, a dollar or more, depending on the amount and difficulty involved.

8. At any checkroom in a hotel specially set up to serve a special affair such as a dance or ball, the attendant receives a quarter per person.

9. A longtime guest in a hotel usually tips the elevator starter, if any, a dollar or more on leaving if he has been helpful and another dollar or more to elevator men who have served him.

10. Hotel managers, as executives, are not tipped. Desk clerks, if they are asked for special services by residents, do expect to be remembered from time to

time. Usually tips are given during the holidays. They may range from two to three dollars to five dollars for them and for telephone operators on such special occasions, depending upon the amount of mail and calls handled.

11. Many hotels make a charge for room service, but on top of this the waiter expects a tip. This is never less than a quarter for an individual small order such as a setup or a pot of tea and toast. For a dinner order, 15 to 20 percent of the bill is expected depending on the quality of the hotel.

12. The dining room waiter is the man in charge of the service in the dining room of a hotel. Transients tip the dining room waiter sometimes, especially if they want to be sure of a good table on their next visit. A dollar is usual every third or fourth trip. Hotel residents tip the dining room waiter the same way as transients do but they give the headwaiter, not normally tipped in hotels by transients, three to five dollars once a month depending on the hotel.

RULES OF THE DANCE—1901

1. As introductions at balls are understood to be for the purpose of dancing, it is not necessary to recognize the person introduced to you afterward, though it is polite to bow.

2. A gentleman must not solicit more than two dances from a young lady whom he has met for the first time that evening.

3. It is very poor taste for a gentleman and lady to place their joined hands against the hip or side of the gentleman. Always keep the hands clear of the body.

4. A gentleman should be constantly on the watch during round dances to see that he and his partner do not collide with other couples. Such an accident would mark him a poor dancer.

5. Noisy talking is improper in a ballroom.

6. Never overlook or refuse to fill an engagement upon your card or erase the name in favor of some other gentleman. It is unpardonable.

7. White kid gloves are worn. Light and very delicate shades are permitted, also. Gloves are removed from the hands at supper.

8. A married couple should not dance together more than once in an evening.

9. If a lady refuses to dance with a gentleman, unless she is previously engaged, she should remain seated until that dance is finished.

10. A lady should not enter the ballroom leaning on the arm of her escort. She should enter first, the gentleman closely following.

11. In asking a lady to dance, the correct form is "May I have the pleasure of the next waltz (or german) with you?" If accepted, the gentleman should enter her name on his card, and his last name on hers.

12. At a large ball any formal leave-taking is unnecessary.

RULES FOR THE SINGING OF THE NATIONAL ANTHEM

1.   When the Anthem strikes up in any public place, men, women, and children should stand at complete attention and should sing it if they possibly can.
2.   If they can't sing they should stand quietly and respectfully without whispering, talking, or fidgeting until the Anthem is finished.
3.   Civilian men and boys remove their hats, hold them with the right hand over their hearts. Women stand st attention or place the right hand over the heart. If in uniform, salute at the first note of the Anthem and retain the position of salute until the last note of the Anthem.
4.   Don't chew gum, eat, or smoke during the playing of the Anthem in public places.
5.   Don't continue making your way to your seat, even if you are in an aisle when the music starts.
6.   The hearing of the National Anthem at home over radio or television does not require the rising of those present if they are gathered informally together in a small group.
7.   The Anthem is never played in private homes merely for entertainment, or improvised upon for dance purposes.

RULES FOR DESIGNING A WOMAN'S VISITING CARD— 1890

1.   Cards shall be moderately large, nearly square, fine in their texture, thin, but not too flexible, and of a soft delicate white that is not intense in its clearness.
2.   Its engraving is script, not large, nor yet small, distinct, and with no ornamentation.
3.   Usually a daughter's card is slightly smaller than that of her mother, but its style of lettering is the same.
4.   It is imperative that Mrs. or Miss be placed before the name upon her engraved card. It is customary to use the husband's complete name, initials being less and less often seen upon visiting cards as the years go by. Except when a complete name is too large to be properly engraved upon a card of customary size, good taste omits initials and uses baptismal names.
5.   The distinguishing convenience of an entire name upon a card, except when the last one is uncommon, is very soon recognized in a city, and sometimes also in towns, if there are many family connections.

6. The oldest married women in the oldest branch of the family may, if she chooses, omit baptismal names from her card, such as: Mrs. Jamison. She, and she only, is entitled to this dignity and simplicity of form.

7. Unless a women is elderly, she usually prefers the prefix of her husband's full name for all ceremonious or social intercommunications, or, at least, she prefers some part or parts of it. Since society is so extended and complex in its interests, an establishment of card usages, and the possession of an unmistakable name and an engraved address, are an immense convenience to overburdened memories. There is small chance of a social blunder being made with a card engraved thus:

Mrs. John Herbert Jamison,

Tuesdays.   15 Porter Place.

8. A city or town is not added except in ink, and then only for use while away from home.

9. If a woman wishes to receive in a more formal manner than by a weekly "at home," or if she has a guest whom she wishes to introduce to her coterie of acquaintances, she may, for example, write the words *From three to six* above *Tuesday,* and the words *Jan. 10th* beneath *Tuesday.*

10. To shorten her season of receiving, it is etiquette to write under the engraved at home day, *Until Lent,* or she may limit the time to any date she pleases.

11. Plates to be used year after year are properly engraved with the receiving month or months beneath the day of the week. This permits a pen to be drawn through the month not devoted to visitors. In the extension of social circles, women in America are beginning to adopt the London and Paris custom of using cards with, for example,

First Tuesdays in
January, February and March.

on their left lower corner.

Such cards provide for absence from home and are most simple and convenient.

RULES OF SEATING IN OFFICIAL
MOTORCADES FOR FOREIGN VISITORS

1. One limousine—one foreign ambassador
   The ambassador, right rear seat
   The mayor, center rear seat
   The local representative of the ambassador, left rear seat
   The ambassador's aide, left rear jump seat

2. One limousine—one foreign ambassasor and wife
   The ambassador, right rear seat
   The wife of the ambassador, center rear seat
   The mayor, left rear seat
   The ambassador's local representative, right jump seat
   The wife of the local representative, left jump seat
   The ambassador's aide, front seat

3. Two limousines—one foreign ambassador and wife
   Lead limousine:
   The ambassador, right rear seat
   The mayor, center rear seat
   The ambassador's local representative, left rear seat
   The ambassador's aide, left rear jump seat
   Second limousine:
   The wife of the ambassador, right rear seat
   The wife of the mayor, center rear seat
   The local representative of the ambassador's wife, left rear seat
   Other woman of the offficial party

4. Several limousines—a foreign President and members of his cabinet and
   their wives
   Lead limousine:
   The President, right rear seat
   The mayor, center rear seat
   Local foreign government representative, left rear seat
   U.S. Office of Protocol representative, left jump seat
   The President's chief security officer, front seat
   U.S. chief security officer, front seat
   Second limousine:
   Minister of foreign affairs, right rear seat
   Minister of defense, center rear seat
   Minister of finance, left rear seat
   Foreign security agent, jump seat
   U.S. security agent, jump seat
   U.S. protocol representative, front seat.

Third limousine:

        Wife of minister of foreign affairs, right rear seat

        Wife of minister of defense, rear center seat

        Wife of minister of finance, left rear seat

        Wife of U.S. officer or protocol representative, right jump seat

        U.S. Security office, front seat

Fourth limousine:

        Other official party members in no particular seating order.

RULES FOR MILITARY MARCHING

1. All steps and marchings executed from the halt, except right step, begin with the left foot.

Forward, half step, halt, and mark time may be executed one from the other in quick or double time.

2. The following table prescribes the length (in inches measured from heel to heel) and the cadence (in steps per minute) of the steps in marching.

Step	Time	Length	Cadence
Full	Quick	30	120
Full	Double	36	180
Full	Slow*	30	
Half	Quick	15	120
Half	Double	18	180
Side	Quick	12	120
Back	Quick	15	120

*This is a special step executed only as the funeral escort is approaching the place of interment. The cadence, in accordance with that set by the band, varies in different airs that may be played. The instructor, when necessary, indicates the cadence of the step by calling one, two, three, four the instant the left and right foot, respectively, should be planted.

3. All steps and marchings and movements involving march are executed in quick time unless the squad be marching in double time or double time be added to the command; in the latter case double time is added to the preparatory command. EXAMPLE: 1. Squad right, double time, 2. MARCH.

4. Quick time—Being at a halt, to march forward in quick time, command: 1. Forward, 2. MARCH. At the command Forward, shift the weight of the body to the right leg without perceptible movement. At the command MARCH, move the left foot straight forward a full step, sole near the ground, and plant it without shock; next, in like manner, advance and plant the right foot; continue the march. Swing the arms about 6 inches to the front and about 3 inches to the rear of the body.

Being in march in double time, to resume the quick time, command: 1. Quick time, 2. MARCH. At the command MARCH, given as either foot strikes the ground, advance and plant the other foot in double time; resume the quick time, dropping the hands by the sides.

5.   Double time—Command: 1. Double time, 2. MARCH. Being at a halt, at the command Double time, shift the weight of the body to the right leg without perceptible movement. At the command MARCH, raise the forearms, fists closed, knuckles out, to a horizontal position along the waistline; take up an easy run with the step and cadence of double time, allowing a natural swinging motion to the arms. Being in march at quick time, at the command MARCH, given as either foot strikes the ground, take one step in quick time and then step off in double time.

6.   To mark time—Command: 1. Mark time, 2. MARCH. Being in march, at the command MARCH, given as either foot strikes the ground, advance and plant the other foot; bring up the other foot in rear, placing it so that both heels are on line, and continue the cadence by alternately raising and planting each foot. The feet are raised 2 inches from the ground. Being at a halt, at the command MARCH, raise and plant first the left foot, then the right foot, and so on as prescribed above.

7.   Half step—Command: 1. Half step, 2. MARCH. Take steps of 15 inches in quick time and 18 inches in double time in the same manner as in the full step.

8.   Side step—Being at a halt or mark time, command: 1. Right (left) step, 2. MARCH. Carry the right foot 12 inches to the right; place the left foot beside the right, left knee straight. Continue in the cadence of quick time. The side step is used for short distances only and is not executed in double time.

9.   Back step—Being at a halt or mark time, command: 1. Backward, 2. MARCH.

EARLY SHAKER RULES FOR CHILDREN ON BEHAVIOR AT THE TABLE

---

1.   First, in the morning, when you rise, Give thanks to God, who well supplies Our various wants, and gives us food, Wholesome, nutritious, sweet, and good:

2.   Then to some proper place repair, And wash your hands and face with care; And ne'er the table once disgrace With dirty hands or dirty face.

3.   When to your meals you have the call, Promptly attend, both great and small; Then kneel and pray, with closed eyes, That God will bless these rich supplies.

4. When at the table you sit down, Sit straight and trim, nor laugh nor frown; Then let the elder first begin, And all unite, and follow him.

5. Of bread, then take a decent piece, Nor splash about the fat and grease; But cut your meat both neat and square, And take of both an equal share.

6. Also, of bones you'll take your due, For bones and meat together grew.

7. If, from some incapacity, With fat your stomach don't agree, Or if you cannot pick a bone, You'll please to let them both alone.

8. Potatoes, cabbage, turnip, beet, And every kind of thing you eat, Must neatly on your plate be laid, Before you eat with pliant blade:

9. Nor ever—'tis an awkward matter, To eat or sip out of the platter.

10. If bread and butter be your fate, Or biscuit, and you find there are Pieces enough, then take your slice, And spread it over, thin and nice, On one side, only; then you may Eat in a decent, comely way.

11. Yet butter you must never spread On nut-cake, pie, or dier-bread; Or bread with milk, or bread with meat, Butter with these you may not eat.

12. These things are all the best of food, And need not butter to be good.

13. When bread or pie you cut or break, Touch only what you mean to take; And have no prints of fingers seen On that that's left—nay, if they're clean.

14. Be careful, when you take a sip Of liquid, don't extend your lip So far that one may fairly think That cup and all you mean to drink.

15. Then clean your knife—don't lick it, pray; It is a nasty, shameful way— But wipe it on a piece of bread, Which snugly by your plate is laid.

16. Thus clean your knife, before you pass It into plum or apple-sauce, Or butter, which you must cut nice, Both square and true as polish'd dice.

17. Cut not a pickle with a blade Whose side with grease is overlaid; and always take your equal share Of coarse as well as luscious fare.

18. Don't pick your teeth, or ears, or nose, Nor scratch your head, nor tonk your toes; Nor belch nor sniff, nor jest nor pun, Nor have the least of play or fun.

19. If you're oblig'd to cough or sneeze, Your handkerchief you'll quickly seize, And timely shun the foul disgrace Of splattering either food or face.

20. Drink neither water, cider, beer, With greasy lip or mucus tear; Nor fill your mouth with food, and then Drink, lest you blow it out again.

21. And when you've finish'd your repast, Clean plate, knife, fork—then, at the last, Upon your plate lay knife and fork, And pile your bones of beef and pork:

22. But if no plate, you may as well Lay knife and fork both parallel.

23. Pick up your crumbs, and, where you eat, Keep all things decent, clean, and neat; Then rise, and kneel in thankfulness To Him who does your portion bless; Then straightly from the table walk, Nor stop to handle things, not talk.

24. If we mean never to offend, To every gift we must attend, Respecting meetings, work, or food, And doing all things as we should.

RULES FOR BEING A GOOD SPORT

1.   Play your best; no matter how far behind you are, keep trying.
2.   Be a generous opponent—slow to take advantage of a technicality for yourself, quick to give another the benefit of the doubt.
3.   Take defeat gracefully: praise the victor's game instead of excusing your own (never "I've been sick!").
4.   Accept victory modestly: find something valid to say about your opponent's game—an unreturnable backhand, not one three-putt green.
5.   Never display "righteous" impatience about the game's being delayed, someone's talking during the play; no glares, sharp words, requests to play the point over.
6.   Accept criticism for breaking a rule with a quick apology.
7.   Call any infringement of the rules on yourself—particularly one not noticed by your opponent.
8.   Never criticize your partner.
9.   Adapt easily—and without complaint—to the house rules of the game when you are a guest.

VICTORIAN RULES OF MOURNING

1.   The Regulation Period for a Widow's Mourning is two years; of this period crape should be worn for one year and nine months, for the first twelve months the dress should be entirely covered with crape, for the remaining nine months it should be trimmed with crape, heavily so the first six months, and considerable less the remaining three; during the last three months black without crape should be worn. After the two years two months half mourning is prescribed, but many people prefer to continue wearing black without crape in lieu of half mourning.
2.   Lawn cuffs and collars should be worn during the crape period.
3.   After a year and nine months jet trimming may be worn.
4.   Widowers should wear mourning for the same period, but they usually enter society much sooner than widows.
5.   For a Parent the period of mourning is twelve months, six months black with crape, four months black without crape, two months half mourning.
6.   Linen collars and cuffs should not be worn during the crape period, but crape lisse only. Neither should jewelry be worn during the crape period, nor until the first two months of black have expired.
7.   For a Son or Daughter the period of mourning is identical with the foregoing.
8.   The Mourning for Infants or very young children is frequently shortened to

half this period and is occasionally only worn for three months; and in this case crape is oftener than not discarded.

9. For a Step-mother—The period of mourning depends upon whether the step-daughters reside at home or not, or whether their father has been long married, or whether their father's second wife has filled the place of mother to them, in which case the period of mourning would be for twelve months, otherwise the period is six months.

10. For a Brother or Sister the longest period of mourning is six months, the shortest period four months. During the longest period, viz., six months, crape should be worn for three months black without crape for two months, half mourning one month. During the shortest period, viz., four months, crape should be worn for two months, and black without crape two months.

11. For a sister-in-law or a brother-in-law the period of mourning is the same as for a brother or sister, and the foregoing are the regulation periods to be observed.

12. For a Grandparent, the longest period of mourning is nine months; the shortest period is six months. During the longest period crape should be worn for three months; black without crape for three months, and half mourning three months. During the shortest period crape should be worn for three months, and black without crape for three months.

13. For an Uncle or Aunt, the longest period of mourning is three months; the shortest period six weeks. During the longest period, black without crape should be worn for two months; half mourning one month. During the shortest period, black without crape for six weeks.

14. For a Nephew or Niece, the periods of mourning are identical with the foregoing.

15. For a First Cousin, the longest period is six weeks, the shortest one month. During the longest period, black for three weeks; half-mourning for three weeks. During the shortest period, black for one month.

RULES OF TABLE SETTING

1.   The center of the dining table should be directly under the central light, unless this position would not permit the waitress to pass between the table and the sideboard.

2.   For dinner, lay the silence cloth upon the table. This cloth may be double-faced cotton flannel, knitted table padding, or an asbestos pad; the latter may be obtained in various sizes. The first two launder well; the last is easily handled and may be protected from soiling by the use of linen covers, which can be bought to fit the pad.

3.   The tablecloth appears to best advantage when ironed with few folds, which must be straight. A tablecloth should be unfolded on the table, not opened and thrown over it, as the latter method tends to crumple the cloth. The center fold of the cloth must form a true line through the center of the table, having the four corners at equal distances from the floor. The cloth never should hang less than nine inches on all sides below the edge of the table.

4.   Place the centerpiece directly in the center of the table, taking care that the thread of the linen runs in the same direction as the thread of.the cloth. Place in the center of this a fern dish, growing plant, dish of fruit, or cut flowers. This is the conventional arrangement, to be varied by individual taste. The decoration varies in elaborateness with the meal served; it should be either so low or so high that an unobstructed view may be had across the table.

5.   Lay the covers, allowing twenty-four to thirty inches from plate to plate. A "cover" consists of the plates, glasses, silver, and napkin to be used by each person.

6.   The covers on opposite sides of the table should be directly opposite each other, not out of line. Mark the position of the covers by laying the service or place plates, which should be not less than ten inches in diameter.

7.   In laying a bare table, the covers are marked by the plate doilies.

8.   Lay a service plate for each person, one inch from the outer edge of the table; this plate remains upon the table until it is necessary to replace it with a hot plate.

9.   Next, lay the silver, which should always be placed in the order in which it is to be used, beginning at the outside and using toward the plate. Silver for the dessert course is never put on with the silver required for the other courses, except for the dinner which is served without a maid, when everything should be done to avoid the necessity of leaving the table. Neither is the table set with more than three forks. If more are required, they are placed with their respective courses.

10.   Either bring the salad or dessert silver in on the plate, or place it from a napkin or tray at the right, from the right, after the plate is placed. Some

persons object to the first-named method, on account of the possible noise.

11. Place the knife or knives at the right of the plate, half an inch from the edge of the table, with the cutting edge toward the plate.

12. Place spoons, with the bowls facing up, at the right of the knife; and forks, with the tines turned upward, at the left of the plate.

13. The spoon for fruit or the small fork for oysters or hors d'oeuvres is placed at the extreme right or on the place containing this course. This statement does not include the serving of oysters or clams on the shell; then the fork is always found at the right.

14. Place the napkin, preferably flat and squarely folded, at the left of the forks. The hem and selvage of the napkin should be parallel with the forks and the edge of the table, this position bringing the embroidered letter, if there be one, in the right place. Napkins are sometimes given additional folds to save space.

VICTORIAN RULES OF DINNER ETIQUETTE

For Hosting

1. Very soon after the last guest has arrived, the servant ought to announce dinner, and the host, after directing the gentlemen whom to take in, should offer his arm to the lady of the highest rank in the room, the gentleman of highest station taking the lady of the house. (This order of precedency in going in to dinner being likely, if violated, to give offense, it is well that the lady of the house should arrange with her husband how to marshal their guests before they arrive.)

2. With respect to persons of title, these take precedence according to their titles; though, as eldest sons of peers have intermediate places in the scale (so to speak), we advise the lady to have by her Lodge's 'Orders for Precedency,' that she may make no mistakes. Foreign ambassadors are given the precedence of our nobility, out of courtesy, and with respect to their mission; archbishops rank with dukes; bishops with earls.

3. Ordinary foreign counts and barons have no precedency of title in England, but rank about with English baronets or great landed proprietors.

For *untitled* precedence:
An earl's grandson or granddaughter, and all near relations (untitled) of the aristocracy precede the esquires or country gentlemen.
Then come:
Wives of country gentlemen of no profession.
Clergymen's wives.
Naval officers and their wives.
Military men and their wives.
Barristers' wives.

4. There is no specified place for physicians or medical men and their wives, who, however, are ranked in the royal household as next to knights, and whose wives therefore would go out after those of barristers.

For Guesting:
1. Take off your gloves, and put them on your lap.
2. Before you, on your plate, will be a table napkin, with a dinner roll in it; take the bread out and put it at the side of your plate.
3. Lay the opened table napkin in your lap, on your gloves, and then listen gracefully, and with attention, to your companion, who will do his best to amuse you till the soup is handed round.
4. Eat your soup from the *side* of your spoon, not take it from the point; that you should make no noise in eating it; that you should beware of tasting it while too hot, or swallowing it fast enough to make you cough.
5. You must begin, or appear to begin, to eat as soon as it is put before you; not wait for other people.
6. Fish follows the soup. You must eat it with a fork, unless silver knives are provided. Break a little crust off your bread, to assist you in taking up your fish, but it is better to eat with the fork only, which you may do if it be turbot or salmon.
7. Put the sauce when it is handed to you on the side of your plate.
8. If you do not wish for soup or fish, decline it with a courteous 'No, thank you,' to the servant.
9. After soup and fish come the side dishes, as they would be called, if they were on the table—the oyster or lobster patties, quenelles, etc. Remember, that for these you use *the fork only*; as, indeed, you should for all dishes which do not absolutely require a knife. You must use a knife, of course, for cutlets of any kind, although they are side dishes. It is proper to eat all soft dishes, as mince, etc., with the fork only.
10. Do not put your hands on the table, except to eat or carve (the latter is not required at a dinner à la Russe). Do not use your handkerchief if you can help it;

if you must do so, let it be as inaudibly as possible.

11. Meat, chicken, or turkey are handed after the made dishes. Then follow game, puddings, tarts, jellies, blancmange, etc.

12. For the partridge or pheasant, of course you use the knife and fork; all sweets are eaten with the fork, or spoon and fork, as you like; but the spoon is only required for cherry tart, or anything of that nature, custard, etc.

13. Ladies scarcely ever eat cheese after dinner, If eaten, remember it should be with a fork, not a knife.

14. You should *never*, by any chance, put a knife near your mouth.

RULES OF BOWLING ETIQUETTE

1. Be punctual. Lanes are crowded these days, and you owe it to teammates and opponents to be on time, ready to start.

2. Be ready to bowl when it's your turn—and not off buying peanuts or chatting.

3. When another bowler takes his stance, be attentive and quiet; say nothing, do nothing that will distract him.

4. Never cross in front of a bowler ready to make his approach.

5. If the bowler on the next lane is ready to bowl at the same time you are, the player on the right should be given precedence.

6. A bowler never, never delivers his ball simultaneously with the bowler on either his left or his right.

7. When it's your turn to bowl, take your time (but not everybody else's!).

8. Using someone else's ball—without permission—is a major bowling offense.

9. Be kind to the equipment. Lofting the ball—dropping it hard on the lane instead of rolling it—not only damages the bed of the lane but also is bad for your game.

10. Bowling shoes—your own or rented ones—are required to save the lanes and also to prevent your slipping on the glossy wood.

SORRY

RULES OF SWIMMING ETIQUETTE

1. Cardinal rule: Never swim alone.
2. Test the depth of pool or pond before diving.
3. Ducking people, tossing the unwary into the water, other forms of potentially dangerous horseplay are to be avoided.
4. Never swim beyond your depth if you're a beginner—and never out of reach of help if you're a strong swimmer. (Anyone can get a cramp, get caught in an undertow, or meet up with a blood-hungry fish in the ocean.)
5. Running around the edge of a pool is universally frowned on; one slip can break a bone and ruin your swimming for the rest of the summer.
6. Most public- and private-pool owners want girls to wear swim caps—not just to keep the water clean but to protect the drainage system from clogging.
7. Shower before swimming in a pool; slosh off grass or sand clinging to your feet.

RULES FOR RIDING ETIQUETTE

1. If you open a gate to ride through, be sure to latch it securely behind you. (Remember all those movies with tragedies that were triggered by the carelessly closed gate?)
2. Never gallop by other riders. Canter, if you will, but give others a wide berth: if you skim by inexperienced riders, their horses may shy and bolt; and never move your horse in close to people on foot: even the most placid horse has his "nerves-on-edge" days and needs to be protected from unnecessary patting and poking.
3. Don't pet or feed someone else's horse without permission.
4. When you're on foot, walk in front of the horse; those who circle in back of a steed often feel the force of a rear hoof.
5. Straight from the horse's mouth: these beautiful beasts can only chomp and cannot nibble daintily like cats and dogs. When you offer tidbits—sugar lump, carrot, apple—hold your hand out flat as a plate with fingers and thumb close together and the tidbit resting on your palm. The horse can mumble it up with his lips, and you will retain all your fingers.

RULES FOR BOATING ETIQUETTE

1. Regardless of sex or age, the skipper is the absolute boss when afloat and is not to be argued with.
2. Be shipshape and tidy; there's no extra room on a boat.

3. Never crush out a cigarette or strike a match on a hull or deck; sailors are unrelenting on the subject of scratches.

4. Sit down when you're told to and on the side you're told to.

5. On a sailboat, remember to duck the boom. And don't grab a line or do anything to help without orders—especially if you're a novice. You might be responsible for a number of friends and lunch bobbing around in the water—and for a lot of wet sail—and for a very angry skipper.

6. Never wear shoes with leather soles or heels on a boat; they wreck the deck.

7. Always wear rubber soles—or go barefoot.

8. Never toss anything overboard to windward—especially cigarettes. If throw you must, pitch it to the leeward, sheltered side so the wind won't boomerang it back into the boat or someone's face.

RULES OF SKATING ETIQUETTE

1. Skate in the same direction others are going.

2. In most rinks, the center is reserved for figure skating; straight skaters have the path around the rink and never cut through the middle.

3. If you are practicing figure, wait till you can get a patch of your own rather than crowding in on someone else's patch. While you have the patch, work at your figures rather than idling with a friend near you—it's maddening to those waiting to see ice going to waste—and, if you see others waiting, surrender your patch after half an hour.

4. Needless to say, no fast skating, racing, acrobatics, or figure skating on the straight-skating path; beginners find that ice both hard and scary.

5. Tag, hockey, crack-the-whip, locomotive, and other ice games should be played when the rink is close to empty except for the gamesters. (Many crowded rinks forbid these at any time, as a matter of safety.)

6. For everyone's safety, don't create hazards by gouging holes or ruts in the ice or by dropping scraps of paper, bobby pins, ice-pops sticks, and such; and food, drinks never go on the ice.

7. If you fall, get up as quickly as you can to avoid pile-ups. Beginners should remember to roll as they fall—rather than land in a lump. Watch the football players to get the idea.

8. Abbreviated fancy costumes are banned in more rinks than Boston's.

RULES FOR GOLF ETIQUETTE

1.   Wear sneakers, flat rubber-soled shoes, or regular golf shoes—never heels that stab holes in costly, hard-to-maintain greens.

2.   Walk on the greens as little as possible; circle around on the apron to reach your ball. If your approach shot has indented the surface of the green, use a tee to raise the dented turf gently to its former level.

3.   Never rest a golf bag or club on the surface of the green.

4.   Silence is the rule when someone else is making a shot—no talking, rattling of clubs.

5.   Keep well away from the person making a shot and out of his line of vision. The best spot on the tee is facing the driver at a distance of four or five feet. This is not always possible on the fairway, where the important rules are not to move during the shot and not to stand where you might get hit.

6.   If your shot veers in the direction of another person, shout "Fore!" as a warning.

7.   The ball farthest from the hole is hit first.

8.   If you have to play out of a trap, you are not permitted to rest your club on the sand when addressing the ball, but you are expected to smooth out footprints and the scuff your club made when you hit the ball.

9.   Taking a divot (a slice of the turf) is usually a sign of a good fairway shot; not replacing the divot and patting it back to grow again is a couldn't-care-less attitude.

10.   Help anyone you're playing with to find a lost ball; keep up the search till he calls it off. If you're the lost one, don't keep the search up too long; it holds up your match and may jam up the progress of other matches.

11.   Keep your score as accurately as you can. If a penalty stroke is incurred, etiquette demands that you call it on yourself. If you're not sure how to score the penalty, ask someone you're playing with.

12.   No temper on the links—not with your fellow players, not with yourself, and especially not with your caddie.

13.   Congratulate your opponent on his good shots; say nothing—particularly nothing sympathetic!—about his dub shots. Try to be Olympian about your own game—not elated by the good play and the good luck, not depressed by the poor play and bad luck. A tall order, but it makes you much nicer to play with.

14.   A twosome should wait to be invited to go through—but a foursome or any slow match is usually obligated to invite a faster match to play through. (Exception: Some clubs do not permit twosomes on weekends or junior members to go through a grown-up match.)

15.   Never, *never* help someone else straighten out his game unless he asks your advice. The tension you create (he smothers his resentment and tries not to show

how vexed he is) only makes his game worse than it was.

16. If you use a golf cart, be fanatic about driving it only within the allowed limits and in the posted directions.

17. Some clubs forbid shorts for both males and females—so ask before going to a club that's new to you. (Short shorts are unacceptable at any golf club.)

RULES OF SKIING ETIQUETTE

1. Beginners should stick to the practice hill or "bunny" slope; once that's mastered, they can move on the the novice slopes and trails. It's folly—and a tremendous hazard to other skiers—to attempt expert or even intermediate terrain until ready and able.

2. Don't ski at a speed you can't control—especially in an unexpected emergency, such as a sudden turn or a possible collision with someone ahead of you who's taken a spill.

3. If you fall while skiing—and you will—get up immediately and smooth the snow over your sitzmark (just what it sounds like: the mark you made in the snow when you sat). (Skiing is so continental for the vocabulary.) If your ski binding has opened or you have gotten your gear tangled up in the spill, move to the side of the slope or to the outside of the curve on a trail while you repair the damage. If you stay smack in the middle of the hill, you're a prime target for oncoming skiers.

4. If you pass fairly close to another skier on your way downhill, call "track right" if you're passing on the right, "track left" if you're going to overtake him on the left.

5. Always ski with runaway straps: these are leather strips (you could use shoelaces) which attach to your boot at one end and your ski binding at the other. Purpose: to keep the ski from flying off downhill if you should fall and break out of your binding. A ski on the wing by itself can gather enough force and momentum to shatter another skier's anklebone; it is actually as dangerous as a hurled spear. Skiing without straps is wickedly careless. If you're ever that careless and you do lose a ski, yell "ski" the minute you see it take off; hopefully, other skiers will be able to get out of its way.

6. Never walk on a slope or trail without skis; you'll break up the surface when you fall. Just remember that Sir Walter Raleigh did not ski—nor will your date haul you out of a snowbank—nor do skiers expect this kind of aid.

7. When you're in line waiting for a lift, keep your place as you would in any line; and never trample on other skiers' skis.

8. How not to be asked again: swing about on chair lifts, play "look-Ma-no-hands" on rope tows, and indulge in other nursery-age tricks.

RULES FOR SALUTING WITH A CANNON

1.   A salute with cannon (towed, self-propelled, or tank-mounted) will be fired with a commissioned officer present and directing the firing.

2.   Salutes will not be fired between retreat and reveille, on Sundays, or on national holidays (excluding Memorial and Independence Days) unless, in the discretion of the officer directing the honors, international courtesy or the occasion requires the exception. They will be rendered at the first available opportunity thereafter, if still appropriate. The interval between rounds is normally three seconds.

3.   The salute to the Union consists of firing one gun for each State. It is fired at 1200 hours, Independence Day, at all Army installations provided with necessary equipment.

4.   The national salute consists of twenty-one guns. It is fired at 1200 hours on Memorial Day. The national flag, displayed at half-staff from reveille until noon on this day, is then hoisted to the top of the staff and so remains until retreat. In conjunction with the playing of appropriate music, this is a tribute to honored dead.

5.   Cannon salutes are rendered on the occasion of the death and funeral of the President and the Vice President of the United States, and other high civil and military dignitaries.

6.   The flag of the United States, national color or national standard, is always displayed at the time of firing a salute except when firing a salute to the Union on the day of the funeral of a President, Ex-President, or President-Elect. On these occasions, the salute will be fired at five-second intervals immediately following lowering of the flat at retreat. Personnel will not salute.

RULES OF WAR ON THE TREATMENT OF THE WOUNDED—1906 GENEVA CONVENTION

1.   Officers, soldiers, and other persons officially attached to armies, who are sick or wounded, shall be respected and cared for, without distinction of nationality, by the belligerent in whose power they are.

A belligerent, however, when compelled to leave his sick or wounded in the hands of his adversary, shall leave with them, so far as military conditions permit, a portion of the personnel and material of his sanitary service to assist in caring for them.

2.   Subject to the care that must be taken of them under the preceding rule, the sick and wounded of any army who fall into the power of the other belligerent become prisoners of war, and the general rules of international law in respect to

prisoners become applicable to them.

The belligerents remain free, however, to mutually agree upon such clauses, by way of exception or favor, in relation to the wounded or sick as they may deem proper. They shall especially have authority to agree:

a. To mutually return the sick and wounded left on the field of battle after an engagement.

b. To send back to their own country the sick and wounded who have recovered, or who are in a condition to be transported and whom they do not desire to retain as prisoners.

c. To send the sick and wounded of the enemy to a neutral State, with the consent of the latter and on condition that it shall charge itself with their interment until the close of hostilities.

3. After every engagement the belligerent who remains in possession of the field of battle shall take measures to search for wounded and to protect the wounded and dead from robbery and ill-treatment. He will see that a careful examination is made of the bodies of the dead prior to their interment or incineration.

4. As soon as possible each belligerent shall forward to the authorities of their country or army the marks or military papers of identification found upon the bodies of the dead, together with a list of names of the sick and wounded taken in charge by him.

Belligerents will keep each other mutually advised of interment and transfers, together with admissions to hospitals and deaths which occur among the sick and wounded in their hands. They will collect all objects of personal use, valuables, letters, etc., which are found upon the field of battle, or have been left by the sick or wounded who have died in sanitary formations or other establishments, for transmission to persons in interest through the authorities of their own country.

5. Military authority may make an appeal to the charitable zeal of the inhabitants to receive and, under its supervision, to care for the sick and wounded of the armies, granting to persons responding to such appeals special protection and certain immunities.

6. Mobile sanitary formations (i.e., those which are intended to accompany armies in the field) and the fixed establishments belonging to the sanitary service shall be protected and respected by belligerents.

7. The protection due to sanitary formations and establishments ceases if they are used to commit acts injurious to the enemy.

8. A sanitary formation of establishment shall not be deprived of the protection accorded by Rule 6 by the fact:

a. That the personnel of a formation or establishment is armed and uses its arms in self-defense or in defense of its sick and wounded.

b. That in the absence of armed hospital attendants, the formation is guarded by an armed detachment or by sentinels acting under competent orders.

c. That arms or cartridges, taken from the wounded and not yet turned over to the proper authorities, are found in the formation or establishment.

9. The personnel charged exclusively with the removal, transportation, and treatment of the sick and wounded, as well as with the administration of sanitary formations and establishments, and the chaplains attached to armies, shall be respected and protected under all circumstances. If they fall into the hands of the enemy they shall not be considered as prisoners of war. These provisions apply to the guards of sanitary formations and establishments in the case provided for in section (c) of Rule 8.

10. The personnel of volunteer aid societies, duly recognized and authorized by their own governments, who are employed in the sanitary formations and establishments of armies, are assimilated to the personnel contemplated in the preceding rule, upon condition that the said personnel shall be subject to military laws and regulations.

11. A recognized society of a neutral State can only lend the services of its sanitary personnel and formations to a belligerent with the prior consent of its own government and the authority of such belligerent. The belligerent who has accepted such assistance is required to notify the enemy before making any use thereof.

12. Persons described in Rules 9, 10, 11 will continue in the exercise of their functions, under the direction of the enemy, after they have fallen into his power.

When their assistance is no longer indispensable they will be sent back to their army or country, within such period and by such route as may accord with military necessity. They will carry with them such effects, instruments, arms, and horses as are their private property.

13. While they remain in his power, the enemy will secure to the personnel mentioned in Rule 9 the same pay and allowances to which persons of the same grade in his own army are entitled.

14. If mobile sanitary formations fall into the power of the enemy, they shall retain their material, including the teams, whatever may be the means of transportation and the conducting personnel. Competent military authority, however, shall have the right to employ it in caring for the sick and wounded. The restitution of the material shall take place in accordance with the conditions prescribed for the sanitary personnel, and, as far as possible, at the same time.

15. Buildings and material pertaining to fixed establishments shall remain subject to the laws of war, but cannot be diverted from their use so long as they are necessary for the sick and wounded. Commanders of troops engaged in operations, however, may use them, in case of important military necessity, if, before such use, the sick and wounded who are in them have been provided for.

16. The material of aid societies admitted to the benefits of this convention, in conformity to the conditions therein established, is regarded as private property, and, as such, will be respected under all circumstances, save that it is subject to the recognized right of requisition by belligerents in conformity to the laws and usages of war.

17. The distinctive Red Cross flag of the Convention can only be displayed over the sanitary formations and establishments which the Convention provides shall be respected, and with the consent of the military authorities. It shall be accompanied by the national flag of the belligerent to whose service the formation or establishment is attached.

Sanitary formations which have fallen into the power of the enemy, however, shall fly no other flag than that of the Red Cross so long as they continue in that situation.

RULES FOR INFURIATING YOUR HOSTESS

1. Use cups, dished, and decorative ornaments, not meant for ashtrays, as receivers or throw dead cigarettes in the dregs of tea, coffee, or a cocktail.

2. Lean back on the rear legs of your chair. This is especially infuriating to antique collectors.

3. Put your shod feet on the bed or on an upholstered chair.

4. Flick ashes onto the floor, into vases, and into the fireplace, followed in the latter case by the butt, *sans doute.*

5. Use the table silver for purposes other than that for which it was intended—drawing on the tablecloth, opening clams.

6. Leave the bathroom in a mess.

7. Discipline the children.

8. Give orders to servants or disrupt them in any manner.

9. Stand on the furniture to reach something.

RULES FOR BEATIFICATION—THE FIRST STEP TOWARD THE CREATION OF A SAINT

1. The candidate's life is investigated with special emphasis on writings, heroic practice of virtue, and the certification of at least two miracles worked by God through his intercession.

2. If the findings of the investigation so indicate, the Pope decrees that the Servant of God may be honored locally or in a limited way in the liturgy.

3. Additional procedures lead to canonization. (See Rules for Canonization.)

OBSCURE RULES OF LAW: COURTSHIP AND MARRIAGE

1. In Nebraska, a husband is justified in slapping his wife if he can show that it was necessary to do so in order to compel her to go out for a ride for the benefit of her health.
2. If a Dixie, Idaho, lady berates her husband in public causing a crowd to collect, the husband shall be fined.
3. Also in Idaho, the legislature passed a law making it illegal for a man to give his sweetheart a box of candy weighing less than fifty pounds.
4. Whitesville, Delaware, deems it disorderly conduct for a woman to offer a marriage proposal during a Leap Year.
5. It is against the law in Portland, Oregon, for anyone to perform a wedding in a skating rink or theater.
6. In Cleveland, you can't get married in a bathing suit.
7. There is a Kentucky law that forbids a housewife to move the furniture in her home without her husband's consent.
8. Another Kentucky law prohibits women from marrying the same man four times.
9. It is against Connecticut law for a man to write love letters to a girl whose mother has forbidden him to see her.
10. Vermont says that a woman cannot walk down the street on a Sunday unless her husband walks twenty paces behind her with a musket on his shoulder.
11. In Lebanon, Tennessee, a husband can't kick his wife out of bed, even though her feet are cold; a wife, however, can kick her husband out of bed anytime, without giving a reason.
12. There is an old Michigan law that says a husband owns his wife's clothes, and if she leaves him he can follow her on the street and remove every article of said clothing.

RULES FOR REGAINING THE AFFECTION OF A LOVED ONE

1. Take cloves, cinnamon, and cardamom and place in a jar.
2. Stand over it and read the "Yasin" chapeter of *Koran* backward seven times.
3. Then fill a basin with rose water and steep your loved on's shirt in it with a parchment containing his name and that of four angels.
4. Heat the basin over fire, and as the mixture boils the loved one should return.

RULES FOR EFFECTIVE PARENTING

1. Let a child know IN DETAIL what you expect him to do. Because children are sticklers for rules. They want to know what the rules are, and just what's going to happen—especially when you take them somewhere.

2. Don't tag along into his world unless you're sure he wants you to. Some kids do, some don't. Sometimes it takes a sensitive eye and heart to know whether they're glad you're aboard or wish you'd get lost.

3. Quit insulting him, as though he were deaf, in front of other people. "Your hands are filthy." "Look at that face!" Many a well-meaning mother hands out a dozen insults a day, then wonders why her child grows up showing a certain ruthless lack of tact, himself.

4. Let him know that pain is sometimes unavoidable. This lesson can keep him one day from biting a dentist.

5. Really listen when he tries to tell you something he thinks is important. That's just good manners with anyone.

6. Cooperate with his burgeoning good manners. There are many heart-warming moments in raising a child, like the moment he learns to cut his own meat, so that you can cut your own before it congeals on the plate.

7. Don't belabor him for not saying "Thank you" when a guest brings him a gift. It's to be hoped that he will. But if his mind is elsewhere, or he is bedazzled by the gift, he may not remember his Magic Words. If he doesn't, let it go. Urging the child embarrasses the guest.

8. When you take him on a jolly toot, let him think it's as much for your pleasure as his. The grim "I'm doing this for your sake so enjoy it!" approach is bad manners as well as a miserable pain in the neck to anyone, any age, any time.

9. Don't laugh at him unless he understands why. It's terribly upsetting to anyone to be laughed at when he doesn't understand the joke.

10. Adopt some minor form of public discipline. When a public reprimand is necessary, the French "tais-toi" or the Spanish "callate" sounds better than the American "shut up," but they still deliver the message. It's wise, too, to perfect a Family Look—perhaps the narrowed eye and the compressed nostril.

11. Don't give more than two of your children names that start with the same letter. If you already have, nickname them. Some families with numerous children major in one initial, like J: Jamie, Junie, Johnny, Jeanie, Joanie. This is mighty cute, but it is disconcerting to outsiders, who are never sure just which one is which, but are embarrassed to admit it.

12. Don't teach a little child to call your grown-up friends Aunt This or Uncle That. It can lead to an embarrassing hiatus when the child grows older and learns he's not really related to them.

RULES FOR RAISING A "GREAT KID"

1. Teach him to say "Please" and "Thank you." You can entwine these words with the word "Mama" or "Mommy" at the same time he learns them. You have him say "Please, Mommy" when he wants something, or he doesn't get it, and "Thank you, Mommy" when he does. This way he'll have them down pat at the age of two or two and a half, which will amaze your friends, and pave the way for "You're welcome"—a subtler concept which comes later and doesn't matter so much anyway.

2. Teach him to go to the toilet immediately before going anywhere else. That is, out to play, over to the neighbor's, to school, or anywhere at all. This will save legwork for everyone.

3. Teach him to stop INTERRUPTING. Unless it's a naturally reticent child—and there do not seem to be as many of them around as there used to—this takes doing. For one thing, you can give him a good example to follow, by remembering to apologize when you interrupt *him*. For another, you can try to see that he gets a fair chance to be heard.

4. Teach him how to tell a fair social lie. Nearly any child can learn quickly to distinguish a Good Lie (told to save people's feelings) from a Bad Lie (told to keep himself out of hot water), once the difference is pointed out. A firm grasp of it will prevent his saying, "Heck, I've already got two of 'em" when he opens a gift, or "No, it's icky" when his hostess inquires if he likes his lunch.

5. Teach him to make no unpleasant personal remarks about people. Children should learn at an early age one of the golden rules of good manners: When in doubt, keep the mouth closed.

6. Teach him to state a preference when he is offered a choice. When his birthday-party hostess says, "Would you like orange juice or milk?" he must say which. His hostess has both, or she wouldn't have asked. She couldn't care less which he picks, just so he picks.

7. Teach him to make a simple introduction. At the age of four, he can get the fundamentals. When he learns to say, "Mommy, this is Jimmy," he has the whole thing in essence: simplicity, with the honored name said first. He can pick up the refinements later.

8. Teach him to call most adults Mr. and Mrs. Somebody, not Steve and Mary. If you encourage a child to call your friends by their first names, you needn't wonder why he never stands up when grown-ups enter the room. It is nice, too, if you can drill into his little head the merits of saying, "Yes, Mrs. So-an-so," once in a while, instead of a flat "yes," or "Uh-huh."

9. Teach him to write his own thank-you letters at Christmas and birthdays. As soon as he learns to print, he can do a simple THANK YOU, AUNT DOTTIE on a piece of paper. Then you can address it and mail it. Bend that twig.

10. Teach him to ask to help when he's a house guest. Set or unset the table. Carry things. Fetch things. Make a pass at making his own bed.

11. Teach him to stay out of other people's private business. Rooms, drawers, closets. And mail. As soon as he can read, he'd better learn not to read other people's letters or what curls out of people's typewriters. (Of course, he won't ever learn this if his parents do it, or if he ever catches Mommy perusing the diary he'd carefully hidden behind his old baseball suit in his bottom dresser drawer. This is excruciatingly bad parental etiquette. This is only basic good manners. Also, people who do it are apt to read something unflattering about themselves, as many an older child from twenty to ninety has learned, to his discomfiture.)

12. Teach him to never answer the telephone with "Who's this?" He can learn, early, to say "Smiths' house."

13. Teach him to understand that some people will like him better than others do. The wound won't go so deep, the first time he's left out of a party, if he realizes that some people may not even like him at all, just as *he* doesn't like some people at all.

RULES FOR SERVING DRINKS IN GLASSWARE

1. If you want to serve a 12-ounce drink, use a "mixing glass." It holds 8 jiggers, or 24 level tablespoons.

2. If you want to serve a 1½-ounce drink, use a "jigger." It holds 3 level tablespoons.

3. If you want to serve a 1-ounce drink, use a "pony glass." It holds 2 level tablespoons.

4. If you want to serve a 2-ounce drink, use a sherry, port, or cocktail glass. They each hold 4 level tablespoons.

5. If you want to serve a 4-ounce drink, use a Bordeaux or Burgundy glass. It holds 8 level tablespoons.

6. If you want to serve a 5-ounce drink, use a champagne glass. It holds 10 level tablespoons.

7. If you want to serve an 8-ounce drink, use a tumbler. It holds 16 tablespoons.

RULES OF METRIC CONVERSION OF MEASURES

1. To find centimeters, multiply total inches by 2.5 or total feet by 30.
2. To find meters, multiply total yards by 0.9.
3. To find kilometers, multiply miles by 1.6.
4. To find grams, multiply total ounces by 28.
5. To find kilograms, multiply total pounds by 0.45.
6. To find milliliters, multiply total teaspoons by 5, or tablespoons by 15, or fluid ounces by 30.
7. To find liters, multiply total cups by 0.24, or pints by 0.47, or quarts by 0.95, or gallons by 3.8.
8. To find temperature degrees Celsius (C), multiply by 5/9 Farenheit, after subtracting 32.

RULES OF CONVERSION FROM METRIC MEASURES

1. To find inches, multiply total millimeters by 0.04 or total centimeters by 0.4.
2. To find feet, multiply total meters by 3.3 or meters by 1.1 to find yards.
3. To find miles, multiply total kilometers by 0.6
4. To find ounces, multiply total grams by 0.035.
5. To find pounds, multiply total kilograms by 2.2.
6. To find fluid ounces, multiply toal milliliters by 0.03.
7. To find pints, multiply liters by 2.1. To find quarts, multiply liters by 1.06.
8. To find gallons, multiply total liters by 0.26.
9. To find temperature in degrees Farenheit (F), add 32 to total degrees Celsius, then multiply by 9/5.

RULES FOR IDENTIFYING AN UNFAITHFUL HUSBAND

1. A change in behavior pattern is the single most important early warning sign that something is happening.
2. Your husband may seem touchy and irritable or lose his temper at the drop of a hat. He may pick on you and the children, criticize you for every little thing.
3. He may just sit by himself indicating he doesn't want to be bothered. He answers questions in one or two words.
4. You may hear him talking quietly into the phone at times, although he usually speaks loudly. He may make a point of picking up the mail.

5. His sexual attitudes might become more liberated. He might even say something like: "I'm not sure the idea of swinging or wifeswapping is so bad after all."

6. The cheating husband might not approach his wife sexually as much as he once did. Some men shower their wives with gifts to cover up their guilt.

7. The man involved in an extramarital affair is likely to be away from home more than ever without letting his wife know where to reach him.

8. He may show an increased interest in his appearance, becoming clothes and weight conscious.

9. There may be a change in your finances. Having an affair usually costs money. Your husband may start looking for all kinds of ways to cut corners—something he never did before.

10. Like most women, when your husband finally admits he has been unfaithful, you are going to be angry. You have a right to be, and you should let your anger out!

RULES FOR KEEPING YOUR HUSBAND FAITHFUL

1. When you quarrel, keep as calm and as reasonable as possible. This is a more efficient way of dealing with conflict than recklessly attacking each other.

2. Don't yell, hurl insults, or bring up past hurts. That only broadens the gap between a couple, thus making it hard to close.

3. Speak honestly. If you don't put your feelings into words, your partner may never know you have them.

4. Try to solve problems and make decisions together. Is your man falling into the habit of discussing matters he previously consulted you about with someone else?

5. Once your man finds someone who is a little more understanding and willing to advise him—not that this person's advice is any better or more valid than yours—it makes it easier for him to become sexually involved with that person.

6. A woman should guard against letting her identity merge into that of her man's to the point where she is completely dependent on him.

7. Be competent. Have interests other than the ones you share with your man. This helps him to recognize you are fully capable of caring for yourself. This will often draw him closer than the "I can't live without you" routine.

8. Give your man some privacy. He might seek solace with someone else because he doesn't have any privacy at home.

9. Accept the fact that you can't be all things to your man at all times. Although it's terribly important to share activities, each partner should feel free to do some things without his partner.

RULES FOR SENDING CHILDREN TO SCHOOL

1. Recognize that the day your child first goes to school is an important event.

2. Provide all the loving support and understanding you can.

3. Take an active interest in what your child tells you about school when he comes home.

4. Be a good listener—allow your child to talk about how he feels about school and the people there.

5. Become acquainted with your child's teacher. If you feel there are things that need to be improved, talk to the teacher and find out how you can help.

6. Praise your child for his accomplishments. You may feel inclined to acknowledge things he has done wrong in his work, but remember there is more to be gained from accenting the positive.

7. Help your child to accept the challenge of being frustrated at school from time to time.

8. Do not compare your child and his school experience with how his brothers and sisters did when they began school.

9. If your child does not do well on his report card as he had hoped, reassure him that he is important to you and that you love him.

10. Give your child lots of time at home to do his own thing. After the structured atmosphere of the classroom, he needs time to relax and play.

11. Plan your day so that you can spend some time with him in the afternoon or evening, or be available when he needs you.

RULES ON LEGAL AGE FOR MARRIAGE

1. Men and women in all states may marry without parental consent if they are twenty-one years or older.

2. Women may marry without parental consent after age eighteen in every state but Florida, Mississippi, and Wyoming (where they must be twenty-one) and Nebraska (where they must be nineteen).

3. Men may marry without parental consent after age eighteen in every state but Alabama, Alaska, Arkansas, California, Florida, Maryland, Mississippi, Missouri, Montana, and New York (where they must be twenty-one) and Nebraska and Alaska (where they must be nineteen).

4. The minimum age for a woman's marriage is sixteen in all states but Kansas (where it is eighteen); Indiana and Washigton (where it is seventeen); Mississippi, Missouri, North Dakota, Oklahoma, and Oregon (where it is fifteen); Alabama, Alaska, New York, and South Carolina (where it is fourteen); New Hampshire (where it is thirteen); and Massachusetts (where it is twelve).

5. The minimum age for a man's marriage is eighteen, except for Alabama, Alaska, Arkansas, Hawaii, Indiana, Mississippi, and Washington (where it is seventeen); Arizona, Colorado, Idaho, Maine, New Jersey, New York, New Mexico, North Carolina, Pennsylvania, South Carolina, Tennessee, Texas, and Utah (where it is sixteen); Missouri (where it is fifteen); and Massachusetts and New Hampshire (where it is fourteen).

RULES FOR OBTAINING A MARRIAGE LICENSE

1. Some type of medical approval is required for issuance of a marriage license in all states but Maryland, Nevada, South Carolina, and Washington.

2. There is no waiting period between applying for and receiving a license in Alabama, Alaska, Arizona, California, Colorado, Delaware, Hawaii, Idaho, Illinois, Louisiana, Nevada, New York, New Mexico, North Carolina, North Dakota, Oklahoma, South Dakota, Texas, Utah, Vermont, Virginia, or Wyoming.

3. There is a waiting period required between obtaining a license and marriage in Delaware, Georgia (if the man or woman is under age), Louisiana, New York, and Utah.

4. Marriage is prohibited in all states between granddaughters and grandfathers, grandmothers and grandsons; mothers and sons, fathers and daughters; aunts and nephews, uncles and nieces; sisters and brothers; half-sisters and brothers.

5. Marriages between first cousins are prohibited in all states but Alabama, Georgia, Maine, Maryland, Massachusetts, Rhode Island, South Carolina, Tennessee, Texas, Vermont, and Virginia.

6. Marriage between stepparents and children are prohibited in Alabama, Georgia, Iowa, Maine, Maryland, Massachusetts, New Hampshire, Oklahoma, Pennsylvania, Rhode Island, South Carolina, South Dakota, Tennessee, Texas, Vermont, and Virginia. All of these states except South Dakota and Oklahoma also prohibit marriages between in-laws.

7. You may marry by proxy or contract under special circumstances in Kansas, Nebraska, New Mexico, New York, Texas, Montana, and South Carolina.

RULES FOR OBTAINING A DIVORCE

1. Adultery and desertion are recognized grounds for divorce and/or separation in thirty-four states—all except Arizona, California, Colorado, Florida, Hawaii, Indiana, Iowa, Kentucky, Michigan, Minnesota, Missouri, Montana, Nebraska, Nevada, Oregon, and Washington.

2. Habitual drunkenness or drug addiction are recognized grounds for divorce and/or separation in thirty-five states—all except Arizona, California, Colorado, Florida, Georgia, Hawaii, Indiana, Iowa, Maryland, New Jersey, Pennsylvania, Texas, Vermont, Washington, and West Virginia.

3. Impotence or a physical defect preventing intercourse are grounds for divorce and/or separation in twenty-two states—Alabama, Alaska, Arkansas, Delaware, Georgia, Idaho, Illinois, Indiana, Maine, Maryland, Massachusetts, Mississippi, New Hampshire, New Mexico, North Carolina, Ohio, Oklahoma, Pennsylvania, Rhode Island, Tennessee, Utah, and Wyoming.

4. Mental cruelty is grounds for divorce and/or separation in twenty-nine states—Alaska, Arkansas, Connecticut, Georgia, Illinois, Kansas, Louisiana, Maine, Maryland, Massachusetts, Mississippi, New Hampshire, New Jersey, New York, North Carolina, Ohio, Oklahoma, Pennsylvania, Rhode Island, South Carolina, South Dakota, Tennessee, Texas, Utah, Vermont, Virginia, West Virginia, Wisconsin, Wyoming.

RULES FOR OBTAINING ANNULMENT OF A MARRIAGE

1. A prior marriage still existing is recognized as grounds for annulment in all states.

2. Prohibited degree of relationship (incest) is regarded as grounds for annulment in all states but California.

3. Underage partners can be regarded as grounds for annulment in all states but Maine, New Hampshire, North Carolina, Oklahoma, Rhode Island, and Virginia.

4. Mental incapacity at the time of marriage is recognized as grounds for annulment in all states but Louisiana, New Hampshire, and Rhode Island.

5. Fraud is considered grounds for annulment in all states but New Hampshire, Oklahoma, and Rhode Island.

6. Inability to consummate the marriage is an allowable grounds for annulment in all states but Alabama, Alaska, Arizona, Arkansas, Connecticut, Florida, Georgia, Illinois, Indiana, Maine, Maryland, Massachusetts, Michigan, Minnesota, Nevada, New Hampshire, New Mexico, North Carolina, Oklahoma, Oregon, Pennsylvania, Rhode Island, South Carolina, Tennessee, Utah, and Virginia.

7. In North Carolina a marriage may be annulled if it was entered into in the mistaken belief that the female was pregnant.

8. In Louisiana a marriage may be annulled if there was a case of mistaken identity.

9. In Georgia there are no grounds for annulment if children are born, or are to be born, as a result of the marriage.

10. In Mississippi a marriage can be annulled if the wife is pregnant by one other than the husband.

RULES FOR TEACHING CHILDREN TO CALL FOR HELP ON THE TELEPHONE

1. Age 2½ to 4: Teach them to tell the operator their first and last name, and the name of the town or section of the city where they live.

2. Age 3 to 6: Have them give first and last name, approximate address, town, or section of city and the need for help.

3. Age 5 to 8: Instruct child to give parent's full name, complete address, and the nature of the emergency—"My mommy is hurt."

Only you can determine how much your children can remember. Don't overestimate.

4. It's important to practice emergency calling. And it's helpful to first tape a small piece of colored paper to make the place to dial "O" for the telephone operator. Then tape down the receiver buttons to stop dial tone during the training.

5. Show the children how to pick up the phone and dial the operator. Then teach them what to say—slowly, clearly, and directly into the mouthpiece. Explain that "O" should be dialed only when help is needed. And that you must be there for any practicing.

6. Other children should be taught to dial "911" if your community has this emergency number. Or to dial other local emergency numbers.

7. If there's a fire in your home, fire departments recommend that you teach your children not to call, but to alert others in the house, get out and go to a neighbor for help.

O = HELP

RULES FOR DRAWING UP A WILL

1. Allow for the unexpected. You assume that you will die first and your children later, but accident or illness may alter the usual pattern. There should be a provision reading "In the event that my beloved child should predecease me . . ." and the names of subsequent beneficiaries.

2. Make provisions for anything out of the ordinary in your family situation. Are there illegitimate children, adopted children, or stepchildren?

3. Consider outstanding debts owed to you. You may wish to make some provisions forgiving the debts.

4. Consider substantial gifts made to beneficiaries during your lifetime. Make a clear statement in your will indicating whether these gifts are to make a difference in the legacies established. (Gifts made within three years of your death will be brought into the decedent's estate and taxed.)

5. In a separate clause of your will, indicate priority of bequests in the event your estate is smaller than you anticipated when making your will.

6. Indicate whether you wish any legacies to be paid free of tax, or, in other words, whether you wish the estate to pay taxes on any of the bequests.

7. Identify any real and personal property adequately, so that there will be no confusion about bequests. Also indicate substitute gifts in the event these properties should have been disposed of before death.

8. When establishing a trust, consider its practicability. Only the income from a trust is available to beneficiaries, and it is necessary to pay someone for management of the trust. Clearly indicate the powers of the trustees.

9. Consider the possibility that the will will be contested, so that your lawyer can take precautionary steps.

10. If you have made a previous will, it is a good idea to include a statement in the new one, revoking one previously signed.

11. Changes in your will may be made by codicils, but more often a completely new will is drawn.

RULES GOVERNING THE LEGAL ENFORCEMENT OF CONTRACTS

1. Contracts to be performed within a year of the date of agreement are regarded as legally binding, whether in writing or not, in all states. In Minnesota they are binding up to fifteen months after the date of agreement, and in Louisiana, North Carolina, and Pennsylvania there is no time limit.

2. Contracts for the sale of goods over $500 must be in writing to be regarded as legally binding in all states but Hawaii, Minnesota, Missouri, Montana, Nevada, New Mexico, and Louisiana. In Missouri written contracts are required

for sales over $30, in Minnesota they are required for sales over $50, in Hawaii for sales over $100, and in Nevada for sales over $200. In New Mexico they are required for the sales of goods in any amount to be enforceable.

3.   Oral leases for periods under a year are regarded as legally binding in all states but Maine, Massachusetts, New Hampshire, Ohio, and Vermont, where all contracts concerning land must be in writing. In Louisiana, all oral leases, no matter how long a time period they cover, are regarded as legally binding.

RULES FOR SECURING A COPYRIGHT

1.   All works receive copyright protection from the moment of creation, rather than from the moment of publication, as was the case previously.

2.   The copyright is in effect for the lifetime of the creator, plus fifty years. Copyrights already in existence under the old law, if renewed, will be extended to last a total of seventy-five years.

3.   All writings and artistic works can be copyrighted, including books, periodicals, newspapers, lectures, sermons, maps, photos, drawings, movies, screenplays, etc.

4.   Works previously copyrighted or in the public domain cannot be copyrighted; however, these can appear in collections with the permission of any copyright owners.

5.   A notice of copyright must appear on published copies of copyrighted works. This consists of ©, or "copyright," followed by the name of the owner and the year of publication.

6.   The copyright in most cases is assigned to the author, or may be assigned to the publisher or proprietor of the work. If the work was made for hire, and the parties agree in writing that this is the case, the employer is regarded as the "author."

7.   If an author has assigned his copyright, he may reclaim it, or renegotiate the contract after thirty-five years.

RULES GOVERNING OUR SEXUAL LIVES

1.   In all but eighteen states (California, Colorado, Connecticut, Delaware, Hawaii, Iowa, Kentucky, Louisiana, Maryland, Montana, Nevada, New York, Ohio, Oklahoma, Oregon, Pennsylvania, South Dakota, Texas) cohabitation without marriage is illegal. Penalties range from $10 (in Rhode Island) to $1,000 and one year of jail (in Georgia and Missouri).

2.   In all but sixteen states (Alabama, Arkansas, California, Colorado, Hawaii, Indiana, Kentucky, Louisiana, Mississippi, Montana, Oregon, Pennsylvania, South Carolina, Texas, Wyoming) adultery is illegal. Penalties range from $10 (Maryland) to $2,000 and four years imprisonment (Michigan).

3.   Sodomy and/or oral copulation are illegal in all states but Hawaii, Ohio, and Texas. In Arkansas the maximum penalty for oral sex is twenty-one years.

4.   Malicious castration bears a possible penalty of sixty years in North Carolina.

5.   Intercourse with an imbecile male bears a possible penalty of twenty-one years in Indiana.

RULES FOR HAVING A HOUSE PARTY

1.   It is up to the host and hostess to establish the atmosphere they wish to prevail at their party.

2.   Plan entertainment or activities that will take into consideration the guests' interests and talents.

3.   Involve people with their fellow guests; introduce new people, arrange the seating to encourage conversation.

4.   Provide seats for all, plan for people movements, and keep the lights on.

5.   Choose a bartender of known discretion. The eager volunteer may turn out to be a pusher who uses the role to give every glass an extra "shot."

6.   Serve drinks at regular, reasonable intervals. A drink-an-hour schedule means good company prevails.

7.   Don't double up. Many people count and pace their drinks. Doubling up isn't hospitality, it's rude.

8.   Let the glass be empty before you offer a refill. Don't rush, especially if someone comes up empty too fast. When a guest says "no, thanks" don't insist.

9.   Push the snacks. Do this while your guests are drinking, not after.

10.   Serve nonalcoholic drinks too. Occasional drinkers sometimes prefer not to drink. So offer a choice of drinks besides alcohol—fruit and vegetable juices, tea, coffee, and soft drinks.

11.   Offer more than drinks. Stir up conversation. Share a laugh. Draw out the guest talent. A good host or hostess has more to give than just food and drinks.

12. Serve before it's too late, if it's a dinner party. After too many drinks, guests may not know what they ate or how it tasted.

13. Set drinking limits. When a guest has had too much to drink, you can politely express your concern for him by offering a substitute drink—coffee, perhaps. This is a gentle way of telling a guest that he has reached the limits you have set for your home.

14. Decide in advance when you want your party to end. Give appropriate cues by word and action that it's time to leave. A considerate way to close the drinking phase is to serve a substantial snack. It also provides some nondrinking time before your guests start to drive home.

RULES GOVERNING ADOPTION IN THE UNITED STATES

1. The child's consent to adoption is required if he is over age fourteen in all states but Alaska, where only adults must give their consent to being adopted. In Hawaii, Maryland, Michigan, New Jersey, New Mexico, North Dakota, the child's consent is required if he is over age ten, and in Arizona, California, Colorado, Florida, Idaho, Kentucky, Massachusetts, Montana, New Hampshire, North Carolina, Ohio, Oklahoma, Pennsylvania, South Dakota, Texas, Utah, and West Virginia, the child's consent must be obtained if he is over twelve.

2. Probationary periods for adoption range from three months (in Kentucky) to a possible thirteen months (in Connecticut). In most states the probationary period is six months.

3. In the absence of a will or other testamentary disposition, adopted children inherit from their adoptive parents in all states.

4. In the absence of a will or other testamentary disposition, adopted children may inherit from their natural parents in Alabama, Arkansas, Indiana, Louisiana, Maine, Mississippi, Montana, Rhode Island, South Dakota, Texas, and Vermont.

5. In most states where inheritance by an adopted child from its natural parents is not provided for, a child adopted by the husband or wife of the natural parent may inherit from its natural parents.

RULES FOR AVOIDING OVEREXERCISE

1. Don't ever exercise to the point of exhaustion.
2. Discover that training short of the point of exhaustion gives far better results than training to exhaustion.
3. Watch for signs of sudden exhaustion and rest for several days before resuming training.
4. Reduce the number of exercises by one third and build up gradually to the former figure if any of these signs occur:

        a) Your heart refuses to stop pounding ten minutes after exercising.
        b) Your breathing is still uncomfortable ten minutes after exercising.
        c) You are still shaky for more than thirty minutes after exercising.
        d) You cannot sleep well the night after exercising.
        e) You carry fatigue (not muscle soreness) into the next day.

RULES OF GOOD NUTRITION

1. *Don't be a hypochondriac or a worry wart*—Worry and concern (about anything, including your health) can help unhinge what good health you already have and can make a good nutritional situation deteriorate into a bad one. Worry is able to alter the working of our body chemistry so that the demands for specific nutrients may become augmented.
2. *Diversify your diet*—Make diet selections from several different types of food and eat substantial portions from each regularly. Choose from among: milk and dairy products; seed (including nut) products; meats (not exclusively muscle) from mammals and fowl; fish and marine products; leafy (green) vegetables; root and tuber vegetables, including carrots and potatoes (yellowness is associated with a source of vitamin A); fruits of all kinds, including melons and tomatoes; fungi—yeast, mushrooms, truffles; eggs.
3. *Use and cultivate your body wisdom*—Develop a strong healthy mind and body through proper living habits. Then, trust your body to tell you what and how much to eat. The healthy body has an amazing capacity to establish its own good nutritional habits if its signals are listened to.

4. *Avoid too much refined food*—Be judicious in your consumption of refined sugar, alcohol, highly milled rice, and, to a lesser degree, products made from white flour, even though it is "enriched."

5. *Use nutritional supplement when, on the basis of informed opinion, it seems desirable*—Such a plan first helps combat ailments of various kinds, including illnesses associated with aging. Parts of our working machinery tend to wear unequally as we age, and the use of supplements may cancel or diminish the difficulties which result. (Treatment of disease or illness should be in the hands of a physician.) The second reason for using nutritional supplements involves insurance against all ills which may have a nutritional basis.

Source: *Nutrition in a Nutshell*, by Roger J. Williams, Dolphin Books, 1962.

RULES FOR GETTING LISTED IN WHO'S WHO

1. Your admission to *Who's Who in America* is based on the extent of your reference interest.

2. You must be on a level of significant achievement, attained in a career of meritorious activity. This should be something that distinguishes you from your contemporaries.

3. You may also be admitted by holding a prominent position of responsibility. These positions include:

- All members of the U. S. Congress.
- All members of the President's Cabinet.
- Federal judges.
- All governors of states, island possessions, and territories.
- All state attorneys general.
- Judges of state and territorial courts of highest appellate jurisdiction.
- U.S. ambassadors and ministers plenipotentiary.
- Heads of the major universities and colleges.
- Officers on active duty beginning with the rank of major general in the Army, Air Force, and Marine Corps; and with rear admiral in the Navy.
- Heads of leading philanthropic, educational, and scientific societies.
- Selected members of the National Academy of Sciences, the National Academy of Design, the American Academy of Arts and Letters, and the National Institute of Arts and Letters.
- Chief ecclesiastics of the principal religious denominations.
- Principal officers of national and international businesses capitalized at or above a certain figure, or of the highest commercial "rating."
- Others chosen because of incumbency, authorship, or membership.

RULES FOR WRITING LETTERS OF COMPLAINT

1. Use a tone that indicates controlled determination. Abuse is likely to get your complaint nowhere except into a wastebasket.

2. Describe clearly the problems, and detail your attempts to get the machine repaired or replaced. Include copies (not originals) of sales slips, repair bills, and correspondence.

3. Address the letter to the customer relations department or the service manager. If you get no satisfaction, write to the president of the company. (If the firm has a hot line, you should be able to get his name from the attendant. If there is no hot line, call the company headquaters and ask the switchboard operator. Or look up the name in a business directory in a library.) Send copies of your letter to as many officials—Better Business Bureau, consumer agencies—as you can think of, not forgetting the subordinate employee who failed to settle your complaint the first time.

4. Consider, some people use their company's letterhead, feeling that the company they work for has more clout than they have as individuals.

RULES FOR ENGRAVING SILVERWARE

1. When buying a set of good silverware of any type, and having it engraved with the family initials, follow these formalities:

> a) *Single Initials.* The initial of either the bride or the groom's family name is used.
>
> b) *Two-Letter Monogram.* The initials of the two family names are used, with a small star or cross between them.
>
> c) *Three-Letter Monogram.* When done in a line or linked, either the initials of the bride's full name or her first and last initials and the initials of the groom's family name are used. In some cases, the initials of the pair's first names are engraved in small letters separated by either a star or a cross, set above a single large initial which is the first letter of the groom's family name.

RULES FROM THE CONSTITUTION

Rules concerning the House of Representatives:

1. The House of Representatives shall be composed of members chosen every second year by the people of the states.

2. Each member must be at least twenty-five years old.

3. Each member must be an American citizen for at least seven years.

4. Each member must be a resident of the state which elects him.
5. The house of Representatives shall have the sole power of impeachment (accusation).

Rules concerning the Senate:
1. The Senate of the United States shall be composed of two senators from each state, for six-year terms.
2. Each senator must be at least thirty years old.
3. Each senator must be an American citizen for at least nine years.
4. Each senator must be a resident of the state which elects him.
5. The Vice President of the United States shall be president of the Senate, but shall have no vote, unless they be equally divided.
6. The Senate shall have the sole power to try all impeachments.

Rules concerning Presidential Powers:
1. The President shall be Commander-in-Chief of the Army and Navy of the United States. Only Congress can declare war.
2. The President shall have power, by and with the advice and consent of the Senate, to make treaties, provided two thirds of the senators present concur.
3. The President shall nominate and, by and with the advice and consent of the Senate, shall appoint ambassadors, public ministers and consuls, judges of the Supreme Court, and all officers of the United States, whose appointments are not otherwise provided for, and which shall be established by law.
4. The President shall give to the Congress information of the state of the Union.

RULES FOR DETERMINING FEES FOR SPECIFIC LEGAL SERVICES

---

1. Accident cases are usually handled on a contingent fee basis. These fees are set by Supreme Court rule and should be discussed by the attorney with the client.
2. Wills and estate planning are often accompanied by set fees. An attorney will usually draft a simple or short term will for a modest fee. Longer, more complicated wills involving marital deductions and trusts will require higher fees.
3. Divorce fees are usually the result of agreements between lawyers and their clients. Any reasonable fee may be agreed upon. Where considerable property and much legal work is involved in the divorce, the fees will be higher.
4. Property transaction fees may very well be part of the largest single purchase you will ever make. In these cases, which involve examining the title and drafting agreements and other documents attending the closing, a flat fee or a percentage may be charged.

RULES FOR ENFORCING PRODUCT WARRANTIES
(Warranty Act—1977)

1. All warranties must be easy to read and understand. They must be written in ordinary language, not "legalese." Fine print isn't allowed.

2. Every term and condition of the warranty must be spelled out in writing. If it isn't there, it isn't part of the warranty.

3. Check what's *written* in your warranty. Beware of spoken explanations of the warranty. What the sales clerk says about the warranty won't count when it comes time for warranty service.

4. If you buy a product "as is," you will have to pay for any repairs. The Warranty Act doesn't make a company give a warranty (though some state and federal laws do require warranties on certain products).

5. If you have a full warranty, you're entitled to:

a) Have a defective product fixed (or replaced) free, including removal and reinstallation if necessary.

b) Have a product fixed within a reasonable time after you complain.

c) Avoid anything unreasonable to get warranty service (such as ship a piano to the factory).

d) Warranty protection as owner of the product during the warranty period.

e) Get your choice of a new product of your money back, if the product can't be fixed (or hasn't been after a reasonable number of tries).

6. If you obtain a "Limited" warranty, be careful—"something's missing." It should:

a) Cover only parts, not labor.

b) Allow only a prorate refund or credit. (You get a smaller refund or credit the longer you had the product.)

c) Require you to return a heavy product to the store for service.

d) Cover only the first purchaser.

e) Include charges for handling.

7. A product can carry more than one written warranty. It can have a FULL warranty on part of the product and a LIMITED warranty on the rest.

8. You are protected by "implied warranties," too. These are rights created by state law, not by the company. All states have them.

The most common implied warranty is the "warranty of merchantability." This means that the seller promises that the product you buy is fit for the ordinary uses of the product.

9. Spoken promises and advertising claims can be warranties too. You have a legal right to get what the company promises. These kinds of warranties are covered by state law only, not federal law.

10. Normally, your warranty rights under these warranties include the right to "consequent damages." This means the company must not only fix the defective product, but also pay for any damage the product did. If your freezer breaks down and the food in it spoils, the company must pay for the food you lost.

RULES GOVERNING YOUNG PEOPLE

1. Young people are legally considered adults at age eighteen in all states but Colorado, Mississippi, and Pennsylvania (where the age is twenty-one); and Alabama, Alaska, Nebraska, and Wyoming (where the age is nineteen).

2. Young people may buy hard liquor at age eighteen in nineteen states: Connecticut, Georgia, Hawaii, Kansas, Louisiana, Maine, Massachusetts, Michigan, Minnesota, Montana, New Hampshire, New Jersey, New York, Rhode Island, Tennessee, Texas, Vermont, West Virginia, and Wisconsin.

3. In Oklahoma, females may purchase beer at age eighteen but males must wait until age twenty-one. Neither may buy wine or hard liquor until age twenty-one.

4. The youngest age at which tobacco may be purchased is fifteen, and then only in Hawaii. Colorado, Connecticut, Maine, New Jersey, Pennsylvania, Rhode Island, South Dakota, and Virginia permit sale of tobacco products to persons sixteen and over.

5. Young people may vote in state elections at age eighteen in all states except Alabama and Alaska (where they must be nineteen) and New Mexico and Utah (where they must be twenty-one).

6. Young people may serve on state juries at age eighteen in all states but Florida, Georgia, Missouri, Nebraska, New Mexico, Rhode Island, and Utah (where the age is twenty-one); and Alabama, Wyoming, and Alaska (where the age is nineteen).

7. Under ordinary circumstances, school is compulsory for young people until age sixteen in all states except Maine, Nevada, New Mexico, Pennsylvania, and Texas (where the age is seventeen); Ohio, Oklahoma, Oregon, Utah, and Washington (where the age is eighteen); and Mississippi (where there is no compulsory(where there is no compulsory education law).

8. Sale or distribution of pornographic materials to persons under age eighteen is prohibited in all states except Colorado, Mississippi, and Pennsylvania (where the age is twenty-one); Nebraska (where the age is nineteen); Arkansas, Connecticut, Delaware, Florida, New Hampshire, New York, and Texas (where the age is seventeen); South Carolina (where the age is sixteen); and Alaska, Hawaii, Kansas, Maine, Oklahoma, Washington, and Wyoming (where there is no provision for minors).

RULES FOR LEGAL DRINKING AGES IN THE UNITED STATES

1. You may drink all alcoholic beverages at age eighteen in: Connecticut, Florida, Georgia, Hawaii, Louisiana, Massachusetts, Michigan, Montana, New Hampshire, New Jersey, New York, Rhode Island, Tennessee, Texas, Vermont, West Virginia, and Wisconsin.
2. It is legal to drink only beer and wine at age eighteen in: Colorado, Kansas, Maryland, Mississippi, North Carolina, Ohio, Oklahoma, South Carolina, South Dakota, Virginia, and Washington, D.C.
3. You may drink all alcoholic beverages at age nineteen in: Alabama, Alaska, Arizona, Idaho, Iowa, Minnesota, Nebraska, and Wyoming.
4. It is legal to drink beer and wine at age nineteen in Illinois.
5. You must be at least twenty years old to drink all alcoholic beverages in Delaware and Maine.
6. You are allowed to drink all alcoholic beverages at age twenty-one in: Arkansas, California, Indiana, Colorado, Illinois, Kansas, Kentucky, Maryland, Mississippi, Missouri, Nevada, New Mexico, North Carolina, North Dakota, Ohio, Oklahoma, Oregon, Pennsylvania, South Carolina, South Dakota, Utah, Virginia, Washington, and Washington, D.C.

RULES FOR WIVES—1845

1. Let every wife be persuaded that there are two ways of governing a family; the first is, by the expression of that will which belongs to force; the second, by the power of mildness, to which even strength will yield. One is the power of the husband; a wife should never employ any other arms than gentleness. When a woman accustoms herself to say *I will*, she deserves to lose her empire.
2. Avoid contradicting your husband. When we smell at a rose, it is to imbibe the sweetness of its odor; we likewise look for every thing that is amiable from women.

   Whoever is often contradicted, feels insensibly an aversion for the person who contradicts, which gains strength by time; and, whatever be her good qualities, is not easily destroyed.
3. Occupy yourself only with household affairs; wait till your husband confides to you those of higher importance, and do not give your advice till he asks for it.
4. Never take upon yourself to be a censor of your husband's morals, and do not read lectures to him. Let your preaching be a good example, and practice virtue yourself, to make him live with it.

5. Command his attentions, by being always attentive to him; never exact anything, and you will obtain much; appear always flattered by the little he does for you, which will excite him to perform more.

6. All men are vain: never wound this vanity, not even in the most trifling instances. A wife may have more sense than her husband, but she should never seem to know it.

7. When a man gives wrong counsel, never make him feel that he has done so, but lead him on by degrees to what is rational, with mildness and gentleness; when he is convinced, leave him all the merit of having found out what was just and reasonable.

8. When a husband is out of temper, behave obligingly to him; if he is abusive, never retort; and never prevail over him, to humble him.

9. Choose well your female friends; have but few, and be careful of following their advice in all matters.

10. Cherish neatness without luxury, and pleasure without excess; dress with taste, and particularly with modesty; vary the fashions of your dress, especially in regard to colors. It gives a change to the ideas, and recalls pleasing recollections. Such things may appear trifling, but they are of more importance than is imagined.

11. Never be curious to pry into your husband's concerns, but obtain his confidence by that which, at all times, you repose in him. Always preserve order and economy; avoid being out of temper, and be careful never to scold. By these means, he will find his own house more pleasant than any other.

12. Seem always to obtain information for him, especially before company, though you may thereby appear a simpleton. Never forget that a wife owes all her importance to her husband.

NEWTON'S RULES OF REASONING IN PHILOSOPHY

1. We are to admit no more causes of natural things than such as are both true and sufficient to explain their appearances.

2. Therefore to the same natural effects we must, as far as possible, assign the same cause.

3. The qualities of bodies, which admit neither intensification nor remission of degrees, and which are found to belong to all bodies within the reach of our experiments, are to be esteemed the universal qualities of all bodies whatsoever.

4. In experimental philosophy we are to look upon propositions inferred by general induction from phenomena as accurately or very nearly true, notwithstanding any contrary hypotheses that may be imagined, till such time as other phenomena occur, by which they may either be made more accurate, or liable to exception.

RULES FOR MAKING DECISIONS

1.   Don't panic! Remember, very few decisions are really final. See the problem in front of you as part of a pattern, but neither its beginning nor its end.

2.   Be optimistic. No decision can be totally wrong.

3.   Be patient and follow through with every decision.

4.   "Keep reminding yourself," according to actress Claire Bloom, "if you make a decision you later regret, you made your decision for reasons that were good, and even if it produced a bad result, the reasons themselves remain good."

5.   Consult all the "experts" but make up your own mind. Decision-making means taking responsibility for yourself.

6.   Consider all alternatives before making a final decision.

7.   Use your imagination; consider as many facts about your choices as possible. But, do not be paralyzed by indecision because you are afraid of things that cannot be foreseen.

8.   Base your decision on what is right for *you*. Make sure it's the "real you" making the decision.

RULES FOR STUDYING FOR AN EXAM

1.   *Budget your time.* Set aside definite hours each day for concentrated study. Adhere closely to this budget. Don't fritter away your time with excessive "breaks." A cup of coffee, a piece of fruit, a look out of the window—they're fine, but not too often.

2.   *Study with a friend or a group.* The exchange of ideas that this arrangement affords may be very beneficial. It is also more pleasant getting together in study sessions. Be sure, though, that you ban "socializing." Talk about friends, dates, trips, etc., at some other time.

3.   *Eliminate distractions.* Psychologists tell us that study efforts will reap much more fruit when there is little or no division of attention. Disturbances caused by family and neighbor activities (telephone calls, chitchat, TV programs, etc.) will work to your disadvantage. Study in a quiet, private room. Better still, use the library.

4.   *Use the library.* Most colleges and universities have excellent library facilities. Some institutions have special libraries for the various subject areas: Physics library, Education library, Psychology library, etc. Take full advantage of such valuable facilities. The library is free from those distractions that may inhibit your home study. Moreover, research in your subject area is so much more convenient in a library since it can provide much more study material than you have at home.

5. *Tailor your study to the subject matter. Skim or scan.* Don't study everything in the same manner. Francis Bacon (1561-1626) expressed it this way: "Some books are to be tasted, others to be swallowed, and some few to be chewed and digested."

6. *Organize yourself.* Make sure that your notes are in good order—also, that your desk top is neat. Valuable time is consumed unnecessarily when you can't find quickly what you are looking for.

7. *Keep physically fit.* You cannot retain information well when you are uncomfortable, headachy, or tense. Physical health promotes mental efficiency. Guarding your health takes into account such factors as these: (a) sufficient sleep, (b) daily exercise and recreation, (c) annual physical examination, (d) a balanced diet, (e) avoidance of eyestrain, (f) mental health.

RULES FOR TAKING AN EXAM

1. *Get to the examination room about ten minutes ahead of time.* You'll start better when you are accustomed to the room. If the room is too cold, or too warm, or not well ventilated, call these conditions to the attention of the person in charge.

2. *Make sure that you read the instructions carefully.* In many cases, test-takers lose credits because they misread some important point in the given directions—example: the incorrect choice instead of the correct choice.

3. *Be confident.* Statistics conclusively show that success is likely when you have prepared faithfully. It is important to know that you are not expected to answer every question correctly. The questions usually have a range of difficulty and differentiate between several levels of skill. It's quite possible that an "A" student might answer no more than 60 percent of the questions correctly.

4. *Skip hard questions and go back later.* First answer the questions you are sure about. Do not panic if you cannot answer a question. Go on and answer the questions you know. Usually the easier questions are presented at the beginning of the exam and the questions become gradually more difficult.

5. *Guess if you are nearly sure.* Gusssing is probably worthwhile if you have an intuition as to the correct answer or if you can eliminate one or more of the wrong options, and can thus make an "educated" guess. However, if you are entirely at a loss as to the correct answer, it may be best not to guess. A correction is made for guessing when the exam is scored.

6. *Read each question carefully.* The exam questions are not designed to trick you through misleading or ambiguous alternative choices. On the other hand, they are not all direct questions of factual information. Some are designed to elicit responses that reveal your ability to reason, or to interpret a fact or idea. It's up to you to read each question carefully so you know what is being asked. The exam authors have tried to make the questions clear. Do not go too far astray in looking for hidden meanings.

7. *Don't answer too fast.* The multiple-choice questions which you will meet are not superficial exercises. They are designed to test not only rote recall, but also understanding and insight. Watch for deceptive choices. Do not place too much emphasis on speed. The time element is a factor, but it is not all-important. Accuracy should not be sacrificed for speed.

RULES FOR REMEMBERING WITH THE HELP OF MNEMONIC PHRASES

1. To tell how many days are in each month:

a) "Thirty days hath September,
April, June, and November;
All the rest have thirty-one,
Excepting February alone,
Which hath but twenty-eight, in fine,
Till leap year gives it twenty-nine."

b) Knuckle Method: By counting on the knuckles of your left hand, you can tell how many days each month has. The knuckles are "31" and the "valleys" between them are "30" (or "28-29," in the case of "February"). Make your left hand into a fist. The knuckles of your left index finger (nearest your thumb) is "January." The "valley" between this knuckle and the next is "February." The knuckle of your second finger is "March" and the following valley "April," etc. When you reach the knuckle of your little finger ("July") go back to the index finger knuckle ("August") and count on to "December."

2. To remember the order of the minerals in Moh's Hardness Scale for Minerals (1. Talc, 2. Gypsum, 3. Calcite, 4. Fluorite, 5. Apatite, 6. Orthoclase, 7. Quartz, 8. Topaz, 9. Corundum, 10. Diamond), remember:

"The Girls Can Flirt And Other Queer Things Can Do."

3. To remember the division in the biological classification system (Kingdom, Phyllum, Class, Order, Family, Genus, Species), Remember:

a) "King Philip Came Over From Greece Saturday."
b) "Kings Play Chess On Folding Glass Stools."
c) "K.P. Comes On Friday, Go Slowly."

4. To remember Ohm's Law ("The current, I, flowing through a resistor, R, depends on the amount of voltage, E" or "IR=E"):

Think of an Indian, a river, and an eagle. The Indian and the river both remain on the ground, while the eagle can fly, so:

I (Indian) $\times$ R (River) = E (Eagle)

and:

$\dfrac{\text{E (Eagle)}}{\text{I (Indian)}}$ = R (River), or the eagle flying over the Indian

$\dfrac{\text{E (Eagle)}}{\text{R (River)}}$ = I (Indian), or the eagle flying over the river

5. To remember the colors of the light spectrum (Red, Orange, Yellow, Green, Blue, Indigo, Violet) remember: Roy G. Biv.

6. To remember the notes on a musical scale for notes falling on lines: (E,G,B,D,F) Every Good Boy Does Fine. For space: (F,A,C,E) Face.

"30 DAYS HATH SEPTEMBER ..."   "30"

RULES FOR DEALING WITH AN OBNOXIOUS PERSON

1. Let them rant and rave. Watch how their craziness manifests itself. Don't put them down, just watch compassionately knowing that whatever set them off comes from their own training and conditioning, their mental programming, and has nothing to do with you.

2. Enjoy the spectacle, but also feel compassion along with wonder at the things people do to themselves. Don't waste a lot of time, though, in wondering what makes them behave this way. It does not mean anything, that's just the way they are.

3. Whoever is being difficult or obnoxious is creating karma for himself (emotional and physical reactions). Don't get sucked into playing that game and creating karma for yourself by doing something you will regret later. Feel free to disagree with anything the person says, if the opportunity comes up to simply state your opinion without getting into a big argument or a lot of justifications and self-defense mechanisms.

4. Deal with the content of what the person is saying, not with the form of it.

5. Refuse to be browbeaten. If they are demanding something you do not want to give, or telling you to do something you do not want to do, stand quietly firm until the storm blows over—don't give in and hate yourself in the morning. "It's only words."

6. Try not to let them give you a lecture. Keep interposing little questions so that there is always the semblance of a dialogue being maintained rather than a one-man show where they have nothing to slow them down or keep them in touch, even minimally, with reality.

7. If you can avoid the temptation to make the other person be wrong (even if they are) and to make yourself right (rather than just let the rights and wrongs fall where they may), you have won half the battle. One sign of making them wrong is if you find yourself attacking them as a person—"You skunk!"—instead of disagreeing with the content of what they say—"I did not agree to that at all."

8. Music has charms to soothe a savage breast, and even for the most difficult person a word of praise or kindness, if honestly applied, can work wonders. Always operate toward the highest level. Always try to respond to the best part of a person, even if that part is very small and hard to find. The good within them, however small, cannot grow without encouragement any more than a seed can grow without water.

9. Do not become discouraged if you fail to see results. Perhaps someday someone else may see them. The difference between people and rosebushes is that if you water a rosebush it gratefully accepts the water. If you attempt to nurture a human being, the response is often that they put up an umbrella.

10. Take away from each encounter with that person whatever of value you can get. Allow yourself consciously to be in the relationship without expecting to be liked and without liking the other person. No one ever said things would always work out perfectly. And after all, you don't have to like each other to work together.

THE 25 RULES OF EFFECTIVE WRITING

1. Write about people, things, and facts.
2. Write as you talk.
3. Use contractions.
4. Use the first person.
5. Quote what was said.
6. Quote what was written.
7. Put yourself in the reader's place.
8. Don't hurt the reader's feelings.
9. Forestall misunderstandings.
10. Don't be too brief.
11. Plan a beginning, middle, and end.
12. Go from the rule to the exception, from the familiar to the new.
13. Use short names and abbreviations.
14. Use pronouns rather than repeating nouns.
15. Use verbs rather than nouns.
16. Use the active voice and a personal subject.
17. Use small, round figures.
18. Specify. Use illustrations, cases, examples.
19. Start a new sentence for each new idea.
20. Keep your sentences short.
21. Keep your paragraphs short.
22. Use direct questions.
23. Underline for emphasis.
24. Use parentheses for casual mention.
25. Make your writing interesting to look at.

RULES FOR UNDERSTANDING THE DEWEY DECIMAL SYSTEM

1. The basic plan of the Dewey Decimal Classification is to assign into ten decimal classes the whole of recorded human knowledge.
2. The ten classes are divided into ten divisions and each division into ten sections; and Arabic numerals are used decimally to signify the various classes of subjects.

The ten classes are:

000 Generalities
100 Philosophy and related disciplines
200 Religion
300 The social sciences
400 Language
500 Pure sciences
600 Technology (Applied sciences)
700 The arts
800 Literature and rhetoric
900 General geography, history, etc.

3. In the process of classification, a book is classified according to its subject matter and is given the number in the classification schedule which stands for that subject.
4. It is further identified by an author number, using the first letter of the author's last name plus Arabic numerals.
5. The title of the book may also be represented by placing the first letter of the title, excluding articles, immediately following the author number.
6. Symbols may be added to indicate that the book is a certain kind of material, as Ref for reference, or J for juvenile.
7. Classification number, author number, and symbol—if any—make the call number of the book.
8. The call number indicates the subject matter of the book and its physical location in the library.

RULES FOR HELPING HOUSEWIVES TO OVERCOME STRESS

1. Investigate and itemize the various stresses which affect you during a typical day. Then ask yourself: What is causing these stresses? How often do they occur? Can any of them be avoided?

2. Isolate these "stresses"—the things which cause the stress. See if there is a way to sit down and try to work out which is most important, and which can be postponed for later.

3. Take a realistic look at your role and your responsibilities. Ask yourself: Are the responsibilities and the role that I have too much to ask of me?

   Find out if there are some things, such as cleaning, you could delegate to the kids or your husband.

4. Don't be afraid to be assertive. Housewives tend to shy away from being assertive, but if you stand up for yourself, this can serve as a real release of tension and can modify or even prevent stressful situations.

5. Get involved in regular physical activity, such as jogging, tennis, or calisthenics. It's a great way to release pent-up stress and will actually increase your level of energy, too.

6. Learn to manage your time. Many housewives try to put too many things into the course of a day to the point where it just won't all fit. Try to distribute your activities as evenly as possible, even if some things get delayed.

7. Find a time each day, between fifteen and twenty minutes, that is yours alone in which to relax. Make sure nothing will disturb you.

RULES FOR UNDERSTANDING CB 10-CODES

10-1	Signal weak		10-21	Call *(Name)* by phone
10-2	Signal good		10-22	Disregard
10-3	Stop transmitting		10-23	Arrived at scene
10-4	Affirmative (OK)		10-24	Assignment completed
10-5	Relay (to)		10-25	Report to (meet)
10-6	Busy		10-26	Estimated arrival time
10-7	Out of service		10-27	License/permit information
10-8	In service		10-28	Ownership information
10-9	Say again (repeat)		10-29	Records check
10-10	Negative		10-30	Danger/caution
10-11	*(Name)* on duty		10-31	Pick up
10-12	Stand by (stop)		10-32	
10-13	Existing conditions		10-33	Help me quick (emergency)
10-14	Message/Information		10-34	Time
10-15	Message delivered		10-35	Reserved
10-16	Reply to message		10-36	Reserved
10-17	En route		10-37	Reserved
10-18	Urgent (quickly)		10-38	Reserved
10-19	(In) contact		10-39	Reserved
10-20	Location			

RULES FOR UNDERSTANDING THE VOCABULARY OF HORSES

1. *Welcome.* This is used to generalize all calls and signs of greeting used between horses, the most common of which is the whicker of welcome. The strength of the call and the vigor of the movement indicate the degree of imperative. The context, and the carriage of the head and tail, indicate the purpose of the welcome.

2. *Who are you?* is used by two strange horses on meeting. It is an extension of the "welcome" phrase and is said by sniffing or more usually blowing at each other. The attitude of the two horses toward each other is indicated by the harshness or the gentleness of the blowing and the carriage of the head and tail. This procedure leads to the submessages (a) *I am a friend*, said by continuation of the gentle blowing and other friendly movements, or (b) *go to hell*, a snap or nip by one or other horse, a stamp on the ground with a front foot, a threat to kick, or a squeal.

3. *What's this?* is used in reference to objects which are close at hand, usually said by a sniff at the object; but a horse may paw the object with his front foot. This gesture leads to the submessages (a) *it's all right*, shown by approaching and inspecting and then ignoring strange objects, or (b) *it's dangerous*, shown by moving away, by shying at the object or attacking the danger.

4. *Look*, used to draw attention to an object and denoted by raising the head and tail and snorting or whinnying to attract the attention of other horses. Similar, and a submessage to "look," is (a) *what is that*, which is said by raising the head high and pricking the ears and looking at a strange object. There is no sound as a secondary reaction to "what is that." The horses will either respond *it is all right* or *it is dangerous*. Another submessage is (b) *let's go this way*. The horse says this by looking in the direction he wants to go and moving in that direction. A second horse responding to "what is that" will look at the object, and if he recognizes it will say (c) *nothing to bother about*, or (d) *look out*, using a snort or a neigh of warning.

5. *Come here.* This starts as a whicker of welcome rising in the imperative, which may also be shown by shaking the head back and forward if there is no response. The message may be changed to *if you do not come here, I will have your guts for garters*, which is shown by a threatening movement and will draw the response (a) *all right I am coming*, usually said by a low whicker.

6. *Is anybody about?* A loud neigh repeated several times. This has an inquiring note and is used with the head and tail held high.

7. *Come on!* This is used when two horses are grazing together or resting, and one wants to move away or play. He will indicate this by nudging his companion or dancing round him and nipping him. He may give a whicker or just walk away hoping his companion will follow. He may get the responses (a) *oh all right*, shown in the reluctant carriage of his companion; or (b) *yes let's*—an enthusiastic response, or (c) *I'm damned if I will!* shown simply by a negative response or even by threatening or snapping.

8. *Go away!* This is a defensive sign and is designed purely to protect. It can be a mild threat, usually made with the teeth or hind legs, possibly only one hind leg. If this is ignored the stronger warning *go away or I will clobber you* follows. This is a definite and hostile movement and quickly becomes *you have asked for it*, which is an attempt to bite or kick the tormentor.

9. *Stop it!* This is a response to an action by another horse or a human. It varies from twitching the skin to striking with the front leg, kicking or biting. This has a response (a) *sorry*, shown by a rapid evacuation of the area with an air of injured innocence or (b) *I will if I want to*, which is shown by intensification of the annoying action.

10. *I love you.* We use this phrase to show affection other than maternal or sexual. There are thirty or more ways of showing this, the most common being a gentle blowing through the nostrils or rubbing with the nose and head. This can draw the response (a) *I love you too*, or (b) *go away*.

11. *I hate you.* The signs and sounds used in this case are different from *go away*, and are of an aggressive rather than a defensive nature. The front legs and teeth will be used, which is a definite sign of antipathy between two horses, and if it draws the response (a) *I hate you too*, a fight will ensue. It may draw the response (b) *I am sorry*, as in message 9: the same sorry signs will be used, but they will also include the defensive actions, that is, the hindquarters will be presented or a pair of heels may be used on the aggressor.

12. *I am king* is the bugle note of a stallion, which is either a challenge, or a call to a group of mares. This will be repeated again as he goes toward the mares.

13. *Come and get it.* This is the horsing mare's neigh in response to the stallion's bugle, and will be used as the horsing mare leaves the group to meet the stallion.

14. *Let us get the hell out of here*, is said with a snort or neigh with the head and tail held high ready for flight, which in turn will draw a response of "yes, let's," or "nothing to worry about."

RULES FOR USING CB RADIOS

Do's

1. Answer all calls for emergencies and motorists' assistance.
2. Switch nonemergencies to another channel.
3. Use your area work channel for all ordinary calling between team members.
4. Use landline to relieve monitor when you take over or in other instances in preference to radio.
5. Insofar as possible, ignore nonemergency users on Channel 9.
6. When it is necessary to handle emergency calls, courteously remind non-emergency callers that Channel 9 is officially limited to emergency calls.
7. Remember, others may be monitoring Channel 9. Respect the rights of others.

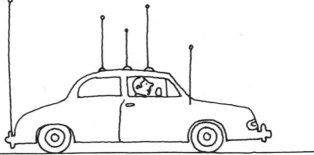

Don'ts

1. Use Channel 9 for non-emergency communications.
2. Argue with other emergency monitors.
3. Continue prolonged communications on Channel 9.
4. Use radio when telephone is available.
5. Dispatch private citizens to scene of emergencies unless requested by authorities.
6. Scold others for abusing Channel 9 rules.
7. Run time checks or "station identification" or frivolous announcements.
8. Call monitor on Channel 9 for ordinary nonemergency callings.
9. Act as if you own Channel 9.
10. Tell public safety personnel what to do. A monitor does not order them around. He does not command them. When you inform a police dispatcher that an accident with multiple injuries has occurred at Second and Main, and when the police respond with all deliberate speed, it is easy to think you have ordered them to go there. You have not. You have merely enabled the police to perform one of their major duties, which is to render assistance as required. You have passed on the information that police presence is required at Second and Main, and you have told the police dispatcher what to expect when they get there.

RULES FOR CORRECTLY PRONOUNCING NUMBERS OVER THE CB RADIO

1. Speak loud and clear.
    - 1- "WUN" . . . with a strong W and N
    - 2- "TOO" . . . with a strong and long OO
    - 3- "TH-R-EE" . . . with a slightly rolling R and long EE
    - 4- "FO-WER . . . with a long O and strong W and final R
    - 5- "FIE-YIV" . . . with a long I changing to short and strong Y and V
    - 6- "SIKS" . . . with a strong S and KS
    - 7- "SEV-VEN" . . . with a strong S and V and well-sounded VEN
    - 8- "ATE" . . . with a long A and strong T
    - 9- "NI-YEN" . . . with a strong N at the beginning, a long I and well-sounded YEN
    - 0- "ZERO" . . . with a strong Z, long E, and a short RO

2. Repeat numbers first individually as integers, and then as the whole number. For example, 1,527,617 is transmitted:

    "One, five, two, seven, six, one, seven (pause)—one million, five hundred twenty-seven thousand, six hundred seventeen."

RULES·FOR A CHINESE WEDDING CEREMONY—1919

The ceremony must follow this sequence:
1. Music.
2. Guests enter.
3. The go-between (matchmaker) enters.
4. The heads of the two families enter.
5. The bride and bridegroom bow twice to each other.
6. The bride and bridegroom exchange tokens and testimonials.
7. The bride and bridegroom face northward and thank the go-between. Two bows.
8. The bride and bridegroom thank the men guests. One bow.
9. The bride and bridegroom thank the women guests. One bow.
10. The bride and bridegroom face northward and honor the family ancestors. They burn incense, offer wines, kneel, make three prostrations, and then rise.
11. The bride and bridegroom offer their respects to their parents.
12. The parents formally acknowledge the presents already received.
13. The family elders acknowledge the gifts. Three bows.
14. Other relatives acknowledge the gifts. One bow.
15. The ceremony is concluded.

RULES FOR RECEIVING AN EMERGENCY RADIO-TELEPHONE CALL

1. *Answer promptly.* Treat each call as an emergency. Put yourself in the place of one who may be ill or suffering from fear or panic. Every ring for that person lasts an eternity. Try to answer within three rings.

2. *Identify yourself and your department.* This insures the caller that he has placed his call properly and thus has a calming influence on him.

3. *Speak directly into the mouthpiece.* This insures that you will be properly understood and will not have to waste time repeating information. Speak up! Don't swallow your words.

4. *Observe telephone courtesy.* A calm, competent, decisive voice that is courteous will reduce chances that the call will be antagonistic. Explain to the caller what action you intend to take and how soon assistance may be expected to arrive at the scene.

5. *Take charge of the conversation.* After the initial exchange and when you sense the needs of the calling party, cut off superfluous wordage by leading the caller into questions to which you need answers; questions as to who, what, where, when. Be courteous but firm.

6. *Take down all information. Write it.* Never leave anything to memory.

7. *Explain waits.* Explain why it will take time to check for information and that you will call back. A party waiting on a "dead phone" may become irritable and uncooperative.

8. *Avoid jargon or slang.* Use good English. Some terms you may use frequently, such as 10-4, ER (emergency room), etc., will not be meaningful to most callers.

9. *Show interest in the person's call.* The person calling has or needs information, and to him it is important. Get the caller's name when possible; it makes him feel you have a personal interest in his call. Do not, however, call strangers by their first name.

10. *Try to visualize the caller.* The telephone is an impersonal thing and we may tend to be curt and less courteous, or we may lose our temper easier than if we were meeting the party in person. Remember, the caller may be under tremendous strain. Try to reassure and calm him.

RULES FOR UNDERSTANDING LIBRARY OF CONGRESS CLASSIFICATIONS

1. The Library of Congress Classification System combines the letters of the alphabet and Arabic numerals. It provides twenty-six main classes compared to ten main classes in the Dewey Decimal Classification System.

2. Main classes are designated by capital letters, subclasses (except Z and E-F) by two capital letters, and further divisions and subdivisions by integral numbers in ordinary sequence.

3. The letters I, O, W, X, and Y are not used at the present time but are reserved for future expansion of the system.

4. The use of letters, numbers, and decimal numbers and letters makes possible the most minute classification.

5. The main classes of the Library of Congress Classification System are:

A   General Works—Polygraphy
B   Philosophy—Religion
C   History—Auxiliary Sciences
D   History and Topography (except America)
E-F   America
G   Geography—Anthropology
H   Social Sciences
J   Political Science
K   Law
L   Education
M   Music
N   Fine Arts
P   Language and Literature
Q   Science
R   Medicine
S   Agriculture—Plant and Animal Industry
T   Technology
U   Military Science
V   Naval Science
Z   Bibliography and Library Science

RULES FOR PRACTICING TO BECOME AN EFFECTIVE PUBLIC SPEAKER

1. Get acquainted. Tell the group who you are, your name and how to remember it, where you work and what you do. About your hobbies or other human-interest facts about yourself. Have fun.

2. Present in detail one single interesting experience. Your most exciting trip. Your most embarrassing situation or the funniest. A fire or accident you saw. Your first job. How you earned your first dollar. Your greatest mistake. If you had your life to live over.

3. Use bodily action. Demonstrate first lessons in gold, tennis, etc., using clubs and racket. First aid to the injured. Parlor tricks. Strokes in swimming. How to tip your hat to the ladies. Good and bad table manners. Show scrapbooks, keepsakes, curios, and mechanical devices. Tell where you got them, what they mean to you, and how they work.

4. Pantomime. Use no words in this exercise: Act out a simple story. Show how you shave, make-up, drive, fish, hunt, bowl, change a tire, build something, dress, hitchhike, escort a date, or portray some other action idea.

5. Argue against your pet peeve. Select a subject about which you really get excited—one that makes you boil or want to fight. Be specific: give plenty of details and examples. Talk about the rude policeman who gave you a ticket. What happened when you lent money to a friend. That raw deal. The used car that turned out to be a "lemon." How you were insulted. Someone at work who annoys you. How you hate war, race prejudice, cruelty to dumb animals.

6. Overcome hecklers. Speak for or against more than two terms for the President of the United States, married women in industry, strikes, uniform marriage and divorce laws, the outlawing of the atomic bomb, yellow journalism, television, prohibition, advertising, radio commercials, etc. Listeners will interrupt the speaker with such questions as, "What do you mean?" "Who says so?" "Explain the point more in detail!" "How do you know?" The audience should put the speaker through the fire, loosen him up, but should not carry the heckling too far. If the speaker is talking with vitality, let up on the heckling. The speaker must keep his head, prevent hecklers from stopping his speaking, and frame answers to silence them. He must be aggressive and never permit the meeting to pass from his control.

7. Emote! Select a nursery rhyme like "Tom, Tom, the Piper's Son," "Old Mother Hubbard," or "Mary Had a Little Lamb." See if you can deliver a rhyme with maximum animation, anger, unexpressiveness, sadness, indignation, or laughter. Whisper the rhyme, shout it, dramatize it, shed tears over it.

94

RULES FOR "SPENDING THE EVENING" WITH A WOMAN

At your place:

1.   Don't make any other telephone calls, particularly calls to other women.

2.   Don't recall all the times and all the women who have slept in her place in that very bed.

3.   Be sure you provide her with such essentials as makeup remover, toothbrush, and body lotion. (She may think such thoughtfulness is for her, but let's face it—it's really for you.)

4.   Close the door when you use the bathroom.

5.   Make sure your apartment is neat. Even if you are a bachelor, a sloppy pad can turn a woman off.

6.   While she undresses, let her know you're watching . . . a word or a gesture will do.

7.   In the morning you make the breakfast bacon, and then take her home, to her office, or escort her to a cab. No woman wants to leave his place without him.

At her place:

1.   Offer to bring a bottle of wine, some cheese, records, or other inducements to lovemaking.

2.   Don't tell her what is wrong with her apartment. If she decorated it, she loves it.

3.   Offer to get up and get extra blankets. Even though it's her house you can extend some courtesies.

4.   Don't ask whether you are the first man she has brought home; she might tell you the truth, and you'd better be sure you can handle it.

RULES REGARDING CHILDREN—THE U.N. DECLARATION

1.   The child shall enjoy all the rights set forth in this Declaration. Every child, without any exception whatsoever, shall be entitled to these rights, without distinction or discrimination on account of race, color, sex, language, religion, national or social origin, property, birth or other status, whether of himself or his family.

2.   The child shall enjoy special protection and shall be given opportunities and facilities, by law and by other means, to enable him to develop physically, mentally, morally, spiritually, and socially in a healthy and normal manner and in conditions of freedom and dignity. In the enactment of laws for this purpose, the best interests of the child shall be paramount.

3.   The child shall be entitled from his birth to a name and a nationality.

4.   The child shall enjoy the benefits of social security. He shall be entitled to grow and develop in health; to this end, special care and protection shall be provided both to him and his mother, including adequate prenatal and postnatal care. The child shall have the right to adequate nutrition, housing, recreation, and medical services.

5.   The child who is physically, mentally, or socially handicapped shall be given the special treatment, education, and care required by his particular condition.

6.   The child, for the full and harmonious development of his personality, needs love and understanding. He shall, wherever possible, grow up in the care and under the responsibility of his parents, and in any case, in an atmosphere of affection and of moral and material security; a child of tender years shall not, save in exceptional circumstances, be separated from his mother. Society and the public authorities shall have the duty to extend particular care to children without a family and to those without adequate means of support. Payment of State and other assistance toward the maintenance of children of large families is desirable.

7.   The child is entitled to receive education, which shall be free and compulsory, at least in the elementary stages. He shall be given an education which will promote his general culture, and enable him, on a basis of equal opportunity, to develop his abilities, his individual judgment, and his sense of moral and social responsibility, and to become a useful member of society.

The best interests of the child shall be the guiding principle of those responsible for his education and guidance; that responsibility lies in the first place with his parents. The child shall have full opportunity for play and recreation, which should be directed to the same purposes as education; society and the public authorities shall endeavor to promote the enjoyment of this right.

8.   The child shall in all circumstances be among the first to receive protection and relief.

9. The child shall be protected against all forms of neglect, cruelty, and exploitation. He shall not be the subject of traffic, in any form.

The child shall not be admitted to employment before an appropriate minimum age; he shall in no case be caused or permitted to engage in any occupation or employment which would prejudice his health or education, or interfere with his physical, mental, or moral development.

10. The child shall be protected from practices which may foster racial, religious, and any other form of discrimination. He shall be brought up in a spirit of understanding, tolerance, friendship among peoples, peace and universal brotherhood and in full consciousness that his energy and talents should be devoted to the service of his fellow men.

PROPOSED U. S. ARMY RULES FOR SENDING SMOKE SIGNALS—1859

1. To raise very dense smokes, kindle a large fire with dry wood and pile on it the green boughs of pine, balsam, or hemlock.

2. When two columns are traveling through a country at such distances that smokes may be seen from one to the other, their respective positions may be made known to each other at any time by two smokes raised simultaneously or at certain preconcerted intervals.

3. Should the commander of one column desire to communicate with the other, he raises three smokes simultaneously, which, if seen by the other party, should be repeated in the same manner. They would then hold themselves in readiness for other communications.

4. If an enemy is discovered in small numbers, a smoke raised twice at fifteen-minute intervals would indicate it: if in a large force, three times with the same intervals might be the signal.

5. Should the commander of one party desire the other to join him, this might be telegraphed by four smokes at ten-minute intervals.

6. Should it become necessary to change direction of the line of march, the commander may transmit this order by two simultaneous smokes raised a certain number of times to indicate the particular direction; for instance, twice for north, three times for south, etc.

7. The previously arranged signals should be written down and copies furnished to the commanders of each party to avoid mistakes.

8. During the day an intelligent man should be detailed to keep a vigilant lookout in all directions for smokes. H should be furnished with a watch, pencil, and paper to make a record of the signals, with their number and the time of the intervals between.

ANCIENT ROMAN RULES OF MARRIAGE

1. Three formalities existed to provide legality to marriage: *Confarreatio*, a religious rite; *Co-emptio*, a higher form of civil marriage, and *Usus*, the lower form of civil marriage.

2. *Confarreatio* was solemnized in the presence of the Pontifex Maximus or the Flamen Dialis (priest of Jove) and ten witnesses.

> a) The pontiff offered a sacrifice of an ox, or of fruits, in the presence of the attending witnesses.
> b) The contracting parties were seated on the same sheepskin.
> c) Certain customary forms of words were uttered.
> d) A salt cake of far or rice was presented as an offering, and tasted by the couple.

From this the ceremony had its name *confarreatio*, from *farreus*, i.e. *farreus panis*, cake of meal or flour. This rice cake indicated the ancient food of Italy, and served as an emblem of their mystic union of mind and body. Or, it may be more correct to say that this was a trace of an ancient usage, by which the wife, partaking of the food of her husband's tribe, became adopted into the tribe, to some extent, while remaining under the tutelage or guardianship of her husband: as the Romans expressed it, *covenire in manum viri*—to come under the hand of her husband. Her position was thus much the same, in fact, as later under the English common law.

3. *Co-emptio* was the solemn binding of the wedding couple to each other, by giving and taking a piece of money.

> a) The wife fulfilled the co-emption by purchasing, with three pieces of copper, a just introduction to her husband's house and household duties.
> b) Co-emptio was a sort of symbolic purchase of the wife by the husband, from the family to which she belonged, *per as et libram*, in the presence of five witnesses, and a sixth as *libripens*, or balance holder.
> c) The precise words and actions used in the co-emptio are not known, but doubtless they resembled those used in the form of sale called *mancipatio*.
> d) The effect of this ceremony was the same as in the *confarreatio*, in bringing the woman under the hand or power of the husband. This was the more frequent marriage custom among the Romans.

4. *Usus*, the third and lowest form of marriage, was without any ceremony being founded, as the word implies, on prescription, by the woman cohabiting with the man as her husband for a whole year, without having been absent from his house for three whole nights in succession.

    a) The uninterrupted possession of a wife for one year gave the husband the same rights he would have acquired at the outset if married with confarreatio or co-emptio.

5.   The Roman principle was that the consent of the parties was required, not only for contracting marriage, but for continuing it, and that hence it could be terminated at any time by either party, by the simple announcement of the fact.

    a) In the case of *confarreatio*, however, a religious rite, called *diffareatio*, was requisite to dissolve the obligation. The result was that the freer form of marriage was resorted to—what might be called the common law form—dispensing with all rites and ceremonies, and this prevailed in the time of Justinian.

    b) This practice, of course, did away with the husband's control over the person and property of his wife, and secured to her great independence as regards both.

RULES FOR KEEPING A CHILD HAPPY

To raise a happy child, it is important that:

1.   He is loved and wanted—and knows it.

2.   He is helped to grow up by not being over- or under-protected.

3.   He is allowed a space of his own.

4.   He is given a feeling of belonging by being made a part of family fun and group activities.

5.   He is exposed to skills—reading, talking, sports, and making things—and his work is admired.

6.   He is disciplined with understanding and he is corrected without being hurt, shamed, or confused.

7.   He has a part in family planning, has duties, and is made to feel needed.

8.   He is made to feel that his parents have no favorites among the children.

9.   He feels free to talk over any problem he has with his parents without feeling afraid or ashamed.

10.   He is given behavior guidelines and standards from infancy, which he must follow or be disciplined, and as he grows older he is given increasing responsibility for his own actions.

11.   He is made to feel that his parents are interested without prying into every facet of his life, that they are doing the best they can for him and they know that he is doing the same for them.

12.   He has something to believe in and work for because his parents have tried to live up to their ideals.

U. S. ARMY RULES FOR PROVISIONING A COVERED WAGON TO BE TAKEN ACROSS COUNTRY BY MULES—1859

1. Wagons with six mules should never, on a long journey over the prairies, be loaded with over two thousand pounds, unless grain is transported, when an additional thousand pounds may be taken, provided it is fed out daily to the team.

2. Every wagon should be furnished with substantial bows and double osnaburg covers, to protect its contents from the sun and weather.

3. Supplies should be put up in the most secure, compact, and portable shape.

4. Bacon should be packed in strong sacks of a hundred pounds each; in hot climates it should be put in boxes and surrounded with bran, which prevents the fat from melting away.

5. Place pork in the bottom of the wagons to keep it cool; if well cured it will keep several months this way, but bacon is preferable.

6. Flour should be packed in stout double canvas bags, well sewed, a hundred pounds in each sack.

7. Butter may be preserved by boiling it and skimming off the scum as it rises to the top, until it is clear, like oil. It is then packed in tin canisters and soldered up.

8. Sugar may be well secured in India-rubber sacks or placed in the wagon where there is no risk of its getting wet.

9. Desiccated or dried vegetables are prepared by cutting them into thin slices and subjecting them to a very powerful press. A small piece of this, about half the size of a man's hand, when boiled swells up to fill a dish and is sufficient for four men.

10. The allowance of provisions for each grown person, to make the journey from the Missouri River to California, should suffice for 110 days. The following is deemed requisite: 25 lbs. bacon or pork and enough beef to be driven on the hoof to make up the meat component of the ration; 150 lbs. of flour or its equivalent in hard bread; 15 lbs. of coffee; 25 lbs. of sugar; salt, pepper, and enough yeast to make up the bread.

11. I would advise all persons who travel for a considerable time without vegetables to carry with them some antiscorbutics; citric acid answers a good purpose. Wild onions, wild grapes, and greens are excellent antiscorbutics. An infusion of hemlock leaves is also said to be an antidote to scurvy.

12. It is true that if persons choose to pass through Salt Lake City, and the Mormons *happen* to be in an amiable mood, supplies may sometimes be procured from them; but those who have visited them well know how little reliance is to be placed upon their hospitality or spirit of accommodation.

RULES FOR SECURING A PATENT FOR YOUR INVENTION

1. Study your invention in relation to other available ways of doing the job, and decide whether the invention provides advantages that make it salable.

2. Get a trustworthy friend to sign his name as witness on a dated drawing or description of the invention, and keep careful records of the steps you take and their dates. Note also, Disclosure Document Program Offered by the Patent and Trademark Office.

3. Make a search to find the most closely related prior patents. This can be done for you by any patent practitioner.

4. Compare the patents found in the search with your invention. Your decision whether to seek patent protection should be based on your own comparison of these patents with the features of your invention which you believe to be new and valuable, and on the advice of your practitioner.

5. If you find that your invention includes valuable features not shown in the patents found in the search, instruct your practitioner to prepare an application for patent and to file it in the Patent and Trademark Office. Help him prepare a good application by giving him all the useful information you can provide.

6. Keep in close touch with the progress of your application in the Patent and Trademark Office. Tell you practitioner promptly of any changes you may make in your invention and of the steps you take to develop and market it. Study the patents which the Patent and Trademark Office may cite against your application. Help your practitioner to overcome rejections by pointing out in what way your invention differs from those described in earlier patents.

RULES FOR BEING AN OFFICIAL GUEST IN A FOREIGN COUNTRY

1. Remember, in some countries an invitation for, say, eight o'clock means exactly eight o'clock; in others, the earliest that guests are expected to arrive for an eight o'clock invitation is nine-thirty. In some countries, multiple courses are served at a meal, or multiple helpings of the same course; to avoid refusing hospitality, only a small portion is taken at a time. At some posts, guests are expected to tip the servants. At official dinners in certain Commonwealth countries, it is rude to smoke at the table before the toast to the Queen. In fact, almost anywhere abroad smoking at the table is to be avoided until the host or hostess indicates it is permissible. In some countries, the right side of the sofa is considered the seat of honor, reserved for the guest of honor or someone specifically invited to be seated in that place by the host or hostess.

2. Be prepared. Americans living abroad will often be confronted with unfamiliar food and drink. In order not to offend the hosts, it is courteous to try to enjoy them.

3. Keep in mind, in addition to variations in local courtesies, there are several general expectations which apply to diplomatic functions. At a reception, for example, a husband may be expected to precede his wife going through a receiving line. At such a party it is as correct and friendly to introduce oneself as it is important to meet and talk with the people of the host country, and to avoid standing in groups with other members of the mission staff.

4. At a seated meal, it is courteous to converse to the right and to the left, and even across a sufficiently narrow table, depending upon the general pattern of conversation set by the host and hostess. No one should be monopolized or isolated.

5. At a dinner party, it is a good idea to leave enough wine in the glass at the end of the meal to join in the drinking of toasts. If you don't care for wine, it is considerate to refuse it or ask for only a small amount rather than leave a full glass untouched. At a formal dinner, a motion of the hand will signal the waiter not to fill your glass. However, if toasts are anticipated, a small amount of the last wine served should always be accepted.

6. Remember, in most (but not all) countries, a guest being toasted remains seated and does not drink; a reply is then made by standing and offering a toast to the host and hostess.

7. It is usually advisable for any guest to leave a party, formal or informal, at a reasonable hour, no matter how pleasant it may be. At some posts, or with certain groups, a party is a protracted celebration and a "reasonable hour" may be a late one.

8. Before leaving, each guest should thank those hosting the party.

9. No guest should leave a formal lunch or dinner party before the guests of honor (unless the guests of honor linger inordinately long) or before the senior representative of one's own Embassy. The guest of honor has an obligation to judge the best time to leave.

10. On the day after a party, unless it was a large reception, "at home," cocktail party, or very informal gathering, it is courteous to say thank you again by writing a note or, if the hosts are good friends, by telephone. A wife may thank the hostess for both her husband and herself. If there was no hostess, a husband thanks the host for both his wife and himself.

11. Thank you notes (and all social and business letters) are signed with the writer's first name, not with "Mr.", "Mrs.", "Ms.", or any other title as an unseparated part of the signature. A married woman, traditionally, signs, "Jane Doe," and to acquaintances who may need further information, she may add "Mrs. John Quincy Doe" in parentheses below her signature, or she may place her title before her name in parentheses, as in "(Mrs.) Jane Doe" or "(Ms.) Jane Doe."

12. Sending flowers or a gift is not usually an obligation but, depending on local custom, it is an excellent way to express thanks, particularly if you are the guest of honor or if there is no other way to reciprocate, such as passing through the country. If flowers are sent beforehand, the hosts can display them at the party. Caution is advised, however; some countries have special rules regarding the sending of flowers and gifts.

RULES FOR MAKING YOUR TELEPHONING EASIER

1. When dialing a phone, release your finger from the hole after dialing each digit. If you keep your finger in the hole to force the dial back, you are likely to get a wrong number.

2. Let the phone ring seven to ten times before you hang up.

3. Hang up carefully after a call is completed. If your phone is even slightly ajar, it may stop calls from reaching you.

4. Be considerate and hang up at once, if you share a party line and comeone breaks in with a need to make a call immediately.

5. Teach children how to use the phone in emergencies. They should know how to call their home phone number and the operator. If you allow them to practice on the home phone, hold down the hook while they are dialing.

6. Keep a list of emergency phone numbers by every phone. Include your doctor, the police, rescue squad, poison control center, fire department, and ambulance center.

7. Avoid busy circuits on special holidays; phone the evening before the holiday.

RULES FOR MATHEMATICAL CONVERSIONS

1. To find acres, multiply hectares by .4047.
2. To find acres, multiply square feet by 43,560.
3. To find acres, multiply square miles by .001562.
4. To find atmospheres, multiply cms. of mercury by 76.
5. To find BTU, multiply horsepower-hrs. by .0003931.
6. To find BTU, multiply kilowatt-hrs. by .0002928.
7. To find BTU/hr., multiply watts by .2931.
8. To find bushels, multiply cubic inches by 2,150.4.
9. To find bushels (U.S.), multiply hectoliters by .3524.
10. To find centimeters, multiply inches by .3937.
11. To find centimeters, multiply feet by .03281.
12. To find circumference, multiply radians by 6.283.
13. To find cubic feet, multiply cubic meters by .0283.
14. To find cubic meters, multiply cubic feet by 35,3145.
15. To find cubic meters, multiply cubic yards by 1.3079.
16. To find cubic yards, multiply cubic meters by .7646.
17. To find degrees, multiply radians by .01745.
18. To find dynes, multiply grams by .00102.
19. To find fathoms, multiply feet by 6.0.
20. To find feet, multiply meters by .3048.
21. To find feet, multiply miles (nautical) by .0001645.
22. To find feet, multiply miles (statute) by .0001894.
23. To find feet/sec., multiply miles/hr. by .6818.
24. To find furlongs, multiply feet by 660.0.
25. To find furlongs, multiply miles by .125.
26. To find gallons (U.S.), multiply liters by 3.7853.
27. To find grains, multiply grams by .0648.
28. To find grams, multiply grains by 15.4324.
29. To find grams, multiply ounces avdp. by .0353.
30. To find grams, multiply pounds by .002205.
31. To find hectares, multiply acres by 2.4710.
32. To find hectoliters, multiply bushels (U.S.) by 2.8378.
33. To find hourepower, multiply watts by 745.7.
34. To find hours, multiply days by .04167.
35. To find inches, multiply millimeters by 25.4.
36. To find inches, multiply centimeters by 2.54.
37. To find kilograms, multiply pounds avdp. or troy by 2.2046.
38. To find kilometers, multiply miles by .6214.
39. To find kilowatts, multiply horsepower by 1.341.

40. To find knots, multiply nautical miles/hr. by 1.0.
41. To find knots, multiply statute miles/hr. by 1.151.
42. To find liters, multiply gallons (U.S.) by .2642.
43. To find liters, multiply pecks by .1135.
44. To find liters, multiply pints (dry) by 1.8162.
45. To find liters, multiply pints (liquid) by 2.1134.
46. To find liters, multiply quarts (dry) by .9081.
47. To find liters, multiply quarts (liquid) by 1.0567.
48. To find meters, multiply feet by 3.2808.
49. To find meters, multiply miles by .0006214.
50. To find meters, multiply yards by 1.0936.
51. To find metric tons, multiply tons (long) by .9842.
52. To find metric tons, multiply tons (short) by 1.1023.
53. To find miles, multiply kilometers by 1.6093.
54. To find miles, multiply feet by 5280.0.
55. To find miles (nautical), multiply miles (statute) by 1.1516.
56. To find miles (statute), multiply miles (nautical) by .8684.
57. To find miles/hr., multiply feet/min. by 88.
58. To find millimeters, multiply inches by .0394.
59. To find ounces avdp., multiply grams by 28.3495.
60. To find ounces, multiply pounds by .0625.
61. To find ounces (troy), multiply ounces (avdp.) by 1.09714.
62. To find pecks, multiply liters by 8.8096.
63. To find pints (dry), multiply liters by .5506.
64. To find pints (liquid), multiply liters by 14732.0.
65. To find pounds apothecaries' or troy, multiply kilograms by .3782.
66. To find pounds avdp., multiply kilograms by .4536.
67. To find pounds, multiply ounces by 16.
68. To find quarts (dry), multiply liters by 1.1012.
69. To find quarts (liquid), multiply liters by .9463.
70. To find radians, multiply degrees by 57.30.
71. To find rods, multiply meters by 5.029.
72. To find rods, multiply feet by 16.5.
73. To find square feet, multiply square meters by .0929.
74. To find square kilometers, multiply square miles by .3861.
75. To find square meters, multiply square yards by 1.1960.
76. To find square miles, multiply square meters by .8361.
77. To find tons (long), multiply metric tons by 1.1060.
78. To find tons (short), multiply metric tons by .9072.
79. To find tons (long), multiply pounds by 2240.0.
80. To find tons (short), multiply pounds by 2000.0.
81. To find watts, multiply BTU/hr. by 3.4129.

RULES FOR AVOIDING POISONING FROM PLANTS

1.   Avoid eating all plants that have milky or colored juices: this includes members of the Milkweed, Poison Ivy, Spurge, and Poppy families. Needless to say, there are exceptions to all general rules, for the young shoots of the Milkweed plant are edible and even Lettuce has a milky juice.

2.   Avoid all unknown white or red fruits. Poison Ivy, Poison Sumac, and some species of Baneberry have white fruits and are poisonous. Strawberries, Apples, and Tomatoes are red, but these are known. The majority of unrecognized red fruits are potentially toxic.

3.   Avoid eating wild seeds, for the seed of the plant usually has the greatest accumulation of chemical which may be toxic. In general the toxicity of plants is greatest in the storage organs of seeds, fruits, roots, and tubers. Young plants or young fruits may be less toxic than the same parts in mature condition. However, some plant poisons are breakdown products, and wilted leaves may often be more dangerous than fresh material.

4.   Avoid all fruits which are three-angled or three-lobed and thereby eliminate the potential dangers of the Spurge, Soapberry, Horsechestnut, Amaryllis, and Lily families. Some of the world's most infamous poisonous plants belong to these families.

5.   Avoid all bulbs that lack the smell of Onions or Garlic. Some members of the Lily and Amaryllis and related families with basal bulbs may kill you if eaten in quantity.

TAKING YOUR PULSE RATE

1.   Remember, proper pulse rate measurement requires comparing heart activity both before and after a period of strenuous activity.

2.   Take your pulse rate properly by following these steps:

        a) Take your pulse rate while sitting at rest.

        b) Then hop fifty times, twenty-five hops on each foot.

        c) Take your pulse immediately after the last hop.

        d) Sit for two minutes, then take your pulse rate again.

        "Normal" rates are:

Resting	60 to 85 beats per minute
Fifty hops	90 to 140 beats per minute
Two Minutes' Rest	60 to 95 beats per minute.

RULES FOR MONITORING YOUR HEALTH

1. If you are eighteen to twenty-four, have an exam once during this period. The exam should include: complete physical, medical, and behavioral history; tetanus booster; tests for syphilis, gonorrhea, malnutrition, cholesterol, and blood pressure; health education in nutrition, exercise, study, career, job, occupational hazards, alcohol, drugs, smoking, and driving.

2. If you are twenty-five to thirty-nine, have an exam twice, at about thirty and thirty-five. The exam should include: complete physical; tests for blood pressure, anemia, cholesterol, cervical and breast cancer; instruction in self-examination of breasts, skin, testes, neck, and mouth; counseling in nutrition, exercise, smoking, alcohol, marital, parental, and other aspects of behavior and life-style related to health.

3. If you are forty to fifty-nine, have an exam four times, once every five years. The exam should include: complete physical and medical history; tests for chronic conditions (high blood pressure, heart disease, diabetes, cancer, vision and hearing impairment); immunizations, as needed; counseling in changing nutritional needs, physical activities, occupation, sex, adjustment to menopause, marital and parental problems, use of cigarettes, alcohol, and drugs. For those over fifty, annual tests for blood pressure, obesity, and certain cancers.

4. If you are sixty to seventy-four, have an exam every two years. The exam should include: complete physical; tests for chronic conditions (see above); counseling regarding changing life-style related to retirement, nutritional requirements, absence of children, possible loss of spouse, and probable reduction in income and physical resources. Annual flu shot. Periodic podiatry treatments, if needed.

5. If you are seventy-five and over, have an exam at least once a year.

RULES TO FOLLOW WHEN YOU DATE A WOMAN WHO IS WILLING TO PAY HER SHARE OF EXPENSES

1. Go Dutch whenever you can afford it. If you always split expenses, you can stay cool about cash and save your emotions for the good stuff.

2. If you're a man who finds she picks up most of the checks, learn to give her a lot of presents—wild flowers, leaves, poems you copy in your own hadwriting. In other words, let her know she is getting her money's worth.

3. Don't think you owe her too much because she pays.

4. Don't take advantage of a woman with money. She'd rather be loved for a lot of other reasons.

RULES FOR MAINTAINING AN ALLERGAN/FREE HOME

1. Vacuum and dust the entire house daily. How much of a job this will be will depend entirely upon how well you have prepared your home from the allergy point of view. Remember your closets are parts of your rooms, and apply the same rules to them that you do to the rest of the house. In your dusting procedure pay special attention to floor moldings, cornices, windowsills, and other exposed flat and rough surfaces (mantels, shelves, shades, and blinds), and to hidden areas such as under beds and under furniture.

2. Do not let "things" accumulate. Magazines, bottles, cans, abandoned toys, outgrown or outworn clothing, used electric bulbs. Give these away to the many agencies that will be grateful for them, or, if you must store them, put them in an out-of-the way place—the garage, cellar, or attic. Get these out of your house as fast as you can—day by day if possible.

3. Pay special attention to the bedrooms. Keep the doors to these rooms shut when you are doing the rest of the house, and clean these rooms last in your daily house-cleaning program. The doors to these rooms should be kept shut at all times when unoccupied.

4. Clean and scrub the frames and open springs of beds at monthly intervals. Be sure to remove the beds from your bedroom when you do these.

5. Sponge-wash impermeable encasings of mattresses and pillows at weekly intervals. Launder bedspreads at two-week intervals. Blankets should be washed at four- to six-week intervals unless they have blanket covers. If so, less frequent washings are permissible. Sheets and pillowcases should be cared for as you do now. Be sure to replace all of the linens at the same time—do not replace one sheet at a time.

6. Go over your medicine cabinets once a week. Remove contents. Get rid of unused or unusable articles such as empty bottles, broken eyedroppers, odd bobby pins, and so on. Wash the shelves.

7. Go over the books in open bookshelves at least weekly. Using a damp cloth, go over the exterior of books one at a time and over the bookshelves.

8. Wash throw rugs and curtains at least once a week.

9. Wash draperies and slip covers at four- to six-week intervals. One of the dust-proofing agents should be used in the wash according to instructions.

10. Remember that these steps are not hard and fast as to intervals. Not only your initial preparation but also the area of the country in which you live will determine these. As a good housekeeper, you should be able to evaluate the frequency of these procedures yourself. If you live in a highly industrial area in which large concentrations of industrial contaminants seep into the house, obviously the maintenance chore will be heavy. If you live out in the country, the situation may be quite different.

11. When you have guests, be sure their outer things are taken off and put into hall and foyer closets before they enter your living quarters. Much that is troublesome can be brought into the house in clothing.

12. Investigate an electronic air cleaner, also known as an electrostatic precipitator. These machines remove 99 percent of all particulate matter from the air by driving the air at a specific rate over an electronic grid. Since all of the particles in the air are electrically charged, when they go over the grid in the air current they are precipitated on the grid plates of opposite charge.

RULES FOR APPROACHING A WOMAN.

1. If you want a lasting relationship, don't look for the woman who is the belle of the bar.

2. Don't be afraid to approach a beautiful woman; she wants love and warmth just as much as the less attractive one you think will accept you. And who knows? That beautiful woman may be able to see beyond your crooked nose into your superior character, intellect, and personality.

3. Learn to talk to a woman the way you talk to a man: with humor, tolerance interest.

4. If you don't seem to hit it off well the first time around and her credentials are good, try again. Maybe the chemistry was wrong the first time. First-rate people deserve a second chance.

RULES FOR TEACHING A BABY

1. Remember, during the first few months you will not be able to spend more than the baby's short waking periods—perhaps a few minutes several times a day. As he gets older, plan fifteen-minute to half-hour lessons, and later, one-hour lessons. It is important that these lessons become part of a structured routine.

2. Choose a convenient time for you and the baby. He should be well-rested, freshly diapered, and comfortable in general.

3. Choose one place for the lessons and use that same place every day. Activities for the first few months may be done in the crib, on the bath table, or on a blanket on the floor. Later a table is preferable to sitting on the floor because it establishes a working situation, good training for the school years ahead. For the baby who is beginning to sit, an infant seat such as a canvas seat within a large table area in which the baby can be strapped to help him sit is suggested.

4. Be sure your baby is comfortably dressed in clothing that is not too heavy. The room should be warm but not hot. It should be quiet and free of distractions.

5. Keep in mind, toys that are used specifically for the daily lessons should be kept in a separate container (laundry basket or carton) out of the baby's reach at other times so that they will have special attraction for him.

6. Keep a small box on the table to hold toys with many small parts, such as beads for stringing.

7. Be positive in your teaching. If you emphasize what your baby can do and realize that what he cannot do is unimportant, you are certain to encourage the child so that he will keep on trying. When you correct a mistake, do not make it seem important; simply show him the right way immediately by encouraging him and showing faith in his ability.

8. Keep a notebook of lesson plans. Plan lessons ahead of time and keep notes on what worked, what did not, and what you think should be repeated. Young children like to do the same things over and over. However, your baby must also be given new things so that he does not develop a rigid adherence to tasks that he finds familiar and easy. You will find your own system for balancing old activities with new and will sense when to go faster to include more activities in one sitting and when to slow down.

9. Show him one toy at a time. Put it back in the box before giving him another. When he gets a little older, let him put the toy back into the box himself.

10. Remember, it is necessary to expand his attention span so that he will work for a long time on the same thing. Show him different ways to play with the

same toy, but be sure to allow him to explore new ways for himself.

11. Break each task to be learned into steps. For example, when giving the child nested cups to put together, first give him two, and when he masters these, give him three, and so on.

12. Stop the lessons while it is still fun, before the baby becomes tired and fusses. Next time he will want more.

13. When a task becomes a chore, work on it for only a short time. If it is too difficult, drop it for a day or a week, or even a month, before trying it again.

14. Remember that you are the teacher and must teach according to your lesson plans. Do not let the child control the situation and tell you which toys he will play with. If you have taken out a puzzle and he then gets a whim to blow bubbles, you can firmly promise that he may blow bubbles just as soon as he is finished with the puzzle. Be quietly firm, not angry, do not say it more than once, and be sure to keep your promise. He will learn that he cannot always have his own way, and also that he has some choice and that you are not stubborn.

15. If the child gets angry for no reason and begins to have a temper tantrum, or simply cries, or is irritable, put away the toys for the day, and work again the next day. You must not be angry yourself or begin a power contest between you in which you say, "You do as I say, or else!" and he says, "I don't have to." Keep your cool and have a smile on your face. He will learn from the consequence of the situation but he will not learn by punishment.

16. He will enjoy his lesson time with you and may cry when it ends. Do not continue because he demands this. Just put him in his playpen and give him a toy to play with by himself. He will gradually learn that there are times that he plays with you and times that he plays alone, and that both are pleasurable.

17. Do not compare your baby with others. Each child does things in his own way and in his own time. Comparisons are dangerous. If you even think, "He is not doing as well as so-and-so," he will know that you do not have faith in him and he will lose faith in himself. It is important, therefore, that you yourself genuinely appreciate your baby's individuality in size and timing and that you be free of anxiety about how he compares with others.

EIGHTEENTH-CENTURY RULES GOVERNING MIDWIFERY

It is ordained that no woman within this corporation shall exercise the employment of midwifery until she has taken oath before the mayor, recorder, or an alderman . . . to the following effect:

1. That she will be diligent and ready to help any woman in labor, whether poor or rich.
2. That in time of necessity she will not forsake the poor woman and go to the rich.
3. That she will not cause or suffer any woman to name or put any other father to the child, but only him which is the very true father thereof.
4. Indeed, according to the utmost of her powers, that she will not suffer any woman to pretend to be delivered of a child who is not indeed her own, neither to claim any other woman's child for her own.
5. That she will not suffer any woman's child to be murdered or hurt.
6. And so often as she shall see any peril or jeopardy, either in the mother or child, she will call in other midwives for council.
7. That she will not administer any medicine to produce miscarriage.
8. That she will not enforce a woman to give more for her service than is right.
9. That she will not collude to keep secret the birth of a child.
10. That she will be of good behavior.
11. That she will not conceal the birth of bastards.

ROMAN RULES COVERING GROUNDS FOR DIVORCE
(A.D. 542)

1. Treason.
2. Attempt on the life of the other spouse.
3. Adultery, or acts creating the presumption of adultery by the wife (for example, going to the theater or to public baths against the husband's will).
4. Abortion.
5. Adultery by the husband if committed with a married woman, or in the common home of the couple.
6. For both parties, idiocy, leprosy, and insanity.
7. Marriage between adulterers is forbidden.
8. The adulterous wife is condemned to five years of celibacy and declared "infamous" if she does not observe the prohibition to remarry.
9. Divorce for any cause not explicitly admitted by the law is punished by certain penalties, such as forfeiture of a part of the responsible spouse's property to the innocent spouse, celibacy for a limited time, banishment.

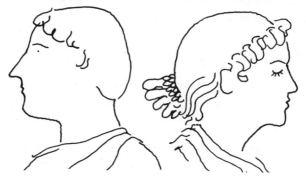

DR. ENDECOTT OF SALEM'S SEVENTEENTH-CENTURY RULES FOR REDUCING THE PAIN OF CHILDBIRTH

1. For Sharpe & Difficult Travel in Women with child Take a Lock of Vergins haire on any Part of ye head, of half the Age of ye Woman in travill.
2. Cut it very smale to fine Powder.
3. Then take 12 Ants Eggs dried in an oven after ye bread is drawne or otherwise make them dry & make them to powder with the haire.
4. Give this with a quarter of a pint of Red Cows milk or for want of it give it in strong ale wort.

RULES FOR TELLING A HUMOROUS STORY

1. Ask whether anybody has heard it before.

"Listen, you all know the story about the old Jewish man?"

It is important that this initial query be as general as possible, so that anybody who has heard the story before should not recognize it and hence have it spoiled for him. The next step is:

2. Ask someone else to tell it.

"Listen, it's a funny story. About an old Jewish man. Al, you tell it."

"I don't know the story you mean, Sylvia."

"Of course you know. Don't you? The story about the old Jewish man. Go ahead, you tell it, Al. You know I can't tell a story properly."

This modesty is very becoming to a performer and will surely be countered with heartfelt cries of denial from your audience. You are now ready to:

3. Explain where you heard the story.

"All right. This story I heard originally from Rose Melnick. You all know Rose? No? Her husband is in dry goods. Melnick. You know the one? All right, it doesn't matter to the story, believe me. Anyway, Rose Melnick heard it from her son-in-law, Seymour, a lovely boy, really. A nose and throat man. Seymour Rosen—you know the name?"

By now your audience has been sufficiently prepared for the story and will be anxious for you to begin. Go ahead and tell it, but be sure to:

4. Begin the story at the ending.

Professional comedians call the end of the story "the punch line." Since this is usually the funniest part of the story, it is logically the best place to start:

"Anyway, there's this old Jewish man who is trying to get into the synagogue during the Yom Kippur service, and the usher finally says to him, 'All right, go ahead in, but don't let me catch you praying.' (PAUSE) Oh, did I mention that the old man just wants to go in and give a message to somebody in the synagogue? He doesn't actually want to go into the synagogue and *pray*, you see. (PAUSE. FROWN) Wait a minute. I don't know if I mentioned that the old man doesn't have a ticket for the service. You know how crowded it always is on Yom Kippur, and the old man doesn't have a ticket, and he explains to the usher that he has to go into the synagogue and tell somebody something, but the usher isn't going to let him in without a ticket. So the old man explains to him that it's a matter of life and death, so then the usher thinks it over and he says to the old man, 'All right, go ahead in, but don't let me catch you praying.' (PAUSE. FROWN. STAND AND BEGIN EMPTYING ASHTRAYS) Ach, I don't think I told it right, Al, *you* tell it."

FOLK RULES REGARDING BABIES

1.   Monday's child is fair of face,
Tuesday's child is full of grace,
Wednesday's child is loving and giving,
Thursday's child must work for a living,
Friday's child is full of woe,
Saturday's child has far to go,
But the child that is born on the Sabbath day
Is blithe and bonny and good and gay.

2.   Dimple in the chin, devil within.

3.   Ugly babies make pretty ladies,
Pretty babies make ugly ladies.

4.   A child born with a caul or a veil is very lucky. He is very intelligent and has the power of healing. So does the seventh son of a seventh son. (But see the rules regarding vampires!)

5.   A child born with an open hand will be generous in life, while a baby born with a closed hand will be stingy.

6.   A baby born between the twenty-first and twenty-forth of any month will have good luck on the thirteenth day of any month.

7.   A baby born between the twenty-first of January and the twenty-first of February will have bowel trouble.

8.   Being born on the twenty-third of June is always lucky.

9.   A baby should see a sunrise before it sees a sunset to ensure long life.

10.   A child will have freckles if rain falls on it during the first year of its life.

11.   To ensure wealth and success, a child should be taken upstairs before it is taken downstairs.

12.   If you crack on a Bible the first louse found in a baby's hair he will become a preacher. Crack it on a tin cup and the child will become a good singer.

13.   A baby born in the light of the moon is more intelligent than one born in the dark of the moon.

14.   A baby born on a stormy night will be cross and nervous.

15.   A child born about four o'clock any afternoon will be moderately wealthy. But, if born about four o'clock on a Saturday it will be extremely wealthy.

16.   A baby with long fingers will play the piano; with a large mouth, a singer; a cowlick, roaringly stubborn.

17.   Give a baby a coin, and if he drops it he will let money slip through his fingers throughout his life. If he grasps it firmly, he will become wealthy.

RULES FOR PROTECTING CHILDREN OF ALL AGES

Birth to Seven Months

1. Keep crib sides up so baby won't roll out.
2. Keep stairs free of objects which can cause you to fall while carrying baby. Tack down extension cords and scatter rugs on floor.
3. Keep hallways and staircases well lighted.
4. Do not leave baby alone for even a moment on a bed, changing table, or any high place.
5. Use a crib and playpen with sturdy sides.
6. Remember, strollers and high chairs should be well balanced and sturdy so they won't tip over easily.
7. Hold baby securely during bath time.
8. Never park carriage/stroller near open stairway, driveway, or incline.
9. Don't put crib or playpen by open window or door leading outside the home.
10. When baby begins to crawl, put gates at stairways, driveways, porches, and seldom-used storage areas. Keep bathroom doors closed. *Never* leave baby alone near open stairway or open doorway to street.

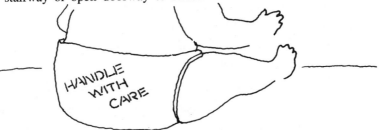

11. Keep a harness or safety strap on an active baby in the carriage/stroller and never leave an active baby alone in the carriage/stroller.
12. Check safety features of any baby play equipment like jumpers, walkers, swings for dangerous springs which might catch and seriously injure baby's fingers.
13. Be sure slats of crib and wooden playpen are spaced no more than two and a half inches apart so baby can't catch his head between them.
14. Keep in mind, filmy plastic sheets or covering on matresses, the use of pillows and harnesses on tiny infants can cause smothering or strangulation.
15. Keep cribs and playpen away from venetian blind cords.
16. When baby begins to sit up, avoid toys that string across crib.
17. Do not let baby chew or suck on a balloon (whether inflated or not).
18. At feeding time: avoid propping bottles (some children spit up and inhale liquids). It is safer not to feed baby while you are in bed—you might doze off and roll over on baby.

19. If baby vomits, lift hips slightly to permit liquid to flow out of mouth. Do not pick child upright at such a time.

20. Keep buttons, pins, beads, bells, small plastic toys and cars with easily detachable pieces—or anything small enough to fit entirely in baby's mouth—safely out of reach.

21. Remove button-type eyes and decorations from dolls or stuffed animals.

22. Use liquid medication when possible. Otherwise, *always* crush pills first and dilute in formula, juice, or water before giving it to baby.

23. Check floor and playpen for small objects before letting child play there.

24. Keep all medicines away from children. Return medicines and household chemicals to safe place *immediately* after using. Don't set it down "for just a moment." You might forget it and babies learn to grab these things very suddenly.

25. Begin now to put everything poisonous in high, locked cabinets. Don't store dangerous, household chemicals under sink or on low shelves.

26. Don't let your child eat or chew on plants, unknown berries, or mushrooms. Many common household plants and outdoor shrubs and flowers are poisonous when eaten. (See: Rules for Avoiding Plant Poisoning)

27. Don't leave an infant alone in the bathtub for an instant.

28. Check temperature of bath water with elbow to prevent scalding.

29. Never leave a child alone in the house.

30. Check materials used in sweaters and blankets for flammability.

Seven to Twelve Months

1. Remove sharp-edged furniture and easily overturned ornaments like lamps and flowerpots.

2. Have household pets immunized against rabies. Watch baby—especially when playing with puppies and kittens.

3. Be cautious if you smoke around baby. He's apt to grab the lighted tip or hot ashes can fall on him. Empty ashtrays before baby does.

4. Place safety guards in front of open heaters, fireplaces, and around floor furnaces and registers.

5. Never leave baby alone in a room with an open, burning fireplace (unless he is protectively enclosed in playpen).

6. Don't let child toddle around kitchen during preparation or serving of meals. He might get spattered with hot grease or you might trip and spill something on him. (Safest place is in playpen or high chair near you.)

7. Keep hot liquids, hot foods, and cords of irons, toasters, and coffepots out of baby's reach.

8. Turn pot handles inward toward back of stove and keep oven doors closed.

9. Avoid tableclothes that hang over the table's edge—the child might grasp it and bring hot, burning foods down on himself.

10. Keep vaporizer or portable heater out of the baby's reach, and do not place such items close to the child or his bedclothes.

11. Get safety plugs for unused electric wall sockets, or cover them over with black electric tape.

12. Never let your child chew on electric cords.

13. Repair frayed electric cords and faulty appliances that may give off shocks.

One to Three Years

1. Remember, this child can open doors. Lock these that lead to danger.

2. Lock gates leading to stairways and doorways faithfully.

3. Don't ever let a child lean out of windows.

4. Store dangerous tools and garden equipment in a safe place.

5. Use no-skid mats on bottom of bathtub.

6. Check outdoor play area for attractive hazards, deep holes, construction, trash heaps, and rickety buildings.

7. Do not allow child in yard while a power mower is in operation. It often throws off missiles like cans, stones, wires, and even broken glass and blades.

8. Teach child to play gently with pets and to avoid strange animals.

9. Never leave trunks, large picnic coolers, discarded refrigerators where child can crawl in and suffocate. If there is an abandoned refrigerator anywhere near a play area, be certain that the doors are removed before letting children play near it.

10. Remove small bones from fish and chicken when your child begins to eat whole table foods.

11. Empty or securely cover wading pools when not in use. (It takes only enough water to cover the nose and mouth to cause drowning.)

12. Be sure all cesspools and wells are securely covered or child carefully isolated from them.

13. Expect a child to seek out interesting water in the neighborhood—the swimming pool, storm sewers, wading pool, or whatever. Make sure such areas are securely fenced off or supervised.

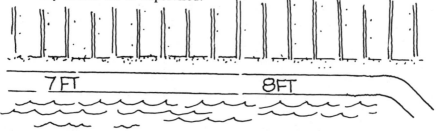

RULES FOR HELPING BABIES LEARN BY LOOKING

1. Give your baby things to look at to help him learn.

2. Hang a toy where baby can see it.

3. To make a hanging toy, crush bright-colored paper into a ball, sew a thread through it, and hang it from a stick or clothes hanger.

4. Lay your baby on his back so he can see.

5. Hang pictures on the wall where baby can see them.

6. Cut a picture from a magazine or hang the pictures older children bring home from school.

7. Give baby something to look at and reach for. Tie a string across his bed. On it hang bright-colored cloth, plastic bottle caps, painted spools, or other things. BE SURE HE CAN'T QUITE REACH THESE THINGS; HE MIGHT PULL THEM DOWN AND SWALLOW THEM.

8. Prop the baby up on the floor, on the bed, or on the couch so he can see around.

9. Hold baby in front of a mirror so he can see himself.

FIFTEENTH-CENTURY RULES FOR CHOOSING A WET NURSE

1. If it happens that from various causes the Mother cannot suckle the child herself, one must choose a nurse for the child.
2. The nurse must be of shapely stature, not too young and not too old.
3. She must at all times be free from illness of eyes or body.
4. Moreover, her nature must be such that there is no defect in her body.
5. Mark also that she must be neither too slim, nor too plump.
6. If there should be any defect in her, the child would incline toward it.
7. She must have a good character, modest, chaste, and clean.
8. Her food should be in conformity with the following directions, so that the milk may remain fully nourishing.
9. She should eat white bread and good meat, also rice and lettuce every day.
10. Almonds as well as hazelnuts she should not do without.
11. Her beverage must be a pure wine.
12. Moderation must be used in bathing.
13. Nor must she do much labor.
14. In case her milk should give out, she must not forget to eat peas frequently and in quantity, also beans, and in addition gruel, which should be boiled in milk beforehand.
15. She must also rest and sleep a good deal so that the child may thrive on the milk.
16. Moreover, she must carefully avoid onions and garlic, as well as any bitter or sour food and any dish containing pepper.
17. She must eat no oversalted food, nor anything prepared with vinegar.
18. Love's intercourse she must also avoid or go in for it very moderately. For in case she should become pregnant, her milk would be harmful to the child.
19. In order that the child may not be harmed in such a case, one must wean it from the milk.

RULES FOR SAFE SKIING

1. Ski under control.
2. When skiing downhill and overtaking another skier, avoid the skier below.
3. When meeting another skier in traversing the slope, pass to the right.
4. Do not stop where you will obstruct a trail or the loading or unloading area of lift, and do not stop where you cannot be seen from above.
5. When entering a trail, or slope from a side or intersecting trail, check for approaching downhill skiers.
6. When standing, check for approaching downhill skiers before resuming run.

7. When walking or climbing in a ski area, wear skis and keep to the side of the trail or slope.

8. Wear ski-retaining devices.

9. Keep off closed trails and posted areas; observe traffic signals and other regulations of the area.

RULES OF CONDUCT FOR MEMBERS OF THE AMERICAN ARMED FORCES

The Code of Conduct

1. I am an American fighting man. I serve in the forces which guard my country and our way of life. I am prepared to give my life in their defense.

2. I will never surrender of my own free will. If in command I will never surrender my men while they still have the means to resist.

3. If I am captured I will continue to resist by all means available. I will make every effort to escape and aid others to escape. I will accept neither parole nor special favors from the enemy.

4. If I become a prisoner of war, I will keep faith with my fellow prisoners. I will give no information or take part in any action which might be harmful to my comrades. If I am senior, I will take command, if not I will obey the lawful orders of those appointed over me and will back them up in every way.

5. When questioned, should I become a prisoner of war, I am bound to give only name, rank, service number, and date of birth. I will evade answering further questions to the utmost of my ability. I will make no oral or written statements disloyal to my country and its allies or harmful to their cause.

6. I will never forget that I am an American fighting man, responsible for my actions, and dedicated to the principles which made my country free. I will trust in my God and in the United States of America.

RULES FOR KEEPING FOSTER CHILDREN

1. See that he has what he needs to keep well: healthy meals, enough rest, suitable clothing, medical and dental care. (The agency provides for health care in addition to the monthly amounts for costs of basic care.)
2. Send the child to school, take an interest in his schoolwork, visit the teachers and join the parent-teachers group.
3. Plan for sports, hobbies, and other recreation, in keeping with the child's interests.
4. Set rules for the child and help him learn to live by them. You will have to discipline him when necessary, in a firm and consistent way but without harshness and without losing self-control.
5. Teach the child good habits, how to do his share of household chores, and how to use money (by helping him use a small allowance when he is old enough).
6. Teach him to set goals, to plan and strive toward an end. For a young child, a goal may be simply to learn to dress himself or to color a picture completely. For a teenager, a goal may be to enter college or a certain occupation.
7. Help him succeed at something, and praise him for it. Many foster children have the feeling that they are somehow "no good" because they are separated from their parents and so are different from other children. Being able to succeed at something and receive honest praise will encourage your foster child to believe in himself. What he succeeds at will, like his goals, depend on his abilities and interests—for example, learning how to spell a set of words correctly, cooking a whole meal for the first time, making the baseball team, etc.
8. Include the child in your family's religious activities, or, if the child's own family is of another religion, see that he receives instruction in the religion.

RULES FOR ENACTING A FEDERAL LAW

1. A senator or a representative introduces a bill and then sends it to the clerk of his house, who gives it a number and title. This is the first reading, and the bill is referred to the proper committee.
2. The committee may decide the bill is unwise or unnecessary and table it, thus killing it at once. Ot it may decide the bill is worthwhile and hold hearings to listen to facts and opinions presented by experts and other interested persons.
3. After members of the committee have debated the bill and perhaps offered amendments, a vote is taken; and if the vote if favorable, the bill is sent back to the floor of the house.

4. The clerk reads the bill sentence by sentence to the house, and this is known as the second reading. Members may then debate the bill and offer amendments. In the House of Representatives, the time for debate is limited by a closure rule, but there si no such restriction in the Senate except by a two-thirds vote for closure. This makes possible a filibuster, in which one or more opponents hold the floor to defeat the bill.

5. The third reading is by title only, and the bill is put to a vote, which may be by voice or roll call, depending on the circumstances and parliamentary rules. Members who must be absent at the time but who wish to record their vote may be paired if each negative vote has a balancing affirmative one.

6. The bill then goes to the other house of Congress, where it may be defeated, or passed with or without amendments. If the bill is defeated, a joint congressional committee must be appointed by both houses to iron out the differences.

7. After its final passage by both houses, the bill is sent to the President. If he approves, he signs it, and the bill becomes a law. However, if he disapproves, he vetoes the bill by refusing to sign it and sending it back to the house of origin with his reasons for the veto. The objections are read and debated, and a roll-call vote is taken.

8. If the bill receives less than a two-thirds vote, it is defeated and goes no further. But if it receives a two-thirds vote or greater, it is sent to the other house for a vote. If that house also passes it by a two-thirds vote, the President's veto is overridden, and the bill becomes a law.

9. Should the President desire neither to sign nor to veto the bill, he may retain it for ten days, Sundays excepted, after which time it automatically becomes a law without signature. However, if Congress has adjourned within those ten days, the bill is automatically killed, that process of indirect rejection being known as a pocket veto.

RULES FOR CONVERSATION

1. Listen sympathetically and interestedly.
2. Ask pertinent questions.
3. Avoid monopolizing the conversation.
4. Think before you speak.
5. Have the discipline to avoid tactless or cruel comments, whiplash wit.
6. Pay attention—so you don't have to interject "what" too often.
7. Say, "I think that . . . " rather than make positive statements.
8. Look for topics of mutual interest.
9. Let a reflective pause happen now and then, rather than keep the conversation going relentlessly.
10. Draw out the other person's opinions, interests, and ideas, rather than hold forth at length about your own.
11. Discuss, analyze, dissect a subject, if you will—enthusiastically, determinedly, heatedly, but never in anger. And end the discussion on a friendly note: "I realize I may be all wrong, you know . . . "
12. Turn a conversation that's becoming bitter, using any number of softening devices. The shock element: "Oh, my word—I forgot my brother's birthday. Excuse me for changing the subject, but what can I get him right now?" The hold-out-a-lollipop switch of subject: "I'm starved; wouldn't anyone like a vanilla frosted?" The temporary peace: "Well, we can't solve the problem today. Let's eat/dance/etc. . . . " The classic tension-breaker: "Oh . . . has anyone read any good books lately?"
13. Never criticize unjustly or destructively. It's true you must criticize sometimes if you are the leader, president, chairman of any group. Try to make the criticism only to the person involved—privately—and with the intention of improving the situation: "Jerry, I think it would be much better if you would concentrate on the sale of tickets and let the decorating committee do its job. Would you do that, please?"
14. Never ridicule or make fun of another person's mannerisms, eccentricities, shortcomings, taste, looks, possessions, relatives, friends, pets.
15. Never wave these conversational red flags: "You always. . . " "The trouble with you is. . . "
16. Never gossip or repeat gossip (a disease that can become chronic and highly infectious to others; males catch it too).
17. Never ask personal questions. These include asking why your family doesn't belong to the club, what's the matter with your little sister who has to repeat second grade, is your mother a real blonde, is your brother ever going to marry Anne, how much insurance your father has, why don't you go on a diet.
18. Never indulge in speculative talk about money. This includes wondering

how much money someone paid for a house, what salary someone probably gets, how much someone paid for a dress, the amount of someone's allowance, whether someone's family can afford to live the way they do, and so on and on.

19. Never, never, never be as funny as you can, especially at someone else's expense.

20. Never dispense wholesale criticism of anyone's politics or religion . . . or of any racial, political, religious, or national group *as a group*.

RULES FOR SPECTATORS AT GOLF TOURNAMENTS

1. Remember it is the players' competition. Treat them as you would like to be treated. A lot is at stake.

2. Be silent and motionless when a player takes his stance and throughout his stroke. If you must speak, do so in a whisper.

3. Give the player plenty of room.

4. Always stay behind the ropes and/or white lines. Never lean on the ropes.

5. If the gallery is large, and if you're in the front row, kneel. Do not call out, "Down in front!" It's the job of the tournament marshals to give instructions.

6. Avoid applause unless really merited. Never applaud while a player is making his stroke.

7. Be fair to players without galleries or with small ones. Do not make it too obvious that you favor one player.

8. Watch where you're going. Keep your head up and never, never run. A golf course can be dangerous to those who are careless.

9. Respect crossover points. Greens and fairways are for the players.

10. Do not walk through traps or bunkers.

11. Never approach a player during play for an autograph or conversation. Wait until his round is completed.

12. Always obey the commands of the tournament marshals. Remember that the marshals are there to see that everything goes smoothly. They are operating according to a plan that will make the tournament more enjoyable for spectators and contestants alike.

RULES OF WEDDING ANNIVERSARY GIFT GIVING

Traditional Wedding Anniversary Gift List
If 1st anniversary give paper.
If 2nd anniversary give cotton.
If 3rd anniversary give leather.
If 4th anniversary give fruit, flowers.
If 5th anniversary give wood.

If 6th anniversary give candy, iron.
If 7th anniversary give wool, copper.
If 8th anniversary give bronze, pottery.
If 9th anniversary give pottery, willow.
If 10th anniversary give tin, aluminum.
If 11th anniversary give steel.
If 12th anniversary give silk, linen.
If 13th anniversary give lace.
If 14th anniversary give ivory.
If 15th anniversary give crystal.

If 20th anniversary give china.
If 25th anniversary give silver.
If 30th anniversary give pearl.
If 35th anniversary give coral.
If 40th anniversary give ruby.
If 50th anniversary give gold.
If 55th anniversary give emerald.
If 60th anniversary give diamond.

Modern Wedding Anniversary Gift List
If 1st anniversary give clocks.
If 2nd anniversary give china.

If 3rd anniversary give crystal, glass.
If 4th anniversary give electrical appliances.
If 5th anniversary give silverware.
If 6th anniversary give wood.
If 7th anniversary give desk sets—pen and pencil sets.
If 8th anniversary give linens, laces.
If 9th anniversary give leather.
If 10th anniversary give diamond jewelry.

If 11th anniversary give fashion jewelry and accessories.
If 12th anniversary give pearls or colored gems.
If 13th anniversary give textiles, fur.
If 14th anniversary give gold jewelry.

126

If 15th anniversary give watches.
If 16th anniversary give silver hollow-ware.
If 17th anniversary give furniture.
If 18th anniversary give porcelain.
If 19th anniversary give bronze.
If 20th anniversary give platinum.
If 25th anniversary give Sterling Silver Jubilee.
if 30th anniversary give diamond.
If 35th anniversary give jade.
If 40th anniversary give ruby.
If 45th anniversary give sapphire.
If 50th anniversary give Golden Jubilee.
If 55th anniversary give emerald.
If 60th anniversary give Diamond Jubilee.

RULES FOR IMPLEMENTING THE DEATH PENALTY

1. In Utah, the convict may choose between hanging and a firing squad. If he will not decide, the sentencing judge must choose the method of execution.

2. In seventeen states (Alabama, Arkansas, Connecticut, Florida, Georgia, Illinois, Indiana, Kentucky, Louisiana, Nebraska, New York, Ohio, Pennsylvania, South Carolina, Tennessee, Vermont, and Virginia) executions must be by electrocution.

3. In nine states (Arizona, California, Colorado, Mississippi, Missouri, Nevada, North Carolina, Wyoming, and Rhode Island) execution must be by lethal gas.

4. In Delaware, Idaho, Montana, New Hampshire, and Washington execution must be by hanging.

5. In Texas execution must be by lethal intravenous injection.

6. In Oklahoma, execution must be by lethal intravenous injection, unless that is ruled unconstitutional, in which case execution must be by electrocution or firing squad.

BASIC RULES OF MUSICAL NOTATION

1.   Music is written on a staff consisting of five lines and four spaces numbered in this order:

> 5th line
> 4th space
> 4th line
> 3rd space
> 3rd line
> 2nd space
> 2nd line
> 1st space
> 1st line

2.   The musical alphabet has seven letters—A, B, C, D, E, F, G.

3.   Notes which fall on the lines of the staff from the bottom upward are: E, G, B, D, F. They can be remembered by the sentence, "Every good boy does fine."

4.   Notes which fall in the spaces from the bottom upward are: F, A, C, E— remembered by the word "FACE."

5.   The musical staff is divided into measures by vertical lines called bars.

6.   The time signature indicated at the beginning of a piece of music shows by the top number the number of beats per measure. The bottom number indicates the type of note receiving one beat. Thus, music written in ¾ time takes three beats to the measure with a quarter note taking one beat.

7.   A note can be shown with up to three parts: a head, either solid or hollow; a stem, a straight vertical line connected to the head; and the flag, a tail-like marking running from the stem off to the right of the note. Used in combination these markings show the length and pitch of a musical tone.

8.   A whole note is shown as a hollow head with no stem. It receives, or is held for, four beats.

9.   A half note is shown as a hollow head with a stem. It receives two beats.

10.   A quarter note is shown as a solid head with a stem. It receives one beat.

11.   An eighth note is shown as a solid head with a stem and a single flag. It receives a half beat.

RULES OF SINGING

1.   Give attention to the position of the body, the separation of the jaws, the shape of the throat, and the breathing.

2.   Position the body straight, well planted on the feet, and without any other support; the shoulders well back, the head erect, the expression of the face calm.

3. The mouth should be opened by the natural fall of the jaw. This movement, which separates the jaws by the thickness of a finger and leaves the lips alone, gives the mouth an easy and natural form.

4. The tongue must be kept limp and motionless, neither raised at the point nor swollen at the root.

5. Finally, the soft palate must be raised as in taking a full breath. The exaggerated opening favors neither low nor high notes. In the later case it may help the vocalist to scream, but that is not singing; the face loses charm and the voice assumes a violent and vulgar tone. The real mouth of a singer ought to be considered the pharynx, because it is in the pharynx that is found the causation to *timbres*. The facial mouth is but a door through which the voice passes. Still, if this door were not sufficiently open, sounds could not issue freely.

6. Those who find it difficult either to diminish or to increase the opening of the mouth will do well to place laterally between the jaws, from back to front, a small piece of wood not thicker than a pencil.

7. It may be added that when the lungs are completely filled with air, the natural tendency is to be quickly rid of the superabundance. Consequently the sounds at the start are strong and often unsteady; then they become weaker with the lessening of the breath. The majority of musical phrases demand the opposite method. On this account, the pupil should begin with a small amount of pressure, increasing it gradually as the supply of air diminishes. The even flow of a long phrase, a long passage of agility, the stability of a long note, all require a continuous and well-managed pressure of the diaphragm. The necessity for a steady pressure is especially felt in large halls and in places bad for sound. Air given out in jerks does not travel. A moderate mass of circumambient air; the faintest sound, given in this manner, if not drowned by the accompanist will reach the ears of the most distant auditor.

RULES FOR INTERPRETING VISUAL LETTER SIGNALS AT SEA

1. The signal *A* means "I have a diver down; keep well clear at slow speed."
2. The signal *B* means "I am taking in, or discharging, or carrying dangerous goods."
3. The signal *C* means "Yes" (affirmative or "The significance of the previous group should be read in the affirmative").
4. The signal *D* means "Keep clear of me; I am maneuvering with difficulty."
5. The signal *E* means "I am altering my course to starboard."
6. The signal *F* means "I am disabled; communicate with me."
7. The signal *G* means "I require a pilot." When made by fishing vessels operating in close proximity on the fishing grounds it means "I am hauling nets."
8. The signal *H* means "I have a pilot on board."
9. The signal *I* means "I am altering my course to port."
10. The signal *J* means "I am on fire and have dangerous cargo on board; keep well clear of me."
11. The signal *K* means "I wish to communicate with you."
12. The signal *L* means "You should stop your vessel instantly."
13. The signal *M* means "My vessel is stopped and making no way through the water."
14. The signal *N* means "No" (negative or "The significance of the previous group should be read in the negative"). This signal may be given only visually or by sound. For voice or radio transmission the signal should be "No."
15. The signal *O* means "Man overboard."

16. The signal *P* means: In harbor, "All persons should report on board as the vessel is about to proceed to sea."

    At sea, it may be used by fishing vessels to mean "My nets have come fast upon an obstruction."
17. The signal *Q* means "My vessel is 'healthy' and I request free pratique."
18. The signal *S* means "My engines are going astern."
19. The signal *T* means "Keep clear of me; I am engaged in pair trawling."
20. The signal *U* means "You are running into danger."

21. The signal *V* means "I require assistance."

22. The signal *W* means "I require medical assistance."

23. The signal *X* means "Stop carrying out your intentions and watch for my signals."

24. The signal *Y* means "I am dragging my anchor."

25. The signal *Z* means "I require a tug." When made by fishing vessels operating in close proximity on the fishing grounds it means: "I am shooting nets."

RULES FOR SPELLING ENDINGS

1. The final *e* after a consonant is usually dropped before adding an ending with a vowel, as in *skate—skating*. The final *e* is retained in some words to prevent confusion, as in *dye—dyeing*; and the *e* is retained after *c* and *g* before a suffix beginning with *a*, as in *peace—*peaceable and *change—changeable*.

2. One-syllable words and words with the accent on the last syllable ending in one consonant preceded by a single vowel usually have the final consonant doubled when a suffix beginning with a vowel is added, as in *swim—swimming*.

3. The plurals of most nouns are formed by adding *s*. However, *es* is added to some words to form the plural so as to make the words easier to pronounce; usually these words end in *s*, *ss*, *sh*, *ch*, *x*, or *z*.

4. A *y* at the end of a word usually changes to *i* when an inflectional ending or suffix not beginning with *i* is added, as in *easy—easily*. To form plurals of nouns ending in *y* preceded by a consonant, the *y* is changed to *i* and *es* is added.

5. The *ks* sound in plural words is not spelled with an *x*; e.g., *ducks*.

6. Words ending in *ful* have only one *l* at the end (and *s* is added after the *l* for plurality).

7. Words ending with short *i* and long *i* sounds usually end in y, as in pretty or sky.

8. Several ending sounds are tricky because they are spelled in four ways although the sound is similar:

> *chun* spelled *tion*, as in *question*
>
> *shun* spelled *cean*, as in *ocean*; *ssion*, as in *mission* and *tion*, as in *nation*
>
> *shun* spelled *sion*, as in *vision*

U. S. ARMY RULES FOR TRACKING INDIANS—1859

1. In following Indian depredators, the utmost vigilance and caution must be exercised to conceal from them the movements of the pursuers.

2. For overtaking a marauding party of Indians who have advanced eight or ten hours before the pursuing party are in readiness to take the trail, it is not best to push forward rapidly at first, as this will weary and break down horses.

3. Scouts should continually be kept out in front upon the trail to reconnoiter and give preconcerted signals to the main party when the Indians are spied.

4. In approaching all eminences or undulations in the prairies, the commander should be careful not to allow any considerable number of his men to pass upon the summits until the country around has been carefully reconnoitered by the scouts, who will cautiously raise their eyes above the crests of the most elevated points, making a scrutinizing examination in all directions.

5. If an Indian should be encountered who has been left behind as a sentinel, he must, if possible, be secured or shot, to prevent his giving the alarm to his comrades.

6. If there be a moon, it will be better to lie by in the daytime and follow the trail at night, as the great object is to come upon the Indians when they are not anticipating an attack.

7. As soon as the Indians are discovered in their bivouac the pursuing party should dismount, leaving their horses under charge of a guard.

8. Before advancing to the attack, so as to advance silently, the men should be instructed in signals for different movements, as, for example, a pull on the skirt of the coat to halt, a gentle push on the back to advance in ordinary time.

9. Great care should be taken that the men do not mistake their brothers in arms for the enemy during a night attack. There should be two passwords, and if there is any doubt as to the identity of two men who meet during night operations, one word should be repeated by each.

10. The men should be impressed with the importance of not firing a shot until the order is given by the commanding officer, so as not to alert the Indians.

EARLY AMERICAN RULES OF DRESS AND HABIT

1.   Don't blow your nose in the presence of others if you can possible avoid it. There are persons who perform the operation with the fingers but his disgusting habit is confined to people of the lowest class. Under any circumstance it is revolting to witness the performance however noseblowing may be done.

2.   Don't gape or hiccough or sneeze in company. When there is an inclination to hiccough or sneeze, hold your breath for a moment and resist the desire.

3.   Don't have the habit of letting your lip drop and your mouth remain open. Breathe through your nostrils and not through your mouth. An open mouth indicates feebleness of character, while this bad habit also affects the teeth and the general health.

4.   Don't keep carrying your hands to your face, pulling your whiskers, adjusting your hair, or otherwise fingering yourself. Keep your hands quiet and under control.

5.   Don't wear your hat in a strictly private office. This is no more justifiable than wearing a hat in a drawing room.

6.   Don't carry a lighted cigar into a private office or into a sales room.

7.   Don't pick up letters, accounts, or anything of private character that is lying on another's desk.

8.   Don't look over another person's shoulder when he is reading or writing.

9.   Don't twirl a chair or other object while either talking or listening to anyone. This annoying trick is very common.

10.   Don't beat a tattoo with your foot in company or anywhere to the annoyance of others. Don't drum with your fingers on a chair. Don't hum. The instinct for making noises is a survival of savagery.

11.   Don't be servile toward superiors or arrogant toward inferiors. Maintain your dignity and self-respect on this point.

12.   Don't wear soiled linen. Be scrupulously particular on this point.

13.   Don't be untidy in anything. Neatness is one of the most important of the minor morals.

14.   Don't neglect details of the toilet. Many persons neat in other particulars, for example, carry blackened fingernails. This is disgusting.

15.   Don't neglect the small hairs that project from the nostrils and grow about the apertures of the ears. These are small matters of the toilet that often are overlooked.

RULES FOR SECURING TRADEMARKS

1. In order to be eligible for registration, your mark must be in use in commerce which may lawfully be regulated by Congress, for example, interstate commerce, at the time the application is filed.

2. You cannot register a trademark if it:

a) Consists of or comprises immoral, deceptive, or scandalous matter which may disparage or falsely suggest a connection with persons, living or dead, institutions, beliefs, or national symbols, or bring them into contempt or disrepute.

b) Consists of or comprises the flag or coat of arms or other insignia of the United States, or of any State or municipality, or of any foreign nation, or any simulation thereof.

c) Consists of or comprises a name, portrait, or signature identifying a particular living individual except by his written consent, or the name, signature, or portrait of a deceased President of the United States during the life of his widow, if any, except by the written consent of the widow.

d) Consists of or comprises a mark which so resembles a mark registered in the Patent and Trademark Office or a mark or trade name previously used in the United States by another and not abandoned, as to be likely when applied to the goods of another person to cause confusion, or to cause mistake, or to deceive.

3. Make a written application to the U. S. Patent Office, Washington, D.C. It should be plainly written on only one side of the paper. Legal-size paper, typewritten double-spaced, with at least a 1 ½" margin on the left-hand side and top of the pages is deemed preferable.

4. Your application should include a request for registration and must specify:

a) the name of the applicant;

b) the citizenship of the applicant; if the applicant is a partnership, the names and citizenship of the general partners or, if the applicant is a corporation or association, the state or nation under the laws of which organized;

c) the domicile and post office address of the applicant;

d) that the applicant has adopted and is using the mark shown in the accompanying drawing;

e) the particular goods on or in connection with which the mark is used;

f) the class of merchandise according to the official classification if known to the applicant;

g) the date of applicant's first use of the mark as trademark on or in connection with goods specified in the application;

h) the date of applicant's first use of the mark as a trademark on or in connection with goods specified in the application in commerce which may lawfully be regulated by Congress, specifying the nature of the commerce;

i) the mode or manner in which the mark is used on or in connection with the particular goods specified.

SAFETY RULES OF THE ROAD FOR CHILDREN

1. Be sure children always enter an automobile on the side opposite the driver, namely, the right side.
2. Caution children to keep their fingers away from car doors. One of the most painful and frequent childhood injuries is a finger pinched in a closing car door.
3. Always get out of cars before children.
4. Do not permit children to stand next to the driver or stand on a car seat in a moving vehicle.
5. Never allow a child to lie on the shelf behind the back seat.
6. Lock all doors before starting the car.
7. Fasten all safety restraints securely.
8. Never permit children to toss around objects such as toys, pillows, or other playthings inside a moving car.
9. Never seat a child on the driver's lap.
10. Teach children to keep their hands off the controls and the dashboard.
11. Never leave a child alone in a parked car.
12. Always carry a first-aid kit in order to manage minor cuts and abrasions that children commonly encounter.
13. Always have available fresh batteries, a flashlight, and an emergency spotlight to alert other drivers in case of an accident.
14. Teach your child to look in all directions before crossing the street.
15. Teach him to cross streets only at marked crosswalks or intersections.
16. Carefully explain to him the dangers of running into the street, running out from behind parked cars, or jaywalking.
17. Teach your child how to read traffic lights, highway signs, and signals.

U. S. ARMY RULES FOR MEETING INDIANS ON THE TRAIL—1859

When alone:

1. It is a safe rule, when a man finds himself alone in the prairies, and sees a party of Indians approaching, not to allow them to come near him, and if they persist in doing so, to signal them to keep away.

2. If the Indians persist in approaching, and if a lone man be mounted on a fleet horse, he should make for the nearest timber.

3. If the Indians follow, and press the lone man closely, he should halt, turn around, and point his gun at the foremost, which will often have the effect of turning them back, but he should never draw trigger unless he finds that his life depends upon the shot; for as soon as his shot is delivered, his sole dependence, unless he has time to reload, must be upon the speed of his horse.

When with a party:

1. When an Indian party is discovered approaching, and are near enough to distinguish signals, all that is necessary in order to ascertain their disposition is to raise the right hand with the palm up front and gradually push it back and forth several times. They all understand this to be a command to halt, and, if they are not hostile, it will at once be obeyed.

2. After they have stopped the right hand is raised again as before and slowly moved to the right and left, which signifies "I do not know you. Who are you?" They will then answer by giving their tribal signal:

> Comanche—the hand makes a waving motion in imitation of the crawling of a snake.
> Cheyenne, or "Cut-arm"—the hand is drawn across the arm.
> Arapahoes, or "Smellers"—the nose is seized with the thumb and forefinger
> Sioux, or "Cut-throats"—the hand is drawn across the throat.
> Pawnees, or "Wolves"—a hand is placed on each side of the forehead, with two fingers pointing to the front, to represent the ears of the wolf.

3. To determine if an Indian party is friendly, raise both hands grasped in the manner of shaking hands, or lock the two forefingers firmly while the hands are held up. If friendly, they will respond with the same signal, if hostile they will probably disregard the command to halt, or give the signal of anger by closing the hand, placing it against the forehead, and turning it back and forth in that position.

4. If the Indians are friendly, their chiefs will ride out to speak with the commanders of the white man's party. They are always desirous of procuring, from whomever they meet, testimonials of their good behavior, which they preserve with great care, and exhibit upon all occasions to strangers as a guarantee of future good conduct.

5. If a small party be in danger of an attack from a large force of Indians, they should seek the cover of timber or a park of wagons, or in the absence of these, rocks or holes in the prairie which afford good cover.

6. In a country infested by hostile Indians, the ground in the vicinity of which it is proposed to encamp should be cautiously examined for tracks and other Indian signs by making a circuit around the locality previous to unharnessing the animals.

JAPANESE RULES OF BUSINESS—1909

1. Luck hovers around the house of smiles.
2. A good speech is a short one, so is a letter.
3. When asked for the chisel, give the hammer also.
4. Of all enemies, your own negligence is the very worst.
5. Wealth and happiness are the productions of effort.
6. One's business ability can be measured by one's borrowing capacity.
7. Great haste spoils achievement, as in the case of the foolish farmer who pulled the rice stalk in order to hasten growth and killed the plant.

RULES FOR USING ARMY TITLES

1. Lieutenants are addressed officially as "Lieutenant." The adjectives "First" and "Second" are not used except in written communications.

2. Other officers are addressed or referred to by their titles, in conversation and in nonofficial correspondence (other than in the address itself), brigadier generals, major generals, and lieutenant generals are usually referred to and addressed as "General." Lieutenant colonels, under the same conditions, are addressed as "Colonel."

3. Senior officers frequently address juniors as "Smith" or "Jones," but this does not give the junior the privilege of addressing the senior in any way other than by his proper title.

4. "Ma'am" is used in addressing a female officer under circumstances when the use of "sir" would be appropriate in the case of a male officer.

5. Chaplains are addressed as "Chaplain" regardless of their grade. A Catholic or Episcopal chaplain may be addressed as "Father."

6. Women officers of the Army Medical Service, as well as those of the Women's Army Corps, are addressed by their military title, and are entitled to the prescribed military salute.

7. The Warrant Officer formally ranks below Second Lieutenant and above Cadet. He is extended the same privileges and respect as a commissioned officer and differs only in that there are certain regulated restrictions on command functions. The Warrant Officer is the Army's top-grade specialist and is addressed as "Mister" or "Miss," as appropriate.

8. Cadets of the United States Military Academy are addressed as "Cadet" officially and in written communications. Under less formal situations, they are addressed as "Mister."

9. Sergeants Major are addressed as "Sergeant Major." A First Sergeant is addressed as "First Sergeant," while a Corporal is addressed as "Corporal." All specialists are addressed as "Specialist." Officers generally address privates as "Jones" or "Smith." The full titles of the enlisted men are used in official communications.

RULES FOR PERFORMING SENTRY DUTIES IN THE U. S. NAVY

1. All Navy sentries must memorize and perform the following:

   a) To take charge of this post and all government property in view.

   b) To walk my post in a military manner, keeping constantly alert, observing everything that takes place within sight or hearing.

c) To report every breach of orders or regulations that I am instructed to enforce.

d) To quit my post only when regularly relieved.

e) To receive, obey, and transmit orders from the commanding officer, executive officer, the officer of the deck, or the officer or petty officer of the guard.

f) To hold conversation with no one, except in the proper discharge of my duties.

g) In case of fire, give the alarm; quit post if necessary to do so.

h) To allow no one to commit a nuisance in vicinity of my post.

i) In any case not covered by instructions, to call the petty officer of the guard.

j) To salute all officers.

k) At night to exercise the greatest vigilance.

2.   When calling for any purpose, challenging, or in communication with any person take the position of port arms.

3.   A sentry on post will not quit his arms except on an explicit order from some officer or petty officer from whom he lawfully receives orders; under no circumstances will he yield his arms to any other person.

4.   Report at once to the petty officer of the guard every unusual or suspicious event noticed.

5.   Between 0800 and sunset, the sentries at the gangway shall salute all officers in uniform, when going or coming over the side. All sentries on the upper decks, or in view from outside, shall salute all commissioned officers passing them close aboard, in boats or otherwise.

6.   Sentries, carrying rifles, salute all commissioned officers by coming to *present*; they salute warrant officers with the rifle salute. Sentries without rifles render the hand salute to all officers.

7.   When relieved, a sentry will repeat in detail to his successor all special orders relating to his post.

8.   The various posts require certain special orders. Before relieving a sentry must make sure that he understands the special orders of his particular post; such special orders are usually posted in the vicinity of the post. Sentries may be detailed for the following posts: the gangways, life buoys, brig, ammunition passage, forecastle, and elsewhere that their services are required.

RULES FOR LANDSCAPING YOUR HOME

1. Make your plan as complete as possible before actually doing any gardening. The location of such things as cesspools (don't plant trees, especially willows, near them) and utility wires are most important to the ultimate success of your plan.

2. Remember to plan for use and enjoyment as well as beauty. A too beautiful landscape that no one can use is virtually worthless. Combine beauty with utility and you have an unbeatable combination.

3. Keep lawn areas uncluttered, especially in front of the house where an unbroken lawn makes the most effective approach. Remember too that the lawn must be mowed, so provide edging strips along which your mower can ride at the edge of each lawn area.

4. Carefully research available trees and shrubs before buying them. Color, shape, growth habit, maximum height, and adaptability to local conditions are important to your selection and ultimate satisfaction.

5. Use restraint in everything you do. Treat each plant as an individual and do not crowd it out with what may soon become too much of a good thing.

6. Use as few drives or walks as possible throughout the property—they chop it up into segments and make the property look smaller. If you must have certain walk areas, pave them. Grass used in walk areas soon becomes worn out and run-down-looking. Keep all walks straight and as short as possible.

7. Plan for adequate storage of gardening equipment, lawn mower, outdoor furniture, snow tires, etc. If possible, plan to build or buy a storage shed and make some attempt to keep it neat and in order.

8. Check with your neighbors on their plans and work with them to develop a nicer neighborhood. If all can agree to keep fences off the front lawn, for example, the wide unbroken expanse of green lawn will be an added asset for the community.

9. Have your property surveyed before putting fences, shrubs, or hedges near any boundary lines. Once surveyed, keep everything of yours within your own property—not on the line.

10. Learn as many tricks and techniques as possible to assure minimum maintenance of your property, and plan all your gardening for the greatest amount of pleasure and the least amount of work.

11. Plan to enjoy outdoor living during the cool of a summer evening. Include weatherproof electrical outlets and garden lighting on your plan so you need not disturb lawns or plants to put in wiring at a later time.

12. Expect to use experts and professionals to do some of the work indicated on your plan. Know your limitations and call in professionals if the task is too exhausting or difficult for you. Doing it yourself is fine for many jobs, but many others are not for amateurs. There is no saving in time, money, or effort if the job must ultimately be redone by an expert.

13. Follow your plan and ad-lib as little as possible. If the plan is flexible, it will allow for changes, additions, and deletions with a minimum of effort. Disregard the plan you have carefully laid out on paper and you court disaster.

14. Don't try to do everything the first year. Follow a timetable and you will be able to enjoy your property even as you work on it.

15. Be patient. Nature will no be rushed. Realize that it will take several years before your newly planted trees and shrubs "grow up."

16. Enjoy new home and all your property—you've earned it!

RULES OF DAILY PROTEIN REQUIREMENTS

1. All children 1 to 3 years of age need 25 grams of protein.
2. All children 3 to 5 years of age need 30 grams of protein.
3. All children 6 to 8 years of age need 35 grams of protein.
4. All children 8 to 10 years of age need 40 grams of protein.
5. Boys 10 to 12 years of age need 45 grams of protein.
6. Boys 12 to 14 years of age need 50 grams of protein.
7. Boys 14 to 22 years of age need 60 grams of protein.
8. Girls 10 to 14 years of age need 50 grams of protein.
9. Girls 14 years to maturity need 55 grams of protein.
10. Adult females (128 pounds) need 55 grams of protein.
11. Pregnant females need 65 grams of protein.
12. Lactating females need 75 grams of protein.
13. Adult males (154 pounds) need 65 grams of protein.

RULES FOR PREVENTING ACCIDENTAL POISONING IN THE HOME

1. Lock cabinets containing medicines, especially those that are candy-flavored or colored. Never refer to aspirin or other medicine as "candy" to children. Check for unused drugs and clean out your medicine cabinet regularly.

2. Replace all torn or lost labels from medicine bottles and cover with transparent tape to keep them legible. Be sure all poisons are prominently marked.

3. Never leave prescription medicines, such as tranquilizers, sedatives, hormones, etc., around the house on tables or dressers or in pocketbooks.

4. Never use beer and sofr-drink bottles to store cleaning fluids, paint thinners, insecticides, or other caustic substances. To a child, a soft-drink bottle means something good to drink. Keep dangerous substances in their original containers with proper labels and safety closures.

5. Never store polishes, waxes, bleaching agents, dry-cleaning fluids, drain cleaners, and ammonia in low cabinets or on shelves that are readily accessible to children. Locked cabinets are the best place for storing solid and liquid poisons if there are children in the home.

6. Make a periodic check of all storage areas in the garage, cellar, or attic for discarded potential poisons that might attract children.

7. Never leave the room, even for a moment, while using a household product that may be a potential poison. Always take the cleaner or polish with you while you answer the door or phone.

8. Never leave a pressurized spray container within easy reach of a child; never dispose of these containers in a furnace or incinerator.

RULES OF LIGHTNING SAFETY

1. Stay indoors, and don't venture outside, unless absolutely necessary.

2. Stay away from open doors and windows, fireplaces, radiators, stoves, metal pipes, sinks, and plug-in electrical appliances.

3. Don't use plug-in electrical equipment like hair dryers, electric toothbrushes, or electric razors during the storm.

4. Don't use the telephone during the storm—lightning may strike telephone lines outside.

5. Don't take laundry off the clothesline.

6. Don't work on fences, telephone or power lines, pipelines, or structural steel fabrication.

7. Don't use metal objects like fishing rods and golf clubs. Golfers wearing cleated shoes are particularly good lightning rods.

8. Don't handle flammable materials in open containers.

9. Stop tractor work, especially when the tractor is pulling metal equipment, and dismount. Tractor and other implements in metallic contact with the ground are often struck by lightning.

10. Get out of the water and off small boats.

11. Stay in your automobile if you are traveling. Automobiles offer excellent lightning protection.

12. Seek shelter in buildings. If no buildings are available, your best protection is a cave, ditch, canyon, or under head-high clumps of trees in open forest glades.

13. Avoid the highest object in the area when there is no shelter. If only isolated trees are nearby, your best protection is to crouch in the open, keeping twice as far away from isolated trees as the trees are high.

14. Avoid hilltops, open spaces, wire fences, metal clotheslines, exposed sheds, and any electrically conductive elevated objects.

15. Drop to the ground immediately when you feel the electrical charge—if your hair stands on end or your skin tingles. Lightning may be about to strike you.

FIRST AID PROCEDURES FOR LIFE-THREATENING CONDITIONS

---

1. Give emergency treatment in this order, as necessary to deal with impaired breathing, heart failure, severe bleeding, and shock:

    a) Clear the air passage.

    b) Restore breathing and heartbeat.

    c) Stop bleeding.

    d) Administer treatment for shock.

RULES FOR HARVESTING

1. *Asparagus* should not be cut for the first two years. The third year, cut all stalks for a period of about one month, and leave uncut the second month. Asparagus that are at least four years old may be cut clean for a two-month period, and then allowed to store food for the next year's growth.

2. *Beans* should be picked at their peak of flavor—when they are young and tender. Pick often and the plant will continue to produce beans for a longer period than if you harvest only once or twice. Beans should not be fat. The young, thin beans taste the sweetest.

3. *Beets* are pulled when they are between one and one half to three inches in diameter, according to variety. Use as quickly as possible after pulling, or keep in a cool moist area until ready to be cooked and eaten.

4. *Broccoli* is cut in the morning when it looks just like green cauliflower. If it is taken with about six inches of stem just before the heads start to separate, broccoli will continue to bear from other shoots that will appear after the first head has been out.

5. *Brussels Sprouts buds* are broken off when they are between one and one half inches in diameter. Keep cool until cooked.

6. *Cabbage heads* are cut when they are firm, but don't allow the heads to get too big or they will split.

7. *Cantaloupe* must be harvested at exactly the correct time to insure peak flavor. Pick melons when the stems separate from the fruit with only a slight pull.

8. *Carrots* are pulled when young and crisp and used as soon as possible. Successive sowing should give continuous harvest.

9. *Cauliflower leaves* should be tied over the head as if forms to blanch vegetable white. Cut about two to three weeks after heads have been covered with leaves. Make sure the head is firm before cutting.

10. *Celery* whether eaten green or blanched white by holding light from stalks with coverings, is harvested by cutting the stalk about three inches below ground.

11. *Corn* is picked when the silks are brown and the kernels milky. Clean outdoors and race into kitchen. Dump immediately into boiling water.

12. *Cucumbers* should not be allowed to get too large or yellow. Keep checking daily, looking carefully under the leaves for newly matured fruits.

13. *Eggplant* is cut from stem with a knife or garden clippers. Pick when skin is dark and shiny and about four inches in diameter.

14. *Lettuce* comes in two forms—leaf and head. Leaf lettuce is harvested as often as leaves are of eating size. Head lettuce should be cut as soon as full and round. Heat will ruin good lettuce so don't wait too long to harvest.

15. *Onions* are ready when tops look dead. Dig up and allow them to remain in the sun for a few days so skins can become tough. This is especially important if onions are to be stored.

16. *Parsley* is picked as required but allow some leaves to remain so growth continues.

17. *Peas* are picked when small, sweet, and tender. If they get too big they become tough. Pick only during cool parts of the day, never in very hot sun.

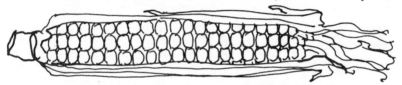

18. *Peppers* are picked when firm, full-sized, and just before they turn red.

19. *Potatoes* are dug up after vines have begun to die. Skins will toughen for better storing if potatoes are allowed to remain on the ground in the sun for a full day.

20. *Pumpkins* are pulled when mature, but do not allow them to become overlarge.

21. *Radishes* are pulled quickly when mature. If you wait too long, they become woody.

22. *Rhubarb stalks* should not be cut; pull when harvesting. Second year harvest lightly, but from the third year on a heavy harvest is okay, and will not hurt roots.

23. *Spinach tops* should be broken when they are four inches long, and new shoots will follow until the first frost. Cool-season types are harvested only once by cutting individual plants.

24. *Tomatoes* are picked when fully ripe and firm to the touch. Do not allow to become soft and overripe.

RULES FOR DONATING BODY ORGANS FOR TRANSPLANTS

1. Realize that donating body parts is up to you. Your decision is a personal one and there is no payment to you or your relatives for donating.

2. Fill out, sign, and carry a Uniform Donor Card.

3. You must be eighteen years of age in most states to be a donor.

4. Filling out the Donor Card does not mean your wishes will be followed automatically. Someone must see that the donation takes place after death. Tell your wishes to your friends, lawyer, clergy, doctor, and, above all, your relatives.

5. It's best to send relatives the following message:

   Dear _____ _____   Date _____ _____

   In the event of my death, I wish to help others by donating body parts. I have signed and am carrying a donor card that tells my wishes. I hope you will remember this message and try to carry out those wishes quickly after I die.

   Signed, _____ _____

6. Have your doctor note in your patient file that you are a donor, and also, if you go into a hospital, ask someone on the medical team to note it in your medical exam.

7. Realize, if you donate for transplant, that the expense of removing the parts is borne by others, but the family bears funeral expenses.

   If you donate your entire body to a medical or dental school:

   The family may choose to have a memorial service without the body's being present. This can be quite inexpensive. Study of your body at the school will take from several months to a year or two. The school will arrange for disposition of the remains without charge to the family.

RULES FOR EATING WITH CHOPSTICKS

1. Put the right fist on the table, thumb up.
2. Open the hand until the fingers are at right angles to the wrist.
3. Lay one of the sticks in the crotch between the thumb and the palm of the hand and between the second and third fingers, so that the middle of the stick rests on the first joint of the third finger and is held down against it by the pressure of the thumb against the hand.

146

4. Do not forget, once in place, this stick is not moved again, the other being manipulated against it.

5. Lay the second stick in place so that it lies across the tip of the forefinger and the ball of the thumb.

6. After having arranged the sticks with the tips meeting, learn to separate them with the first and second fingers and then to bring them together again.

7. Proceed, when perfect at this to the picking up of a bean and getting it as far as the mouth without actually bending over the dish. A nonchalant ease is not likely to be acquired in a day, but diligent practice will at least enable one to appreciate the deftness of Oriental fingers.

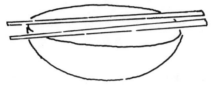

RULES FOR REDUCING THE DANGERS OF SMOKING

1. Choose a cigarette with less tar and nicotine; the difference between brands can be more than two to one. See how your brand compares. Find out how much you can reduce your tar and nicotine intake by switching to another brand, or to another version of the brand you are now smoking.

2. Don't smoke your cigarette all the way down; you get the most tar and nicotine from the last few puffs. Smoke halfway and you get only about 40 percent of the total tar and nicotine. The last half of the cigarette will give you 60 percent. The sooner you put your cigarette out, the lower your dose of those harmful ingredients.

3. Take fewer draws on each cigarette and you'll cut down on your smoking without missing it.

4. Reduce your inhaling. Don't inhale as deeply; take short shallow drags or just puff. Practice on a big cigar.

5. Smoke fewer cigarettes each day. Pick a time of day when you promise yourself not to smoke. Maybe you won't start smoking till after breakfast; maybe you won't smoke on the way to work; or between three and four o'clock, or on the way home. Make it a habit. Don't think of it as cutting down, think of it as postponing. It's always easier to postpone a cigarette if you know you'll be having one later.

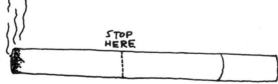

RULES FOR PLANTING TREES

1. Don't try to plant trees with trunks over four inches in diameter. This is a job for an experienced nurseryman. Trees of this size are too big to handle, require huge planting holes and too much manual labor for the beginning gardener.

2. Dig your planting hole about twice as wide and twice as deep as the earth ball. Fill the hole about half full of a well-mixed combination of topsoil and well-rotted manure and tamp well before placing the tree and earth ball into the hole.

3. Young trees should be staked to maintain stability until the roots take hold in their new home. Drive the stake into the hole before placing the tree so that the roots are not cut or disturbed by the stake.

4. While maneuvering the earth ball into the hole, or moving it at any time, pick it up by the earth ball and not by the tree trunk. Handle the tree and the earth ball carefully so they go into the ground intact and no roots are exposed or damaged.

5. Plant the tree at the same depth, give or take an inch, as it was at the nursery.

6. Fill the hole about halfway and water well so soil can fill in around roots and eliminate air pockets that dry out the roots. Add more dirt and more water until the hole is filled to about two or three inches below ground level. Leave this saucer-shaped depression to hold rainwater and keep the roots moist. Apply a layer of mulch to the saucer after it has been thoroughly watered, and keep this moist also.

7. Do not fertilize the first year, except with well-rotted manure mixed with the topsoil used to fill the hole.

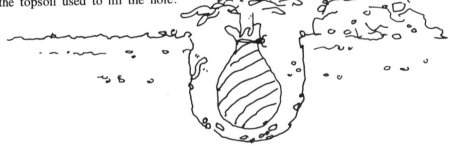

RULES FOR OBTAINING NATURAL VITAMINS

1. Get vitamin A from fish-liver oils, liver, butter, cream, whole milk, whole-milk cheeses, egg yolk, dark-green leafy vegetables, yellow vegetables, yellow fruits, fortified products.

2. Get vitamin D from fish-liver oils, fortified milk, activated sterols, exposure to sunlight.

3. Get vitamin E from plant tissues—wheat germ oil, vegetable oils (such as soybean, corn, and cottonseed), nuts, legumes.

4. Get vitamin K from green leaves such as spinach, cabbage, cauliflower and also from liver.

5. Get vitamin C from citrus fruits, tomatoes, strawberries, cantaloupe, cabbage, broccoli, kale, potatoes.

6. Get folic acic from liver, kidney, yeast, deep-green leafy vegetables.

7. Get thiamine from pork, liver, and other organs, brewer's yeast, wheat germ, whole-grain cereals and breads, enriched cereals and breads, soybeans, peanuts, and other legumes, milk.

8. Get riboflavin from milk, powdered whey, liver, kidney, heart, meats, eggs, green leafy vegetables, dried yeast, enriched foods.

9. Get niacin from lean meat, fish, poultry, liver, kidney, whole-grain and enriched cereals and breads, green vegetables, peanuts, brewer's yeast.

10. Get vitamin B_6 from wheat germ, meat, liver, kidney, whole-grain cereals, soybeans, peanuts, corn.

11. Get vitamin B_{12} from small daily intakes of animal protein.

12. Get biotin from liver, sweetbreads, yeast, eggs, legumes.

13. Get pantothenic acid from plant and animal tissue. Liver, kidney, yeast, eggs, peanuts, whole-grain cereals, beef, tomatoes, broccoli, salmon.

14. Get choline from egg yolk (best source), liver, heart, sweetbreads, milk, meats, nuts, cereals, vegetables, soybeans.

RULES OF MATH SIGNS

1. Addition: When the signs are the same, keep the sign and add the absolute values of the numbers; when the signs are different, keep the sign of the number with the larger absolute value and find the difference between the absolute values of the numbers.

2. Subtraction: Change the sign of the subtrahend (bottom number) and with the new sign, apply the addition laws.

3. Multiplication: $(+)(+) = +$; $(+)(-) = -$; $(-)(+) = -$; $(-)(-) = +$.

4. Division: $(+) \div (+) = +$; $(+) \div (-) = -$; $(-) \div (+) = -$; $(-) \div (-) = +$.

RULES FOR ADMINISTERING MOUTH-TO-MOUTH ARTIFICIAL RESPIRATION

1.   Position victim on his back. If it is necessary to roll the victim over, try to roll him over as a single unit, keeping the back and neck straight. This is to avoid aggravation of any possible spinal injury.

2.   Kneeling at the victim's side, tilt victim's head back so his chin is pointing up by placing one hand under the neck and the other hand on the forehead.

3.   Quickly glance in victim's mouth for any obstruction (e.g., food, tobacco, blood, dentures). If an obvious obstruction is present, carefully turn the victim on his side, tilt his head down, and sweep his mouth out with your fingers. When the mouth is clear, move the victim onto his back again and tilt his head back.

4.   For at least five seconds listen and feel for air exchange and look for chest movements.

5.   Check for breathing by bending over the victim, placing your ear close to victim's mouth and nose.

6.   If the person is not breathing, pinch the nose closed, form an airtight seal by placing your mouth over the victim's mouth and breathe into the victim's mouth until the chest rises. (If using the mouth-to-nose method, seal the victim's mouth with your hand and breathe in through his nose.)

7.   Breathe into the patient a total of four times as quickly as possible. If you feel or hear no air exchange, retilt his head and try again. If you still feel no air exchange, again sweep the mouth of foreign objects (Rule 3), and breathe into the victim again. If you still have no air exchange, turn victim on side and slap the victim on the back between his shoulder blades. Again sweep his mouth to remove foreign matter. (Note: If none of the above steps clears the air passage, repeat the blows to the back and tilt the head.)

8.   Repeat breathing. Remove mouth each time to allow air to escape. Repeat twelve times per minute for an adult—twenty times for a small child or infant. Use deep breaths for an adult, less for a child, gentle puffs of the cheeks for infants. As the victim begins to breathe, maintain head tilt.

RULES FOR SMOKING UNDERWATER

1.   The swimmer smokes a pipe or cigar until it is well alight, and takes up his stand on the side of the pool or on the divingboard.

2.   The lungs should then be inflated, the head sunk over as for a dive, and, just before the feet leave the diving board, the bowl of the pipe, or, in the case of a cigar, the lighted end, thrust rapidly into the mouth. Particular care must be taken not to draw inward.

150

3. When once in the water the breaststroke must be used, and at each stroke of the arms the swimmer should blow gently at the pipe or cigar. This will cause the smoke to issue from the mouthpiece and curl upward to the surface of the water.

4. After going about ten yards a turn to the side should be made. As the head comes to the surface, the smoke may be blown out, the body well raised, and the pipe or cigar quickly removed, care being taken that the lighted end is not wetted.

5. Then the return can be made to the starting point, smoking above the surface, by swimming on the side.

RULES FOR DETERMINING DISTANCES AT SEA

1. A 5-foot-high object may be seen at three miles.
2. A 10-foot-high object may be seen at four miles.
3. A 20-foot-high object may be seen at six miles.
4. A 50-foot-high object may be seen at nine miles.
5. A 100-foot-high object may be see at thirteen miles.
6. A 220-foot-high object may be seen at eighteen miles.
7. A 300-foot-high- object may be see at twenty-three miles.
8. A 500-foot-high object may be seen at thirty miles.
9. An 800-foot-high object may be seen at thirty-seven miles.
10. A 1,000-foot-high object may be seen at forty-two miles.

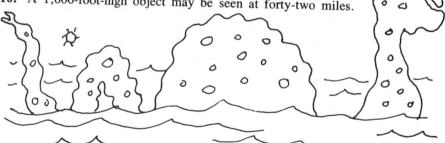

RULES FOR GIVING MEDICINE TO CHILDREN

1. Follow the instructions for administering prescribed medication *exactly*. If prescribed "as necessary," give *only* as necessary.

2. Some medications can safely be kept on hand, such as nose drops, decongestants, antihistamines, cough medicines, stomach settlers, and laxatives. Others should be disposed of as soon as medication is stopped.

3. To give medicines, administer nose drops, or clear out a child's nose with an aspirator, place him on a kitchen counter, press his right arm against your body, hold his left arm with your left forearm and control his head with your left hand. This leaves your right hand free for handling the medication.

4. Use a medicine dropper or a disposable injection syringe (with needle removed) to squirt liquid medication into the side of an infant's mouth. Measure the correct amount into a teaspoon, and suck it up into the dropper or syringe from that.

5. Be firm with children who resist medication. Don't give up. They must learn that there is no alternative to taking their medicine.

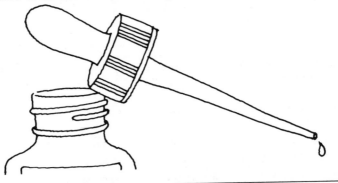

RULES OF COOKERY FOR A SMALL HOUSE—TURN-OF-THE-CENTURY ENGLAND

1. Cooking ought not to take too much of one's time. One hour and a half to two hours for lunch, and two and a half for dinner is sufficient, providing that the servant knows how to make up the fire in order to get the stove ready for use. Most girls will quickly learn to do that and how to put a joint properly in the oven. You must not leave the kitchen while the cooking is going on—unless of necessity and only for a very few minutes at a time.

2. The bane of life in a small house is the smell of cooking. Very few are free from it. And yet it need not be endured at all. This evil yields to nothing more heroic than a simple but scrupulous care in all the processes in making food ready for consumption. That is why your constant presence in the kitchen is

152

recommended. Unremitting care should be directed to the following points:

a) No saucepan should be allowed, of course, to boil over.

b) No frying pan should ever be put on the fire without the butter or lard being first placed in it, and that not before the pan is required for use.

c) No joint should be placed in the oven so high as to allow the fat to splutter against the roof of the oven.

d) No joint should be baked in a tin which is too small for it.

e) No vegetables should be cooked without a sufficient amount of water in the saucepan and no green vegetables should be cooked with the lid on.

f) No frying pan while in use should be allowed to remain on the fire with only the fat in it. A piece of whatever you are frying, bacon, fish, fritter should be left in till another piece is placed in the fat.

g) The pan must be removed directly when finished with.

h) No fat once used for frying should be kept for future use. The economy is not worth making. The fat, for instance, in which potatoes have been fried will always contain a certain amount of moisture and the next lot of potatoes fried in it will turn out greasy and flabby.

i) Fried potatoes should be crisp and melting in the mouth and if properly prepared make a delicate dish for a discriminating palate.

RULES OF FIREARM SAFETY

1. Treat every gun with respect and always point the muzzle in a safe direction.
2. Always keep the safety on until you are ready to fire, and never fire until you are absolutely sure of your target.
3. Never shoot at a hard, flat surface or at water; that can cause ricochets.
4. Load your gun only in the field or when you are ready on the range.
5. Never climb or jump over anything with a loaded gun.
6. Unload the gun when you are not using it, and keep the action open.
7. Store guns and ammunition separately.
8. Keep your gun in top shape, and always make sure you are using the right ammunition for your gun.

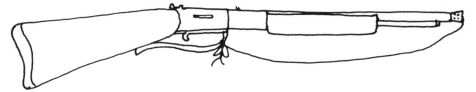

RULES FOR IMMUNIZING CHILDREN

1. Be careful, vaccines work best when they are given at the recommended time and on a regular schedule. Measles vaccine, for example, is not usually given to infants before they reach the age of fifteen months. When it is given earlier than that, it may not be as effective. Oral polio and DPT vaccines must be given over a period of time, in a series of properly spaced doses. Scheduling is important.

2. Follow this schedule:

a) At two months child should receive diphtheria/pertussis/tetanus vaccines and oral polio.

b) At four months child should receive second series of diphtheria/pertussis/tetanus and oral polio.

c) At six months child should receive third in series of diphtheria/pertussis/tetanus. Third oral polio at this level is optional.

d) At fifteen months child should receive measles, rubella, and mumps vaccine.

e) At eighteen months child should receive fourth diphtheria/pertussis/tetanus and oral polio vaccine.

f) At age four to six years the final diphtheria/pertussis/tetanus and oral polio vaccines are administered.

3. Be aware of these facts: Measles, rubella, mumps can be given in combined form, at about fifteen months of age, with single injection. Children should receive a sixth diphtheria/pertussis/tetanus injection (booster) at age fourteen to sixteen years.

RULES FOR EATING UNDERWATER (1893)

1. If this feat be executed in a bath, a spot where the water is about three or four feet deep should be selected.

2. A sponge cake should be held in the left hand, which is kept out of the water, the rest of the body being sunk below the surface, one knee resting on the bottom.

3. The right arm should be brought out of the water and a piece of the cake broken off.

4. The piece should then be sharply carried under the water to the mouth, and, just as it is placed in, a gentle exhalation should be made so that the water may not enter the mouth.

5. After properly eating the first piece, the rest of the cake should be taken and eaten in a similar manner.

6. Then the left hand should be sunk below the surface, and the head raised gently out of the water.

7. Before descending below the surface, the lungs should be inflated, because if this precaution be neglected the swimmer will not be able to stay under long enough to eat all the cake, and the feat is spoilt if the mouth has to be raised above the water for an inspiration.

RULES FOR CARVING A TURKEY

1. When your turkey is done, let it stand for about fifteen minutes. It firms the flesh, making it easier to carve.

2. Heat serving plates in the meantime.

3. Remember, proper carving will insure more attractive, uniform slices.

4. Cut across the grain for short fibers, which are more tender. Be sure to count how many servings are needed before the actual carving.

5. Begin carving by grasping the drumstick firmly with fingers or carving fork and pulling drumstick away from body of turkey. Cut through meat between thigh and backbone. With tip of knife, disjoint leg bone from backbone.

6. Holding leg vertical, large end down, slice meat parallel to bone and under some tendons, turning leg for even slices. Or, first separate thigh and drumstick. Slice thigh meat by cutting slices parallel to bone. Slice drumstick as described.

7. Before carving white meat, make a deep horizontal cut into breast close to wing.

8. If you wish to remove the wing, brace turkey with fork inserted in breast and cut vertically between wing and body.

9. Cut thin, even slices from top of breast down to horizontal cut with straight, even strokes. Final smaller slices can follow curve of breastbone. If desired, cut an opening through thin layer of meat where thigh was removed to reach stuffing.

10. Repeat above steps with the other side of the bird. You will find that carving only one side of the turkey at a time helps retain the heat and protects the full flavor. It's usually best to start carving on the side facing the guests and to carve only enough for everyone to have one serving; then fill dinner plates. Second servings may be carved later.

RULES FOR KNOWING WINE AND LIQUOR BOTTLE CAPACITIES

1. Remember liquor is usually packed in terms of quarts and fractions thereof, though in some countries, ounces may be used. The common liquor bottles are:

> Pint   = 16 oz.
> Fifth = 26 oz.
> Quart = 32 oz. (American)
>   = 40 oz. (British and Canadian)

2. Be advised to consult wine bottle labels to learn the amount in the bottle, though there is some standardization in the field. There is, perhaps, more discrepancy here than in any other field. This is because wine is grown in so many different countries, causing many different traditions and bottling techniques to develop.

In Europe, the standard wine bottle, if there can be said to be such a thing, usually contains about 26½ fluid ounces. The amount is based on the reputed wine quart, which is one sixth of an imperial gallon (160 ounces). There are also quarter bottles and half bottles, based on this bottle.

Many elaborate and outsized bottles have been developed, the larger ones being used more for display purposes than anything else. These bottles have acquired nicknames, and their capacity is commonly a multiple of the basic 26 2/3-ounce bottle.

NAME	CAPACITY
Magnum	2 bottles
Double Magnum	4 bottles
Tappit-Hen	3 imperial quarts
Jeroboam	4 bottles
Rehoboam	6 bottles
Methuselah	8 bottles
Salmanazar	12 bottles
Balthazar	16 bottles
Nebuchadnezzar	20 bottles

Certain wines have become associated with certain bottle shapes, and, in some cases, these shapes have been standardized as to capacity. These figures especially apply in America.

Vermouth bottle	30 oz.
Chianti bottle	30 oz.
Champagne bottle	24 to 26 oz.
Champagne half-bottle	12 to 13 oz.

RULES FOR GAINING WEIGHT

1. Concentrate a little more on the fatty foods and starches, without slighting the proteins to too great an extent—don't unbalance your diet.

2. Remember, fatty foods, such as all fat meats, butter, cheese, nuts of all kinds, chocolate, potatoes, peanuts, crackers, cream, sugar, oatmeal, and dozens of other well-known flesh builders, should play an important role in your daily diet.

3. Eat bananas or crackers with milk between meals.

4. Cod liver oil is thought to be an effective weight-gaining supplement.

5. If your appetite is normal, don't stuff yourself in efforts to put on a few pounds.

RULES FOR CLEANING YOUR TEETH

1. Do a good cleaning job at least once a day, preferably at night, taking five to ten minutes to do a thorough job. The goal is to remove all plaque. A good cleaning requires flossing and brushing.

2. Use a piece of dental floss or tape. Wind one end around the first or second finger of each hand, holding them not more than a half inch apart.

3. Work the floss gently up and down between the teeth twice, cleaning the side surface of each tooth, including the area below the gumline. Be careful not to cut into the gum. Clean between all the teeth. Move your fingers to change the angle.

4. When you have finished flossing your teeth, rinse your mouth with water to wash away any debris dislodged by the cleaning.

5. Brush the inside of the front teeth with an up-and-down motion.

6. Brush the inside of the back teeth and the chewing sufaces with short back-and-forth strokes.

7. Brush where your teeth meet your gum.

8. Brush the outside surfaces of all teeth with short back-and-forth strokes.

RULES FOR AQUA DYNAMICS . . . PHYSICAL CONDITIONING IN THE SWIMMING POOL

1. Before starting this conditioning program, you should have a medical examination.

2. Adapt this program to your indfvidual tolerance level—the level at which you can perform comfortably and without undue distress.

3. To achieve maximum potential, use a combination system of training with both "change of pace" and "interval training."

> a) "Change of pace" consists of the shifting from one activity to another involving a different set of muscles or type of stress and the changing of the intensity of the work.
>
> b) Interval training is interspersing repeated periods of physical work with recovery periods during which activity of a reduced intensity is performed.

4. During a workout, the body should be warmed up by light conditioning and stretching exercises before heavier activities are attempted. Deck exercises including flexibility and strength activities with heavy breathing are appropriate. Various strokes may be simulated. Participants should begin with light rhythmical work at a slow pace. A tempo should be gradually accelerated, alternating slow with faster work, until one nears perspiration.

5. Specific back-stretching exercises should be completed both at the beginning and end of the workout. For maximum benefit, the individual should stand with legs apart, extending the hands high over head and reaching as high as possible. After approximately 5 to 10 seconds in the arms-over-head reaching position, one should bend the trunk forward and down, flexing the knees, and the bending and stretching position should be held for approximately 20 to 30 seconds, then the high reaching followed by the bending and stretching action should be repeated.

6. Be aware that through proper warm-up, the body's deep muscle temperature will be raised and the ligaments and connecting tissues stretched, thereby preparing the body for vigorous work. This will help avoid injury and discomfort. Swimming is unique in that age is no hindrance and individuals of varying exercise tolerance levels can utilize this activity to develop organic vigor and to improve flexibility, strength, and the blood circulation.

7. Individuals in poor condition must work slowly and progressively. It has taken many years for most adults to get out of shape. One should be patient and realize that rebuilding the heart, lungs, and body may take a long period of time. A commitment to regularity and gradual buildup will pay off. *Train, don't strain!*

158

RULES FOR FIRST AID TREATMENT FOR PROFUSE BLEEDING

1.   Cover wound with the cleanest cloth immediately available, or your bare hand, and apply *direct pressure* on the wound. Most bleeding can be stopped this way.

2.   Elevate a bleeding arm or leg as you apply pressure, if there is no broken bone.

3.   Remember, digital pressure at a pressure point can be used if it is necessary to control bleeding from an arterial wound (bright red blood spurting from it). Apply your fingers to the appropriate pressure point—a point where the main artery supplying blood to the wound is located. Hold pressure point tightly for about five minutes or until bleeding stops. The three pressure points in the head and neck should only be used as a last resort if there is a skull fracture and direct pressure can't be used. If direct pressure can be used, it will stop bleeding on the head in about 95 percent of the injuries.

4.   Apply a tourniquet to an arm or leg *only* as a *last resort* when all other methods fail. A tourniquet is applied between the wound and the point at which the limb is attached to the body, as close to the wound as possible but never over a wound or fracture. Make sure it is applied tightly enough to stop bleeding completely.

5.   In the case of an improvised tourniquet, wrap the material twice around the extremity and half knot it. Place a stick or similar object on the half knot and tie a full knot. Twist the stick to tighten the tourniquet only until the bleeding stops—*no more*. Secure the stick or level in place with the loose ends of the tourniquet, another strip of cloth, or other improvised material.

6.   Once the tourniquet is put in place, *do not* loosen it. Mark a "T" on the victim's forehead and get him to a medical facility as soon as possible. Only a doctor loosens or removes a tourniquet.

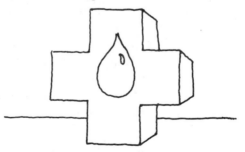

Note: A tourniquet can be improvised from a strap, belt, handkerchiefs, necktie, cravat bandage, etc. (Never use wire, cord, or anything that will cut into the flesh.)

RULES FOR ACCEPTING THE NEW CAR YOU'VE JUST PURCHASED

1. Read the Owner's Manual carefully. Sit in the driver's seat and, before you start the car, have the salesman explain the starting procedure, the dashboard gauges and warning lights, and the operation of all controls and accessories. Read the warranty carefully and note the services that are free and those for which you must pay. No warranty, however, will cover normal wear or abusive use.

2. Examine the exterior for dents, irregularities, or paint scratches.

3. Check the interior for wrinkled or misfit floor mats; look at the seats, door panels, and headlining for scuffs, tears, or crooked seams.

4. Open and shut the doors to see if they fit the frames and latch properly.

5. Roll the windows up and down. Do they work smoothly and close all the way?

6. Look in the trunk for the spare wheel and tire, the tire jack, and the lug wrench. Ask the salesman or service manager to show you how to operate the jack.

7. Look in the engine compartment. Is it clean and new-looking? Ask the salesman to show you how to check the oil and coolant levels.

8. Start the engine and listen for any roughness or noise after it has warmed up.

9. For an automatic transmission, set the emergency brake and then shift to "drive." The engine should continue to run smoothly and not stall.

10. Road test the car. It should accelerate without jerks or hesitations, the brakes should work evenly and effectively, and the steering should be responsive and smooth.

11. Try the horn and the windshield wipers and washer. Have the salesman try all the lights and the turn signals while you stand outside the car and check their operation.

12. If the car fails to satisfy you on any of these points, insist that the fault be corrected before you accept delivery. In addition, be sure you understand the warranty provisions. What free repairs and services does it offer? When must you bring in the car for check and adjustments?

VICTORIAN DRIVING RULES

1. When asking a lady to drive, do so only on an advanced acquaintance, and do not keep her out after dark.

2. Take care not to allow the whip to dangle in her face, and, in urging on the horses, do so in an easy manner, without that sudden start which throws the lady so violently back in her seat.

3. Do not talk about horses; it is a very poor subject, and savors of poor taste.

4. In calling for a lady do not keep her waiting, but have the vehicle at the door on time.

5. If possible to leave the reins loose on the horses, step out and help the lady into the vehicle, then pass round to the other side and take your seat, carefully adjusting the lap robe over both.

6. Do not keep up a continuous chuckle to the horses, as it is a very monotonous sound, but use the whip.

7. A full driving suit should always be worn if a lady accompanies you. Always wear gloves in driving.

8. If you have spirited horses to handle, it is not necessary while driving to take off the hat when recognizing a person; a smile and an inclination of the head are sufficient, for taking off the hat interferes considerably with your management of the animals, and has often resulted in serious accidents.

9. Do not take a lady riding in the morning. The afternoon from three till five is the proper time.

10. Never on any account drive on Sunday.

11. Never take a lady in a light wagon or buggy, or out with fast horses, in the city, for it is not stylish; in fact, such turnouts are common, as in use only by sporting men or horse lovers.

12. Riding should be confined to the morning as much as possible, and a complete outfit worn upon all occasions. Especially is this urged when with a lady.

13. Always keep head and neck of your own horse beyond your companion's; if a lady, in view of being able and prepared to assist her in case of fright or accident to her horse.

14. Always assist her in mounting and alighting from her horse.

RULES FOR EXERCISING TO FORESTALL FLABBY FACES

1. Hold your index finger against your lips, as if you were signaling hush. Blow your cheeks out, pushing you index finger hard against your lips to keep air from escaping. Count up to six to yourself while blowing out your cheeks. Doing this exercise ten times will firm up your cheeks.
2. Purse your lips as for whistling; while keeping them in that position try to wrinkle up your nose. You will feel the tension of the muscles along the sides of the nose if you hold the whistle position of the lips while wrinkling. Repeat ten times. This exercise helps to erase the lines at the sides of the cheeks near the nose.
3. Stick out your tongue as far as you can, arching it as high as you can while you do so. If you place index and third finger under your chin, back close to your neck you will be able to feel the tension in the muscle. The exercise is unbeatable for keeping a firm chin line. Do it 10 times.
4. Close your eyes and look up toward the ceiling. Count five while you hold them in this position. Do this ten times. Now close them again and look down, again holding them in the position. Do this ten times. You can do the eye exercises without closing your eyes, but this tends to wrinkle the forehead. If you touch the area just beneath the eye while you are doing the first part of this exercise you will feel the tension in the muscle there. You will feel the same with the second part of the exercise if you touch your eyelid while you are doing it. This exercise prevents bags from forming under the eyes, and also helps to relax and rest them too.
5. Remember, the muscles in the neck respond so quickly to a little exercise, and firmness in the neck improves your appearance tremendously.
6. Interlace your fingers and place the interlaced palm sides against your forehead. While you count up to five, push against your hands with your head back with the interlaced palms of your hands.
7. Now place the interlaced fingers at the back of your head, palm sides against your hair. Push and resist, counting up to five.
8. Now place the palm of your right hand against the right side of your head, against the hair, just behind your temple and just above the ear. Push and resist, counting up to five. Do the same with the left hand on the left side of the head.

RULES FOR MAKING A MEAL OF A PORCUPINE

1. Procure a club and approach the animal cautiously so as not to frighten it. Getting within range is not too difficult to achieve; this rodent seems to be

162

somewhat nearsighted and he doesn't pay too much attention to cautiously moving objects. But, if he is startled by a sudden motion or sound, he will usually head for a tree. He is an excellent climber and will quickly find his way to branches that are too flimsy to support the weight of a man.

2.   When proximity is achieved, stun the animal by a sharp blow to the nose, and a couple more to the skull will finish him.

3.   Be aware skinning and dressing the animal requires caution if the hunter is to come off unpunctured. The directions should be followed carefully.

4.   Turn the body on its back with the club. Press the point of your knife deeply through the lower jaw so that the brain is penetrated. Cut the throat; then hang up the body by one hind leg until bleeding ceases.

5.   The next step is to skin the porcupine. With your knife make a long incision in the outer layer of skin on the unquilled belly. Do not cut through the inner skin, or the abdominal wall. Insert your fingers into the opening and pull and cut the skin loose from the carcass. (This is a slippery job. Rub a little cornmeal or even sandy soil on your hands; it will help you to get a grip on skin and carcass.) Be sure to work from the inside of the skin so that the quills do not touch your hands. Sever the bones of the tail, feet, and neck. Cut away the glands of reproduction and the anal region. (This is important; if it is not done thoroughly the meat will have an objectionable flavor.) Now draw the carcass away from the skin; the appendages are left attached.

6.   Now disembowel the carcass—or this operation may be accomplished at the time of making the first incision. However, the job is less messy if this method is followed. Be sure that all internal glands and organs are removed.

7.   Wash the carcass, disjoint the legs, and cut up the body as you would a rabbit. Although not absolutely necessary, the meat will be more tender if it is parboiled. The pieces may be stuck on a pointed stick and broiled over an open fire.

8.   Be cautious in skinning the porcupine since you may be stuck by some of the quills. These should be removed from the wound immediately as they tend to work farther into the flesh. If the penetration is slight a good tug will pull then out. If they are in deeply, work some oil or fat of any sort into the quills as closely as possible to the skin. (Melted fat from the carcass will do.) The oil softens the barbs and allows them to be removed more easily, and less painfully.

RULES FOR PREVENTING ACCIDENTAL DROWNING IN A POOL

1. Put up a fence that is at least six feet high and built with vertical or solid segments. Fences with fancy basket weaves, split railings, or chain links, which children can easily climb, should be avoided. To be a safety measure, a fence must be properly designed to keep small children out and make it difficult for older children to trespass.

2. Be sure the fence has self-closing and self-latching gates with the mechanism out of reach of children. The gate should be securely locked when pool is not in use.

3. Remember, a pool cover can serve as protection for a child who trespasses when the pool is not being used.

4. Clearly mark the shallow and deep ends of the pool to show safe jumping and diving areas. Diving into pools and striking the pool bottom or its walls has caused serious head injuries, paralysis, and death.

5. Remember, the pool bottom should slope gradually. A float line is essential to keep younger swimmers in the shallow end.

6. Be certain there are clear and strict instructions prohibiting any horseplay around the slippery pool area.

7. Teach children swimming, floating, and water survival techniques at an early age.

8. Prominently display poolside rescue equipment to use in case of an accidental drowning. Emergency numbers of local rescue squads, ambulances, and physicians should be posted on a nearby telephone.

9. Clean and repair your pool regularly. Slippery bottoms, faulty float lines, and burned-out underwater lamps account for a number of pool accidents.

10. Consider, an alarm system in the pool which will sound an alert in case someone falls into the pool by accident. It can be an excellent safety precaution.

RULES FOR PLANNING YOUR FLOWER GARDEN

1. Keep in mind, flowers are most effective when grouped—several of a single variety—in a relatively small area.

2. Find out the mature height of the plants and place low-growing ones in front and tall varieties in the rear.

3. Don't forget, flowers will stand out better and be more attractive when placed in front of a green background. Especially in borders or other semiformal or formal gardens, use evergreen shrubs or other dense green plants as background material.

4. If flowers are primarily for cutting, plant them away from the house where the cut stems will not detract from the appearance of the house or other plantings.

5. Keep the overall effect in mind at all times. Clashing colors, overpowering varieties and plants with unsightly growing habits can ruin an otherwise beautiful garden.

6. Remember the other parts of the plant as well as the flowers when planning. Foliage and stems can either enhance or detract from an otherwise nice planting.

7. Balance your enthusiasm with the knowledge of what plants look like before, during, and after flowering. If they do not fit in with the overall plan, relegate them to cutting gardens or other out-of-the-way spots.

8. Balance all the elements of the planting. Colors, sizes, and types should be balanced for pleasing effect, but not to the point of fanatical symmetry.

9. Don't expect to be able to buy or grow every flower that appeals to you. Too much of anything is usually no good, so select the best and show them off to their best advantage.

10. Select flowers with a good chance of growing in your locality, especially in borders or foundation planting. Experiment with different varieties and select from these the additions or substitutions for the old standbys you've developed.

RULES FOR LIFTING

---

1. Look over the object to decide the best way to grasp it.
2. Place your feet close to the object to be lifted.
3. Get a good grip on the load.
4. Bend your knees, keep your back straight.
5. Keep the load close to your body.
6. Be sure you can see past the load.
7. Get help for large or heavy objects.
8. In team lifting, cooperate with your buddy.

TREATING FROSTBITE

1. Remember, frostbite can occur whenever body parts are exposed to cold weather conditions. The most frequently frostbitten parts of the body are the fingers, toes, nose, and ears.

2. Recognize the symptoms of frostbite: pale or grayish-yellow skin coloration; body parts feeling cold and numb; and frozen parts feeling "doughy."

3. Wrap the victim in woolen cloth and keep him dry until he can be brought inside.

4. Do not rub, chafe, or manipulate frostbitten parts.

5. Place frostbitten victim in warm water (102–105°F) and make sure temperature remains warm. Never thaw if victim has to go back out into the cold because affected area could be refrozen and permanently damaged.

6. Do not use hot-water bottles or heat lamps and never place victim near a hot stove.

7. Do not allow victim to walk if feet are affected.

8. Have victim gently exercise parts, once thawed.

9. Seek medical aid for thawing in severe cases because pain will be intense and tissue damage extensive.

RULES FOR SURVIVING SNOW AVALANCHES

If you are caught in an avalanche:
    1. Discard all equipment.
    2. Get away from your snowmobile.
    3. Make swimming motions. Try to stay on top; work your way to the side of the avalanche.
    4. Get your hands in front of your face and try to make an air space in the snow as you are coming to a stop.
    5. Try to remain calm.

If you are a survivor:
    1. Mark the place where you last saw victims.
    2. Search for victims directly downslope below the last seen point. If

they are not on the surface, scuff or probe the snow with a pole or stick.

3. Remember, you are the victim's best hope for survival.

4. Do not desert victims and go for help, unless help is only a few minutes away. Remember, you must consider not only the time required for you to get help, but the time required for help to return. After thirty minutes, the buried victim has only a 50 percent chance of surviving.

If there is more than one survivor:

1. Send one for help while the others search for the victim. Have the one who goes for help mark the route so a rescue party can follow back.

2. Contact ski patrol, local sheriff, or Forest Service.

3. Administer first aid.

4. Treat for suffocation and shock.

RULES FOR DRYING FRUITS

1. Use only fully ripened fruit, since drying does not improve the quality of fruit. If it is not suitable for eating fresh, it is not suitable for drying.

2. You may dry fruits in the oven, in the sun, or in a dehydrator. Drying fruits is not very different from drying vegetables.

3. Remember, oven drying is not recommended for sulfured fruits because of the objectionable odor of the sulfur fumes.

4. Keep in mind, packaging dried fruits is also similar to packaging dried vegetables. Note: Sulfuring does not prevent insect infestations, so pack the dried product immediately just as you would unsulfured fruit.

5. Do not use metal lids with sulfured fruits unless a cellophane or polyethylene sheet is placed under the lid to prevent sulfur fumes from reacting with the lid.

6. Store fruit in plastic bags. Tightly sealed, they will help keep the original fruit color.

RULES FOR DELIVERING A BABY WITHOUT MEDICAL ASSISTANCE

1. Be sure the doctor or ambulance has been called.
2. See that the mother is comfortably lying down.
3. Wash your hands thoroughly.
4. Do not touch the area around the vaginal entrance.
5. Place a clean towel under the mother's hips for the baby to come onto. If you have time, protect the bed with newspapers.
6. Let the baby come naturally.
7. If the bag of waters has not broken, and the baby is born inside the sac, puncture the sac with a pin or tip of scissors. Wipe the sac and fluid away from his face and head with the inside of a clean handkerchief.
8. As soon as he is born, wipe the baby's mouth, nose, and face with the inside of a clean handkerchief.
9. Move him carefully to a clean spot between the mother's legs, with his head elevated a little and away from any fluid or secretions. Do not stretch the cord. Let it remain a little slack.
10. If the doctor has been called and is on his way, you do not need to tie the baby's cord. Leave it attached. Leave the baby in a clean spot between the mother's legs, but cover his body with a blanket or towel to prevent chilling. Leave his head uncovered so he can breathe.
11. If you have not been able to reach the doctor, or if he cannot get there within an hour, the cord should be tied.

> a) Tie the cord *tightly* in two places about two inches apart with clean pieces of tape or strong twine. The tie nearest the baby should be about six inches from the navel.
>
> b) Cut the cord between the two ties with a clean pair of scissors.
>
> c) Wrap the baby in a clean flannel square or blanket, with his face uncovered, and lay him on his side in a warm place.

12. Let the afterbirth come by itself. Do not pull on the cord to make it come out. Save the afterbirth in a basin or newpapers for the doctor to examine.
13. As soon as the afterbirth has passed out, place your hands over the mother's uterus (a firm lump just below the mother's navel).
14. Cup your hands around the mother's uterus and massage the uterus several times to keep it firm. If it does not stay firm, hold your hands around it until it does.
15. Clean the mother's buttocks and lower thighs, but do not touch the area around the vaginal entrance.
16. Make the mother comfortable and see that the baby is warm and breathing. Give the mother a hot drink, such as tea, if she wishes.

FOLK RULES FOR REMOVING WARTS

1. Stick the hand which has warts on it into a bag and tie it up. The first person who opens it will get your warts.

2. Get something like a penny that someone would want to pick up. Put some blood from the wart on it and throw it into the road. When someone picks it up, the wart will go away.

3. Wet your finger and make a cross on the wart.

4. Take a persimmon stick and put as many notches on it as you have warts. They will go away.

5. Count them, touching each one as you do, and say a verse which is secret and known only to you, the conjuror.

6. Tie a horsehair around it.

7. Rub the wart with the skin of a chicken gizzard, then hide the skin under a rock. The wart will disappear.

8. Count the warts. Tie as many pebbles as there are warts in a bag and throw the bundle down in the fork of a road. They will soon go away.

9. Steal a neighbor's dishrag. Wipe it across the warts and bury it in the woods.

10. Wash the affected area with water from a rotten chestnut stump for nine mornings in a row before breakfast.

11. Rub the warts with a rock and put it in a box. Whoever opens the box will get the warts.

12. Rub a flint rock three times over the warts and put it back where you got it from. They will disappear.

13. Cut the wart, make it bleed, and put one drop of the blood on a grain of corn. Feed the grain of corn to a chicken or rooster and the wart will disappear.

14. Put a small piece of bacon or salt pork on the wart. Wrap it up and sleep with it that way. In the morning the wart will be gone if you have faith.

15. Prick the wart with a needle, and put a few drops of the blood on some fat meat. Bury the meat, and when it rots the wart will go away.

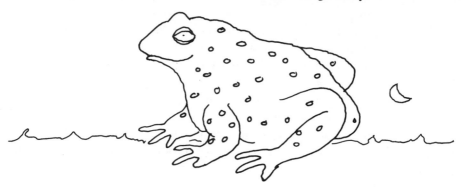

RULES OF FLOWER ARRANGEMENT

1. Make sure your design consists of a planned relationship among flowers, foliage, and container, with a definite relation to the location of the arrangement in the house.

2. Achieve scale by selecting materials reasonably related in size to one another and to the container, and of both to the location of the arrangement. Consider the visual weight of material and container. Suggested measurements: Arrangement's height should be 1½ times the container's width for a horizontal container, 1½ times the container's height for a vertical container.

3. Ensure harmony in texture—surface quality—among plant material, background, and container: smooth or rough, shiny or dull, coarse or fine. Harmony in texture can lend added emphasis to harmony in line or colors.

4. Balance the materials within the pattern so that an impression of calm and stability is created. Balance is achieved by working from light, delicate forms (buds and foliage tips) at the edges of the arrangement to darker, heavier materials at the center. Balance is of two types: symmetric—the two sides of the same or compensating weight; asymmetric—the two sides are distinctly different but have equal visual weight and therefore balance each other. A properly balanced arrangement looks well from any viewpoint.

5. Group colors carefully.
    a) Group color is more effective than spotty or mixed colors.
    b) Dark, full-blown, heavy flowers are best at the base or center, with buds and lighter flowers at the edges.
    • c) Striking effects may be obtained by using all warm or all cool colors.
    d) Grouping different shades of one color from pale to dark makes an interesting arrangement.

6. Place materials so the eye is led to a center of interest or focus. Make sure that there is a highlight of choicest plant material, never a void, where the main lines of the design cross.

7. Achieve rhythm, a feeling of motion in the arrangement, by making graceful lines which curve through the arrangement and lead to the center.

8. Accent a special area of the composition by giving it unusual prominence. Accent is achieved by contrast in color, size, form, or texture, or by incorporating unusual but harmonious material.

9. Use added decorative accessories to complete or enhance the design, or to suggest a theme. Make sure the accessories are in proper proportion to the rest of the arrangement.

RULES FOR PERSONAL HYGIENE—U. S. NAVY, 1940

1. Take a daily cold bath followed by a brisk rub. It is beneficial to health.
2. Wash the hands before each meal, and immediately after using the head.
3. Brush teeth at least twice a day, especially at night.
4. Avoid exposure to venereal disease but, if exposed, wash parts immediately with soap and water; then use prophylactic treatment.
5. Avoid intemperance in eating and drinking. Men who drink alcoholic liquor are more apt to get sick than those who abstain.
6. Remember daily exercise is conducive to good health.
7. Follow periods of work with periods of relaxation, rest, or recreation.
8. Allow sufficient time for meals; the food should be chewed thoroughly.
9. Air bedding as often as practicable. Sunlight kills disease germs.
10. Keep the hair short and the fingernails trimmed and clean.
11. Avoid contact with the sick unless duty requires it.
12. Drink plenty of water, but do not drink a large amount at any one time, especially when overheated.
13. Remember, underclothes, shirts, and socks should be clean. This is especially important before going into battle, as soiled clothes predispose to wound infection.
14. Do not forget, the mental attitude has a close relationship to health. Worrying and anxiety over trifles should be avoided; to accomplish this the mind should be kept occupied and interest maintained in work and recreation.

RULES FOR DRINKING UNDERWATER (1893)

1. Half-fill a small lemonade bottle with milk and cork it.

2. After taking the bottle underwater, uncork it with great care, so as to prevent the surrounding water from getting into it.

3. The mouth of the bottle should be placed between the lips, and the cork pulled out sideways with the right hand.

4. As soon as the cork is withdrawn, the drinking should be commenced.

5. If the milk does not enter the mouth easily, a little air should be blown out through the nostrils, and the contents of the bottle will then be quickly emptied into the mouth.

6. Before coming to the surface, the bottle should be recorked.

RULES FOR PREVENTING ELECTRICAL ACCIDENTS

1. Never use a radio, TV, heater, or any other electrical appliance near a tub, sink, or pool. Keep hands dry when operating electrical tools, switches, or appliances. Remember, water and electricity don't mix.

2. Check electric cords periodically and repair any worn or exposed wires. Handle electrical wires as though they were powerful and in need of continuous care.

3. Cap unused electric wall outlets or seal with electric tape to prevent children from inserting metal objects into them.

4. Never use a knife or fork to pry toast from a plugged-in toaster.

5. Never leave an extension cord plugged into wall when disconnected from the appliance. Always unplug the cord at the wall outlet after using the appliance.

6. Remember, major appliances should be installed and repaired by professional servicemen.

7. Do not overload your electrical appliance. Fuses blow because they are the safety valves of your electrical circuits. If the fuses continue to blow, have a qualified electrician locate the trouble.

RULES FOR DETERMINING YOUR IDEAL WEIGHT

1.   When you get up in the morning, after urinating and defecating, and before dressing you should weigh within the ranges shown below:

WOMEN

HEIGHT (WITH 2″ HEELS)	SMALL FRAME	MEDIUM FRAME	LARGE FRAME
4 ft 10 in	92–98	96–107	104–119
4 ft 11 in	94–101	98–110	106–122
5 ft 0 in	96–105	101–113	109–125
5 ft 1 in	99–107	104–116	112–128
5 ft 2 in	102–110	107–119	115–131
5 ft 3 in	105–113	110–122	118–134
5 ft 4 in	108–116	113–126	121–138
5 ft 5 in	111–119	116–130	125–142
5 ft 6 in	114–123	120–135	129–146
5 ft 7 in	118–127	124–139	133–150
5 ft 8 in	122–131	128–145	137–154
5 ft 9 in	126–135	132–147	141–158
5 ft 10 in	130–140	136–151	145–163
5 ft 11 in	134–144	140–155	149–168
6 ft 0 in	138–148	144–159	153–173

MEN

HEIGHT (1″ HEELS)	SMALL FRAME	MEDIUM FRAME	LARGE FRAME
5 ft 2 in	112–120	118–129	126–141
5 ft 3 in	115–123	121–133	129–144
5 ft 4 in	118–126	124–136	132–148
5 ft 5 in	121–129	127–139	135–152
5 ft 6 in	124–133	130–143	138–156
5 ft 7 in	128–137	134–147	142–161
5 ft 8 in	132–141	138–152	147–166
5 ft 9 in	136–145	142–156	151–170
5 ft 10 in	130–150	146–160	155–174
5 ft 11 in	144–154	150–165	159–179
6 ft 0 in	148–158	154–170	164–184
6 ft 1 in	152–162	158–175	168–189
6 ft 2 in	156–167	162–180	173–194
6 ft 3 in	160–171	167–185	178–199
6 ft 4 in	164–175	172–190	182–204

RULES FOR EXERCISE AND WEIGHT CONTROL

1. Realize that the key to effective weight control is keeping energy intake (food) and activity energy output (physical activity) in balance. When the calories consumed in food equal those used to meet the body's needs, weight will remain about the same. When one eats more than this amount, one will put on fat unless physical activity is increased proportionately. Lack of exercise has been cited as the most important cause of the "creeping" obesity found in modern mechanized societies.

2. If you add thirty minutes per day of moderate exercise to your schedule, it can result in a loss of about twenty-five pounds in one year, assuming food consumption remains constant.

3. If you are trim and want to keep that way, exercise regularly and eat a balanced, nutritious diet which provides sufficient calories to make up for the energy expended.

4. If you are a thin individual and want to gain weight, exercise regularly and increase the number of calories you consume until the desired weight is reached.

5. If you are overweight, decrease the food intake and step up the amount of physical activity.

EDITOR'S NOTE: All exercise should be sufficiently vigorous to use up the required number of calories, and to some degree, it must be sustained. To the extent possible, one should meet one's needs for regular activity through sports and other forms of physical recreation that are enjoyable; otherwise the activity is likely to be abandoned or played only irregularly.

6. Pick activities that can be done regularly. They needn't be the same ones every day; in fact, variety adds spice to an exercise schedule.

7. Be aware of two basic fallacies that have been widely held with respect ot exercise and weight control:

> a) The first is that a great deal of time and effort is required to use up enough calories to affect weight materially.
>
> b) The second is that exercise increases the appetite and so will increase, not decrease, weight.

Scientific experiments on animals and man have demonstrated the falsity of these assumptions.

8. Remember, increasing exercise doesn't give license also to increase one's diet! Step up the exercise, but keep the diet well balanced, the calorie intake the same—or a little less—for the best long-range results.

The reader is advised to choose his daily food requirements from the Basic Four: 1. Milk Group, 2. Meat Group, 3. Vegetable-Fruit Group, 4. Bread-Cereal Group.

9. Each individual should commit himself to a planned program of exercise and stick with it. This means setting aside thirty minutes to an hour a day about five times per week for physical activity.

10. An exercise program should be balanced just as a diet should be balanced. Some parts should be designed primarily to exercise the heart and lungs in a way that will develop endurance. Brisk walking, jogging, and swimming relatively long distances are good for this purpose. Other parts of the program should be directed toward the improvement of strength, agility, flexibility, balance, and muscle tone.

11. Start easily. Keep a record of what is done and how many times it is done. Gradually increase the amount of exercise until a reasonably good level is reached. Most people, especially those who wish to lose weight, should supplement the scheduled exercise with additional physical recreation. Gardening on weekends, a pleasant walk, bird watching, bowling, etc., provide recreational benefits and a bit of exercise as well.

RULES FOR AVOIDING CARBON MONOXIDE POISONING

1. Have all heating systems checked annually for operating efficiency. Make sure vents, pipes, and chimneys are tight.

2. Make sure that your heating plant is not starved for air.

3. Make sure that all heating devices designed for venting are properly vented to the outside.

4. Never use hibachis indoors.

5. Never tamper with the ducts or vents of a heating device to produce more heat.

6. Never close your fireplace damper until you are certain that the fire is out.

7. Be sure that the garage is sealed from the house; never run the car in a closed garage.

8. Use your nose to detect the smoke that often accompanies carbon monoxide.

RULES FOR BOILING AND PREPARING A LOBSTER

1.   Have salted water, or whatever other liquid the recipe calls for, boiling rapidly in a large fish kettle.
2.   Plunge the lobster into the boiling liquid, head first, one at a time, bringing the liquid back to the boiling point between each addition. Lobsters should be entirely immersed in the liquid.
3.   Cook the lobster about 15 to 20 minutes depending on the size. Do not stop the rapid boiling as this will make the meat tough.
4.   In opening a cooked lobster, first remove the large claws, then the small claws and tail.
5.   Be alert, the tail meat may sometimes, after a little practice, be drawn out whole with a fork or a skewer, but more often it is necessary to cut the thin shell in the underpart of the tail with a pair of kitchen scissors before the tail meat can be removed.
6.   Divide the tail meat through the center and remove the small intestinal vein which runs along the entire length.
7.   Hold the body of the shell firmly in the left hand and, with first two fingers and thumb of the right hand, draw out the body, leaving in the shell the stomach, which is not edible.
8.   Eat the green liver; it is in particular a delicacy.
9.   Discard the lungs.
10. Break the body through the middle, and separate the body bones, picking out the meat that lies between them, which is the sweetest and tenderest part of the lobster.

RULES FOR HANDLING HAZARDOUS SUBSTANCES

1.   Read the directions and warning statements carefully before each use. Never depend on your memory.

2. Use only as directed. Never experiment or combine two or more products.
3. Store in the original container. Never put poisons in food or beverage containers. Label the new container if it is necessary to transfer contents.
4. Store out of the reach of children. Never underestimate a child's curiosity. Keep poisons under lock and key.
5. Destroy empty containers. Never leave them for children or pets to discover.

RULES FOR PREPARING FOR THE JOB MARKET AS A COLLEGE FRESHMAN

1. Get elected to or volunteer for student government offices or committee chairmanships. Companies look for people with leadership potential or experience. Everybody is involved in extracurricular activities; it's your role in them that counts.

2. Organize something (and we're not talking about a sit-in in the dean of students' office). Be the catalyst in getting special services added to your university health department or mastermind a T-shirt and poster-selling business. Not only will you be making campus living more pleasant and maybe earning money, but you'll be gathering experience for your resume.

3. Get related job experience even if it has to be on a volunteer basis; hang out at your local radio/TV station, newspaper, ad agency, hospital.

4. Make friends with future contact, i.e., guest lecturers, artists-in-residence, returning alumnae, friends of friends.

5. Read or subscribe to professional journals and other publications in your field, for instance, *Variety, Women's Wear Daily, Oil and Gas Journal,* so you can keep track of current happenings.

6. Make sure that your professors know who you are, by sight and name, so they know whom they're talking about when they're eventually asked to write recommendations for you.

7. Enter job-related contests.

RULES FOR BUYING A FARM

1. Decide on the value of the farm depending on:

      a) Its worth as a place to live.

      b) The value of the products you can raise on it.

      c) The possibilities of selling the property later on for suburban subdivision.

2. Decide what the place is worth to you and your family as a home in comparison with what it would cost to live in town. Take into account the difference in city and county taxes, insurance rates, utility rates, and the cost of travel to work.

3. Estimate the value of possible earnings of the farm. To do this, set up a plan on paper for operating the farm. List the kind and quantity of things the farm can be expected to produce in an average year. Estimate the value of the produce at normal prices. The total is the probable gross income from farming.

4. To find estimated net farm income, subtract estimated annual farming expenditures from probable gross income from farming. Include as expenditures an allowance for depreciation of farm buildings and equipment. Also count as an expense a charge for the labor to be contributed by the family.

5. To figure the value of the farm in terms of investment income, divide the estimated annual net farm income by the percentage that you could expect to get in interest if the money were invested in some other way.

6. Realize that whether you can buy a farm for the amount of its value to you as a home plus its value as an income producer will depend, among other things, on its nearness to a city. A farm within commuting distance of a city—roughly within thirty miles of it—is likely to be one half to two thirds more expensive than one farther out. A farm near one of the larger cities will cost more than one near a smaller city. Land located on a hard-surfaced road is likely to cost 10 to 30 percent more than comparable land served by a dirt road.

7. Compare the price asked with the probable cost of a comparable house in town, making allowances for difference in heating system, water supply, and sanitary facilities. Prices asked for small farms suitable for part-time farming reflect primarily the size and condition of the house. The alternative to buying a place that already has a house is to buy a piece of land and build the kind of house you want. When this is done, the cost of the land is likely to be only a small part of the total cost of setting up the part-time farm.

8. If you can pay cash for the land, it is usually easier to obtain financing for the cost of a new house on it than to finance the purchase of a place that already has buildings; a new house is a better security for a loan than an old one.

9. Know that many savings and loan associations and local banks provide financing for new residences on part-time farms. The Farmers Home Administration also has a special credit program for farm housing that is well adapted to the needs of part-time farmers. Other possible sources of loans for part-time farmers are the Farm Credit Administration and some insurance companies.

RULES OF PROFESSIONAL MEDICAL PRACTICE
(THE OATH OF HIPPOCRATES, c. 460—377 B.C.)

1. I swear by Apollo the healer, invoking all the gods and goddesses to be my witnesses, that I will fulfill this oath and this written covenant to the best of my ability and judgment.

2. I will look upon him who shall have taught me this art even as one of my own parents.

3. I will share my substance with him, and I will supply his necessities if he be in need.

4. I will regard his offspring even as my own brethren, and I will teach them this art, if they would learn it, without fee or covenant.

5. I will impart this art by precept, by lecture, and by every mode of teaching, not only to my own sons but to the sons of him who has taught me, and to disciples bound by covenant and oath, according to the law of medicine.

6. The regimen I adopt shall be for the benefit of the patients according to my ability and judgment, and not for their hurt or for any wrong.

7. I will give no deadly drug to any, though it be asked of me, nor will I counsel such, and especially I will not aid a woman to procure abortion.

8. Whatsoever house I enter, there will I go for the benefit of the sick, refraining from all wrongdoing or corruption, and especially from any act of seduction, of male or female, of bond or free.

9. Whatsoever things I see or hear concerning the life of men, in my attendance on the sick or even a part therefrom, which ought not to be noised abroad, I will keep silence thereon, counting such things to be as sacred secrets.

10. Pure and holy will I keep my life and my art.

RULES FOR STORING PERISHABLE FOODS IN THE HOME

1. BREAD—Store in original wrapper in breadbox or refrigerator. Use within five to seven days. Bread will also retain its original quality for two to three months if frozen in the wrapper and stored in the home freezer.

2. EGGS—Store promptly in refrigerator. To insure best quality and flavor, use eggs within a week. If held too long, the white may thin and the yolk membrane may weaken and break when opening the shell. If eggs are cracked, use them only in foods that will be thoroughly cooked.

3. FRESH MEATS (Roasts, steaks, chops, etc.)—Cover loosely and store in the coldest part of the refrigerator. Use within three to five days. Ground meats such as hamburger are more likely to spoil than others because more of the meat surface has been exposed to contamination from air, handlers, and machines. This meat should be lightly covered and used in one or two days.

4. FRESH MILK—Store in refrigerator at about 40° F. Keep covered so milk will not absorb odors and flavors of other foods. For best quality use within a week and only take out of refrigerator long enough to get amount needed. Return immediately to refrigerator.

5. CHEESES—Keep in refrigerator. Wrap tightly to keep out air. This way hard cheeses can be kept for several months. If mold develops, simply cut off molded section. Cheese inside is still edible.

6. VEGETABLES—Sort vegetables before storing them. Use immediately any vegetables that are bruised or soft. The vegetables crisper in your refrigerator performs better if it is at least two thirds full. Keeping vegetables in plastic bags will insure freshness.
   The fresher the vegetable the better it is when eaten. With few exceptions, vegetables will keep best in the refrigerator. (Exceptions: potatoes, onions, eggplants, squashes, and rutabagas.)

7. FRUITS—Plan to use fresh fruits promptly when they are most flavorful. Because fruits are fragile, they need special handling to keep from being bruised or crushed. Softened tissues of fruit permit the entrance of spoilage

organisms that can quickly break down quality. Sort fruit before storing and eliminate bruised or decayed fruits. Apples, grapes, cranberries, plums, and cherries should be stored in the refrigerator immediately after purchase and are best eaten within a week. Avocados, bananas, pears, apricots, nectarines, peaches, and melons should be allowed to ripen at room temperature and then stored in the refrigerator. These fruits are best if eaten within three to five days.

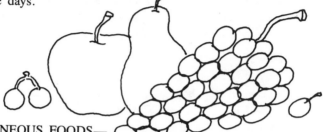

8. MISCELLANEOUS FOODS—
Peanut butter—After the jar has been opened it is best to keep peanut butter in the refrigerator. Remove it from the refrigerator a short time before using to allow it to soften and spread more easily.
Nuts—Best if kept in airtight containers in the refrigerator or freezer. Because of their high fat content, nuts require refrigeration to delay development of rancidity. Unshelled nuts may be stored at room temperature for about six months. Shelled nuts, in moisture-proof wrapping, can be refrigerated up to six months.

RULES FOR BIRTHSTONE GIVING

1. In January give garnet. It represents constancy and fidelity in every engagement.
2. In February give amethyst. It prevents violent passions.
3. In March give bloodstone. It stands for courage, wisdom, and firmness in affection.
4. In April give sapphire to provide freedom from enchantment.
5. In May give emerald for insuring true love.
6. In June an agate insures long life, health, and prosperity.
7. In July give ruby. It corrects evils resulting from mistaken friendship.
8. In August give sardonyx. It insures conjugal felicity.
9. In September give chrysolite. It suggests freedom from evil passions and sadness of the mind.
10. In October give opal to denote hope, sharpen the sight, and inspire the faith of the possessor.
11. In November give topaz. It prevents bad dreams and solidifies friendship.
12. In December give turquoise, for prosperity in love.

RULES FOR GETTING THE BEST SERVICE ON YOUR CAR

1.   During the warranty period, have the car serviced exactly as recommended. Routine maintenance may be performed at an independent garage or service station without violating the warranty agreement; but be sure to keep a receipt showing the mileage reading, the date, and the nature of the service. For repairs under warranty, you must take the car to an authorized dealer.

2.   When repair or service is necessary after the warranty period, be sure to take the following steps:

> a) Inquire if the shop offers a warranty on service and replacement parts and how long it is effective.
> b) Tell the service manager, the service adviser, or the mechanic *all* the car's symptoms and problems, and be sure he understands what you are saying.
> c) Then, find out exactly what work is to be done and, if possible, obtain a written estimate. At least write out a list for yourself and keep it. *Insist that the shop obtain your approval before doing any additional work.*

3.   When you pick up the car after repairs, check each item on the list or estimate. Do not accept the car unless everything is complete and satisfactory. If parts have been replaced, ask for the old ones to take with you. If they are too large or messy to carry, ask to see them.

4.   Road test the car before you drive home, and return it to the garage immediately if it is not performing well. Don't wait until tomorrow; you claim for corrective service will be weakened.

5.   Try to use the same mechanic every time you have your car serviced.

6.   When work is good, stop by and tell the dealer or the service manager, and ask him to pass on your compliment to the mechanic.

7.   At a dealership, talk to the owner about poor service or inadequate repairs. If he refuses to give you satisfaction, consult your Owner's Manual or the warranty for the address of the nearest district office of the company, and write or telephone the customer service representative.

8.   At a private garage or service center, also talk with the owner about a complaint. If the problem is not resolved, check to see if a municipal, county, or state consumer agency can help you. You can also appeal to the local office of the Better Business Bureau or write to the U.S. Office of Consumer Affairs, Washington, D.C. 20201.

9.   As a last resort, pay the bill and then see a lawyer.

RULES FOR DRYING VEGETABLES

1. Select your vegetables carefully. If they are not fresh and are not in prime condition for cooking, they are not suitable for drying.

2. Blanch vegetables by heating sufficiently to inactivate enzymes. Enzymes are the biological catalysts that facilitate chemical reactions in living tissue. If certain enzymes are not inactivated, they will cause color and flavor to deteriorate during drying and storage. Blanched vegetables, when dried, will have better flavor and color than unblanched ones. Blanch with hot water or with steam.

3. Dry in the kitchen oven or in a dehydrator. However, sun drying may be used under proper conditions.

4. Remember, drying in the sun is unpredictable unless temperatures are over 100° F, and the relative humidity is low. If the temperature is too low, humidity too high, or both, spoilage will occur before drying is achieved.

5. Be aware dehydrated vegetables are free from insect infestation when removed from the dehydrator or oven. However, they are immediately susceptible to contamination and should be packaged as soon as they are cool.

6. Keep in mind that, despite precautions, sun-dried vegetables may be contaminated by insects. Therefore, the packaged dried vegetables should be placed in the home freezer for forty-eight hours to kill any possible insects or their eggs.

7. Store containers of dried vegetables in a dry, cool, and dark place. Low storage temperatures extend the shelf life of the dried product.

8. Remember, all dried vegetables deteriorate to some extent during storage. losing vitamins, flavor, color, and aroma. For this reason, they will not retain their appeal indefinitely.

9. Keep in mind, carrots, onions, and cabbages deteriorate at more rapid rates than do other vegetables, and will generally have a shelf life of only six months. Some vegetables, however, will be good after a year's storage.

10. Don't forget, fresh vegetables provide man with bulk, energy, minerals, and vitamins. Bulk is provided by the indigestible fiber, and energy is provided by the starch, sugar, and fat. Neither bulk nor energy is affected by the drying process.

RULES FOR DETERMINING AN ALCOHOLISM PROBLEM

If you should honestly answer "yes" to any one of these questions, that is a definite warning that you may be an alcoholic; to any two, the chances are you are an alcoholic; to three or more, you are an alcoholic.

a) Do you lose time from work due to drinking?

b) Is drinking making your home life unhappy?

c) Do you drink because you are shy with other people?

d) Is drinking affecting your reputation?

e) Have you ever felt remorse after drinking?

f) Have you gotten into financial difficulties as a result of drinking?

g) Do you turn to lower companions and an inferior environment when drinking?

h) Does your drinking make you careless of your family's welfare?

i) Has your ambition decreased since drinking?

j) Do you crave a drink at a definite time daily?

k) Do you want a drink the next morning?

l) Does drinking cause you to have difficult in sleeping?

m) Has your efficiency decreased since drinking?

n) Is drinking jeopardizing your job or business?

o) Do you drink to escape from worries or troubles?

p) Do you drink alone?

q) Have you ever had a complete loss of memory as a result of drinking?

r) Has your physician ever treated you for drinking?

s) Do you drink to build up your self-confidence?

t) Have you ever been to a hospital or institution on account of drinking?

RULES FOR KEEPING FAMILY HEALTH RECORDS

1. Start with a good health record with the names of the members of your family and their dates of birth. A place for your current address is important in case the record is lost. Keep a listing of your doctors and dentists with their

addresses and telephone numbers and a list of your health insurance policies with the name of the company and the number of the policy.

2. Remember, because heredity can play an important role in some diseases, it is important for your doctor to know of any serious illnesses in your family background. Include incidence of diseases such as cancer, heart disease, epilepsy, diabetes, etc., in the immediate family of both husband and wife. If family members are deceased, cause of death should also be noted. Include any other family medical data which might be important.

3. Be aware, maternity records can be a good indication of your general health. So for every pregnancy, it is a good idea to know the specifics of each pregnancy. Include: doctor, delivery date, place, birth difficulties, method, etc. If the pregnancy was terminated, include space for the date, the reasons for the termination, and other pertinent information.

4. You should know the rate at which a baby's or child's height and weight increase play an important role in maintaining good health and early detection of potential problems. During a baby's first year, these measurements should be recorded regularly every two to four months, then at least once a year thereafter until the child reaches maturity.

5. Remember too, normal weights for adults will vary by age, sex, and body build. Your doctor is the best source of this information. He will probably also tell you that any drastic change in weight should receive immediate attention; it may be a sign of some yet-undetected illness. Even healthy adults should keep a yearly record of their weight.

6. Record all childhood diseases. Since a person cannot get a common contagious disease such as chicken pox or measles more than once, it is helpful to know, in later life, whether or not exposure to these diseases should be avoided. A doctor may also use this information as a clue to diagnosing another disease. For example, scarlet fever can lead to nephritis or a rheumatic heart.

7. Carefully record injuries because of accidents since they may result in disabling conditions or may, years later, be the long-forgotten cause of illness. A record of accidents and injuries may become important years after the incident.

8. Record such acute ilnesses as influenza, pneumonia, or severe infections, plus any chronic illness (heart disease, diabetes, cancer, etc.) and surgical operations.

9. Start your immunization program on time—usually when a child is two to three months old—and keep it up-to-date. That can go a long way toward raising a healthy family. By recording the dates of each, you will know when anyone in your family needs a "booster" to renew protection.

10. Remember hay fever, asthma, hives, and other allergic reactions often result from breathing certain pollens or after eating specific foods. Some insect bites and medications can also bring reactions to allergy-prone persons. You can help your doctor find cause(s) of such reactions by recording any sensitivities.

RULES FOR DEALING WITH A CHILD POISONING EMERGENCY

1. Keep calm, you will act more effectively.

2. Find out what kind of poison was taken and how much by examining the container or any remaining contents.

3. Observe the child's symptoms.

4. Call the doctor, the police, or the poison control center nearest you. If you cannot reach the poison control center in your area, call the New York number, 212-340-4494, which is operative twenty-four hours a day, seven days a week.

5. Decide whether to induce vomiting. Vomiting is to be avoided if:

  a) The child has swallowed a corrosive poison or petroleum product. (Burns around the mouth may indicate that the child has taken a corrosive poison.)

  b) The child is unconscious or having convulsions.

  c) The child complains of acute pain.

6. If the child has taken a corrosive or caustic substance, attempt to reduce the absorption of the poison by coating the stomach wall with a demulcent · (soothing) substance such as raw egg white or milk. If the skin and clothes are contaminated, flush the skin thoroughly with water and remove the clothes. If the eyes are contaminated, hold the eyelids open and flush with a gentle stream of cool water.

7. If the poison is not corrosive or a petroleum product, induce vomiting by:

  a) Inserting your finger into the child's throat, or

  b) Administering syrup of ipecac (never with activated charcoal). Two or three teaspoonfuls will cause vomiting within five ·to fifteen minutes. This dose may be repeated in twenty minutes if vomiting does not occur. You may also use two tablespoonfuls of salt in a glass of warm water.

8. After the child has vomited, neutralize the poison remaining in his stomach by administering one or two tablespoonfuls of activated charcoal USP in eight ounces of tap water. GIVE ACTIVATED CHARCOAL ONLY AFTER VOMITING.

9. If the child has stopped breathing, administer mouth-to-mouth resuscitation.

> a) Clear the child's mouth with your fingers. Keep his tongue from being swallowed. Place the child on his back, lift his neck, tilt his head back.
>
> b) Place your mouth tightly over the child's mouth, closing off the nostrils at the same time to prevent the escape of air. The mouth and nose of an infant or young child should be tightly covered by your mouth.
>
> c) Breathe into the child's mouth or nose until you see his chest rise, then remove your mouth and listen for him to exhale. Repeat, removing your mouth each time to allow the air to escape. For children, small puffs of air repeated about twenty times per minute should be continued until the child breathes for himself.

RULES FOR RECOGNIZING A SERIOUS HEADACHE

1. Check any sudden severe headache which strikes out of the blue.

2. Be aware, any headache accompanied by convulsions is a very serious indication.

3. If you get a headache and then find yourself running a fever for no discernible reason, it means it's time to call the doctor in a hurry.

4. Remember, headache accompanied by mental confusion or any drop in conscious awareness or alertness could prove dangerous.

5. See a doctor if you get a headache along with localized pain in an eye or ear or a specific area.

6. If you have a bad fall and strike your head, or have a heavy object fall onto your unprotected head, then a headache is a warning to get a prompt medical examination.

7. Keep in mind, the occasional headache is something we must all live with, but frequently recurring headaches are a danger sign in a normally headache-free adult.

BREAST CANCER: SELF-EXAMINATION

Follow these steps to examine your breasts regularly once a month. This is best done after the menstrual period.

1. Stand in front of a mirror with the upper body unclothed. Look for changes in the shape and size of the breast and for dimpling of the skin or "pulling in" of the nipples.

2. Be aware, too, of any discharge from the nipples or scaling of the skin of the nipples.

3. Because abnormality in the breast may be accentuated by a change in position of the body and arms, examine yourself from the following positions:

    a) Stand with arms down.

    b) Lean forward.

    c) Raise arms overhead and press hands behind your head.

    d) Place hands on hips and tighten chest and arm muscles by pressing firmly inward.

4. Lie flat on your back with a pillow or folded towel under your shoulders and feel each breast with the opposite hand in sequence. With the hand slightly cupped, feel for lumps or any change in the texture of the breast or skin; also, note any discharge from nipples. Avoid compressing the breast between the thumb and fingers as this may give the impression of a lump which is not actually there.

5. Place the left arm overhead. With the right hand, feel the inner half of the left breast from top to bottom and from nipple to breastbone.

6. Feel the outer half from bottom to top and from the nipple to the side of the chest. Pay special attention to the area between the breast and armpit including the armpit itself.

7. Repeat this same process for the right breast using your left hand to feel.

8. Feel gently, carefully, and thoroughly. If you find something which you consider abnormal, contact your doctor for an examination. Most breast lumps are not serious, but all should come to the doctor's attention for an expert opinion after appropriate examination.

9. Follow your doctor's advice—as your early recognition of a change in your breast and his thoughtful investigation will determine the safest course.

10. Keep up this important health habit even during pregnancy and after menopause.

RULES FOR CARING FOR YOUR FEET

1. Keep your feet clean and dry in order to help prevent infections. When you are wearing shoes, use a foot powder or talcum.

2. Dry between your toes thoroughly after bathing. This helps to prevent athlete's foot. Never wear another person's shoes, as athlete's-foot fungi are easily transmitted this way.

3. If your feet tend to be dry and scaly, lubricate them regularly with a foot cream or hand lotion.

4. Go barefoot whenever you can on sand, grass, carpeting or other resilient surfaces. Avoid walking on concrete, asphalt, tile or wood floors without protective padding.

5. Be sure that socks are roomy and comfortable. Change them regularly—twice a day if your feet perspire a lot.

6. Have at least two pairs of shoes to wear on alternate days, and allow them to dry between wearings. Use shoe powder to stop dampness.

7. Trim toenails often with a special clipper made for this purpose.

8. Rub corns and calluses with a lava stone and use foot creams if they are frequent problems. Never cut corns or calluses with a razor or scissors. Even self-treatment with commercial corn removers can aggravate problems. See a podiatrist if lava stones don't help.

RULES FOR EATING CORRECTLY

1. Eat quietly with the lips closed.
2. Do not lean on elbows while eating.
3. Keep lips and fingers clean while eating.
4. Do not put arm around plate while eating.
5. Keep your elbows near your body.
6. Cut only enough food for one bite, never an entire plateful at once.
7. Never use your own fork to help yourself from a serving platter.
8. When soup is served in soup plates, leave your spoon in the plate; but when served in cups, the spoon should be left in the saucer under the cup.
9. Never place knives, forks, and spoons on the table after being used. They are placed on their respective plates. When an extra piece of silverware is used, it should be left on the bread and butter plate, or on the meat plate.
10. Leave a teaspoon in the saucer under the cup, never in the cup.
11. When buttering a piece of bread, hold it over the bread and butter plate or over the meat plate, not in the air. Butter only enough bread for one bite. When hot biscuits are served, break (do not cut) apart, and butter straight across.

RULES FOR FEMALE EXECUTIVE SUCCESS

1. *Establish your priorities*—If you wish to become an executive, that goal must be the most important commitment in your life. You are competing with others who have made the quest for executive power the overriding factor in their lives. To compete with them, you must devote equal time and attention to your goal, if not more, as most executive women believe. Often you will be required to sacrifice your weekends or evenings, and you may have to curtail some of your other interests. Preparing to be an executive means establishing your priorities. Your career ambitions must come first.

2. *Be assertive*—Being assertive is a prerequisite for gaining executive power. This may mean reprogramming yourself. You must be assertive in the supervision of your employees, and you will be respected for it. At all times you must maintain the upper hand with them. You must be assertive in standing up for your rights and demanding equality. To management, you must be assertive about letting your demands be known. In all aspects of your life, you must know how to say no. You cannot be the self-effacing stereotype of the submissive woman.

3. *Speak up*—Speaking up falls into the category of being assertive, but it deserves special attention. Your executive skills must include the ability to speak before others. As long as you sit in a business meeting being seen and not heard, you are doing nothing to further your executive image. If you want to be noticed for more than your legs, you should be able to speak out and express your opinions, and you should do so at every available opportunity.

4. *Take risks*—Women have been culturally trained away from taking risks, and tend to be more cautious than male counterparts. However, taking calculated risks is an important element in executive decisions-making, and top executives are judged on their willingness to do so. If you're ever going to score big in business, you must have the courage to gamble. In fact, you should enjoy it.

5. *Maintain career visibility*—Taking a risk is one way to gain visibility within your organization. Being the first person to hold a new job will also help you get noticed. And just being a woman helps. As a minority member of the executive ranks, you are more apt to be noticed than a man, and you should augment this advantage by participating in other activities that will enhance your career visibility.

6. *Focus on the relevant*—The necessity for relevancy applies to two distinct areas. The first is within your job tasks. You will always have more to do than you seemingly have time for. If this weren't the case, your company wouldn't need you to begin with. Only a portion of these duties are truly important. The rest may be traditional busywork. You must isolate the matters which are pressing and relevant from those that can wait. To accomplish this, you must

understand how your job fits into the scheme and what the true function is that management expects you to fulfill. To be a successful executive, you must perceive which tasks are relevant to your job and which are not.

The second need for relevancy centers upon your job as a whole. Are your responsibilities vital to the continuing success of the firm, or are they nonessential? If you are stuck in a routine, busywork job, you are less apt to be noticed in a favorable light by management, and you will be overlooked when it comes time for promotions. Having relevant responsibilities is a way to gain power within organizations, and it is also a method to gain career visibility.

7. *Accept responsibility for your actions*—If you are going to be an executive, you must be master of your own destiny. If you make a mistake, excuses are unacceptable. And you must shoulder the responsibility for your subordinates as well. These are the traits of a strong leader. Management and your subordinates will be watching you to see if you display the strength of character to accept full responsibility for your actions.

8. *Learn to live with trial and error*—Often, we tend to procrastinate for fear of making the wrong decision, but in doing so we often make the worst decision of all—no decision. No one expects you to be perfect. Part of your learning process involves trial and error. Accept it, and don't let your mistakes become a source of frustration. So much of management is educated guesswork that trial and error is about the only method you have to improve your job skills.

Learn from your mistakes, and then forget them. Don't allow a few errors in judgment to erode your self-confidence. Expect to live with trial-and-error learning.

9. *Be patient*—The new executive woman is the glamour symbol of our time. But don't expect is instantly. The really glamorous jobs are few and far between, and the competition is keen. Seniority is often a factor, and women are just beginning to gain the experience that will qualify them for the top jobs.

Many younger women have come into business expecting too much too soon and have been disappointed at their seemingly slow process. We must pay our dues too. It takes from fifteen to twenty-five years for a manager to become a top executive. Establish high goals, but be realistically patient about achieving them. Business success rarely happens overnight.

10. *Be strong*—Being an executive requires an inordinate amount of courage and a strong sense of self-confidence. Moreover, as a woman, you are pursuing a life-style that is contrary to the norm, and the price you pay is partial nonacceptance. Often you will experience loneliness and frustration, resentment and prejudice, and sometimes you will question whether it is all worth it. Men share those feelings too.

11. *Look out for yourself*—Corporations can indeed be jungles full of predatory monsters eager to wipe you out. To survive, you must be savvy to the politics transpiring around you, and, most important, you must learn to look out for yourself. Don't naïvely assume that everyone can be trusted or that everyone is your friend. The competitive spirit is the catalyst for the business system. But often it brings out the worst in people.

12. *Help other women*—In the long run, it will be easier for you if women executives are not a rarity. By helping other women, you are helping yourself.

You need to help create a women's job network that can compete and counterbalance the old boys' network that has helped men so much. If men will not let women become a part of theirs, they must create one of their own.

WOMEN'S RULES FOR GOING AWAY FOR THE WEEKEND

1. First, be realistic. Go somewhere that interests you both. There's no point in setting off for the snow if he's a ski fanatic and you never venture outdoors.

2. Start by going away with another couple, or, better still, by visiting out-of-town friends. It's a risk to set off into the sunset together unless both of you are completely at ease. Learn to relax with each other first.

3. Be honest with each other. If you don't like the idea of three days camping out, tell him. Far better for him to have that sort of holiday later than for both of you to go and have a lousy time.

4. Don't ever let him take you somewhere he used to go with another girlfriend. Disappointment—for both of you—is inevitable. Find places of your own.

5. Don't panic if you find there are great gaps when neither of you has anything to say. Relax and enjoy the breaks in the conversation.

6. If things start to go badly don't balk at bringing them out into the open. It is far better, if you want to salvage the relationship, to talk over the problem.

7. Allow some time to be alone. Everyone needs some solitude and there's no need to feel guilty about it. Overexposure to each other is a dangerous preliminary to trouble.

8. Be flexible. If you want to suggest, or if he suggests, a minor change to the day's plans don't feel compelled to stick to the original planned schedule.

9. Determine sleeping arrangements in advance. If your relationship hasn't reached the stage of sharing a bed, then make that clear before you leave. And if you are staying with friends, make certain that they are aware of the situation.
10. Don't blame each other if things go wrong. The more you ask, "Whose idea was it to come here? Whose fault is it that everything has gone wrong?" the more convinced each one of you will be that it really is the other one's fault.
11. Make allowances for each other.

RULES GOVERNING THE BROTHELS OF AVIGNON (FOURTEENTH CENTURY)

1. On the 8th of August, in the Year 1347, our good Queen Jane gave Leave that a publick Brothel should be set up at Avignon, and ordered that the Wenches, who play'd there, should not walk the Streets, but keep themselves confined within the Brothel, and by Way of Distinction wear a tied knot upon their left shoulders.
2. If any Girl has thus offended and persists in her Offence, that then the Claviger, or Chief of the Beadles, shall lead her through the city by Beat of Drum, a red knot hanging at her Shoulder, back to the Brothel, and shall prohibit her from walking about any more, under the Penalty of being lash'd privately for the first Offence, and of being whipp'd publickly and turned out of the House for the second.
3. Our good Queen orders that this Brothel shall be erected in Broken-bridge-street, near the Convent of the Augustin Friars as far as to Peter's-gate, and that the Entrance shall be toward the Street, and the Door locked, that no youth may have admittance to the Wenches without Leave from the Abbess or Governess, who is to be chosen every Year by the Directors.

RULES OF NORMAL SEQUENCE OF SEXUAL INTIMACY

1. *Eye to body rule.* The most common form of social "contact" is to look at people from a distance. In a fraction of a second it is possible to sum up the physical qualities of another adult, labeling them and grading them mentally in the process.

2. *Eye to eye rule.* While we view others, they view us. From time to time this means that our eyes meet, and when this happens the usual reaction is to look away quickly and break the eye "contact." This will not happen, of course, if we have recognized one another as previous acquaintances. In such cases, the moment of recognition leads instantly to mutual greeting signals, such as sudden smiling, raising of the eyebrows, changes in body posture, movements of the arms, and eventually vocalizations. To perform prolonged staring is in itself an act of aggression between unfamiliar adults. The result is that two strangers normally watch one another in turn, rather than simultaneously. If, then, one finds the other attractive, he or she may add a slight smile to the next meeting of glances. If the response is returned, so is the smile, and further, more intimate contact may ensue. If the response is not returned, a blank look in reply to a friendly smile will usually stop any further development.

3. *Voice to voice rule.* Assuming there is no third party to make introductions, the next stage involves vocal contact between the male and female strangers. Invariably the initial comments will concern trivia. It is rare at this stage to make any direct reference to the true mood of the speakers. This small-talk permits the reception of a further set of signals, this time to the ear instead of the eye. Maintaining this communication at the level of irrelevant small-talk enables either side to retreat from further involvement, should the new signals prove unattractive despite the promise of the earlier, visual signals.

4. *Hand to hand rule.* This stage may take place quickly, in the form of the introduction handshake, or it is likely to be delayed for some considerable time. If the formalized, nonsexual handshake does not come into operation, then the first actual body contact to occur is likely to be disguised as an act of "supporting aid," "body protection," or "directional guidance." This is usually performed by the male toward the female and consists of holding her arm or hand to help her cross a street, or climb over an obstruction. Again, the use of acts which are irrelevant to the true mood of the encounter is important. If the body of the girl has been touched by the man in the act of assisting her in some way, either partner can still withdraw from further involvement without loss of face. The girl can thank the man for his help and leave him, without being forced into a position where she has to deliver a direct rebuff. Only when the growing relationship has been openly declared will the action of hand-holding or arm-holding become prolonged in duration. It then ceases to be a "supportive" or

194

"guiding" act and becomes an undisguised intimacy.

5. *Arm to shoulder rule.* Up to this point the bodies have not come into close contact. When they do so, another important threshold has been passed. Whether sitting, standing, or walking, physical contact down the side of the body indicates a great advance in the relationship from its earlier hesitant touchings. The easiest method employed is the shoulder embrace, usually with the man's arm placed around the girl's shoulders to draw the two partners together. This is the simplest introduction to trunk contact because it is already used in other contexts between mere friends as an act of nonsexual companionship. It is therefore the smallest step to take, and the least likely to meet rebuff. Walking together in this posture can be given the air of slight ambiguity, halfway between close friendship and love.

6. *Arm to waist rule.* A slight advance on the last stage occurs with the wrapping of the arm around the waist. This is something the man will not have done to other men, no matter how friendly, so that it becomes more of a direct statement of amorous intimacy. Furthermore, his hand will now be in much closer proximity to the genital region of the female.

7. *Mouth to mouth rule.* Kissing on the mouth, combined with the full frontal embrace, is a major step forward. For the first time there is a strong chance of physiological arousal, if the action is prolonged or repeated.

8. *Hand to head rule.* As an extension of the last stage, the hands begin to caress the partner's head. Fingers stroke the face, neck, and hair. Hands clasp the nape and the side of the head.

9. *Hand to body rule.* In the post-kissing phase, the hands begin to explore the partner's body, squeezing, fondling, and stroking. The major advance here is the manipulation by the male to the female's breasts. Further developments mean increasing difficulty in breaking off the pattern without continuing to completion, and if the bond of attachment has not reached a sufficient level of mutual trust, more advanced sexual intimacies are postponed.

10. *Mouth to breast rule.* Here the threshold is passed in which the interactions become strictly private. For most couples this will also have applied to the last stage, especially where breast manipulations are concerned, but advanced kissing and body fondling does occur frequently in public places under certain circumstances. Mouth-to-breast contacts are the last of the pregenital intimacies and are the prelude to actions which are concerned not merely with arousal, but with arousal to climax.

11. *Hand to genitals rule.* If the manual exploration of the partner's body continues, it inevitably arrives at the genital region. After tentative caressing of the partner's genitals, the actions soon develop into gently, rhythmic rubbing that stimulates the rhythm of pelvic thrusting.

12. *Genitals to genitals rule.* Finally, the stage of full copulation is reached. There is also, for the first time, the possibility of an irreversible act, namely that of fertilization, which puts this concluding act in the sequence onto an entirely new plane. Each stage will have served to tighten the bond of attachment a little more, but, in a biological sense, this final copulatory action is clearly related to a phase where the earlier intimacies will already have done their job of cementing the bond, so that the pair will want to stay together after the sex drive has been satisfied.

RULES FOR BIRTH CONTROL

"The Pill"
1. You must take the pill regularly and exactly as instructed for it to be effective. Of 100 women who use the pill for one year, 2 to 3 will become pregnant.
2. Avoid taking The Pill if you have had a heart attack, stroke, angina pectoris, blood clots, cancer of the breast or uterus, or scanty or irregular periods.
3. If you think you are pregnant, avoid The Pill because it increases the risk of defect in the fetus.
4. After childbirth, consult your doctor before resuming use of The Pill. This is especially true for nursing mothers because the drugs in The Pill appear in the milk and the long-range effect on the infant is not known.

Intrauterine Device (IUD)
1. Be sure a competent physician inserts the IUD. Of 100 women using an IUD for one year, 1 to 6 will become pregnant.
2. Check to see that the IUD is in position at regular intervals. The user can check it herself but should have a physician check it once a year.
3. Consult a physician if heavy or irregular bleeding occurs.

196

4. If you have had any of the following prior to getting an IUD: cancer of the uterus or cervix; bleeding between periods; heavy mentrual flow; infection of the uterus, cervix, or pelvis; recent pregnancy; abortion or miscarriage; venereal disease; fainting attacks; abnormal "Pap smear," tell your doctor. These conditions may affect the prescription of the IUD.

5. An infection of the pelvis may occur in some cases and could result in your future inability to have children.

Diaphragm

1. If you use the diaphragm with a spermicidal jelly regularly for one year, your chances of becoming pregnant are 2 to 20 out of 100.

2. You must insert the diaphragm before each intercourse and keep it in place for at least 6 hours afterward.

3. Have a physician check the fit of your diaphragm yearly, and after each childbirth or abortion.

4. You may have difficulty using the diaphragm if the vagina is greatly relaxed or if the uterus has "fallen."

Foam, Cream, or Jelly Alone

1. Use this chemical form of contraception and your chances for becoming pregnant are 2 to 29 out of 100.

2. You must apply the chemical barrier one hour or less before intercourse.

3. Wait 6 to 8 hours after intercourse before douching.

Condom (Rubber)

1. Your male partner must interrupt foreplay to fit the condom in place before sexual entry. Chances for pregnancy are 3 to 36 out of 100.

2. Be careful that the condom does not split, or tear, or spill during removal from the vagina.

3. Your partner may want to switch to a natural skin condom if the rubber causes an allergic reaction (burning, rash, swelling, etc.)

Coitus Interruptus (Withdrawal)

1. The male partner *must* withdraw the penis from the vagina before ejaculation.

Warning: The failure rate with this method is extremely high and it should not be considered effective for preventing pregnancy.

Rhythm Method

1. You must determine the time of ovulation for a high degree of effectiveness. This can be done by the calendar method, a method based on body temperature, and a mucus method.

2. Refrain from intercourse on days surrounding the predicted time of ovulation. Chances of pregnancy with this method are 14 to 47 out of 100.

3. Be careful! If you are using this method you may find it difficult to refrain from intercourse as required to maximize effectiveness.

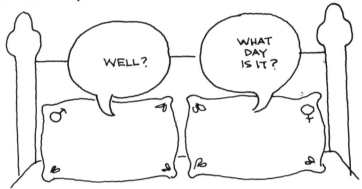

RULES FOR WASHING DISHES

1. Before the dishes are stacked, they should be scraped as clean as possible. If they contain any material, such as egg yolk, that will harden, they should be rinsed off while it is still soft.

2. Empty cups and glasses and rinse with clean water.

3. Stack the dishes carefully, so that there is no possibility of any two becoming stuck together, or of the pile toppling over.

4. Give china or glassware that has held ice or other cold substances an opportunity to gradually warm before being placed in the water.

5. Use water as hot as the hands will bear.

6. Use detergents according to the directions on the box, and if soap is used, there should be adequate suds, but no free soap floating in the water.

7. Wash glassware first, before anything else is placed in the water. It is best to handle glassware individually, to prevent breakage through jostling.

8. Chinaware comes next, and common sense will indicate how much should be placed in the dishpan at any one time. Mere soaking is not enough; each item should be well scrubbed with a cloth or brush.

9. Silverware is washed next, before the cooking utensils.

10. If at any time during the operation the water becomes too cool, dirty or greasy, change it. Greasy water in particular is hazardous, for it is apt to coat everything with a thin grease film. It may be found necessary to add further soap or detergent as the washing process, but this should not be used as a substitute for fresh water.

11. Wash sharp knives individually, for otherwise the hands may be cut as they grope about in the water.

12. Never place a heavy object on top of a fragile one in the water.

13. After washing dishes rinse them in hot, clear water, and then dry. They may be rinsed by immersion or by pouring the water over them.

14. If soap is used, dry dishes by hand, lest water spots or soap film be left on the surface, but air drying is permissible with some of the detergents. For appearance' sake, a final polishing may be given with a clean, dry cloth.

15. Remember, because they are most subject to grease and charred foods, cooking utensils require special care. It is well to prepare each vessel as soon as it is released from use by scraping it out and filling it with water to soak.

16. Pour out as much of the grease in frying pans as possible, fill with water, and leave to simmer while the other dishes are being washed. This water is poured down the drain, and will be found to carry most of the grease with it.

17. When food has burned in a vessel, much of the char can be removed by soaking and simmering, though care should be taken not to let substances like macaroni, noodles, etc., get down the drain where they might clog the pipes.

18. Use steel wool to remove stubborn particles, provided that the utensil is made of a suitable material. Silver polish can be used to remove stains on chromium plating, etc.: Knives and similar sharp, pointed instruments should not be used to scrape, for they cause scratches and gouges in the surface.

19. Cooking vessels present particular problems because they often have rivets, rims, folds, and other hard-to-clean areas. In addition, they may be made up of components that require different individual care.

20. Take care at all times to make certain that the water does not become too dirty or greasy to properly clean.

21. Grease is the big problem in dishwashing. The only answers to grease are plenty of *hot* water, soap or detergent, and vigorous scrubbing. Wherever possible, the grease should be removed in solid form.

RULES OF WATER SAFETY

1.   Never swim alone, except in areas protected by a lifeguard. If there is no lifeguard, one of your swimming companions should be a qualified lifesaver.
2.   Never jump or dive into unfamiliar waters. Enter cautiously, checking the bottom for trash, weeds, or sudden drops.
3.   When diving, be aware of other swimmers; stay away from diving boards and platforms when you swim.
4.   Supervise children constantly around deep water; the very young should wear flotation jackets.
5.   Master "survival floating," which enables you to stay afloat without swimming or using much energy; take a deep breath and relax your body, floating vertically with your face forward in the water. When you need another breath, exhale through your nose; then lift your head out of the water either by pressing your arms down or by bringing your legs together. Inhale through your mouth; relax, and return to the face-down floating position.

RULES OF WATER RESCUE

1.   Keep in mind, a swimming rescue is dangerous and should be attempted only by a trained lifeguard.
2.   If the person in trouble is close enough, extend a board, pole, tree branch, towel, or article of clothing for him to grab. Pull him to safety, making sure you stay low to avoid being pulled into the water yourself.
3.   If the swimmer is farther away, toss him a life preserver, a board, or anything else that floats and will support him until help comes.

RULES FOR MOVING

Do-it-yourself:
1. Plan the move well in advance.
2. Insure that the required vehicle will be available at the time needed and that it is in good and safe working order and properly licensed.
3. Obtain proper packing materials and rent pads for furniture protection.
4. Line up necessary assistance for the day of the move.
5. Buy adequate insurance for protection of household goods and the vehicle used.
6. Keep flexible for changes in the weather and other surprises.
7. Don't expect the entire operation to be a snap. The professional who makes the job look easy has experience and capabilities the average person lacks.

Hiring a professional mover:
1. Before the move—plan to be flexible. Try to avoid moving during peak periods—the summer season and those days preceding the first of the month when many households are being shifted.
2. Decide what you intend to move, which material (such as fragile and unusually valuable possessions) you will transport yourself, which articles you will pack, which articles you wish to have packed (for a fee), the time span available for the move.
3. Select moving companies with good reputations in the community and ask for estimates (without charge). Make certain that estimators are aware of everything that must be moved. Remember that the charge for interstate moves will be based on weight and distance according to tariffs on file with the ICC. The actual weight and not the estimated weight will determine the cost that must be paid—no more and no less.
4. Ask for a written estimate. You still must pay a cost based on the actual weight, but the written estimate can have an effect on the amount of cash necessary for delivery of your shipment.
5. Determine what degree of legal protection is needed for the safety of your household goods. From acceptance to delivery of your goods, the carrier is responsible for your shipment.
6. Remember, carrier negligence may have to be proven before any reinbursement takes place. Perhaps an act of God, rather than negligence, was the cause of the loss. In such situations the carrier may have no liability. A good starting point here is to recognize the difference between insurance and carrier liability. Carriers do not sell household goods insurance. This must be purchased through your insurance agency. You must determine if it is worthwhile.
7. Be sure that agreements between you and the carrier are in writing and on

the Order for Service and the Bill of Lading which the carrier will provide.

8. Decide which of your belongings you wish the mover to pack (for a fee) and what you intend to pack yourself. Agree on the time when the packers will do their work. Give them space to operate and provide a table on which to pack things.

9. When the driver arrives, and before the loading begins, insist on exchanging information necessary for the transaction to run smoothly. Obtain his name, home office location and telephone number of the carrier, vehicle license and equipment numbers, location of the scale he will use to weigh your shipment, his route, expected arrival time and where he can be reached en route, let him know your plans, and provide an address and a telephone number where he can contact you.

10. Have someone accompany the mover's representative who writes up the inventory of your goods, and their condition. If there is disagreement over the described condition of an article, note this in writing before signing off after completion of an inventory.

11. Verify that the tare weight is listed. This represents the weight of the vehicle before your goods were loaded. The difference between the loaded and tare weights will establish the weight of your shipment.

12. Plan to be at the delivery site on or before the agreed delivery time. Movers need wait only three hours for you to accept your goods, and less time if the move is under two hundred miles. The driver, however, cannot show up for an early delivery without your consent.

13. Remember, if the mover has met all his obligations but delivery cannot be made because of your inability to pay the lawful charges or accept delivery within the free waiting period, your household goods could wind up in storage— at your expense. Redelivery cost will add to the bill.

14. Upon delivery, have a family member check each article against the inventory and examine for any damage. Before signing the delivery receipt or the inventory, make sure they include written notations of loss or damage, and be specific.

RULES FOR KEEPING HOME RECORDS

1. Since there are many occasions when the information on your birth certificate will be needed, it is important that you keep it in a safe place, preferably in a safe-deposit box.

2. By the same token, there will be a death certificate for every person someday. These will be needed occasionally and should also be kept in the safe-deposit box.

3. Other family-type records that are important documents, and that ought to be kept in your safe-deposit box, include marriage certificates, divorce or other legal papers regarding dissolution of marriage, adoption papers, citizenship records, service papers, and any other document that is either government- or court-recorded.

4. The original copy of a will, in most cases, is kept in the safe of the attorney who prepared it. This is highly desirable, since it may save complications later. The client receives the two carbon copies, one of which may be put into his or her own safe-deposit box. The third copy should be kept at home where it is readily accessible.

5. Investment papers, securities, and government bonds should be kept in a safe-deposit box. Among other investment-type documents that require safekeeping are papers that serve as proof of ownership, such as deeds for real estate, other mortgage papers, important contracts, automobile titles, leases, notes, and such special papers as patents and copyrights.

6. Many items can be replaced rather easily. Copies of insurance policies can be obtained from your insurance companies. Copies of canceled checks are usually available at your bank.

7. While it isn't necessary to keep all canceled checks, it's important to keep any checks and receipts that may be needed for income tax purposes or as proof of payment on installment debts.

8. Among your important records will be a household inventory. Before this is of much value, in case of fire or burglary, you'll need to supply some details. Be sure to list the item, date bought, purchase price (not including credit charges), model number if it applies, brand name, dealer's name, and general description (color, size, style, electric or gas, etc.). Don't forget to include a realistic lump sum in your list for clothes and jewelry if you don't itemize these.

9. It's a good idea to make several copies of your household inventory. One copy should be put in your safe-deposit box; and you may wish to give a copy to your insurance company. The third copy can be kept in a convenient place at home. This information is quite helpful for insurance claims, fire, or finding property stolen from you.

CONSUMER RULES FOR OLDER PEOPLE

1.   Before you buy anything by mail, see if you can get a better deal at a local store. Be careful about mail that offers an "easy" way to make money at home, or a "bargain" retirement home in the sun. Check first with your local postal inspector, your lawyer, local senior citizens center, or the Legal Aid Society.

2.   Don't fall for the "gimmicks" or for the "free" gift offers. When a salesman comes to your door and wants you to buy something right now, DON'T! Ask him to come back tomorrow, then check with the Better Business Bureau, Legal Aid Society, local community action agency, or the local police station.

3.   Before you sign a contract or an agreement, ask yourself these questions: Do I understand everything it says? Do I agree with everything it says? If your answer to either question is "No," don't sign. If the contract is for something you really want, check it with a lawyer or the Legal Aid Society.

4.   Don't be fooled by talk about "low" monthly payments. Find out the total amount you'll be paying over the life of the loan. Subtact the cost of the item you are buying. The difference is what you pay in interest. If it seems to be too much, check with a local bank, a credit union, or the local community action agency.

5.   Don't buy a health product or health machine just because someone says it's good. The only way to know for sure is to check with your doctor or local health clinic. Check first. And don't use anyone else's medicine.

6.   Don't buy glasses and hearing aids until you see your doctor or local health clinic. And don't buy them at a bargain price unless your doctor says okay. They need to be properly fitted, and a bargain isn't a bargain if it won't help you. You can also get advice from the local vocational rehabilitation office.

7.   If someone comes to your door and wants to fix up your home, be suspicious. Don't sign anything until you do these things: (a) make sure repairs are needed, (b) get other estimates, (c) make sure salesman is legitimate, (d) check with the Better Business Bureau. If you do sign a contract, READ IT ALL! Make sure you are not mortgaging your home for a few dollars worth of repairs.

8. Don't be afraid to say no. Don't let yourself be high-pressured into buying something you don't want or need.

9. Get a receipt. Whenever you buy something, make sure you get a receipt, and read it all the way through.

10. Don't be afraid to check on sellers. The only ones who object to this are the ones who are trying to take advantage of you.

RULES FOR SAFELY USING CLEANING PRODUCTS

1. Remember, ammonia or products containing ammonia (i.e., window and toilet bowl cleaners, etc.) should not be used.in combination with products containing chlorine (i.e., bleach, scouring powder, etc.). The combination produces deadly chlorine gas.

2. Don't use laundry products containing enzymes with bleach, as the enzymes become deactivated.

3. Do not soak aluminum utensils in ammonia. They become unfit for use thereafter

RULES FOR TRAPPING ANIMALS

1. Obtain the landowner's permission before trapping on another's land.
2. Avoid setting traps in areas where domestic animals may get caught.
3. Set traps to kill quickly, utilizing water sets where possible.
4. Check traps regularly—preferably in the early morning.
5. Identify and record trap locations carefully and accurately.
6. Dispose of animal carcasses properly so as not to offend others.
7. Make an effort to concentrate trapping in areas where animals are overabundant for the supporting habitat.
8. Promptly report the presence of diseased animals to wildlife authorities.
9. Assist farmers and other landowners who are having problems with predators.
10. Support and help train new trappers.
11. Support strict enforcement of regulations including the reporting of all takes to state game agencies.

RULES FOR PREPARING AN OUTDOOR SURVIVAL KIT

Matches
1. Carry the long, wooden, strike-anywhere, kitchen variety—they are both handiest and most durable.
2. Pack your emergency matches in an unbreakable, waterproof container that can be fastened to clothing with a safety pin.
3. Carry two supplies of matches at all times, perhaps one in a pocket, one in a pack.
4. Waterproof a large sealed container of matches with paraffin, for extended trips, to assure a supply in case the regular box becomes wet.
5. Consider buying a metal match, if you're trying to reduce your kit to the bare minimum. These durable, waterproof and fireproof, stubby, gray sticks will light one to three thousand fires, depending on size.

Compass

1. Carry at least one compass, even if familiar woods. In wild country, carry a spare pinned to your clothing.

2. Choose a compass that is waterproof, accurate, and durable, and has a luminous dial, or at least a luminous needle.

3. Wear a watch. In an emergency, this can be used to determine direction.

Glasses

1. Carry a spare pair of glasses, in a substantial protective case, if you need prescription lenses to get around.

2. Carry sunglasses if you expect to find yourself in snow, desert, or high country.

First Aid Equipment

1. Carry a supply of Band-Aids. These can be used to repair equipment, as well as covering cuts and blisters.

2. Include plain white gauze and plastic tape (for an extended trip).

3. Carry a suction snake-bite kit.

4. Carry a small bar of soap for washing cuts.

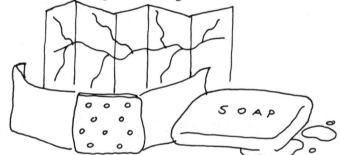

Maps

1. Carry contour maps of areas you expect to be passing through.

Knife

1. Choose a rugged sheath knife with a substantial leather case. Ideally the case will have a separate compartment to hold Carborundum.

2. Remember, the Carborundum block should be fine on one side, coarser on the other.

3. Carry kerosene, light machine oil, or salve to lubricate the Carborundum.

Ax

1. Choose a Hudson Bay ax—it is light, because it has a cut-away butt, but it has a regular-sized cutting surface.

2. Be careful; if you ax does not have a leather sheath, wrap the blade carefully before packing it.

Saw

1. Choose a lightweight sawblade of ribbon-like thin steel. This can be rolled into a small bundle and packed in canvas.

2. Pack a two-piece, tubular steel handle, or take two butterfly bolts and make yourself a handle by bending a stout green sapling on the spot.

Guns and Ammo

1. Pack a light, adequately sighted, accurate big game repeating rifle for living off a big game area indefinitely.

2. Pack a .22 caliber, in a small game area.

Plastic

1. Take a sheet of light plastic, 8′ × 4′, or two 6′ square sheets. These serve innumerable purposes and fit into a shirt pocket.

RULES FOR SHARPENING A KNIFE

1. Lubricate the Carborundum with kerosene, light machine oil, or salve.

2. Place the knife diagonally on the sharpening stone.

3. Raise the side of the blade away from the surface of the stone to an angle of about twenty degrees.

4. Keeping the edge of the blade to the surface of the hone, holding both the diagonal position and the twenty-degree angle, sweep the edge across the hone from hilt to point, always toward the edge.

5. Turn over the blade and repeat the operation.

6. Continue sharpening on alternative sides of the blade, one stroke at a time. Be sure to use even, sweeping strokes and to maintain the same angle on both sides of the blade throughout each stroke. Lessen the pressure as the edge is restored.

7. Hone off a "wire" edge, if it develops, by giving the blade a few light sweeps across the fine-grit hone at a high angle of about sixty degrees.

208

SPECIAL RULES FOR ALLERGY-PROOFING THE NURSERY

1. Make floor coverings linoleum or synthetic material tile.
2. Paint walls in odorless rubber or plastic-based paint. They should not carry wall hangings, pictures, photographs of any kind. If you wish pictorial decor, you might have small murals painted.
3. Remember, bedding and curtains should as far as possible be made of synthetic fiber materials. Pillows and mattress, regardless of what material they are made, should be covered with encasings of impermeable material. DO NOT USE PLASTIC. It is hot, makes noise, has a high odor, cracks, collects perspiration, and is slippery so that the pillow covers tend to slip off. (The same instructions should be followed for the perambulator.)
4. Allow no overstuffed furniture in the room. Furniture should be of simple wood or metal painted with the same type of paint as that used for the walls.
5. Permit no fur-bearing or feathered pets.
6. Be certain toys are wood or plastic. Fuzzy toys are undesirable.
7. Permit only currently used toys out in the open. The others should be kept in a toy chest or on enclosed shelves.
8. Buy early baby books of washable cloth. Others should be kept behind enclosed shelves or out of the room entirely.
9. If possible, have a separate dressing and bathing room. Take both your and the baby's street clothes off before entering his sleeping room.
10. Keep talcs, powders, bath oils, and soaps on enclosed shelves. These articles should be of the simplest type and preferably unscented.
11. Do not use insecticides in this room—especially highly scented or odoriferous ones.
12. Do not use pungent antimoth spays or other forms of moth killers in baby's closet.

13. Do have simple filters for the windows. If this room is heated by hot air (which is very bad), then place filters behind the hot-air gratings.

14. Keep the baby out of the room when it is being cleaned.

15. Keep the door to this room shut as much as possible, especially when the baby is out of it.

16. Avoid marked temperature drops in this room. This may be facilitated by the use of a well-placed electric heater for winter nights.

17. Do not use venetian blinds. Simple, washable window shades are preferable.

18. Maintain the humidity as evenly as possible.

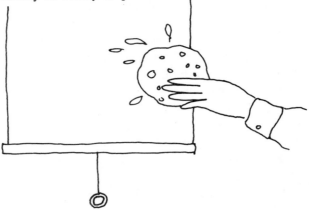

RULES FOR THE CARE OF BOOKS AND DOCUMENTS

1. Do not fold papers that are expected to endure, since the physical act of folding breaks some fibers. Store unfolded in file folders or document containers.

2. Open new books gently. Separate the pages a few at a time, and run your finger lightly down the center line.

3. Use a bookmark to mark your place in a book. Never turn down a corner of a page or lay the book open, face down, on a flat surface.

4. Remove dust accumulating on books by vacuum cleaning or by dusting with a soft brush.

5. Remember, cloth and buckram bindings require very little attention, but leather bindings should be treated with a leather dressing compound at least every two years. A suitable dressing may be prepared as follows:

> Melt two parts of lanolin in a double broiler; add three parts of neat's-foot oil; and stir the mixture until the consistency is uniform. A small quantity of cedar oil may also be added. Apply a small amount, and work into the leather with a cloth. (Lanolin may be found in most drug stores, and neat's-foot oil may be found in hardware or drug stores.)

6. Do not pack books too tightly on a shelf. They tend to stick together, and removal may cause damage to the book spines.

7. Do not pack or shelve books, such as dictionaries, with the long facing edge (fore edge) down. This puts a heavy strain on the binding and may cause a separation at the glue line.

8. Keep in mind, documents may be damaged by storing them in unbleached envelopes or in contact with newsprint or very acidic paper. Impurities can migrate from one sheet of paper to another.

9. Call in an exterminator if insects are a problem.

10. Do not store a publication fastened with staples next to bound books, as imperfectly stapled publications can easily be torn, and can also damage adjacent books.

11. Do not keep books in sunlight, strong indirect natural light, strong artifical light, high temperature or high humidity. Also, attics, basements, and other locations of extreme temperature variation.

12. Remember, air conditioning is very helpful in maintaining temperature and humidity at reasonable levels.

RULES FOR SURVIVAL DURING AN EARTHQUAKE

1. Try to stay cool and take in what's happening. An earthquake is really a marvel, unless you are standing under a tottering wall. The roaring and rolling can be very terrifying, but unless something falls on you, it probably won't hurt you. The earth does not swallow whole neighborhoods and close up again.

2. If you're indoors, stay there. Get under a heavy table or desk to protect yourself from falling debris; or move into a doorway or against inside walls. A doorframe and the structural form of the building are its strongest points, and least likely to collapse on your head. Stay away from glass; the rocking motion can shatter it.

3. If you're outside when the shaking starts, get away from buildings and electrical wires. Falling debris can kill you. Stay in the open.

4. Don't stop on or underneath a bridge or overpass if you're in a moving car. Don't stop where buildings can come crashing down on you. If in the open, pull off the road, stop the car, and stay inside until the shocks stop.

RULES FOR SURVIVING TIDAL WAVES

1. Remember, not all earthquakes cause tidal waves, or tsunamis, but many do. If you're near the ocean or tidal inlet following an earthquake be alert for tidal waves. Move inland.

2. Keep in mind, the earthquake may generate a series of higher-than-normal, fast-moving waves. Listen for tidal wave warnings, and stay out of danger areas until an "all-clear" is issued.

3. Don't ignore a warning that a tsunami is coming. The tsunami of May 1960 killed sixty-one people in Hilo, Hawaii, who thought it was "just another false alarm."

4. Don't go down to the beach to watch for a tsunami. If you are close enough to see the wave coming, you probably are too close to escape.

5. Remember, approaching tsunamis are sometimes heralded by a noticeable rise or fall of coastal water. This is nature's warning. Believe it.

6. Cooperate with your local emergency organizations during a tsunami emergency; they are trying to save your life.

7. Don't forget, sooner or later tsunamis visit every coastline in the Pacific. Warnings can apply to you if you live in any Pacific coastal area.

RULES TO FOLLOW IMMEDIATELY AFTER AN EARTHQUAKE

1. Don't forget, earth movement can break water, gas, and electrical lines. If there is a gas line into your home or building, turn off burners, including pilot lights. Don't light candles, matches, or lighters until you're sure there are no gas leaks. If you smell gas, open the windows. Leave the house or building and report the leak to the fire department. A gas leak can cause an explosion. Stay out of the building until the leak is fixed.

2. Turn on your radio or television to get official emergency information and instructions.

3. Don't use the telephone unless you have a real emergency to report. Don't tie up lines that are urgently needed for emergency operations.

4. Stay out of damaged buildings. Aftershocks can cause sudden collapse.

5. Don't go sightseeing. The area probably will be cluttered enough, and you will hamper emergency work.

RULES OF GENTLEMANLY ATTIRE—1890

1. A gentleman should never leave his room without a complete attire, as it is essential that he present the same appearance before a servant as a lady.

2. The same rule should apply when he risks encountering unknown gentlemen, or acquaintances, as it should be his desire to receive respect at the hands of both sexes.

3. The body coat should never be removed in the presence of ladies, no matter how ready they may be to approve of the act, unless it is their express and unanimous desire, in which case the better policy, in choosing between the alternative of positive rudeness and a fall of dignity, is to take the course requested.

4. An overcoat should never be worn in a private house unless the temperature is such as makes the act compulsory in order to preserve the health, and then only on receiving approval from the majority of those ladies (only) who may be present. It is immaterial if it be worn in a hotel, exceptions being made to the parlors, ballroom, dining rooms, or apartments.

5. The overcoat should be removed immediately on entering a theater or music hall if the intention is to remove it at all, as it is the height of rudeness to rise in the seat to remove it if the act cause discomfort to, or obscures the view of, parties occupying rear or adjoining seats.

6. Never add to your comfort by making your appearance displeasing to others. And under this head I would state that the pockets of either coat, vest, or trousers should never be bulged out with articles so as in any way to spoil the effect of neatness and cut of the clothing.

7. The clothes should not be allowed to wrinkle; if carefully worn, or when not in use hung smoothly on stretchers, wrinkles can be avoided.

8. The hands should never be carried awkwardly, and especially must care be taken to keep them out of the pockets; such habits mar the appearance of the gentleman.

9. Underwear may be flannel, balbriggan, or silk.

10. White is the proper color, because it is pure and clean.

11. Such colors as pink, or blue, or black may be worn.

12. Have 'the drawers fit tight, or the trousers will set ill.

13. Half hose should fit very tight.

14. They should match the shirt and drawers in material and color.

15. Half hose should be in solid colors only.

16. For morning wear and afternoon dress, white or black is the most elegant; other shades may be worn, if desired. They should match the underwear.

17. For evening dress, white or black only. White half hose with white underwear only. Black half hose with white or black underwear only.

18. Half hose supporters are made to hold up half hose. They are of white silk.

19. Other colors may be worn.

20. Underclothing should be changed at least twice a day.

21. Silk is worn always with evening dress.

22. Indulge in baths as frequently as possible.

RULES FOR BECOMING A STUDENT PILOT

1. You must get a medical certificate prior to any solo flight. You must also have a student pilot certificate. A combination medical certificate and student pilot certificate is issued by the medical examiner upon the satisfactory completion of a physical examination. Student pilot certificates may be issued by FAA inspectors or designated pilot examiners if you already possess a valid medical certificate.

2. Be aware that to qualify as a student pilot, you must be:
   a) at least sixteen years of age.
   b) able to read, speak, and understand the English language and
   c) qualify for at least a third-class medical certificate.
Operating limitations may be imposed in lieu of requirement b).

3. Your medical and student pilot certificate expires at the end of the twenty-fourth month after the month in which it was issued.

4. You cannot renew a student pilot certificate, but a new one may be issued by the medical examiner upon completion of the required examination, or by an inspector or pilot examiner if you already hold a valid medical certificate.

5. The endorsement to solo does not permit you to make solo cross-country flights. The student pilot certificate must be specifically endorsed for solo cross-country flights by the flight instructor.

6. You must carry your student pilot certificate on your person when you are piloting an aircraft in solo flight.

7. You must carry your medical certificate on your person when you are piloting an aircraft in solo flight.

8. Prior to receipt of your private pilot certificate, you are not permitted to carry passengers with you.

9. Persons operating aircraft radios must have at least a Restricted Radiotelephone Operator's Permit issued by the Federal Communications Commission.

10. To qualify for a private pilot certificate with an airplane rating, you must be at least seventeen years of age and have had at least a total of forty hours of flight instruction and solo flight time which must include the following:

    a) twenty hours of flight instruction from an authorized flight instructor, including at least:

        A. three hours of cross-country;

        B. three hours at night, including ten takeoffs and landings for applicants seeking night flying privileges; and

        C. three hours in airplanes in preparation for the private pilot flight test within sixty days prior to that test;

    b) twenty hours of solo flight time, including at least:

        A. ten hours of airplanes;

        B. ten hours of cross-country flights, each flight with a landing more than fifty nautical miles from the point of departure, and one with landings at three points, each of which is more than a hundred nautical miles from each of the other two points; and

        C. three solo takeoffs and landings to a full stop at an airport with an operating control tower.

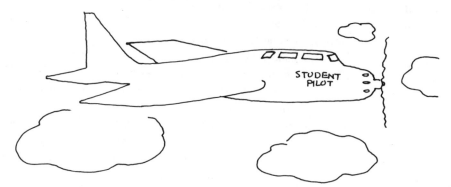

RULES TO INCREASE THE LIFE OF CAR TIRES

1. Do not drive at excessive speeds.

2. Avoid fast turns on curves and around corners.

3. Do not drive over curbs, chuckholes, other obstructions.

4. Avoid "jackrabbit" starts and "panic" stops.

5. Slow down on rough "washboard" roads.

6. Stay off the edge of the pavement.

RULES FOR SURVIVING AN AIRCRASH ON LAND

1.   Get clear of the airplane until the engines have cooled and spilled gas has evaporated.

2.   Check yourself for injuries and administer first aid. Make other injured survivors comfortable and give first aid.

3.   If weather is inclement, get all victims out of wind and rain and set up a temporary shelter. If fire is needed, start one at once.

4.   Now, relax and rest until you and others are over the shock of the crash. This will enable you to think clearly.

5.   After you have rested, organize the camp. Appoint individuals to specific duties. Pool all food and place one person in charge. Locate a water supply, and possible source of animal and plant food.

6.   If in "rugged" country, mountains, or thick forest terrain try to locate a mirror and signal upward and outward at regular intervals.

7.   If a radio on the plane is operating, try to determine your position by the best means possible and transmit it. If position is based on celestial observations, transmit this information also.

8.   Stay with the airplane and utilize it and its contents for shelter if at all possible. Do not venture forth unless you know that you are within easy walking distance of help. If you travel, leave a note giving planned route the group will take and stick to it so that rescuers can locate you.

9.   SPECIAL CONDITIONS:

        a) Snow/Cold—Stay dry and keep snow out of your clothing. Avoid snow blindness and check for frostbite. In mountain terrain, rope party together before walking and probe the snow in front of your to detect crevasses covered by thin snow.

        b) Desert/Tropics—Do not waste water. Keep head and back of neck covered and keep sweating and water loss to a minimum. Travel only at night. Protect yourself against insect bites.

SAFETY RULES FOR HUNTERS

1. Store guns unloaded, under lock and key, out of reach of children and others not qualified to handle them.

2. Lock up ammunition also, preferably separate from the guns.

3. Keep guns well cared for and inspect before use. Ammunition should also be checked for age and condition of casings. A malfunction could result in a misplaced shot and possible serious injury to yourself or to your companions.

4. Prepare yourself for the elements in the area you will cover by wearing boots and clothing that is adequately warm.

5. Wear clothing which is highly visible to avoid being mistaken for game.

6. Carry a compass, small flashlight, reliable lighter or matches in a waterproof case, strong knife, first aid kit, and a map of the area where you will be hunting. Also carry a loud whistle to summon aid if needed.

7. Let someone—a friend or relative—know where you are going and when you plan to return.

8. Remember, both law and courtesy require a hunter to ask permission to hunt on private property. The landowner can advise the location of other hunters and the whereabouts of livestock. When leaving the property, notify and thank the landowner.

9. In open field or brush, walk abreast, making sure no one gets out in front. A left-handed marksman should walk at the right end of the group because of his tendency to swing right.

10. While walking, carry the gun cradled in the arm with the muzzle pointing down in case of a fall.

11. Check the gun muzzle frequently to make certain it hasn't been accidentally plugged with mud, earth, or weeds; a plugged barrel could explode or split when fired, with disastrous results. But be careful: never look directly into the muzzle of a loaded weapon.

12. Never try to cross a fence with gun in hand. If alone, open the action or unload the gun, push it laterally under the fence, than climb through or over the fence at the butt end of the weapon.

13. When crossing a fence with a companion, one should hold the weapons while the first crosses and then pass the weapons across, muzzle up, before crossing himself.

14. Wait until your target is fully visible and a good shot is possible before pulling the trigger; an overanxious shot at movement or noise can result in a wounded animal wandering off to die a slow death, dead livestock, or, worse, a dead fellow hunter.

15. Approach downed game with caution; the animal may only be stunned. Bear, elk, and moose can kill a man, and even a deer is extremely dangerous.

16. Don't carry game over your shoulders. A pair of antlers emerging from brush or trees is a perfect target for another eager hunter. Drag the animal out, carry it on a travois, or dress it out, quarter it, and bring out the pieces.

OBSOLETE RULES FOR TREATMENT OF SNAKEBITE

Early American Treatments (Please don't try these)

1. "Catch a toad and squeeze his pee into the wound, then kill the toad and leave wound soaked with pee. This will kill the snakebite."

2. Administer alcohol,* preferably straight whiskey. A half pint of bourbon every five minutes until a quart had been taken was recommended. Strong wine with pepper was an alternative prescription. (One physician, having administered a quart of brandy and a gallon and a half of whiskey over thirty-six hours, reported seriously that his patient was seen after recovery looking for another rattlesnake to bite him.)

3. Apply a solution of potassium permanganate to the wound, or inject it into the surrounding tissue. (This was a potentially dangerous treatment, but potassium permanganate was a standard item in snakebite first aid kits until around 1930.)

4. Soak the wound in kerosene.

5. Clap the split body of a freshly killed chicken onto the bite.

6. Suck the venom from the bite by mouth. (The danger of absorbing poison through cavities or sores in the mouth was remote, but infection was often introduced in this way.)

7. Suck the venom from the wound with a "snakestone" or "madstone." Made of porous minerals, semiprecious stones, bone, horn, kidney or bladder stones, these sometimes commanded such a high price that they were bought communally.

8. Amputate the bitten limb *quickly*, before the poison had a chance to circulate through the body.

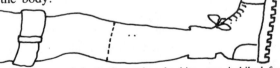

---

*Alcohol was also considered a prophylactic for rattlesnake bite—one imbibed freely to maintain immunity. Sufficient whiskey in the bloodstream was thought not only to save the man but kill the snake.

RULES FOR CORRECTLY TREATING SNAKEBITES

Modern Day Treatments (Accepted today.)

1.   Place a ligature between the bite and the rest of the body, make incisions around the bite and suck the venom from it with a mechanical device (preferably sterile).

2.   Administer correct antivenin.

3.   Administer EDTA (a chemical which reduces local tissue damage by deactivating venom enzynes), antihistamines or corticotropins and corticosteroids (cortizone).

4.   Apply ice packs or immerse wound in ice water to retard absorption of venom and inhibit enzme action.

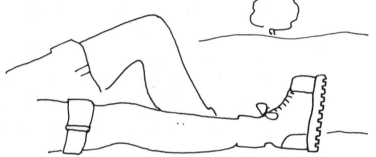

RULES FOR TRAFFIC SIGNS AND ROAD MARKINGS

1.   Diamond-shaped signs signify a warning; rectangular signs with the lower dimension vertical provide a traffic regulation.

2.   Rectangular signs with the longer dimension horizontal contain guidance information.

3.   An octagon means stop.

4.   An inverted triangle means yield.

5.   A pennant means no passing.

6.   A pentagon shows the presence of a school.

7.   A circle warns of a railroad crossing.

8.   Yellow lines on the pavement delineate the separation of traffic flow in opposing directions.

9.   The center line on two-way roadways is dashed yellow to differentiate from the dashed white lines used on multilane one-way roadways. This warns drivers who leave one-way roadways that traffic will be opposing them to the left of the yellow line.

SPECIAL RULES FOR SAFE DRIVING ON ICE AND SNOW

1. Keep a pair of sunglasses or yellow lenses in your car and use them. Snow produces a glare which can adversely affect vision. The sun, shining on the snow, makes the problem worse.
2. Follow cars in front at a safe following distance, when driving under cold-weather conditions or when the roads are slippery. Increase your following distance to allow enough room to stop, if you have to.
3. Know how and when to brake. When possible, use the braking power of the engine by downshifting to a lower gear rather than by using the brakes. When you must brake, do not jam on the brakes—tap and release them in a pumping motion. Don't brake in the middle of a curve. If your vehicle goes into a skid, take your foot off the brake.
4. Don't panic during skids. Don't oversteer. Don't jam on the brakes. Ease up on the accelerator and steer in the direction the rear of the vehicle is skidding; e.g., if the rear of the vehicle is skidding toward the right, turn the steering wheel to the right. When you are able to regain steering control you may be able to resume braking by pumping the brakes lightly.
5. Start out slowly if parked on a slippery surface to retain traction and avoid skids. If your wheels start spinning, let up on the accelerator until traction is returned.

   Before going up a hill, increase speed (within reason) to build up momentum to help you climb.

   Before going down a hill, especially a steep one, slow down by shifting into a lower gear. Don't use your brakes going down a slippery hill.
6. Use your JUDGEMENT. By observing what other vehicles are doing, it may be apparent that the hill is too slippery and dangerous. Pull over to the side as far as you can without the risk of getting stuck, and wait for a salt or sand truck.

YELLOW

RULES TO FOLLOW IN CASE OF AN AUTO ACCIDENT

1. Protect your car from further accidents by waving oncoming cars past.

2. Ask someone to call the police immediately.

3. Comfort the injured, but do not move them until a doctor, ambulance, or the police arrive.

4. If a child or adult is trapped but can easily be released, do so without tugging.

5. In case of severe bleeding apply a tourniquet at the site of the bleeding. If the blood is gushing from a deep wound, apply a pressure dressing with a folded cloth. Always keep the patient warm until medical help arrives.

6. Always use a flashing police-type light to warn off oncoming cars. Always keep one of these in your car in case of emergency.

7. Avoid the use of light flares near the car and permit no one to smoke—there may be a possibility of fire or explosion.

BICYCLE SAFETY

1. Obey all traffic regulations, signs, signals, and markings. Bikes should be driven as safely as any other road vehicle and they are subject to the same rules of vehicular traffic . . . A good rule of thumb is to avoid congested streets and use bikeways, lanes, or paths where possible.

2. Observe all local ordinances pertaining to bicycles. Registration and licensing, inspections, driving on sidewalks, etc., may all be covered by local laws.

3. Keep right: Drive with traffic, not against it. Drive single file. Keep as close to the curb as possible. When driving two abreast, a minor swerve could force you into traffic.

4. Watch for drain grates, soft shoulders, and other surface hazards. Be careful of loose sand or gravel . . . watch out for potholes.

5. Watch for car doors opening or for cars pulling into traffic.

6. Use hand signals. Let the motorist know what you plan by giving the appropriate hand signals for turning left or right or for stopping.

7. Protect yourself at night with required red reflectors and lights. State laws vary. Check the ones applying to you. Use maximum night protection.

8. Drive your bike defensively. Observe the car in front of you and the one in front of him. Leave yourself room and time to take defensive action.

9. Drive a safe bike. Have it inspected to insure good mechanical condition. Make sure your bike fits you. Have checked regularly brakes, pedals, lights, reflectors, shifting mechanisms, sounding devices, tires, spokes, saddle, handlebars, and all nuts and bolts.

10. Be extremely careful at intersections, especially when making a left turn. Most accidents happen at intersections. If traffic is heavy, get off and walk your bike with pedestrian traffic.

RULES FOR SURVIVING WINTER STORMS

1. Listen to and heed the latest Weather Service warnings and bulletins on radio and television.

2. Check battery-powered equipment, emergency cooking facilities, and flashlights before the storm arrives so you won't be without heat or light.

3. Check your supply of heating fuel, because fuel carriers may not be able to move if the storm buries your area in snow.

4. Stock an extra food supply. Include food that needs no cooking or cooling in case of power failure. The food in your freezer and refrigerator is safe from spoilage for a minimum of two days if you don't open your refrigerator or freezer at all.

5. Prevent fire hazards by preventing your stove, heater, or furnace from overheating. Don't leave a fireplace unattended.

6. Stay indoors during cold snaps and storms unless you are in top physical condition. If you must go out, don't overexert. Particularly, don't kill yourself shoveling snow. If you're out of shape, it can bring on a heart attack, a common cause of death during and after winter storms.

7. If outdoors, dress in loose-fitting, lightweight, warm clothes in several layers, because you can remove layers to prevent perspiring and subsequent chill, and layers trap warm air close to your body.

8. Get your family's car winterized before the storm season. Keep water out of the fuel by keeping the tank filled.

RULES TO FOLLOW IF YOU'RE TRAPPED IN A BLIZZARD

1. Avoid overexertion and exposure. Strenuous acts like pushing your car, shoveling snow, and so on can cause a heart attack in extreme weather conditions.

2. Stay in your car. Disorientation happens fast in blowing snow, and you are sheltered and more likely to be found in your car.

3. Don't panic.

4. Keep fresh air in your car. Freezing wet and wind-driven snow can seal the passenger compartment and suffocate you. Keep the *downwind* window open, when you run the motor and the heater.

5. To avoid freezing, exercise by clapping hands and moving arms and legs vigorously from time to time. Don't stay long in one position.

6. Turn on dome light at night to make the car visible.

7. Keep watch. Don't allow all the people in the car to sleep at once, or all of you may freeze to death.

FIRST AID RULES FOR FRACTURES AND DISLOCATIONS

1. If fracture is suspected, immobilize.

2. "Splint them where they lie."

3. Handle as gently as possible. This work should be done in pairs, one person to immobolize the limb and one to apply the splint.

4. Place a fracture in as near normal position as possible by applying slight traction. Traction is applied by grasping the affected limb gently but firmly, with one hand above and below the location of the fracture, and pulling the limb between your hands. This is maintained until the splint is secured in place. *Caution*: Never try to straighten if a joint of spine is involved.

5. Immobilize dislocated joints in the position they are found; do not attempt to reduce or straighten any dislocations.

6. Follow these rules for splints:

    a) They should be long enough to support joints above and below fracture or dislocation.

    b) They should be rigid enough to support the fracture or dislocation.

    c) Improvised splint should be padded enough to insure even contact and pressure between the limb and the splint and to protect all bony prominences.

    d) Splints are of these types: air splint, padded boards, rolled blankets, tools, newspapers, magazines.

7. To apply improvised splint:

    a) Apply slight traction to the affected limb.

    b) A second person (if available) should place the padded splint under, above, or alongside the limb.

    c) Tie the limb and splint together with bandaging materials so the two are held firmly together. Make sure the bandaging material is not so tight that it impairs circulation. Leave fingers and toes exposed, if they are not involved, so that circulation can be checked constantly.

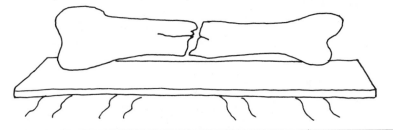

RULES FOR PREVENTING HOME BREAK-INS

1. Notify your local police when you will be away from home for extended periods of time.

2. Stop deliveries of newspapers, milk, etc., or have a reliable neighbor pick up these items for you.

3. Do not chat idly with strangers about your plans for leaving home for a vacation or a visit.

4. Be sure to close and lock all windows to protect your home from burglary.

5. Double-lock the doors.

6. Notify the post office to hold your mail, or ask a neighbor to to get it for you.

7. Give the appearance that someone is home by arranging for someone to mow your lawn in the summer, and shovel snow from your drive in the winter.

8. Put an automatic timer on one or two lamps to give your home or apartment a "lived-in" look. Set the timers to go on and off according to your usual schedule.

RULES OF BORROWING AND LENDING

If you borrow:
1.   Return the item in good condition at whatever time you promised to return it (right away, Sunday, in a week, whenever).
2.   If you've harmed it, replace it or have it repaired (first telling the owner you're going to, since she might want a particular shop to fix it).
3.   If you've lost the borrowed item—gloves you needed for a play—buy your friend a new pair that's as much like the old as possible (but don't give her money instead).
4.   Try not to borrow fragile, expensive, or irreplaceable items. If your friend shows the slightest hesitation, quickly and firmly stop the transaction.

If you lend:
1.   Don't lend anything you'd be shattered to have damaged or lost.
2.   Try to laugh off the damage or loss of anything you do lend.
3.   Refuse chronic borrowers.
4.   Pursue the nonreturning borrower doggedly but politely until that which was loaned is returned (but don't discuss the matter with others).
5.   Be sure you're not pressing loans on others to bolster your own self-esteem. Sometimes excessive lending or offering to do favors is a thinly disguised way of showing off or trying to gain friendship.

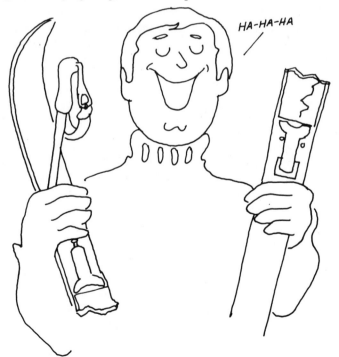

RULES FOR KEEPING FOODS IN YOUR REFRIGERATOR/FREEZER

1. Wrap fresh meat loosely, just enough to allow air to circulate but not enough to let the product dry out.
2. The rule is reversed for leftovers: they should be tightly covered.
3. Do not wrap raw poultry. Place it on a dish, and cover. Giblets must be wrapped and stored separately. Also, stuffing must never remain in meat and poultry; warm dark cavities are ideal areas for growth of dangerous toxins.
4. Close or cover all containers.
5. Cover leftover yolks with cold water and refrigerate with a cover. (They should be used within two to four days.) Whites don't need the water.
6. Wrap all items tightly in moisture-resistant materials, such as freezer paper or foil for freezing.
7. Remember, where you put the food is important for three reasons: a) Some should be kept colder than others; (b) Food placement affects air circulation and efficiency of the refrigerator; (c) Foods that should be used quickly need to be in full view so they're not easily forgotten.
8. Remember, the coldest part of the refrigerator is the area nearest the freezing compartment. Milk, meats, and most leftovers should be in that area.
9. Do not stack foods. Refrigerator shelves should never be covered with foil or any material that keeps down air circulation.
10. Hold produce in the lower compartments to prevent crystallization.
11. Arrange food, both in the freezer and the refrigerator, so that the oldest is used first. This is important for safety as well as flavor and nutrition.

RULES FOR EATING CERTAIN FOODS

1. You may always eat these foods with your fingers: salted nuts, radishes, raw vegetables served as a relish, celery, and olives.
2. You may eat certain foods with your fingers under certain conditions. For example, pickles are eaten with the fingers at a picnic, and with a fork at the table.
3. Break open baked potatoes with your fingers and the fork. French fried potatoes are eaten with a fork.
4. Eat chicken, chops, and bacon with the fingers at a picnic, and with a knife and fork at the table. At the table, as much meat as possible should be cut from the bone; but the meat should never be eaten directly from the bone. It is very unappetizing to see people holding food in their fingers while at the table.
5. Eat corn-on-the-cob by breaking the ear in half. It is held in one hand and

only as much as can be eaten in two or three bites is buttered and salted at a time.

6. Break off celery with the fingers rather than bite off portions from a very long stalk.

7. Peel banana skin down a little at a time and break off the banana with the fingers or fork.

8. Cut sandwich by holding the knife in your right hand and steadying the sandwich with the fingers of the left hand. Triple-decker sandwiches and moist sandwiches may be broken in half with the fingers and eaten that way.

9. Never squeeze a grapefruit at the table to get more juice from it.

10. Eat oysters whole with an oyster fork; never cut in half.

11. Crack a lobster well before serving. The meat is eaten with a fork; the claws with the fingers.

12. Eat lettuce and salads of all kinds with a knife and fork. There is no reason why the knife should not be used to cut lettuce, rather than the fork, which may cause it to jump off the plate. As a silver knife stains, it should not be used with a vinegar salad dressing.

13. Eat stewed prunes. peaches, and plums with a spoon, which should be used first to remove the pit from the fruit while it is still in the plate.

14. Place pits from grapes, cherries, and alives in the fingers after leaving the lips, and put on the plate.

15. If a pit or a fish or poultry bone is found in the mouth, it should be removed with the fingers. Never hide behind your napkin, as it is permissible to remove such particles quickly and naturally.

16. Learn to eat as many different foods as possible so that you will know how all foods taste. It shows consideration to a hostess to be able to eat whatever may be served. It is not polite to criticize the food.

RULES FOR MAKING COFFEE AND TEA

Coffee
1. Know the most important thing in coffeemaking is the cleanliness of the pot. It should be scrubbed well after each use and washed with soap and water.
2. Follow the recommended proportions for making coffee: ¾ cup water to 1 coffee measure. This proportion applies whether the pot is drip, percolator, filter, or whatever. If on the other hand you find that the coffee thus produced is too weak for your taste, then by all means increase the quantity of coffee; or if it too strong, then reduce the quantity.
3. When the coffee is drunk, empty the pot, pour out the grinds, and wash the pot well. The grinds, incidentally, may in almost all circumstances be put down the drain of the kitchen sink. They will not clog it.

Tea
1. Be aware, absolute cleanliness is not as essential in a teapot as it is in a coffeepot but the teapot, nonetheless, should be washed frequently and thoroughly after one or two uses.
2. Remember, the essential thing in making tea is that the water be brought to a furious boil. Purists will heat the teapot first by pouring some of the boiling water into the pot, letting it stand briefly before emptying. This is unnecessary for all practical purposes. Simply put 1 teaspoon of tea into a teapot and pour in a cup of the boiling water.
3. When you discard used tea leaves, empty them onto paper toweling or waxed paper, which may then be rolled into a ball for discarding.

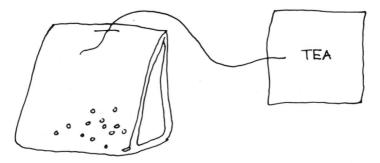

RULES FOR SELECTING AND KEEPING WINE

1. Serve chilled Champagne, Dubonnet, Sherry (dry), or Vermouth with an appetizer or alone.
2. With soup, serve chilled Sherry or Vermouth.

228

3. If you serve eggs, a Chablis (white Burgundy), kept in the cellar or chilled, is recommended.

4. For light main course dishes a cellar-stored or chilled Graves (white Bordeaux) is proper.

5. Serve chilled Moselle with fowl.

6. With seafood, chilled Rhine Wines, dry Sauterne, or other white table wines are acceptable.

7. Serve a Burgundy from the cellar with all cheese dishes.

8. For wild game, including dark fowl meat, Chianti from the cellar or stored at room temperature is suggested.

9. Serve Claret (Red Bordeaux) at room temperature, with main courses.

10. When serving meat and pasta (spaghetti) any red table wine is adequate.

11. For desserts, select chilled Champagne if the dish is not overly sweet. A chilled Haut (Sweet) Sauterne or Sparkling Burgundy are quite complimentary or Tokay, Port, and Muscatel (all served at room temperature).

12. Serve Port, at room temperature, when offering a selection of nuts.

13. Alone, at the end of nice meal, serve cellar-stored or chilled Sherry Sparkling Wine . . . any sweet dessert wine.

RULES FOR UNDERSTANDING ROMAN NUMERALS

1. Learn the seven basic symbols: I=1, V=5, X=10, L=50, C=100, D=500, M=1,000.

2. If a letter is repeated it indicates a doubled value. Example: CC=200.

3. When a letter follows one of greater value, it adds to it. Example: XII=12.

4. If a letter precedes one of greater value, it is then subtracted from it. Example: IX=9.

5. When a dash appears over a letter, it multiplies that number by 1,000. Example: $\bar{X}$=10,000.

I	1	XI	11	XXX	30	CD	400
II	2	XII	12	XL	40	D	500
III	3	XIII	13	L	50	DC	600
IV or IIII	4	XIV	14	LX	60	DCC	700
V	5	XV	15	LXX	70	DCCC	800
VI	6	XVI	16	LXXX	80	CM	900
VII	7	XVII	17	XC	90	M	1,000
VIII	8	XVIII	18	C	100	$\bar{V}$	5,000
IX	9	XIX	19	CC	200	$\bar{X}$	10,000
X	10	XX	20	CCC	300	$\bar{M}$	1,000,000

The year 1979 would be written MCMLXXIX.

RULES FOR DRINKING THIN

1. Prefer 80-proof liquor to 86-, 90-, or 100-proof. It's cheaper and lower in calories.

2. Remember this rule when drinking whiskey, vodka, gin, and most other distilled spirits: Each ounce of liquor contains one calorie for every degree of proof. If you're drinking 80-proof vodka, you're getting 80 calories per ounce; if you're drinking 100-proof vodka, you're getting 100 calories per ounce.

3. Prefer dry manhattans to sweet manhattans; prefer dry martinis to regular martinis, and vodka martinis to gin martinis.

4. Always order cocktails "on the rocks." They'll stay cold longer, and as the ice melts the alcohol will be diluted—you'll get just as relaxed, but you'll spend more time on the drink, and will be less tempted to have a second (or third).

5. Prefer highballs to cocktails. The mixes—wine, sugar, juice, cream, whatever—add more calories than ever . . . and besides, a highball takes longer to drink.

6. Highballs should be mixed with water, soda, or a low-calorie soft drink. (You can make your own low-calorie "tonic" water by adding 2 teaspoons lemon juice to 6 ounces of club soda.)

7. Avoid the exotic but extraneous garnishes many bartenders (including home bartenders) add to cocktails: maraschino cherries, olives, etc. If you must have something decorative with your drink, use a lemon peel or a cocktail onion.

8. When "trading" calories, ask yourself this: "Am I getting the best deal in this trade?" If you're giving up the calories in a steak or salad for the calories in a martini, you're cheating yourself and endangering your health. If you're trading the calories in a roll, a potato, or a rich dessert, you're all right—providing you eat that steak and salad.

9. When ordering your drink (or making it at home) be sure that dinner is under way. Too many careless drinkers blame lazy waiters or forgetful wives or thoughtless hostesses for that second, or third, or fourth drink. If you're dining at a friend's house, there's not much you can do about hurrying up the dinner except: (a) Ask for more ice or more water and drink more slowly; and (b) If your friend has the habit of a prolonged cocktail hour, plan to arrive late—very

230

late, if necessary. Your're being no more rude than your host. There is nothing polite about forcing guests to sit through two or three hours of drinking before serving them dinner.

10. Keep in mind, it is both pleasant and wise to have snacks while you are enjoying the cocktail hour. They keep you from attacking the dinner like a starving refugee, and they counter the hazardous effects of alcohol on an empty or nearly empty stomach. But often too many of these snacks—pretzels, potato chips, crackers, creamy dips—are your enemies, high in calories, low in nutrients. There's not much you can do about this when you're at the home of a friend. But when entertaining yourself you can serve a good many tasty and applause-winning canapes and appetizers that will keep the hunger pangs down without keeping your weight up.

RULES FOR FALLING ASLEEP

1. Get plenty of exercise! If you are capable of exercise, it should be several hours or more before bedtime and should produce a mild degree of physical exhaustion. The preference is tennis rather than golf. If you are very competitive and ruminate over your play, try jogging.

2. Have large meals a number of hours before going to bed. Most people are uncomfortable after having a large meal and should expect to have some difficulty falling asleep, particularly if the meal is in any way disagreeable (onions, garlic, etc.) to them.

3. Do something routine in the hour before bed; read a dull book or watch a dull television program.

4. Don't bring business into your bedroom.

5. Once in bed, finding yourself not able to fall asleep, don't stay in bed, get up, fully out of bed, and go to a chair and read—something dull; watch a nighttime talk show.

6. Don't sleep in a warm room. If the climate is dry, try to have a humidifier going so that your throat doesn't become dry; this is aggravating and makes it difficult to sleep.

7. Try to screen out extraneous noise if at all possible.

8. Alter your life so that the strains are minimized and ask yourself what are you driving yourself for. Many people, however, will argue that the gains of meeting a goal are worth the toll taken out on their body.

9. Finally, avoid stimulants such as coffee and tea in the evening hours.

RULES FOR RECEIVING CALLERS IN YOUR OFFICE

1. When more than one visitor is expected, be sure there are enough comfortable chairs in your office before they arrive. Scrambling about for additional chairs while your guests stand and wait is time-consuming and disconcerting.

2. Smoking has become one of those irksome problems that are producing a new crop of vocal disapprovers. Even if you are a nonsmoker, clean ashtrays should be available for the guests who smoke.

3. If you are a shirt-sleeve worker, it is polite to put on your jacket, whether your caller is a man or a woman. There are some diehard organizations, especially in the eastern metropolitan areas, where it is de rigueur for executives to wear jackets under all circumstances and under all conditions.

Even with the advent of air conditioning, more and more companies are tolerating jacketless executives. As with the use of first names, the rule of thumb is: large corporations are more formal than smaller companies. Geography also dictates the style an executive should pursue. In the Midwest, Southwest (Texas in particular), and on the West Coast, etiquette in general is more informal, and this is carried over into the business environment.

Any young executive who has maverick compulsions will have to postpone them until such time as he is in a position to name the rules. For the time being he has to conform to top management's whims and fancies and, in any case, should always don the jacket when callers come.

4. Circumstances beyond your control are the only valid excuse for keeping a guest, who has a definite appointment with you, cooling his impatience in the reception room until you get ready to see him. If you know you will be late, the ideal thing, of course, is to notify him in advance and arrange the appointment for a later hour. If this is not possible, and if there is no way of avoiding the delay, make sure your caller is notified the moment he arrives that you will be late and that you extend your apologies, and hope he doesn't mind waiting for you. Wasting the time of any businessman is equivalent to robbing his wallet. Keeping him waiting is bad business practice and bad manners.

5. If you cannot make your apologies in person, your secretary should explain the circumstances, and ask him if he would mind waiting. The secretary might usher him into your private office, take his coat and hat, see that he is seated and is comfortable. He might be asked if he would like a magazine to read, or coffee or tea, or a soft drink while he is waiting for you.

This is routine in many organizations. In some of the larger corporations, especially in the new high-rise buildings, automatic vending machines are located on each floor with refreshments for employees as well as for visitors.

Secretaries are known to keep a till of petty-cash coins to feed the machines. It is not unlikely that during a meeting in the boss's office a request will be made for refreshments, and an efficient secretary is prepared to oblige.

6. When the receptionist telephones you that your caller has arrived, the polite gesture is to have your secretary go to the reception room and escort the visitor to your office. If he is important and requires VIP treatment, you might go to the reception room yourself.

7. Your secretary should be on hand in your office to accept the visitor's hat and coat, especially if there is more than one visitor. Many companies have special compartments to hang visitors' coats. A cluttered, untidy office is a distraction and not always conducive to relaxed discussions.

8. When a visitor enters your office, you are the host and you naturally stand up. A firm handshake is a warm greeting of welcome, whether the caller is a male or female. In Emily Post's day it was considered courteous for the man to wait for the woman to extend her hand first; you will make her feel she belongs without offending her feminity by offering your hand first.

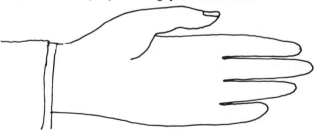

9. One of the least endearing traits is to accept telephone calls when you have visitors in your office, even if there is only one visitor and his rank is of no particular consequence. No person is comfortable sitting in your office professing indifference while you are carrying on a telephone conversation that is of no concern to him. Courtesy is an extension of one's character. Good breeding and consideration of others know no distinctions, and courtesy should, therefore, be a natural unforced outgrowth of an innate sense of decency.

While you are in conference, your secretary, of course, will take messages. If a call comes through which is important and requires your immediate attention, you might be buzzed twice.

Before you answer the telephone, you might take a moment to apologize to your visitor, explaining that this call is important and that otherwise your secretary would not ring you.

10. Your visitor may turn out to be a long-winded, nonstop talker. The pressure of many urgencies you still have to attend to may be building up. Your nerves may become taut and your temper severely tried. You can dispose of him with tact.

> a) If you have a prearranged signal system, you might unobtrusively, signal your secretary who can enter and say, "I'm sorry to interrupt you, but you'll be late for your meeting," or words to that effect.
> b) A quicker and surer method is to stand up, telling your visitor how interesting and valuable you find your discussion and how much you wish you could continue it, but you are sorry, you have another appointment.

11. When you rise to say good-bye, a warm handshake and a pleasant smile will send your visitor on his way with the best possible impression of you and, of course, of your company. If he is a customer, or important to the company, you might escort him out of your office.

RULES OF GOOD PRACTICE FOR FUNERAL DIRECTORS

1. Make available in advance of need full information about funeral prices and services.

2. Provide a continuing opportunity to all persons to make funeral arrangements in advance of need.

3. Offer funeral services in as wide a range of price categories as possible so that any person may select a funeral service which is within his means.

4. Be prepared to furnish, as represented, any and all services and goods which have been advertised.

5. Maintain an establishment, including a suitable selection of caskets and other merchandise, equipment, facilitiesm and trained personnel, fully capable of providing services and goods offered.

6. Respect all religious faiths, creeds, and customs.

7. Provide dignity and competence in the conduct of all services.

8. Treat with reverence and respect decedents entrusted to our care.

9. Assure each purchaser complete freedom to excercise his preference in selecting a funeral service within his means.

10. Plainly mark the prices charged for all funeral services offered; disclose affirmatively and in a conspicuous manner the caskets, services, and facilities comprising the funeral services so offered and withhold from no one the privilege of inspecting and freely considering each of them.

11. Furnish to every purchaser at the time of purchase a memorandum or other document which contains an accurate accounting of all charges, including all merchandise, services, and facilities listed in the offered price, and to charge for no further or additional items of expense except with the express authorization of the purchaser.

12. Charge nondiscriminatory prices to all purchasers.

13. Avoid any representation, written or oral, which may be false or misleading.

14. In case of hardship, accept as a community responsibility the obligation of providing a funeral service within the financial means of the family, however limited.

RULES FOR DAILY NUTRITIONAL REQUIREMENTS

1. Choose four or more servings every day from the *Vegetable-Fruit* group. This group includes all vegetables and fruit.

2. Remember, good sources of vitamin C are: grapefruit or grapefruit juice, orange or orange juice, cantaloupe, guava, mango, papaya, raw strawberries, broccoli, brussels sprouts, green pepper, sweet red pepper.

3. Remember, fair sources of Vitamin C are: honeydew melon, lemon, tangerine or tangerine juice, watermelon, asparagus tips, raw cabbage, cauliflower, collards, garden cress, kale, kohlrabi, mustard greens, potatoes and sweet potatoes cooked in the jacket, rutabagas, spinach, tomatoes or tomato juice, turnip greens.

4. Be aware, sources of Vitamin A include dark-green and deep-yellow vegetables and a few fruits, namely: apricots, broccoli, cantaloupe, carrots, chard, collards, cress, kale, mangoes, persimmons, pumpkins, spinach, sweet potatoes, turnip greens and other dark-green leaves, winter squash.

5. Remember, fruits and vegetables are valuable chiefly because of the vitamins and minerals they contain. Vitamin C is needed for healthy gums and body tissues. Vitamin A is needed for growth, normal vision, and healthy condition of skin and other body surfaces.

6. Include in your four or more servings; one serving of a good source of vitamin C or two servings of a fair source, and one serving, at least every other day, of a good source of vitamin A. If the food chosen for vitamin C is also a good source of vitamin A, the additional serving of a vitamin A food may be omitted.

The remaining one to three or more servings may be of any vegetable or fruit, including those that are valuable for vitamin C and vitamin A.

7. Remember, foods from the *Milk* group include:

Milk . . . fluid whole, evaporated, skim, dry, buttermilk.
Cheese . . . cottage, cream, cheddar-type—natural or processed.
Ice cream.

8. Consider, milk is our leading source of calcium, needed for bones and teeth. It also provides high quality protein, riboflavin, vitamin A (if milk is whole or fortified), and other nutrients.

9. Keep in mind, some milk every day is recommended for everyone. Recommended amounts are given below in terms of whole fluid milk:

	8-OUNCE CUPS
Children under nine	2 to 3
Children nine to twelve	3 or more
Teenagers	4 or more
Adults	2 or more
Pregnant women	3 or more
Nursing mothers	4 or more

Part or all of the milk may be fluid skim milk, buttermilk, evaporated milk, or dry milk. Cheese and ice cream may replace part of the milk.

RULES ON HOW TO AVOID UNNECESSARY SURGERY

1. Don't go directly to a surgeon for medical treatment. If at all possible start out by going to a general practitioner or internist. Go to your regular family doctor—a general practitioner or internist—for any initial diagnosis or treatment.

2. Make sure any surgeon that is to perform surgery on you is Board certified. This means his competency as a surgeon has been certified by one of the American Specialty Boards, after a vigorous oral, written, and clinical examination.

3. Make sure the surgeon you are to use is a Fellow of the American College

of Surgeons (F.A.C.S.). There are about twenty-five thousand surgeons who are designated Fellows. The American College of Surgeons has membership qualifications that keep out the less-competent surgeons, and the College also stresses programs of continuing education.

This is not an infallible rule, of course, but it is one that is well worth applying in selecting any surgeon.

The equivalent organization for Osteopaths is the American College of Osteopathic Surgeons located at 1550 South Dixie Highway, Suite 216, Coral Cables, Florida 33146.

4. Consider getting an independent consultation or opinion before subjecting yourself to surgery, even if your family doctor and surgeon agree that surgery is necessary.

Consultations, according to some studies, reduce operations by as much as 20 to 60 percent. You may be in that 20 to 60 percent. And you have a right to seek consultation.

5. Make sure any surgery is performed in an accredited hospital and, if possible, select a hospital that gives staff privileges (i.e., the right to practice in the hospital) to both your doctor and surgeon. The Joint Commission on Accreditation of Hospitals (J.C.A.H.) certifies that institutions it accredits meet certain minimum requirements designed to assure quality patient care.

Osteopathic hospitals may be accredited by their own group—the American Osteopathic Association—or by the J.C.A.H.

Another method of assuring quality hospital and surgical care is to make sure the hospital you go to is affiliated with a medical school, and your doctor and surgeon are on the staff of that hospital. Medical school hospitals and their affiliates have a reputation for excellence, and for keeping their medical staffs on the ball.

6. Don't push a doctor to perform surgery on you. If you insist on surgery, even if it is unnecessary, you are likely to find a surgeon willing to perform it. There are "overtreaters" who are willing to perform unnecessary surgery, so don't ask for trouble.

7. Make sure your doctor and surgeon explain both the alternatives to surgery and the possible benefits and complications of surgery.

Any doctor or surgeon should do so and you'll be able to make a more intelligent decision on surgery when you have the facts. As a matter of fact, a doctor who fails to disclose the risks of surgery may open himself up to a malpractice suit. Under the legal doctrine of informed consent, a patient who has not been fairly advised about the risks of surgery has not legally consented to it. He may, therefore, sue any doctor for malpractice who operates on him without fairly disclosing the risks incurred.

8. Frankly discuss the fee for surgery with your doctor. You should know what the surgery is going to cost. Futhermore, most surgeons prefer that the patient understand the cost of surgery in advance. So, forget all about the mistaken notion that it's somewhat improper to inquire about the cost of surgery.

Any surgeon worth his scalpel will gladly discuss fees. If he is not willing to do so, then he doesn't know much about his obligation to the patient and the patient's right to know. Under Phase II of the Federal Wage Price Stabilization Program, every doctor must post a notice that a record of all his fees is available on demand.

9. Check out the surgeon with those who know him or have used him. This includes other patients as well as associates of the surgeon.

You might want to check on his background in the Directory of Medical Specialists. What school did he go to? Where did he take his residence? How long has he practiced, etc.?

One good way to find the best surgeon is to find out who doctors see when they need surgery for themselves or their families. The greatest compliment to a surgeon is when his is used by a doctor or his family.

10. Make sure the surgeon knows and is willing to work with your general practitioner or internist. To assume complete, continuous, and quality care, close contact between the surgeon and your doctor is vital.

If they can't work as a team, you may be the loser.

11. Consider a surgeon who is part of a group practice and preferably a group that includes internists, surgeons, and other specialists. This involves doctors who work together on all their cases, and freely consult and communicate with each other. With a general practice, you are more likely to have a doctor available at all times who is familiar with your case and you have the built-in benefits of consultation.

Some patients are critical of group practice, however, if they get a feeling that they are being passed from one doctor to another.

12. Select a surgeon who is not too busy to give patients enough time and attention. Surgeons who handle too many cases are bad news for the patient for obvious reasons.

The best surgeons are likely to be busy. But the "best" surgeon who must rush through an operation and must hurry past his patients is not likely to get good results.

13. Be especially on guard if some of the operations that are most often unnecessarily performed are proposed to you. These include hysterectomies, hemorrhoidectomies, and tonsillectomies. These operations have been referred to as "remunerectomies" by some cynics (a fancy Greek derivative from the word "remuneration").

14. Listen to the experts. But remember, it's still your decision. You're entitled to have the facts you need and you're entitled to decide whether or not to go ahead with the surgery. The patient, not the doctor or the surgeon, is supposed to and is entitled to make the decision on whether to have surgery.

RULES FOR CLASSIFYING PEOPLE BY OBSERVING THEIR HANDS

First Impressions

1. People with large hands are fond of details and people with small hands are only interested in the big design of life, business, etc.

2. Soft hands are ruled by imagination and belong to the class of artists, while men with hard hands are practical workers.

3. A thin hand shows timidity, meanness, and poverty of intellect. A thick hand belongs to the laborer.

4. A very hollow hand indicates a financial failure.

5. Cold hands indicate a reserved and unemotional nature. Warm hands show vivacity and personal magnetism.

6. A medium-sized hand shows coolness in emergency.

7. A dead-white hand shows lack of ardor. A pink hand indicates a gentle and sympathetic spirit. Red hands show ardor and intensity.

8. A wet hand shows warm-bloodedness and vivacity of spirit. A dry hand indicates lack of spirit and enthusiasm.

A Closer Study

1. When a person keeps his hands as closed as possible, he has a dark side to his character.

2. When the hand hangs down naturally but the fingers are partially closed, the person is cautious but trustworthy.

3. When the fists are firmly closed, it indicates a bully.

4. A person who carries his hands awkwardly up and down betrays an uncertainty of purpose.

5. A person who waves his hands purposefully betrays caution and watchfulness.

6. Toying with hanky, watch, button, etc., betrays a temporary excitement.

7. Hands clasped in front show a calm and quiet temperament.

8. Rubbing hands together shows an untruthful and hypocritical temperament.

9. Hands clasped behind show extreme caution.

VICTORIAN RULES OF HYGIENE

1.   The first step which should be taken for the prevention of disease is to make provision for the health of the unborn child. Greater care should be exercised with women who are in a way to become mothers. Those who are surrounded by all the luxuries which health can bestow indulge too much in rich food, and take too little exercise; while the poor get too little nourishment, and work too hard and too long. A woman in this condition should avoid overexertion, and all scenes which excite the passions or powerful emotions. She should take moderate exercise in the open air; eat moderately of wholesome food, and of meat not oftener than twice a day; take tea or coffee in limited quantities, and avoid the use of all alcoholic liquors; she should go to bed early and take not less than nine hours' sleep; her clothing should be loose, light in weight, and warm. She should take every precaution against exposure to contagious or infectious diseases.

2.   There is no better method for preventing the spread of contagious diseases than perfect isolation of the infected, and thorough disinfection of all articles of clothing or bedding which have been in contact with the infected. Many persons erroneously believe that every child must necessarily have the measles, and other contagious diseases, and they, therefore, take no precautions against the exposure of their children. The liability to infection diminishes as age advances, and those individuals are, as a rule, the strongest and best developed who have never suffered from any of the contagious diseases. Although vaccination is the great safeguard against pox, yet it should never prevent the immediate isolation of those who are suffering from this disease.

3.   To avoid the injurious effects of impure air, the following rules should be carefully observed. The admission of air which contains anything that emits an unpleasant odor into closed rooms should be avoided. The temperature of every apartment should be kept as near 70° Fahrenheit as possible, and the air should not be overcharged with watery vapor. Provisions should be made for the free admission into and escape of air from the room at all times. When an apartment is not in use, it should be thoroughly ventilated by opening the windows. Those who are compelled to remain in an atmosphere filled with dust should wear a cotton-wool respirator.

4.   To insure a healthy condition of the body, the diet of man ought to be varied, and all excesses should be avoided. The total amount of solid food taken in the twenty-four hours should not exceed two and a half pounds, and not more than one third of this quantity should consist of animal food. Many persons do not require more than one pound and a half of mixed food. To avoid parasitic diseases, meat should not be eaten rare, especially pork. The amount of drink taken should not be more than three pints in the twenty-four hours. The

excessive use of tea and coffee should be avoided. Pickles, boiled cabbage, and other indigestible articles should never be eaten.

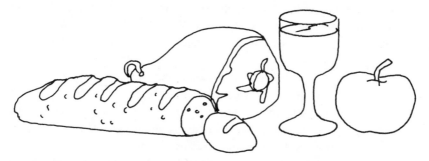

5. To avoid the evil effects of alcoholic liquors, perfect abstinence is the only safe course to pursue. Although one may use spirituous liquors in moderation for a long period of time and, possibly, remain healthy, yet such an indulgence is unnecessary and exceedingly dangerous. A person who abstains entirely from their use is safe from their pernicious influence; a person who indulges ever so moderately is in danger; a person who relies on such stimulants for support in the hour of need is lost.

6. While the use of tobacco is less pernicious than alcohol in its effects, yet it exerts a profound disturbing influence upon the nervous system, and gives rise to various functional and organic diseases. This is the verdict of those who have given the subject the most study, and who have had the best opportunities for extensive observation. Suddenly fatal results have followed excesses in the use of tobacco. Therefore, the habit should be avoided, or if already acquired, it should be immediately abandoned.

7. The clothing should be light and porous, adapted in warmth to the season. It is especially important that persons in advanced life should be well protected against vicissitudes of heat and colds. Exposure is the cause of almost all those inflammatory diseases which occur during winter, and take off the feeble and the aged. The undergarments should be kept scrupulously clean by frequent changes. Corsets of bands which impede the flow of blood, compress the organs of the chest or abdomen, or restrict the movements of the body, are very injurious, and should not be worn. Articles of dress which are colored with irritating dyestuffs should be carefully avoided.

8. It matters not how varied a person's vocation may be, change, recreation, and rest are required. It is an error to suppose that more work can be done by omitting these. No single occupation which requires special mental or physical work should be followed for more than eight hours out of the twenty-four. The physical organism is not constructed to run its full cycle of years and labor under a heavier burden than this. Physical and mental exercise is conducive to health and longevity, if not carried too far. It is erroneous to suppose that excessive physical exertion promotes health. Man was never intended to be a running or a jumping machine. In mental work, variety should be introduced. New work calls into play fresh portions of the brain, and secures repose for those parts which have become exhausted. Idleness should be avoided by all. Men should never retire from business as long as they enjoy a fair degree of health. Idleness and inactivity are opposed to nature.

9. The average length of time which a person ought to sleep is eight hours out of twenty-four, and, as a rule, those who take this amount enjoy the best health. The most favorable time for sleep is between the hours of 10 P.M. and 6 A.M. All excitement, the use of stimulants, and excessive fatigue tend to prevent sleep. Sleeping rooms should be well ventilated, and the air maintained at an equable temperature of as near 60° Fahrenheit as possible. An inability to sleep at the proper time, or a regular inclination to sleep at other than the natural hours for it, is a certain indication of errors of habit, or of nervous derangement.

10. Prominent among all other measures for the maintenance of health is personal cleanliness. Activity in the functions of the skin is essential to perfect health, and this can only be secured by thoroughly bathing the entire body. Strictly, a person should bathe once every twenty-four or forty-eight hours. The body should be habituated to contact with cold water at all seasons of the year, so that warm water may not become a necessity. The simplest and most convenient bath is the ordinary sponge bath. An occasional hot-air or Turkish bath exerts a very beneficial influence. It cleans out the pores of the skin and increases its activity.

11. The emotions and the passions exert a powerful influence over the physical organism. It is important, therefore, that they be held under restraint by the reasoning faculties. This rule applies equally to joy, fear, and grief; to avarice, anger, and hatred; and, above all, to the sexual passion. They are a prolific source of disease of the nervous system, and have caused the dethronement of some of the most gifted intellects.

RULES FOR VASSALS DURING THE MIDDLE AGES

1.   He who swears fealty to his lord ought always to have these six things in memory: what is harmless, safe, honorable, useful, easy, practicable.

    a) Harmless, that is to say, that he should not injure his lord in his body.

    b) Safe, that he should not injure him by betraying his secrets or the defenses upon which he relies for safety.

    c) Honorable, that he should not injure him in his justice or in other matters that pertain to his honor.

    d) Useful, that he should not injure him in his possessions.

    e) Easy and practicable, that that good which his lord is able to do easily he make not difficult, nor that which is practicable he make not impossible to him.

2.   That the faithful vassal should avoid these injuries is certainly proper, but not for this alone does he deserve his holding; for it is not sufficient to abstain from evil, unless what is good is done also.

3.   It remains, therefore, that in the same six things mentioned above he should faithfully counsel and aid his lord, if he wishes to be looked upon as worthy of his benefice and to be safe concerning the fealty which he has sworn.

RULES FOR DEALING WITH OBSCENE PHONE CALLS

1.   Hang up the telephone immediately. Don't say one word. Most annoyance calls are placed to see what response they will get. If you give callers no satisfaction, they will usually stop.

2.   Report obscene or nuisance calls to your telephone's business office if they persist.

3.   Call the police if you fear personal harm.

4.   Don't identify yourself before recognizing callers or asking them to identify themselves.

5.   Don't tell unknown callers that your husband is out of town.

6.   Teach children and baby sitters to be cautious with unkown callers. They should not say that they are alone in the house. Instead, ask them simply to take a message.

RULES FOR SECURING A U.S. PASSPORT

1.   Be sure to have a passport whenever you depart from or enter the United States and most foreign countries. The exceptions generally relate to travel between the United States and certain countries in North, South, and Central America and the Caribbean, except Cuba.

2.   Apply early for your passport, preferably a few months in advance of your departure date.

3.   Personally present a completed Form DSP-11 "Passport Application," at one of the passport agencies; at any federal or state court of record accepting applications; or at a post office which has been selected to accept passport applications.

4.   Apply by mail if you had a previous passport and wish to obtain another passport.

5.   Show proof of U.S. citizenship to obtain a passport by showing a previously issued passport; a birth certificate if you were born in the United States, a Certificate of Citizenship issued by the Immigration and Naturalization Service if citizenship was acquired through naturalization or a parent or parents; a Report of Birth Abroad of a Citizen of the United States of America. (Form FS-240), A Certification of Birth (Form FS-545 or DS-1350), or a Certificate of Citizenship should be submitted if citizenship was aquired by birth abroad to a U.S. citizen parent or parents.

6.   Present two (2) identical photographs of yourself plus (2) identical group photographs of any inclusions which have been taken within six months of the date of your apllication.

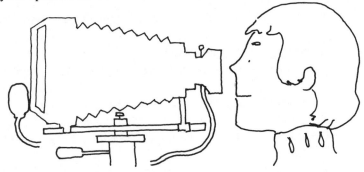

7.   Present group photograph of inclusion when more than one person is to be included.

8.   Sign all photographs. Individual photographs must be signed both on the front left side without marring the features and in the center on the reverse of the photograph. The two (2) additional photographs of any inclusion must be signed only on the reverse.

9. Photographs shall all be 2x2 inches in size. In individual photographs, the image size measured from the bottom of the chin to the top ot the head (including hair) shall be not less than 1 inch or more than 1⅜ inches. In group photographs, the images should be of sufficient size for identification purposes.

10. Acceptable passport photographs can be black and white or in color but not retouched to a point where appearance is changed.

11. Photographs should be taken in normal street attire without a hat and should include no more than your head and shoulders or upper torso. Dark glasses are not acceptable unless medically required. (Newspaper and magazine prints are not acceptable.)

12. Pay a fee of $10 for a passport. No passport fee is charged for Armed Forces personnel or their dependents who submit Department of Defense form DD-1056, civilian employees of the U. S. Government or their dependents proceeding abroad on official business with letters of authorization from the government agency. An execution fee of $3.00 must be paid to the official executing the application. No execution fee is required when applying for a passport by mail.

13. When applying at a passport agency, Federal Court or authorized post office, the $10 passport fee and the $3.00 execution fee should be included in one remittance made payable to the Passport Office.

14. When applying at a state court, the $10 passport fee should be made payable to the Passport Office and the $3.00 execution fee paid by whatever means the state court requires.

15. Do not submit coin or currency unless application is made at one of the passport agencies.

16. Establish your identity to the satisfaction of the person executing your application. A wife or husband to be included in a passport must also be identified.

17. Provide these acceptable documents of identity if they contain your signature and if they readily identify you by physical description or by photograph: previous U.S. passport, Certificate of Naturalization or of Citizenship; Driver's license (not temporary or learner's license); governmental (federal, state, municipal) identification cards or pass.

18. Bring an identifying witness who has known you for at least two years, and who is a U.S. citizen or a permanent resident alien of the United States. If you are not able to present the above acceptable documents, the identifying witness must sign an affidavit in the presence of the same person who executes the passport application.

19. You may include in your passport: your husband/wife; any children under the age of thirteen years, including stepchildren and adoped children; any brothers or sisters under the age of thirteen years. Animals may not be included in your passport even though they might travel with you.

20. All persons must appear in person before the clerk or agent executing the application if he is the bearer of the passport and is thirteen years of age or older; a wife or husband to be included in a passport.

21. Apply by mail if you are a bearer of previous passport (form DSP-82).

22. Order either a 48-page or a 96-page passport at the time of application if you are planning to travel abroad extensively.

23. Turn in mutilated or altered passports to passport agents, clerks of courts, authorized postal employees, or U.S. consular offices abroad. All changes must be made by an authorized official.

24. Immediately report the loss or theft of a valid passport to the Passport Office, Department of States, Washington, D.C. 20524, to the nearest Passport agency, or the nearest American consular office. The loss or theft should also be reported to local police authorities.

RULES OF WALKING—1890

1. When walking alone a quick step is to be taken; the toes must be turned out.

2. Never run into a person, if ordinary care can prevent it, and especially give way to a lady, no matter how you may meet.

3. Always keep to the right of the sidewalk, and never pass in front of a lady coming at right angles at a street corner, unless a distance of six feet intervene between said lady and the crossing point when you reach it.

4. In bowing when alone the hat should be carried quickly down to the right, or left if left-handed, till the back of the hand strikes the hip, then slowly replaced on the head. The taking off of the hat is to be accompanied by a slight forward inclination of the body and a smile of recognition.

5. Unless the cause of the act is known to the lady as well as yourself, never cut her, that is, do not look at her and refuse absolutely to return her bow, but recognize it in an indifferent manner sufficient to convey the fact that something is wrong, and that the return bow was forced, while still it is polite.

6. If you know a lady whom you dislike and have no desire to recognize, never look at her in passing, as you would thus invite recognition, and would be exceedingly impolite in cutting her.

7. When you meet a person walking, and that awkward dodging in the effort to pass occurs, always stop and turn slightly to the right till the other has passed on. If it be a lady, the expression "Pardon" is to be used as she passes.

8. If you step on a man's foot, address him with an apology merely; if on a lady's, the apology must be accompanied by a slight bow.

9. Never carry a parcel of any kind: if a hat is to be taken to the store, carry it in a leather case; if articles of wear, carry them in a satchel.

10. Do not wear too large a boutonniere; a few dozen violets or two or three pinks, or a few sprays of lily of the valley, or a few pansies, or a very small red rosebud for afternoon, and as few leaves as possible. For the evening a few sprays of hyacinth or lily of the valley is the only proper buttonhole bouquet.

11. When walking with a lady keep either a military step, or if her step is too short for your comfort, then take a Newport drag pace, taking care that the body does not rise much, thus preventing a seesaw appearance.

12. Always walk on the side nearest the curbstone, except in the case of a very crowded street, when it may be the most convenient for the lady to walk on your right.

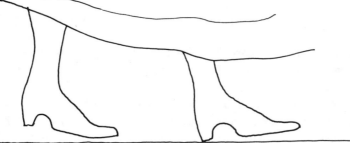

13. A distance of half a foot should be kept between the lady and yourself at all times when the walk is not crowded; this is necessary always in the daytime, and also in the evening unless the acquaintance is such as permits taking arms.

14. Never lock arms in the daytime.

15. Always pay attention if your companion is speaking; your mind should not be distracted by persons or objects passing; there is nothing more unsatisfactory and disagreeable to a young lady than for her to realize that she in unheard and unheeded.

16. When with a lady it is unnecessary to stop at all to permit another lady to pass when coming at right angles, as is necessary when alone.

17. If she has a satchel or large parcel when you meet her, immediately offer to carry it.

18. When joining a lady, if coming toward her, wait till she has passed; then turning, join her with usual or intended salutation, without stopping her. Never come intentionally face to face to join her; she will, presumably, think that you wish to stop, and it is a settled conclusion that a lady and gentleman should never stop to talk on the street; in a party it is permissible only if the several persons thereof have chanced to meet, or are in the act of parting.

19. When joining a lady in the morning on the street only accompany her a few blocks, for the morning is shopping time, and escorts are seldom desired.

20. When raining always hold the umbrella; when sunny never offer to, or hold a parasol, unless expressly requested to do so; a sunshade is for a lady to hold, and looks out of place in a gentleman's hand, unless it is a particularly heavy one, or the wind is too strong to permit of the lady carrying it comfortably.

21. Never fail to raise the hat on leaving a lady on the street, or at doors or windows.

22. When it is muddy, cross before a lady that she may profit by your action, by crossing in your footprints. If very muddy, offer your hand for her support in finding a good footrest.

23. Never carry the cane in the hand next the lady if it is possible to carry it in the other; if not possible, because the other is the useful one, then it should be carried under the arm next to her with that hand placed at the cane head. The reason for this rule will be understood on reflecting that if the cane is carried in the useful hand, it must necessarily be conveyed to the other every time a man bows; it is a poor action, and presents an awkward appearance, especially if the cane drops. This rule also applies to umbrellas when rolled. Of course, this is plain, as it is not supposed that a gentleman who is promenading carries any but these two articles. Never let a lady carry your cane in the city.

24. When entering a door or passageway, allow the lady to precede you, as is done indoors.

25. When with a lady, and she bows, your bow should be less marked than when alone; the hat is to be raised and carried quickly to the front as low as the chin, then as speedily replaced. When you consider the side you occupy, the advisability of this manner of bowing is at once seen on reflecting that a sweeping bow would more or less interfere with the continuation of your companion's recognition of the third party, which is a complaint the majority of young ladies set up.

26. In giving a lady soda-water or other cooling drink, do not allow her to use her own kerchief, but insist upon her using one of your own; a gentleman should always carry two. Also, in view of the fact that many pockets in dresses are difficult to discover immediately, the gentleman should thus be prepared for emergencies.

27. If walking in the afternoon with a lady, and you are overtaken by darkness, do not continue, but immediately board a horse car, enter a stage, or have your carriage follow and meet you, and thus return. This rule is on the principle that ladies and gentleman should not walk the streets after dark, and this principle is universally approved of by society.

28. The walk to and from cars to attend theaters in the evening is a different matter entirely and cannot be offered in opposition to the above rule (as many have claimed), as it is confined to only a few particular streets, and has nothing whatever to do with avenue promenades; besides, it is understood that crossing to theaters is compulsory, and so excusable.

29. In taking a lady for a walk, you should always provide her with a fair-sized bouquet of violets, if popular, or, if not, of roses to harmonize with her type, whether blonde or brunette; or any class of flowers which you know would suit her taste, provided they are not out of style, or unsuited to the season or for street wear, or perhap too loud for her general appearance.

RULES FOR WORLD OBSERVANCE OF HUMAN RIGHTS AS ESTABLISHED BY THE UNITED NATIONS DECLARATION—1948

1. All human beings are born free and equal in dignity and rights. They are endowed with reason and conscience and should act towards one another in a spirit of brotherhood.

2. Everyone is entitled to all the rights and freedoms set forth in this Declaration, without distinction of any kind, such as race, color, sex, language, religion, political or other opinion, national or social origin, property, birth or other status.

Furthermore, no distinction shall be made on the basis of the political, jurisdictional, or international status of the country or territory to which a person belongs, whether it be independent, trust, non-self-governing or under any other limitation of sovereignty.

3. Everyone has the right to life, liberty, and the security of person.

4. No one shall be held in slavery or servitude; slavery and the slave trade shall be prohibited in all their forms.

5. No one shall be subjected to torture or to cruel, inhuman, or degrading treatment or punishment.

6. Everyone has the right to recognition everywhere as a person before the law.

7. Everyone has the right to an effective remedy by the competent national tribunals for acts violating the fundamental rights granted him by the constitution or by law.

8. All are equal before the law and are entitled without any discrimination to equal protection of the law. All are entitled to equal protection against any discrimination in violation of this Declaration and against any incitement to such discrimination.

9. No one shall be subjected to arbitrary arrest, detention, or exile.

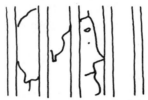

10. Everyone is entitled in full equality to a fair and public hearing by an independent and impartial tribunal, in the determination of his rights and obligations and of any criminal charge against him.

11. Everyone charged with a penal offense has the right to be presumed innocent until proved guilty according to law by public trial at which he has had all guarantees necessary for his defense.

No one shall be held guilty of any penal offense on account of an act or omission which did not constitute a penal offense, under national or international law, at the time when it was committed. Nor shall a heavier penalty be imposed than the one that was applicable at the time the penal offense was committed.

12. No one shall be subjected to arbitrary interference with his privacy, family, home or correspondence, nor to attacks upon his honor and reputation. Everyone has the right to the protection of the law against such interference or attacks.

13. Everyone has the right to freedom of movement and residence within the borders of each State. Everyone has the right to leave any country including his own, and to return to his country.

14. Everyone has the right to seek and to enjoy another country's asylum from persecution.

This right may not be invoked in the case of prosecutions continually arising from non-political crimes or from acts contrary to purposes and principles of the United Nations.

15. Everyone has the right to a nationality. No one shall be arbitrarily deprived of his nationality nor denied the right to change his nationality.

16. Men and women of full age, without any restriction due to race, nationality, or religion, have the right to marry and to found a family. They are entitled to equal rights as to marriage, during marriage, and at its dissolution. Marriage shall be entered into only with the free and full consent of the intending spouses. The family is the natural and fundamental group unit of society and is entitled to protection by society and the State.

17. Everyone has the right to own property alone as well as in association with others. No one shall be arbitrarily deprived of his property.

18. Everyone has the right to freedom of thought, in science and religion; this right includes freedom to change his religion or belief, and freedom, either alone or in community with others and in public or private, to manifest his religion or belief in teaching, practice, worship, and observance.

19. Everyone has the right to freedom of opinion and impression; this right includes freedom to hold opinions without interference and to seek, receive, and impart information and ideas through any media and regardless of frontiers.

20. Everyone has the right to freedom of peaceful assembly and association. No one may be compelled to belong to an association.

21. Everyone has the right to take part in the government of his country, directly or through freely chosen representatives. Everyone has the right to equal access to public service in his country. The will of the people shall be the basis of the authority of government; this will shall be expressed in periodic and genuine elections which shall be by universal and equal suffrage and shall be held by secret vote or by equivalent free voting procedures.

22. Everyone, as a member of society, has the right to social security and is entitled to realization, through national effort and international cooperation and in accordance with the organization and resources of each State, of the economic, social, and cultural rights indispensable for his dignity and the free development of his personality.

23. Everyone has the right to work, to free choice of employment, to just and favorable conditions of work and to protection against unemployment. Everyone, without any discrimination, has the right to equal pay for equal work. Everyone who works has the right to just and favorable remuneration, ensuring for himself and his family an existence worthy of human dignity, and supplemented, if necessary, by other means of social protection. Everyone has the right to form and to join trade unions for the protection of his interests.

24. Everyone has the right to rest and leisure, including reasonable limitation of working hours and periodic holidays with pay.

25. Everyone has the right to a standard of living adequate for the health and well-being of himself and of his family, including food, clothing, housing and medical care and necessary social services, and the right to security in the event of unemployment, sickness, disability, widowhood, old age, or other lack of livelihood in circumstances beyond his control. Motherhood and childhood are entitled to special care and assistance. All children, whether born in or out of wedlock, shall enjoy the same social protection.

26. Everyone has the right to education. Education shall be free, at least in the elementary and fundamental stages. Elementary education shall be compulsory. Technical and professional education shall be made generally available and higher education shall be equally accessible to all on the basis of merit. Education shall be directed to the full development of the human personality and to the strengthening of respect for human rights and fundamental freedoms. It shall promote understanding and friendship among all nations, racial or religious groups, and shall further the activities of the United Nations for the maintenance of peace. Parents have a prior right to choose the kind of education that will be given to their children.

27. Everyone has the right freely to participate in the cultural life of the community, to enjoy the arts and to share in scientific advancement and its benefits. Everyone has the right to the protection of the moral and material interests resulting from any scientific, literary, or artistic production of which he is the author.

28. Everyone is entitled to a social and international order in which the rights and freedoms set forth in this Declaration will be fully realized.

29. Everyone has duties to the community in which the free and full development of his personality is possible. In the exercise of his rights and freedoms, everyone shall be subject only to such limitations as are determined by law solely for the purpose of securing due recognition and respect for the rights and freedoms of others and of meeting the just requirements of morality, public order, and the general welfare in a democratic society. These rights and freedoms may in no case be exercised contrary to the purposes and principles of the United Nations.

30. Nothing in this Declaration may be interpreted as implying for any State, group, or person any right to engage in any activity or to perform any act aimed at the destruction of any of the rights and freedoms set forth herein.

RULES FOR INTERPRETING CHARACTER FROM HANDWRITING

Analyzing the Lines:

1. If the lines are straight, level, and parallel to the top of the paper, the writer is level-headed, somewhat self-assertive, and independent. He seldom becomes extremely emotional.

2. Optimism and ambition are usually indicated by rising lines, although if the upward slant is extreme, the writer may be too visionary. If the lines rise in the middle after a straight or downward beginning, caution is shown.

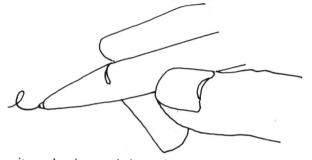

3. The writer who is worried or despondent tends to make his lines go downward. If the lines descend after a straight upward beginning, he seldom finishes what he starts.

4. Unreliability and a tendency to exaggerate are shown by lines that are wavy, zigzag, or undulating. If the lines wander all over the paper, uncertainty is indicated.

5. Even spacing between the lines is a sign of an orderly mind, although the writer who leaves much space unnecessarily between them may be somewhat extravagant. If the lines run into other lines above or below, moodiness and carelessness are shown.

6. If the lines are heavy, showing the writer used an unusual amount of pressure, great perseverance and resolve are indicated. Light, thin lines made with light pressure signify refinement and a sensitive, idealistic nature. Even pressure (neither heavy nor light) denotes a systematic, energetic person.

Analyzing the Margins

1. When the margins on both sides of the page are unnecessarily wide, the writer is apt to be careless and extravagant. If the margin at the right is too wide, a tendency to be extreme is indicated. Originality and generosity are shown by wide margins at the left.

2. The writer whose margin widens as it progresses down the paper is not sufficiently careful with his money.

3. Avarice and extreme caution or stinginess in regard to money are signified when both margins are too narrow. Such a writer's judgment is apt to be inaccurate. If only the right margin is too narrow, the writer is versatile as well as cautious.

4. If the margins are even and in correct proportion to the size of the paper, neatness and good taste are indicated.

5. Instability and unpredictable nature are shown by varying margins that weave or undulate down the left side of the paper.

Analyzing the Words

1. If the word endings are long and have an upward slant, the writer is inventive, original, and imaginative. Long, straight endings denote a tendency to be too generous.

2. An economical, prudent nature is indicated by short word endings, but if they are too short, the writer is apt to be miserly.

3. If the word endings are in the form of a graceful, ascending curve, the writer is considerate, kind, and gracious. When the endings curve back and under each word, thoughtlessness is denoted.

4. The writer who brings his word endings forcefully downward has a domineering nature. Temperamental difficulties are shown by lighter downward endings and by endings which are brought abruptly down after being straight nearly to the end.

5. When the size of each word increases so that the latter part is larger than the beginning, the writer is frank, conscientious, and naïve.

conscientious

6. Reserve and secretiveness are indicated by words that grow smaller toward the end.

7. If just enough space for good legibility is left between words, the writer is cautious and economical. Very little space denotes an unemotional, reserved nature. A great deal of space signifies clear thinking and a tendency to be extravagant.

Analyzing the Letters

1. When the letters slant to the right, the writer has a well-balanced mind and is affectionate; if the slant is extreme, however, an emotional, nervous nature is shown. Letters which slant to the left denote originality and reserve. A variable slant (with some letters to the right and others to the left) signifies indecision.

2. If the letters are straight up-and-down or vertical, the writer is calm, deliberate, and his careful judgment enables him to make wise decisions.

3. If the letters are rounded, the writer has an impressionable, peaceful nature, and makes friends easily because of his amiable disposition.

4. An energetic, alert nature is shown by angular, sharp letters, but if there are no rounded letters whatever in the writing, a tendency to austerity is indicated.

5. Frankness, generosity, and restlessness are signified by large letters. If the letters are small, refinement, caution, and unusual powers of concentration are shown. A writer whose letters are of medium size is practical and neat. Letters of uneven, irregular size denote a changeable nature and a quick temper.

6. When letters are decorated with flourishes the writer is somewhat vain and self-centered.

7.　If the letters in a work are not connected, so the word appears to be broken into two or more parts, a lack of concentration is shown; the writer is so energetic that he attempts too many tasks at the same time.

8.　When letters such as o and a are open at the top, the writer is so outspoken and candid that it is difficult for him to keep a secret. Very wide openings signify a tendency to gossip.

9.　Tact, discretion, and dignity are characteristics of the person who closes the top of his "o's," "a's," and other letters. If such letters are closed with a loop, secretiveness is indicated.

10　A well-balanced, unaggressive nature is shown by a "t" stem of the usual type, but if the "t" stem is looped, the writer is apt to be sensitive; stubbornness is shown if the looped stem is pointed.

11.　Impatience, curiosity, and a quick mind are shown by a "t" bar placed to the right of the stem. If placed to the left, the "t" bar shows caution and a tendency to procrastinate. Absentmindedness and imagination are shown if the "t" bar is high above the stem. A long "t" bar denotes enthusiasm, while a short one signifies preciseness. If the "t" bar is unusually low, the writer has remarkable willpower.

12.　A religious, sytematic nature is shown if the looped letters usch as "b", "l", and "y" have loops of equal, medium size. Very long loops denote a tendency to exaggerate. If straight lines are used in place of loops, the writer is decisive and not easily deterred from his purpose. Clannishness is shown if the loops are very small, like circles.

13.　Large capital letters signify self-respect; however, if the capital "I" is unusually large, egotism is indicated. A modest, quiet, and efficient nature is shown by small capital letters.

14.　If the letters are written as if they had been printed by a printing press, neatness, originality, and refinement are signified.

Analyzing Punctuation

1.　If the dots are usually omitted from the letters "i" and "j", the writer has a poor memory in regard to details. Vivacity and the habit of procrastination are also shown if the writer appears hurried.

2.　When the dots and other punctuation marks are heavy, a violent temper and great ambition to make money are shown. If the pressure varies so that some dots are heavy and others are light, the writer is apt to be impetuous and changeable.

3.　Concentration and caution are indicated by dots that are low and directly above the letters. If they are high above, the writer is enterprising and inquisitive.

4.　The writer who prefers to use dashes instead of punctuation marks is animated, cautious, and apt to be suspicious.

RULES OF BUSINESS ETIQUETTE FOR THE WOMAN EXECUTIVE

Raising consciousness levels and breaking down old traditions requires constant attention to detail. The new woman executive should follow these rules of etiquette to keep her upward mobility mobile:

1. Introductions

The name of the person with the highest business status is said first. Therefore, unlike social etiquette, a woman may be presented to a man, depending on their relative status within the corporate hierarchy. When you are in doubt about their relative status, say the older person's name first.

2. Introducing Yourself

When you are introducing yourself, also give your company affiliation, and position if it is relevant. When you enter an unfamiliar office because you have an appointment, say to the receptionist, "Good afternoon. I am Tammy Tycoon, and I have a three o'clock appointment with Mr. Bridgenose." Also give the receptionist your business card. If you do not have an appointment, tell the receptionist the purpose of your visit so the information can be relayed to the person you wish to see.

3. Who Goes First

Ladies before gentlemen went out with garter belts. Those with the highest status walk first. If you are hosting guests, then they always walk first, no matter who has the highest status. The remainder of the time, it makes no difference.

4. Holding Doors

The same rules apply as to who goes first. Hold the door open for those with higher status than you. If you are hosting guests, then hold the door for them, no matter what their status. Other than that, the first person to the door holds it open for others.

5. When to Rise

Always rise when you are being introduced or are greeting a visitor. Stand up when a person comes into your office, offer him a chair and remain standing until he is seated. Rise again when he starts to leave, and accompany him to the door.

6. Shaking Hands

Even if you have to walk across the room always shake hands with a person to whom you've been introduced. After the initial introduction, if you see the person on a regular basis (such as another employee in your department), it is unnecessary to shake hands or rise each time you see him. If the situation dictates handshaking, then offer your hand first, because a gentleman will usually wait for you to make the first move. When you have been with outsiders, most business people also shake hands at the end of the meeting.

7. What to Say

When you are being introduced, say, "How do you do, Ms. Bigwig?" or "I've heard some very nice things about you, Ms. Bigwig, and I've looked forward to meeting you." Whatever you choose to say, use the person's name while looking into her eyes. This helps you remember the name.

8. Your Business Name

It is proper for a married woman to keep her maiden name in business if she chooses to do so. If you marry after your career has been established, always keep the name with which you started.

9. Use of Ms.

Marital status has no bearing on your career, and you should adopt the use of Ms. Some women, however, are offended by it. If you are addressing a letter to an executive woman, and you do not know her preference, have your secretary check with her office.

10. Name on Business Card

A man never uses Mr. before his name on business cards, and neither should you. (Sorry, Amy Vanderbilt.) Use no designation, just your business name. You may still use a form of address before your name on your social cards but look for that custom to change.

11. Exchanging Business Cards

Although many people break this rule, it is proper etiquette to exchange business cards at the end of a meeting, not at the beginning.

12. Use of First Names

The use of first names varies according to geography and industry. Adopt the custom of the other executives in your industry. For example, the atmosphere around most advertising agencies is casual, and first names are used almost exclusively. In banking, however, the opposite is true, and last names are used. If you are meeting a person substantially older than yourself, always use his last name until he asks you to do otherwise.

13. Writing Letters

Make your written communications concise and brief. All business correspondence, except handwritten thank-you notes, should be typed on company letterhead. Many business people have adopted the use of personalized letterhead with their name on the left side. A status symbol, the letterhead is 7"×10" instead of 8½×11", and is called executive-sized stationery.

14. Telephone Manners

The telephone has replace the letter as the most frequent means of business communication. Most executives have their secretaries answer their phones and screen the calls, but the trend is away from that. Whoever answers your phone, there are some rules of phone etiquette that you should observe.

Answer the phone immediately and identify yourself. Even though you may be in the middle of a rush report, switch your voice to a friendly, relaxed tone. The person who originates the call is also the one who ends it, so wait for the caller to say good-bye. Hang up gently.

When you are the caller, you will first go through the company's receptionist, and then the person's private secretary before you reach your party. No need to identify yourself to the company receptionist, just ask for the party. If you are calling an unfamiliar office, when you reach the secretary, identify yourself by your name, title, company affiliation, and the nature of your business.

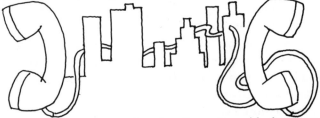

If you are about to embark on a lengthy discussion with the person you are calling, ask him first if he has a few minutes to talk. You may have caught him at a bad time, and while you are communicating your message, he may be preoccupied. On the phone, it is harder to keep a person's attention.

If someone important has called you at an inconvenient time, take the call anyway, tell him you are exceedingly busy, and ask if you can call him later. Unless it is an emergency, never take phone calls when there are guests in your office. It is rude.

15. You and Your Supervisor

Wait for your boss to set the stage for the degree of formality in your relationship. Call him by his last name unless he requests otherwise. Respect his working time. Unless you have a crisis on your hands, accumulate several items you need to discuss, and cover them all at once. Keep your interruptions to a minimum.

On the other hand, keep your boss informed by sending him carbon copies of correspondence and memos. Check with him before making important decisions such as hiring, firing, large expenditures, or budget cuts. But even then, get right to the point, and tell him of your decision. Do not justify your decision unless he asks you to do so.

You have the right to disagree with your boss, but do it in a way that won't antagonize him. This is the proper time to justify your argument, and do it calmly and objectively. If you have ample justification, have thought out the solution, and have a boss who is interested in the growth of his managers, he will allow your decision to stand. Whatever the outcome of the disagreement, however, his decision is the ultimate one, and you must respect that. Above all, be cooperative.

RULES FOR SERVING WINE

1. Always allow wines to rest a day or so after being brought home from the store, to give any sediment that might be present a chance to settle. In handling, they should never be agitated or sloshed about, and the cork should be withdrawn with care.

2. First remove any foil or cellulose around the cork by cutting, since that leaves a neat-looking band around the neck of the bottle. The neck of the bottle and the exposed cork are carefully wiped before the corkscrew is inserted, and the cork is withdrawn with as steady and smooth a motion as possible. If possible, the cork should be removed in one piece.

3. Wipe the bottle mouth after the cork has been extracted to minimize the dangers of dust or sediment.

4. When you pour wine a little bit is always first poured into the host's glass. This is done every time a bottle is opened, and only on the first pouring from a bottle. It is not a violation of the general rule of hospitality that says the host should be served last, but serves several rather practical purposes. If there are any bits of cork, dust, or sediment floating on the surface of the bottle's content, the host, and not the guests, will get them. It also gives the host an opportunity to first inspect, smell, and taste the wine to make certain it is of a quality worthy to be set before his guests.

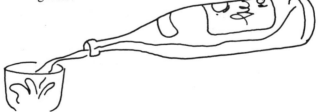

5.   Fill wineglasses to the half, two-thirds or three-quarters level, but never to the brim. This is done to leave an area of glass exposed, enabling the drinker to roll the wine around, wetting this area and thus releasing the aroma, an important part of true wine enjoyment. On succeeding rounds, it is customary to fill every glass to this level, whether it has been emptied or not.

6.   Pour the bottle carefully so as not to disturb the sediment. Usually it is gripped in the vicinity of the label to insure a steady hold and even pouring. Dripping may be prevented by gently twisting the bottle as the last drops are poured into a glass and the neck raised.

If a bottle is properly poured, only a little wine will remain amoung the lees, dreg, or "heel" in the bottle.

7.   There is no need to wrap a towel or napkin around a bottle while pouring; indeed, there are those who might think that the host is ashamed of the quality of the wine and is trying to conceal the label. The only purpose of the towel is to absorb the moisture found on the surface of chilled bottles, especially those that have been packed in ice. This moisture can just as well be wiped off before pouring.

8.   Take care with heavy sediment. As previously explained, some wines form sediment in the bottle while aging. Special steps must be taken in pouring these wines, to keep them clear. They, in particular, should be well rested before they are served. They should be gently withdrawn from the shelf, and, when carried, held at the same angle as the one in which they had lain. Bottle baskets or cradles made of wicker are sometimes used for this purpose. They are so constructed that the bottle rests in them on its side, and they have a handle so the bottle may be carried in them, placed on the table, and then poured without removal or disturbance. Cradles are made in different sizes for different bottles, so if one is used, it should be the proper size for the bottle, else the bottle may slip. If the wine has been agitated, or merely as a precautionary measure, it may be decanted instead of directly poured.

9.   Decant when a wine has a heavy sediment, or when bits of cork or other foreign bodies have fallen into the bottle. It may also be done simply for appearance' sake. Decanters are usually made of cut crystal and are shaped along the lines of a full-bodied bottle. They are equipped with a stopper, usually also of glass. Decanting consists in pouring the wine into a decanter or similar stoppered container, straining it through a piece of fine linen or cambric cloth as it is poured. Wines, especially of high alcoholic strength, may be left in a decanter for reasonable periods of time without suffering, but never for an undue period. The wine dealer should be consulted if a wine is intended to be left in a decanter more than a day or so, to learn how long it would be safe for that particular wine.

10. Keep in mind, the technique of handling a bottle of champagne or other sparkling wine differs somewhat because of the effervescent nature of the wine. There is considerable pressure within the bottle and the cork is usually held in place by means of a wire hood beneath the foil wrapping. There is a special wire loop attached to the hood enabling both the hood and the foil to be removed in one motion. When the hood is removed, a thumb is held on the cork to keep it from inadvertetly popping out.

a) The bottle is held at a 45-degree angle and the cork removed by twisting gently until the internal gas pressure forces it out. A firm grip should be kept on the cork at all times to keep it from flying off and striking someone as it is forced out. There are two opposing schools of thought on the matter of champagne corks. Some prefer to have them emerge with a loud, spectacular bang, while the older, traditional school holds that a properly removed champagne cork will emerge soundlessly.

b) Once uncorked, the wine is poured in two motions; the glass filling with foam on the first pouring, being brought to the proper level (two thirds to three-quarters full) with the second, once the foam has subsided. Between servings, the champagne is kept in an ice-filled bucket to keep it at the proper temperature.

11. Remember, wines are served at three general temperature levels: cellar, room, and chilled.

a) Cellar temperature is slightly lower than that of the room, being wine that is brought directly from the cellar and promptly served.

b) Wines are brought to room temperature by letting them stand in the room for a few hours before serving. Under no circumstances should a wine be warmed over a fire or otherwise heated to bring it to the proper temperature. Some wines improve in flavor if they are opened during this standing period, others should remain corked until the time of serving.

c) There is no exact temperature for a chilled wine, for it varies too greatly with taste for general rules. The temperature should be somewhere around 45 degrees, however. Wines are easiest chilled by placing them in a refrigerator some time before serving. They may also be packed in ice, usually held in a metal bucket. If a wine is not prechilled, usually twenty minutes in the ice bucket will bring it to the proper temperature.

12. Never place ice in wine, unless the wine is served in the form of a mixed drink containing other ingredients. This rule can be broken at the dictates of personal taste, but the host should never put ice in a guest's wine without first consulting him, for the vast majority of wine drinkers look on this practice as the ruination of wine.

RULES FOR WINNING SWEEPSTAKES

1. Separate the tasks of entering sweepstakes. If you divide up the tasks of entering the sweepstakes, you'll find that you get more done in less time. For instance, first put all the stamps on the envelopes, then fill out all the qualifiers. You might even be able to get the rest of the family involved in this. Set up an assembly-line production. Have one person sponge on the stamps. Have another person print out the block-letter proofs of purchase. Have another person fill out entry forms. Have another person fill envelopes and seal them. Remember, the key to winning is entering often. And this way you can enter twice as often in the same amount of time.

2. Abbreviate as much as possible. Find a way to abbreviate your name and address. Again, in this way you'll find that you can enter more often. Obviously "NE" for Nebraska is going to take a lot less time than spelling out the word "Nebraska." But here, a word of caution: make sure that it's a common abbreviation, one that's known to the judging organization. If the judge can't understand what you've written, he'll disqualify your entry. Don't ever invent abbreviations. If you have a question, look up words in the dictionary. It will take more time the first time, and less time later on.

3. Try to limit your entries to national contests. It's sometimes worthwhile to enter small local contests. Often the number of entries is small in relation to the number of prizes. But if you do enter, make sure you're dealing with a company or organization that you know and trust. One of the reasons why it's better to enter national contests is that they are usually judged by independent judging organizations. Thus, you are assured of a great deal of fairness and integrity on the parts of the judges.

4. Mail to the different box numbers you may notice in different newspapers, magazines, or on different entry blanks. These are key numbers so that the manufacturer understands where most of the entries are coming from. Mail entries to each of these different box numbers. This provides an even distribution of your entries and helps assure you of a maximum chance of winning.

5. Read the rules to make sure the promotion is legal in your state. Various states at various times have some legislation restricting sweepstakes. If on close reading of the rules you are to find that in the state of Florida, for example, the sweepstakes is void, and you are a resident of that state, it would be silly to waste your time and postage to enter that sweepstakes, for even if your entry was drawn it would immediately be disqualified. One reason for the voiding of certain states at times is that the company does not market its products there. But approximately 90 percent of the time, voiding occurs simply because the particular kind of prize promotion that company is offering isn't allowed in the state.

6. Enter often. As incredible as it sounds, most people who have never won a sweepstakes simply haven't entered often enough. The statistical fact of life is that the more you enter, the better chance you have to win. Most people will enter once, twice, three times. Yet the real professional sweepstakes entrant will sit and write out hundreds of entries. Naturally, his or her opportunity to win is much greater.

7. Follow the rules. In many sweepstakes 25 percent of the entries are disqualified on the basis that entrants failed to follow the rules. The rules are so simple in most sweepstakes that the average eight-year-old could follow them without any trouble. Yet, incredibly, many potential winners are disqualified. Anyone in the sweepstakes business will also tell you about the thousands of entries that are received after the closing date of the promotion, simply a waste of the postage money on the part of the contestants, something they could easily have avoided by following the rules. Often, rules say print your name and address clearly. Again, every sweepstakes judge can tell you of situations where a name or address was illegible, or, even more tragic, was simply left off of the entry form. There is hardly a sweepstakes that goes by in which some "winner" is chosen only to find his name and address has been left off the entry blank, and there is absolutely no way of telling who the entrant was. Remember, too, that if the rules say "hand print," then don't type. If the rules say "type or print," either choice is acceptable, but it may be preferable to type, simply because typing is the easiest thing in the world to read. Script is almost never acceptable. Be very cautious on this point, since it's sure to make a difference if your entry is drawn.

8. Know where to spend your time, money, effort, and postage. By this, simply examine the sweepstakes and decide whether this sweepstakes is really for you. Don't enter just to be entering. If you have time to enter a sweepstakes a hundred times, you're definitely better off entering the sweepstakes that you're really interested in than twenty-five different sweepstakes that you're marginally interested in. Why? The value of prizes in sweepstakes may vary from $5,000 to $1,000,000. Assuming the sweepstakes contest receives the same number of entries, it's silly and a waste of time to enter those that only offer a few, small prizes.

If you're a smart contestant, you'll spend your time factoring in the following two situations. First, what is your feeling as to the number of entries that will be received, and you can guess at this by deciding how widely the promotion is advertised. If you see a sweepstakes in every national magazine you pick up, obviously there will be a great number of entries. It's not unusual for upward of 3 percent of a magazine's circulation to enter. Therefore, if you see a sweepstakes advertised in *TV Guide*, *McCall's*, *Ladies' Home Journal*, and other big-circulation magazines, it's safe to assume there will be hundreds of thousands or millions of entries. On the other hand, if you see it only on a take-one form in a supermarket, then chances are there will be fewer entries. Second, what is the value of the prizes and do you really want to receive them?

9. Always remember that all that foibles of human beings unfortunately are present among judging organizations just as much as they are anywhere else. Judges are human, and you can take advantage of this fact. It seems that no matter how well, how carefully people are trained, they are still subject to human error. How can the contestant use this fact in her favor? Well, there are number of ways. The idea of judging a sweepstakes probably sounds very exciting to you. It probably is exciting the first, second, or maybe even the third time. But after a while, it becomes a dull and repetitive task.

When the judge does a drawing, it's his job to draw from hundreds of thousands of entries. Among those drawn, he will probably have to redraw at least 25 percent, because at least that many people make mistakes on their entry forms. Needless to say, after the first few drawings, the judge will be looking for ways to brighten up his day. And you can help.

A large and colorful envelope will sometimes work to the advantage of the contestant. Most sweepstakes are drawn from sealed envelopes. If the judge is not blindfolded, the larger surface area of the envelope is likely to attact attention. Remember that the 3"×5" requirement of the entry form usually only applies to the entry itself, not the envelope. As long as you've correctly followed all the rules of the sweepstakes inside, you can do what you want with the outside.

Another thing, sweepstakes winners are usually chosen in multiple drawings. This is because the thousands and thousands of entries in a national sweepstakes will more than fill a drum. This makes a single drawing highly impractical.

Most companies train their people to take an equal sampling from all the mailbags. But again, human nature intervenes. Sometimes the judges are lazy. They don't take as many entries as they need from the early mailbags, and they end up taking most of them from the last mailbag received. Therefore, you'd be wise to wait until later in the promotion to enter, and probably if you do so, you'll increase your chances of winning.

You might think of other ways to attract the attention of the judges. These factors, the color and size of the envelope and the timing of your entry, are not supposed to influence the judges, but sometimes they do.

Of course, it's important to note that independent judging organizations have a very high degree of integrity. Although you should try to influence the judges, don't try anything illegal or unfair. Bribery, or suggested bribery, for example, is out of the question.

10. Be on the lookout for sweepstakes. Your chances of winning are, again, a function of how often you enter. One way to find sweepstakes entry blanks is to join a sweepstakes service. Some of these services are, however, extremely expensive. One of the best ways is to watch for them in your local supermarket. You can ask the check-out clerks or even the manager to help you. Check window displays. Read the newspapers, magazines, and all your so-called junk mail. To you, no mail is junk. Once you get in the sweepstakes mood, you will constantly be looking for new and different sweepstakes. Remember, your chances of finding the really exciting sweepstakes are a function of your keeping a good watch.

11. Set aside a certain amount of time each day or evening for your hobby. Once you have decided which contests and sweepstakes you wish to enter, you must give yourself enough time to enter correctly. Decide to spend a certain amount of time each day filling out entry forms, addressing envelopes, sponging stamps. Start well in advance of the closing date, and decide exactly how many times you will enter. The number of times you enter should be a sensible figure—not so many times that you'll go stark raving mad filling out forms. And not so few that you don't have a good chance of winning. If you're entering a sweepstakes, you'll send in more entries than if you're entering a contest which requires some skill. And remember, the more difficult the contest, the less steep the competition. This is one factor that really makes contests worth your while.

RULES TO HELP YOU SELECT A NURSING HOME

Administration Policies:

1. A nursing home should have the required current license from the state or letter of approval from a licensing agency.

2. The administrator should have a current state license or waiver. (This is required for nursing homes cooperating under Medicaid.)

3. The home must be certified to participate in the Medicare and Medicaid programs.

4. The home should provide (if needed) rehabilitation therapy or a therapeutic diet.

5. The general atmosphere of the nursing home should be warm, pleasant, and cheerful.

6. The administrator(s) should be courteous and helpful.

7. The staff members should be cheerful, courteous, and enthusiastic.

8. The staff members should show patients genuine interest and affection.

9. Patients should be well cared for and generally content.

10. The patients should be allowed (if they so desire and are able to) to wear their own clothes, decorate their rooms, and keep a few prized possessions on hand.

11. There should be a place for private visits with family and friends.

12. There should be a written statement of patient's rights. As far as you can tell, these points should be an actuality.

13. The patients, other visitors, and volunteers should generally speak favorably about the home.

General Physical Considerations:

1. The nursing home should be clean and orderly.

2. The home should be reasonably free of unpleasant odors.

3. The toilet and bathing facilities should be easy for handicapped patients to use.

4. The home should be well lighted.

5. The rooms should be well ventilated and kept at a comfortable temperature.

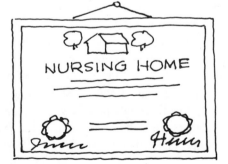

Safety:
1. The home should provide wheelchair ramps where necessary.
2. The nursing home should be free of obvious hazards, such as obstacles to patients, hazards underfoot, unsteady chairs.
3. There should be grab bars in toilet and bathing facilities and handrails on both sides of hallways.
4. The bathtubs and showers should have nonslip surfaces.
5. There should be an automatic sprinkler system and automatic emergency lighting.
6. There should be portable fire extinguishers.
7. Exits should be clearly marked and exit signs illuminated.
8. Exit doors should be unobstructed and unlocked from inside.
9. Certain areas should be posted with no-smoking signs. Make sure to notice that staff, patients, and visitors observe them.
10. There should be an emergency evacuation plan posted in prominent locations.

Pharmaceutical Services:
1. The pharmaceutical services should be supervised by a qualified pharmacist.
2. A room should be set aside for storing and preparing drugs.

Medical, Dental, and Other Services:
1. The home should have an arrangement with an outside dental service to provide patients with dental care when necessary.
2. A physician should be available at all times, either on staff or on call, in case of medical emergencies.
3. The home should have arrangements with a nearby hospital for quick transfer of nursing home patients in an emergency.
4. Emergency transportation should be readily available.

Nursing Services:
1. There should be at least one registered nurse (RN) or licensed practical nurse (LPN) on duty day and night.
2. There should be a RN on duty during the day, seven days a week.
3. There should be a RN serving as director of nursing services.
4. The nurse call buttons should be located at each patient's bed and in toilet and bathing facilities.

Food Services:

1.   The kitchen should be clean and reasonably tidy. The food should be kept refrigerated, not left standing out on counters. The waste materials should be properly disposed of.

2.   At least three meals should be served each day. The meals should be served at normal hours, with plenty of time for leisurely eating. Ask to see the meal schedule.

3.   No more than fourteen hours should be allowed between the evening meal and breakfast the next morning.

4.   Nutritious between-meal and bedtime snacks (could/should) be available.

5.   The food should look appetizing. The patients should be given enough food.

6.   The food should be tasty and served at the proper temperature. Sample a meal.

7.   The meal being served should match the posted menu (with few, if any, necessary exceptions).

8.   Special meals should be prepared for patients on therapeutic diets.

9.   The dining room should be attractive and comfortable.

10. Patients who need it should get help in eating, whether in the dining room or in their own rooms.

Rehabilitation Therapy:

1.   A full-time program of physical therapy should be available for patients who need it.

2.   There should be occupational therapy and speech therapy available for patients who need them.

Special Services and Patient Activities:

1.   There should be social services available to aid patients and their families.

2.   The nursing home should have (if possible) a varied program of recreational, cultural, and intellectual activities for patients.

3.   There should be an activities coordinator on the staff.

4.   There should be suitable space available for patient activities. Tools and supplies should be provided.

5.　There should be suitable activities offered for patients who are relatively inactive or confined to their rooms.

6.　Some activities should be provided each day. Some activities should be scheduled in the evenings. Look at the activities schedule.

7.　Patients should have an opportunity to attend religious services and talk with clergymen both in and outside the home (if so desired).

8.　A barber and beautician should be available.

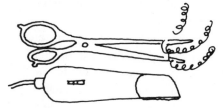

Patients' Rooms:

1.　All the rooms should open onto a hallway.

2.　They should have a window to the outside.

3.　Each patient should have a reading light (if they want to read), a comfortable chair, and a closet and drawers for personal belongings.

4.　Fresh drinking water should be within reach.

5.　There should be a curtain or screen available to provide privacy for each bed whenever necessary.

6.　Bathing and toilet facilities should have adequate privacy.

Other Areas of the Nursing Home:

1.　There should be a lounge where patients can chat, read, play games, watch television, or just relax away from their rooms.

2.　There should be a public telephone available for patients' use.

3.　The nursing home should have an outdoor area where patients can get fresh air and sunshine.

Financial and Related Matters:

1.　The estimated monthly costs (including extra charges) should compare favorably with the cost of other homes.

2.　A refund should be made for unused days paid for in advance.

3.　The visiting hours should be convenient for patients and visitors.

4.　These and other important matters should be specified in the contract.

RULES FOR INTERPRETING CHARACTER FROM THE SHAPE OF THE HEAD

Numbers indicate locations in figure.

1. This area is commonly known as the *amative center*, which concerns the mating instinct, the capacity for romance and physical love, and energy. A well-developed amative center denotes an effectionate nature strongly influenced by persons of the opposite sex.

2. Fondness for children is indicated when this area, called the *parental center*, is prominent. It also shows a desire to protect children from harm and to have offspring of one's own. If a mother who has a large parental center is childless, she is apt to adopt a baby.

3. A sociable disposition and a dislike of being alone are signified when this area, called the *gregarious center*, is well developed, The person is happiest when in the company of congenial friends.

4. Known as the *concentrative center*, this region pertains to the ability of the person to devote his attention exclusively to a single task or plan, and to complete it in an efficient and methodical way.

5. If this area—the *destructive center*—is well developed, the person must guard against a tendency to destroy things unnecessarily, and should control his temper at all times, since he is apt to be caustic and to hurt others by his severity.

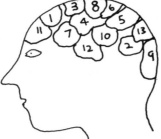

6. Unusual courage, an aggressive nature, and the ability to argue or debate effectively are shown by a prominent *center of combativeness*, which is located in this area.

7. Often called the *acquisitive center*, this region concerns the wish to collect things either as a hobby or a vocation.

8. This area is the *secretive center*—the indication of prudence, restraint, and the ability to keep a secret. It is not wise to confide in anyone who has an underdeveloped secretive center.

9. The *self-respective center*, which is in this area, denotes the extent of the person's self-esteem and confidence. When it is well developed, it indicates pride, dignity, and sometimes a sense of superiority.

10. An unusual fondness for compliments and praise of any kind is shown by a well-developed *center of approbation*, which occupies this part of the head. It denotes a sincere desire to please others and to gain favorable recognition for all one's efforts.

11. Known as the *constructive center*, this area concerns the wish and ability to make or build things, and is often characteristic of an inventive nature or a talent for architecture or engineering.

12. Watchfulness, caution, and level-headedness are indicated by a prominent *watchful center*, which is located in this area and enables the person to be constantly on his guard.

13. The *firmness center*, located in this region, pertains to the amount of determination and self-control which the person exercises. A well-developed firmness center denotes a strong will, perseverance, and the patience and courage needed to overcome obstacles.

14. This area is the *benevolent center*—the sign of kindness, a benign and pleasant disposition, and unselfishness.

15. Fairness and a strong sense of justice are shown by a well-developed *conscientious center*, which is in this portion of the head. Such a person is often qualified to serve as a judge or referee.

16. The *veneration center*, located in this area, concerns the feeling of respect and high regard for anyone who the person believes is superior to himself. It does not signify an inferiority complex. Anyone who has a prominent veneration center is usually a devout church member.

17. Known as the *ideality center*, this part of the head pertains to an artistic, original nature and the ability to appreciate the aesthetic things in life to the fullest extent.

18. The *hope center* is found here, and if prominent it shows a cheerful, hopeful nature, indicating that its owner is not easily discouraged and does not allow disappointments to dampen his outlook on life.

19. An unusual faculty for making witty remarks and a bright sense of humor are signified by a well-developed *humor center* which is located here and makes its owner fond of mirth and gaiety.

20. This area is called the *wonder center*; it concerns a belief in the supernatural, a superstitious nature, and a strong feeling of curiosity and awe in regard to miracles, the occult, and all weird events.

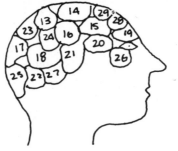

21. Here may be found the *observation center*, which has to do with the faculty of noticing and carefully distinguishing between persons or articles at a brief glance. A large observation center makes its owner observant of all details, attentive, and constantly alert.

22. The ability to mimic or imitate others is shown by a prominent *imitation center*, which occupies this part of the head.

23. Often called the *balance* or *weight center*, this area concerns the sense of balance and general equilibrium. If the center is well developed, its owner is generally graceful, agile, and lithe.

24. A remarkable memory for faces, strong eyes, and an excellent sense of touch are denoted by the *form center*, if it is prominent. The eyes of a person with these faculties are generally far apart.

25. This area is the *size center*, which concerns the ability to perceive the difference in size between two or more things which may look exactly alike to anyone whose size center is not well developed.

26. The *mathematical center* is found here, at the outer angle of the eye. When this center is sufficiently developed, its owner is adept at addition, subtraction, and division without using a pencil. Such persons are valuable as accountants or bookeepers.

27. An unusual memory for localities and an almost infallible sense of direction are denoted by a well-developed *locality center*, which is to be found in this part of the head.

28. Here may be seen the *neatness center*, which concerns the desire and ability to be orderly in all habits. People who have large neatness centers are seldom haphazard in any undertaking.

29. The *color center*, located in this area, concerns fondness for attractive color combinations. A well-developed color center is often characteristic of decorators, painters, and florists.

30. The *tune* or *music center* is found here, and is usually prominent on the heads of musicians and others who appreciate music, since this center pertains to the ability to recognize beautiful melodies.

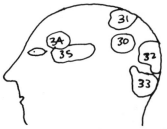

31. In the center of the forehead is the *eventuality center*, which (if well developed) signifies that its owner is inquisitive and can learn a certain amount concerning a variety of subjects. However, it is difficult for him to master completely any one field of study.

32. This area is known as the *reason center*, since it concerns the faculty of logical reasoning.

33. A good sense of timing and an accurate memory for dates are shown if this region, known as the *time center*, is well developed. It does not necessarily denote punctuality, however.

34. The *discrimination center*, located in this part of the forehead, concerns the faculty of comparing and arranging objects such as books, plants, etc., and of decisive thinking to sort out various ideas to form an orderly plan.

35. In the upper portion of the eye is the *language center*, which (if prominent) signifies not only ability to learn foreign languages easily, but also to express one's thoughts clearly in words.

RULES FOR PUNCTUATION

1. Use the semicolon (;) to link subject-predicate groups that could otherwise occur as separate sentences, especially if they are parallel in structure and emphasis.

> This is an excellent soup; you should try some.
>
> I am going to the grocery; I'll get some flour.

2. Use the semicolon to link word groups containing heavy internal comma punctuation.

> I took a skillet, one pot, and a bucket; a sleeping bag, pillow, and an air mattress; and a gun.

3. Use the omission period or dot to indicate omission of several letters, especially if the words are abbreviated.

> Mr. F. C. Wright
>
> M.D.
>
> The I.R.S. has changed its rules again!

4. Use triple periods or dots (. . .) to indicate a more or less extensive omission of material at the beginning of, or within, a quoted passage; followed by a period (. . . .) they indicate omission at the passage's end.

> . . . the difficulty with scrupulous conformity . . . is that it makes even the slightest deviation from the norm appear . . . aberrational at best. . . .

5. Use triple periods to indicate omissions deliberately left to the reader's imagination.

> The fire spread through the forest . . . when it had passed, not a living thing remained.

6. Use the dash to indicate the deliberate suppression of letters in a person's name in order to avoid positive statement of identification.

> The noble personage, Lord _____ , swore that he had witnessed no miscarriage of justice.

7.   Use brackets (. . .) as a special kind of parentheses, or to insert pronunciations written in the symbols of the International Phonetic Association (IPS).

> According to the judge, "It (the new law) will be extremely difficult to interpret unless it is written in more specific terms."
>
> The correct pronunciation of *suave* is (swav).

8.   Use quotation marks (". . .") to enclose direct quotations from speech, and to enclose references to specific words, slang expressions, hackneyed expressions, familiar and well-worn phrases, and terms you do not like.

> "This is no joke," said the teacher, "and you'd better stop laughing."
>
> "Inter-animal density" refers to the spacing between individuals in a colony.
>
> The "rakes" of the period wore lavender gloves and hats tilted at a jaunty angle.
>
> According to the students, passage of the bill is a "sure thing." The "co-eds" at Davidson are a powerful minority.

9.   Use the apostrophe (') to indicate the omission of a letter no longer pronounced or deliberately suppressed in pronunciation.

> He's going to Maine and he'll get some good pictures.
>
> Could ye le' me ha' a look at your bicycle, ma'am?
>
> He'll be returnin' home soon.

10.   Use the apostrophe before the "s" in plurals of figures, signs, symbols, and letters, and before the "s" in plurals of words that ordinarily have no plural.

> Young children have an especially difficult time writing 5's and r's.
>
> When it comes to helping with the church suppers, the congregation separates itself into "Will's" and "Won't's."

11.   Use the apostrophe after the "s" to form the possessive plural of nouns and to form the possessive singular of nouns already ending in "s".

> The dogs' kennels need to be cleaned.
>
> Willis' statements get more and more absurd!

12.   Use the apostrophe before an "s" to form the possessive singular of nouns.

> David's guns need cleaning.
>
> Williams, Prang and Son's law offices are being redecorated.

13.   Use the colon (:) to emphasize a word group or the word that follows it.

> The trip went exactly as planned: we were back by 3:30.
>
> The solution was simple: we replaced the cord.
>
> There was just one thing I needed: food.

14.   Use the dash to connect a subsidiary word group or word to a primary one. The dash directs the reader's attention backward.

> The place was absolutely deserted—desolate and lonely.
>
> One chance at a blue ribbon—that's all I ask.

15. Use a hyphen to link parts of words together, and to link the elements of compound numbers and fractions.

> a well-liked game
> free-swimming larvae
> a come-hither attitude
> fifty-four dollars
> one-quarter cup

16. Use the period to separate subject-predicate sentences from each other.

> The river is tidal. It is also slightly salty.

17. Use a question mark to indicate a question.

> Why aren't we going to Grandma's house for Christmas?
> We aren't going to Grandma's house for Christmas?

18. Use an exclamation mark to indicate that a group of words or a word is charged with emotion.

> This is the worst traffic I've ever been in!
> Golly! That's really expensive.

19. Never use a comma between a subject and a verb, a verb and a complement, or between two complements.

> The convicts escaped from the prison without difficulty.
>
>   subject   verb   complement   complement

20. Always use a comma after each word or word group in a series terminated by "and" or "or".

> I bought two books, a ruler, and five pencils.
> Either cornmeal, flour, or cracker crumbs may be used.

21. Use a comma between subject-predicate word groups linked by "and," "but," "or," "not," "yet."

> This salad is really good, and it has few calories.
> The trip was long, yet worth the trouble.

22. Use a comma before a modifying word or word group that is out of its normal sentence order.

> Miss Harper, kind and gentle, will help with the Sunday School.
> Meat, we have; it's drink we're missing.

23. Use a comma after an introductory word, word group, transitional adverb, or vocative expression.

> However, the chores remained undone.
> Martha, this is my friend Nancy.

24. Use a comma between elements in sentences and word groups which might cause confusion if thought of as combined.

> The wallpaper has flat, white flowers.
> The dogwood tree has flat, white flowers.

25. Use commas between items in dates, addresses, book and author references, etc.

> January 17, 1979
> David Vass, Montreal, Canada
> *Game of Kings*, by Dorothy Dunnett

26. Used paired commas (, . . . ,) to enclose modifying word groups not regarded as essential to the identification of the word they modify, and to enclose interpolated words and word groups.

> The cookies, which the children finished up before you got home from work, were really very good.
> This discrepancy, in fact, is what suggested that the man died by murder rather than suicide.

27. Use paired dashed (— . . . —) to enclose elements less closely related to the main thought of the sentence than those enclosed by paired commas, or whenever the enclosed word group has heavy comma punctuation of its own.

> The neighbors—mostly older, retired people—have been so friendly.

28. Use parentheses to enclose material which is obviously outside the main scope of the sentence.

> My great-uncle, William Scott, was a mason, and worked until the end of his life (he was eighty-seven when he died).

RULES FOR RANKING
GUESTS AT OFFICIAL FUNCTIONS

This is the order of precedence as established by Official Protocol of the U.S. Department of Defense:

The President
The Vice President
Governor of a State (when in his own State)
The speaker of the House of Representatives
The Chief Justice of the Supreme Court
Former Presidents of the United States
The Secretary of State
Ambassadors of foreign powers accredited to the United States (in order of the presentation of credentials)

Ministers of foreign powers accredited to the United States (only those ministers who are chiefs of diplomatic missions; in order of the presentation of credentials)

Associate Justices of the Supreme Court (by date of appointment)

The Cabinet (other than the Secretary of State)

    The Secretary of the Treasury

    The Secretary of Defense

    The Attorney General

    The Postmaster General

    The Secretary of the Interior

    The Secretary of Agriculture

    The Secretary of Commerce

    The Secretary of Labor

    The Secretary of Health, Education, and Welfare

    The Secretary of Housing and Urban Development

    The Secretary of Transportation

The president Pro Tempore of the Senate

Senators

Governors of States (when outside their own State. Relative precedence among governors, all of whom are beyond their State perimeters, is determined by their State's date of admission to the Union, or alphabetically by State)

Acting heads of executive departments (e.g., Acting Secretary of Defense)

Former Vice Presidents of the United States

Congressmen (according to the length of continuous service. If the latter is the same, arrange by date of their State's admission to the Union or alphabetically by State.)

Chargé d'affaires of foreign powers

Former Secretaries of State

The Under Secretaries of executive departments (e.g., The Deputy Secretary of Defense)

Secretaries of the military departments (Army, Navy, Air Force, in that order)

Chairman, Joint Chiefs of Staff

Members, Joint Chiefs of Staff (by dates of appointment to JCS)

Commandant of the Marine Corps

Five-star generals and admirals

Director of Defense Research and Engineering

U.S. ambassadors (on assignment within the United States)

Assistant Secretaries of executive departments (by date of appointment

Judges of the U. S. Court of Military Appeals

Under Secretaries of the military departments (Army, Navy, Air Force, in that order)

Four-star military

Assistant Secretaries of military establishments (Army, Navy, Air Force, and by date of appointment within each service)

Deputy Under Secretaries of military departments

Assistants to executive departments

Three-star military

Deputy Director, Defense Research and Engineering

General counsels of the military departments (Army, Navy, Air Force, in that order)

Former foreign ambassadors

Former U. S. ambassadors and ministers to foreign countries

278

Ministers of Foreign Powers (not accredited heads of missions)
Deputy Assistant Secretaries of executive departments and deputy counsels
Counselors of foreign embassies
Consuls general of foreign powers
Two-star military (rear admiral, upper half)
Deputy Assistant Secretaries of military departments (by date of appointment)
Heads of offices, Office of the Secretary of Defense

RULES FOR RECOGNIZING THE COMING OF MENOPAUSE

1.   Understand the only signs and symptoms which are uniquely characteristic of the menopausal period are hot flashes and genital atrophy.

a) *Hot flashes*, or sudden waves of heat, are generally felt on the upper chest and arms, neck and head. Frequently this sensation is accompanied by reddening of the skin, or hot flushes, and is followed by profuse sweating. In most instances these symptoms are not severe or especially troublesome. Occasionally, they can become severe and frequent enough to interfere with a woman's sleep or routine.

b) *Genital atrophy* refers to the degenerative changes that can occur in the vagina and external sex organs. The tissues and structures of the external sex organs shrink and lose some of their fat.

THE ORIGINAL JUDEAN TEN COMMANDMENTS

1. Thou shalt have no other gods before me.
2. Thou shalt not make unto thee any graven image, or any likeness of any thing that is in heaven above, or that is in the earth beneath, or that is in the water under the earth: thou shalt not bow down thyself to them, nor serve them: for I the Lord thy God an a jealous God, visiting the iniquity of the fathers upon the children unto the third and fourth generation of them that hate me; and shewing mercy unto thousands of them that love me, and keep my commandments.
3. Thou shalt not take the name of the Lord thy God in vain; for the Lord will not hold him guiltless that taketh his name in vain.
4. Remember the sabbath day, to keep it holy. Six days shalt thou labour, and do all thy work: but the seventh day is the sabbath of the Lord thy God: in it thou shalt no do any work, thou, nor thy son, nor thy daughter, thy manservant, nor thy maidservant, nor thy cattle, nor thy stranger that is within thy gates: for in six days the Lord made heaven and earth, the sea, and all that in them is, and rested the seventh day: wherefore the Lord blessed the sabbath day, and hallowed it.
5. Honour thy father and thy mother: that thy days may be long upon the land which the Lord thy God giveth thee.
6. Thou shalt not kill.
7. Thou shalt not commit adultery.
8. Thou shalt not steal.
9. Thou shalt not bear false witness against thy neighbour.
10. Thou shalt not covet thy neighbour's house, thou shalt not covet thy neighbour's wife, nor his manservant, nor his maidservant, not his ox, nor his ass, nor anything that is thy neighbour's.

RULES FOR
DISPLAYING AND USING THE AMERICAN FLAG

1.   It is the universal custom to display the flag only from sunrise to sunset on buildings and on stationary flagstaffs in the open. However, when a patriotic effect is desired, the flag may be displayed twenty-four hours a day if properly illuminated during the hours of darkness.

2.   The flag should be hoisted briskly and lowered ceremoniously

3.   The flag should not be displayed on days when the weather is inclement, except when an all-weather flag is displayed.

4.   The flag should be displayed daily in or near the administration building of every public institution and during school days in or near every school.

5.   The flag, when carried in a procession with another flag or flags, should be either on the marching right, that is the flag's own right, or, if there is a line of other flags, in front of the center of that line.

6.   The flag should not be draped over the hood, top, sides, or back of vehicle, train, or boat. When displayed on a motorcar, the staff shall be fixed firmly to the chassis or fender.

7.   When displayed against a wall, the union of blue field of the flag should be uppermost and to the flag's own right, that is to the observer's left. In a window display of the flag, the union should be to the left of the observer in the street.

8.   The flag should never be displayed with the union down, except in instances of extreme danger to life or property as a signal of dire distress.

9.   The flag should never touch anything beneath it, such as the ground, floor, water, or merchandise.

10. The flag should never be used as wearing apparel, drapery, or bedding. Never place upon it or mark it in any way with an insignia, letter, mark, word, figure, design, or picture.

11. The flag should never be used for advertising purposes. It should not be printed or impressed on napkins, boxes, or anything for temporary use to be discarded.

RULES FOR INTRODUCTIONS

In all introductions follow three simple rules:

1.   Introduce the younger person to the older.
2.   Introduce the less important person to the more important.
3.   Introduce the male to the female.

RULES FOR DEALING WITH BATS IN YOUR ATTIC

1. When you discover a bat in your attic, don't jump out the window.
2. Remember, bats won't hurt you, according to the experts. In the next breath the experts say that you shouldn't pick up a "sluggish" bat because it may have rabies and bite you. They don't bother to explain the difference between a sluggish bat and one who's just goofing off, a slugabed bat. Experts are like that. They also tell you that vampire bats live only in South and Central America. But suppose that thing hanging up there is visiting?
3. Remember, a bat won't get caught in your hair unless—but there's no sense going into all that now. A calm retreat is the best policy.
4. Pretend to ignore the bat and casually stroll back to the attic hatchway.
5. Then gracefully leap through to the floor below, slamming the trapdoor behind you.
6. The solution to bats in the attic is a simple one. Keep the attic closed at all times. Don't go up there. Bats have their territory; you have yours.

RULES FOR QUALIFYING AS FOSTER PARENTS

1. You should have a natural liking for children, enjoy playing and talking with them, and like taking care of them.
2. You should be able to see each child as a different, interesting person with his own needs.
3. You must be able to give affection and care to a child without expecting him to be loving and grateful in return right away.
4. Your marriage should be stable, and basically happy. Both you and your husband or wife should want the foster child.
5. You should be able to get along with other people, and be dependable about your responsibilities.
6. You should be able to accept the fact that your foster child is not entirely yours—his own parents and the child welfare agency have important places in his life. When the time comes for the child to go back to his parents or to an adoptive home, you should be ready to help prepare him for it.
7. You must have tolerance and understanding for the foster child's own parents. A disapproving attitude will be sensed by the child, and this will damage his ties with his parents and his feelings about his own worth.
8. Keep in mind, only occasionally is a widow or a single woman with experience in child care accepted as a foster mother, for example, for temporary care of infants. But for most foster children the agency will consider only homes with both a mother and father.

282

9. You may have children of your own at home and still have foster children. Of course, it is unwise for a family to have so many children, especially very young ones, that the home is overcrowded or the mother and father cannot give enough attention to each child.

10. You must be in fairly good health, so that you will be able to give constant care to the child. Midical examinations of family members may be required, including tests for diseases that can be spread to children. The foster child will also usually receive a medical examination before coming to stay with you.

11. The foster father should have steady employment, and your family income should be large enough to meet family needs, before taking into account foster children and foster care payments.

12. Agencies need foster parents of all races. There are many Negro, Puerto Rican, Indian, and Spanish-American children who need foster care in different parts of the country.

13. Many kinds of homes are used for foster care, from city apartments to homes in suburbs and rural areas. In any case, the home and neighborhood should be safe for children, and the home should not be overcrowded. A child needs a bed of his own and a place to keep personal possessions—clothes, pictures, favorite toys.

RULES FOR MEMORIZING DIFFICULT SPELLING

To spell this word: Remember, this sentence:

affect . . . . This verb has an *a* for action.

all right . . . . To write this as one word would be *all wrong*.

believe . . . . Strange but true, there is a *lie* in *believe* and *belief*.

capitol . . . . In the spelling of this building, there is an *o* as in its *dome*.

friend . . . . This word ends in *end*.

girl . . . . Every G.I. has a girl.

grammar . . . . Write *gram*; repeat the last three letters, but in reverse.

hear . . . . I *hear* with my *ear*.

marriage . . . . One must be a certain *age* to have a *marriage*.

meat . . . . We *eat meat*.

meet . . . . You *greet* those you *meet*.

piece . . . . This is a *pie* to cut and eat.

principal . . . . He is a *pal* of yours.

stationery . . . . . . There is an *er* in this word as there is in the *paper* for the stationery.

their . . . . Don't let the *ir irk* you.

there . . . . This usually tells you *where*, or *here* or *there*.

which . . . . "*Which* witch has the sandwich?"

283

MARIO PUZO'S GODFATHERLY RULES FOR WRITING A BEST-SELLING NOVEL

1. Never write in the first person.
2. Never show your stuff to anybody. You can get inhibited.
3. Never talk about what you are going to do until after you have written it.
4. Rewriting is the whole secret to writing.
5. Never sell your book to the movies until after it is published.
6. Never let a domestic quarrel ruin a day's writing. If you can't start the next day fresh, get rid of your wife.
7. Moodiness is really concentration. Accept it because concentration is the key to writing.
8. A writer's life should be a tranquil life. Read a lot and go to the movies.
9. Read criticism only in the beginning. Then read novels to learn technique.
10. Never trust anybody but yourself. That includes critics, friends, and especially publishers.

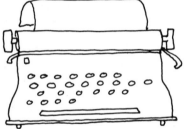

RULES FOR READING POETRY

1. *Read a poem more than once*—A good poem will no more yield its full meaning on a single reading than will a Beethoven symphony on a single hearing. Two readings may be necessary simply to let you get your bearings. And if the poem is a work of art, it will repay repeated and prolonged examination.

2. *Keep a dictionary by you and use it*—It is futile to try to understand poetry without troubling to learn the meanings of the words of which it is composed. One might as well attempt to play tennis without a ball.

3. *Read so as to hear the sounds of the words in your mind*—Poetry is written to be heard: its meanings are conveyed through sound as well as through print. Every word is therefore important. The best way to read a poem is just the opposite of the best way to read a newspaper. One reads a newpaper as rapidly as he can; one should read a poem as slowly as he can. When you cannot read a poem aloud, lip-read it: form the words with your tongue and mouth though you

do not utter them. With ordinary material, lipreading is a bad habit; with poetry it is a good habit.

4. *Always pay careful attention to what the poem is saying*—Though one should be conscious of the sounds of the poem, he should never be so exclusively conscious of them that he pays no attention to what the poem means. One should make the utmost effort to follow the thought continuously and to grasp the full implications and suggestions. Because a poem says so much, several readings may be necessary. But on the very first reading one should determine which noun goes with which verb.

5. *Practice occasionally reading a poem aloud*—Read it affectionately, but not affectedly. The two extremes which oral readers often fall into are equally deadly. One is to read as if one were reading a tax report or a railroad timetable, unexpressively, in a monotone. The other is to elocute, with artificial flourishes and vocal histrionics. It is not necessary to put emotion into reading a poem. The emotion is already there. It only wants a fair chance to get out. It will express *itself* if the poem is read naturally and sensitively.

RULES FOR BEING FUNNY

---

1. Learn to tell the difference between funny and not funny situations. Traction is funny. Open heart surgery is not.

2. Learn a few Yiddish words.

3. If you must set a joke in a geographical area, set it in New Jersey. New Jersey is the only funny state.

4. Learn to tell funny names from not funny ones. Ethel is funny. Susan is not.

5. Learn to identify funny sounds. The "ch" sound is especially funny. So is the "k". "Chicken" is surefire.

6. Always work in threes. A priest and a rabbi on a raft are not funny. A priest, a rabbi, and a swami are.

7. If you don't have a sense of timing, don't tell anything but Polish jokes.

8. Be willing to bomb. Being funny is taking a chance. You can protect yourself a little by using deadpan humor. If nobody laughs, you can pretend it wasn't a joke.

RULES FOR PURCHASING FISH AND SHELLFISH

1. Know that whole or round fish are marketed just as they come from the water. Before cooking, they must be scaled and eviscerated. Usually, head, tail, and fins are removed.

2. Know that drawn fish are marketed with only the entrails removed. They need to be scaled, and head, tail, and fins are removed before cooking.

3. Know that dressed or pan-dressed fish are both scaled and eviscerated; usually head, tail, and fins are removed and they are ready for cooking. Smaller fish, called pan-dressed, usually have head and tail left on, and are ready for cooking. Larger, dressed fish are frequently cut into steaks or fillets.

4. Know that steaks are cross-section slices of the largest types of dressed fish. They are ready to cook as purchased.

5. Know that fillets are the sides of dressed fish, cut lengthwise away from the backbone. They are practically boneless, may be skinned, and require no preparation before cooking.

6. Know that butterfly fillets are two sides of fillets of the fish held together by the uncut belly skin and are usually boneless.

7. Know that fish sticks are pieces of fish cut from frozen fish blocks into uniform portions usually about one inch wide and three inches long. They weigh up to one and a half ounces.

8. Know that fish portions, so very popular today, are cut from frozen fish blocks into uniform portions weighing not less than one and a half up to six ounces.

9. Know that shellfish (such as clams, lobsters, oysters, and some varieties of crabs) should be alive if purchased in the shell.

10. Know that shucked shellfish have shells removed.

11. Know that shrimp are usually sold headless. "Green" shrimp applies to raw, headless shrimp in the shell in most areas. Peeled shrimp are headless shrimp with the shells removed. Deveined shrimp are shrimp with the intestinal track or black vein down the back removed. Cooked shrimp, available fresh, frozen, and canned, is usually sold peeled and deveined, ready to use.

RULES OF ETIQUETTE FOR THE JUNIOR EXECUTIVE

1. Be friendly but not intimate. Too deep a personal involvement in business makes it difficult to maintain an objective attitude. Moreover, an intimate knowledge about yourself and your private affairs may turn into a weapon in the hands of an overambitious, unscrupulous, or scandalmongering associate.

2. Don't encourage intimate confidences on the part of a fellow worker. His problems may impose a personal obligation upon you which may affect your rational judgment in a crisis situation. If he reveals too many confidential details about himself, you are bound to become personally involved and you will lose your objectivity.

3.   You may have the gift of mimicry and like to show off your talents before an appreciative audience. If any of your associates are present, whether the occasion is a working or a nonworking one, never use any of the executives or other sacred cows of the organization as your subjects. Word is sure to get around, and no-nonsense executives would take a dim view when they learn that they have been the butt of your humor, however innocent or clever.

4.   Under the guise of friendship, an associate may ask you a business question that is improper. Don't brush him off with indignation. Be noncommittal and as nonchalantly courteous as you can. He has been indiscreet and tactless, but you need not follow suit.

5.   An associate may ask you for material from your files that you are not sure he ought to have. Find some excuse. Tell him your superior has the folder, or that your secretary is in the midst of doing something urgent and you cannot disturb her. Stall him until you can query your boss as to whether it is okay for you to give him the information he wants.

6.   On the other hand, if a high-ranking executive asks you for material when your superior is not available, you may have no alternative other than to give it to him without delay. But be sure you tell your superior about it when he returns.

7.   You may on occasion have to work in confidential reports, or keep restricted information on your desk. Keep these papers in a folder in the event an associate or an unexpected visitor comes into your office. It would be the natural thing for you to close the folder without appearing to be rude.

8.   You and your associates may be in the habit of having lunch together. Should you be fortunate enough to be promoted ahead of the others, appear to take it in your stride without bursting your shirt buttons in front of your associates. You will have to walk a tightrope to maintain the friendship of your associates without seeming to patronize them. You never know when your executive levels may coincide again, or collide. In the meantime, with your new exalted position, there will be some changes in your relationships. These changes should take place gradually; there should be an evolution rather than a revolution in your attitude toward your former associates.

It might be a good idea for you to arrange to give them a "celebration" luncheon. If they give you a celebration treat, you go ahead with your plans anyhow. In a way, it is your friendly gesture of farewell because in your new position your luncheon commitments will more likely be with individuals of another echelon. Your associates will get the message that it is not your intention to pull rank, but the SOP (standard operating procedure) is breaking the continuity of your quasi-social meetings.

RULES FOR INSURING A GOOD LAWYER-CLIENT RELATIONSHIP

1. Don't withhold information from your lawyer. Give your lawyer an objective statement of all the facts and let him present them in your best interest.

2. Don't expect simple or quick answers to complicated questions. Lawyers are justifiably cautious in drawing conclusions or answering complex legal questions. They know that the law is rarely an "open and shut" case.

3. Keep your lawyer advised of all new developments in the case. Your lawyer needs this information to make progress on your case.

4. Never hesitate to ask your lawyer about any matter relevant to the case. But remember, lawyers are not psychiatrists, doctors, marriage counselors, or financial advisers.

5. Follow your lawyer's advice. Don't work against your lawyer. In contested cases, the last thing a lawyer needs is another adversary to make matters more difficult.

6. Be patient. Don't expect instant results. Trust your lawyer to follow through on the case but don't hesitate to ask for periodic progress reports. You always have a right to know exactly what your lawyer is doing for you.

RULES TO AVOID BEING NOT-FUNNY

1. Don't put a lampshade on your head at a party.

2. Don't tell ethnic jokes to an ethnic if that's the ethnic you're joking about.

3. Remember, if you're a woman, leave insult humor to Don Rickles. What is called "wit" in men is often called "cattiness" in women.

4. Do not go too far in telling jokes at your own expense. At a certain point, people stop laughing and start believing.

5. Don't tell a joke with your mouth full.

6. Don't tell the punch line first.

7. Be sure you remember the joke before you start telling it.

8. Don't preface your joke with, "Wait till you hear this. It'll kill you." You're setting yourself up for a big fall.

9. Don't try too hard when you're telling a joke. It should sound easy, natural, spontaneous.

10. When you've told one good joke, don't try to top yourself.

RULES GOVERNING STATUTORY RAPE

1. Women may not consent to sexual intercourse under age sixteen in all states except Arizona, California, Florida, Idaho, Illinois, Nebraska, Tennessee, Wisconsin, or Wyoming (where the age is eighteen); Louisiana, New York, and Texas (where the age is seventeen); North Dakota and Virginia (where the age is fifteen); Georgia, Maine, and Maryland (where the age is fourteen); Minnesota, New Hampshire, New Mexico, and Utah (where the age is thirteen); Delaware, Mississippi, and North Carolina (where the age is twelve).

2. In Maryland, males may not consent to sexual intercourse if under fourteen with a female who is eighteen or older.

3. In Utah, if a male if under fourteen, his physical ability must be proved before he can be convicted.

4. In Tennessee a female may be considered consenting if she is over twelve and "bawd, lewd, or kept."

5. In Mississippi no female between twelve and eighteen, of previously chaste character, can consent to sexual intercourse with a male older than she is.

DEALING WITH YOUR OWN PERSONAL EMOTIONAL PROBLEM

1. Define the problem.

2. Accept the idea that for the most part you learned how to think, feel, and act this way and *therefore you can unlearn it*.

3. Devise a way of measuring the problem to see how often it occurs or to what degree it occurs. For example, you would check for the frequency of a disturbing thought, the amount you are overweight.

4. Devise a way of lessening the frequency or the severity, while also increasing those positive and adaptive elements that will enhance your happiness. This latter step requires imagination and practice, and in fact you may feel at this point you would like a consultation with a trained person who is more accustomed to thinking this way.

5. Admit to yourself that if you continue to feel, act, and think a certain way—the way that gives you problems—you are choosing to be that way when you could in fact find out how to change and make the special effort to change.

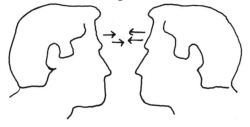

VICTORIAN RULES FOR DANCING AS A GENTLEMAN

1. Remember there is one custom which above all others is essential to every man who has any desire to play the role of a thorough social success, and that requirement is dancing.

2. There is not one thing which a society gentleman performs, which gives so much enjoyment not only to himself, but to others.

3. Nothing is more closely criticized, nothing more prominent when in execution; nothing more benefiting as an exercise, and nothing more satisfactory to the performer, than dancing. By that word is meant any performance which has the name of dance, and which has the requisites of "grace," "ease," and "perfect performance."

4. To be a perfect dancer the above expressions in reference to your dancing should be won from your admirers.

5. do not think, because you have an idea of how to dance, that you really do so perfectly.

6. The first requirement to good dancing is grace. If you are graceful you cannot appear awkward to onlookers, for your step is firm, body quiet, and arms still. The arm is never pumped, and the feet are barely lifted off the floor.

7. To have ease, a dancer should appear confident of his ability, and show that ability by a correct and actual performance of the dance in the above-explained graceful way.

8. To have a perfect performance of a dance, both of the former requirements are to be exercised, with these additional requisites, viz.: use a long decided glide, never jump or hop, always reverse equally as much as you turn the original way, keep to the side of the room, direction to the right from the entrance.

9. Do not collide with other couples, or at least protect your partner from sudden collisions, and on no account allow her to slip.

10. The right hand should be at the lady's back, between the lower ends of the shoulder blades, and should always carry a silk handkerchief.

11. Never in dancing hold a lady close to you, for it is the most disagreeable position for her, and looks decidedly improper.

12. Hold your partner at all times at arms' length; this gives you freedom of speech, space to use the feet, and allows you to glide more easily.

13. In a Waltz, always take a long, sweeping glide, with as little rise as possible.

14. Any step between a Boston dip and the Philadelphia glide, if used as a sort of an imperceptible, sweeping dip, will apear to great advantage on the floor.

15. A Polka should either be glided or walked through; never skip, and not take too long a step, and do away entirely with all fancy variations of the dance.

16. Keep strictly to the original Polka form and you will avoid all awkward appearances.

17. The same rule applies to the Yorke, Galop, etc.

18. The Schottische is a beautiful dance, if performed gracefully as in the Waltz, only much more care should be exercised in the forward steps.

19. Do not use that once popular, but awkward manner of skipping in this dance, but the more modern three running steps.

20. Those familiar with all these popular dances will comprehend the importance of my criticisms.

21. The Caprice is the combination dance of Waltz and Polka, and necessitates more care and attention than any other. Nothing but the glide step should be used in this dance.

RULES FOR ACCOMMODATING A MISTRESS

1. Discretion is not necessary in a lot of cases because the thinking of people today accommodates a variety of living arrangements, only one of which is a man and woman not married to one another.

2. Meeting the family is a no-no for a married man with a woman friend. Women who love should be spared the discomfort of making small talk with His Wife, a woman she hates before she meets.

3. Take vacations with her when you can. When you can't, don't show her the slide . . . especially the ones with your wife in a bikini.

4. If you're not with her on holidays, make sure you call her. If you are married, you have to be doubly sure she feels pampered, cherished, worthwhile—all the things a second-place woman is concerned about.

5. Marry her. Or stop talking about it, for God's sake.

RULES FOR DETERMINING WHEN NOT TO GET MARRIED

1. Don't get married if:

  a) You are escaping from your family.

  b) All your friends are married, and you want to be like your friends.

  c) You hate the Chinese laundry.

  d) You think you ought to be a father.

  e) You need someone to talk to (remember, a psychiatrist is cheaper).

  f) You like her sister better.

  g) You aren't sure you love her, but you think you may learn. (P.S. You won't.)

MARTIN LUTHER'S RULE FOR FREQUENCY OF INTIMACY

A week two
Is the woman's due.
Harms neither me nor you,
Makes in a year, twice fifty-two.

RULES FOR LIVING (THE LATEST DECALOGUE)

Written in the mid-nineteenth century by Arthur Hugh Clugh, one of England's "poets of doubt."

Thou shalt have one God only; who
Would be at the expense of two?
No graven images may be
Worshipped, except the currency.
Swear not at all; for thy curse
Thine enemy is none the worse.
At church on Sunday to attend
Will serve to keep the world thy friend.
Honor thy parents; that is, all
From advancement may befall.
Thou shalt not kill; but need'st not strive
Officiously to keep alive.
Do not adultery commit;
Advantage rarely comes of it.
Thou shalt not steal; an empty feat,
When it's so lucrative to cheat.
Bear not false witness; let the lie
Have time on its own wings to fly.
Thou shalt not covet, but tradition
Approves all forms of competition.

RULES FOR LIVING (DESIDERATA)—1692

- Go placidly amid the noise & haste, & Remember what peace there may be in silence.
- As far as possible without surrender be on good terms with all persons.
- Speak your truth quietly & clearly; and listen to others, even the dull & ignorant; they too have their story.
- Avoid loud & aggressive persons, they are vexations to the spirit.
- If you compare yourself with others, you may become vain & bitter; for always there will be greater & lesser persons than yourself.
- Enjoy your achievements as well as your plans.
- Keep interested in your career, however humble; it is a real possession in the changing fortunes of time.
- Exercise caution in your business affairs; for the world is full of trickery. But let this not blind you to what virtue there is; many persons strive for high ideas; and everywhere life is full of heroism.
- Be yourself; Especially, do not feign affection.
- Neither be cynical about love; for in the face of all aridity & disenchantment it is perennial as the grass.
- Take kindly the counsel of the years, gracefully surrendering the things of youth.
- Nurture strength of spirit to shield you in sudden misfortune, But do not distress your self with imaginings. Many fears are born of fatigue & loneliness.
- Beyond a wholesome discipline, be gentle with yourself.
- You are a child of the universe, no less than the trees & the stars; you have a right to be here. And whether or not it is clear to you, no doubt the universe is unfolding as it should.
- Therefore be at peace with God, whatever you conceive Him to be, and whatever your labors & aspirations, in the noisy confusion of life keep peace with your soul.
- With all its sham, drudgery & broken dreams, it is still a beautiful world.
- Be careful.   • Strive to be happy.

RULES FOR TREATING EPILEPTIC SEIZURE

1. Recognize these signs/symptoms:
    a) Loses consciousness.
    b) Convulsions.
    c) Severe spasms of the muscles of the jaw (may bite tongue).
    d) Victim may vomit.
    e) Face may be livid, with veins of the neck swollen.
    f) Breathing may be loud and labored with a peculiar hissing sound.
    g) Seizure usually lasts only a few minutes but it may be followed by another.

2. Provide this first aid treatment:
    a) Keep calm.
    b) Do not restrain victim; prevent injury by moving away any object that could be dangerous.
    c) Place light padding under victim's head to protect from rough ground (jacket, shirts, rug).
    d) Remember, there is a danger of the victim biting his tongue so place a padded object between his jaws on one side of his mouth. A shirttail and a stick can be used for the padded object. However, do not try to force jaws open if they are already clamped shut.
    e) When the seizure is over loosen clothing around the neck.
    f) Keep the victim lying down.
    g) Keep victim's airway open.
    h) Prevent his breathing vomit into lungs by turning his head to one side or by having him lie on his stomach.
    i) Give artificial respiration if breathing stops.
    j) After the seizure, when consciousness is regained allow the victim to sleep or rest.

FIRST AID RULES FOR IMPALED OBJECTS IN THE EYE

1. Leave object in victim; it should only be removed by a doctor.
2. Place sterile gauze around eye, apply no pressure.
3. Cover with paper cup or cardboard cone to protect it and prevent object from being farther driven into eye.
4. Cover both eyes, and explain to victim why both eyes are covered: one eye cannot move without the other eye moving. Calm and reassure the victim—he may panic with both eyes covered.

RULES TO AVOID BEING EATEN BY SHARKS

1.   Avoid attracting or annoying sharks. Most of them are scavengers, continuously on the move for food. If they don't get it from you, they will lose interest and swim on.
2.   Use shark repellent if sharks are in the vicinity.
3.   Keep your clothing and shoes on.
4.   If your group is threatened or attacked by a shark, bunch together and form a tight circle.
5.   Face outward so that you can see an approaching shark.
6.   If the sea is rough, tie yourselves together.
7.   Ward off actual attack by kicking or stiff-arming shark.
8.   If you are apparently undetected, stay as quiet as you can.
9.   Float to save energy.

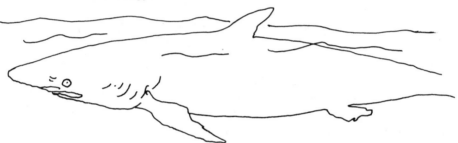

10.   If you must swim, use strong, regular strokes; don't make frantic, irregular movements.
11.   When swimming alone, stay away from schools of fish.
12.   If a single large shark threatens at close range:

> a) Use strong, regular swimming movements; try feinting toward the shark—he may be scared away.
>
> b) Don't swim away directly in the shark's path; face him and swim quickly to one side to avoid him.
>
> c) As a last resort, kick or stiff-arm a shark to push him away.
>
> d) Make loud sounds by slapping the surface of the water with cupped hands. Use regular strokes.
>
> e) Use knife at close quarters in a showdown. Stab the shark in gills or eye.

13.   If a shark threatens to attack or to damage the raft, discourage him by jabbing snout or gills with oar (be careful not to break the oar and don't take roundhouse swings that may upset you).

> a) Fire a pistol above a shark—it may frighten him away.
>
> b) Look for sharks around and under your raft before you go into the water.

RULES FOR ATTRACTING BIRDS TO YOUR YARD

1.   Provide places for birds to feed, sing, court, nest, rest, and hide. They like a choice of places for these activities—from crowns of tall trees to low-growing flowers and grasses. They also like a choice of foods—seeds, fruits, berries, and flower nectar.

2.   Add more plants and a great diversity of plant species and heights, attract more kinds of birds. Plants of varying heights are especially important. If you want to attract certain birds or groups of birds, find out their particular food and cover preference so you can select appropriate trees, shrubs, vines, grasses, flowers, and other plants. Consider the bird appeal of the plants now in or bordering your yard and make needed additional plantings. Yards that have only deciduous trees and shrubs can be improved by adding pines, junipers, cedars, yews, and other evergreens that provide winter shelter for birds. Fruit-bearing shrubs and trees are helpful additions you can plant.

3.   Select plant species with staggered flowering and fruiting periods, so you can have a succession of floral displays and bird food throughout much of the year. By intermingling different species, shapes, and sizes, you can create varied and attractive landscaping patterns

4.   Use flowers and other annuals to increase the kinds of bird food, to balance landscape spacing, and to fill in along walls and other structures. A small pond or pool will further enhance your yard's attractiveness for you and your birds. Cutting a small clearing into the margin or in the middle of a wooded area creates an edge effect that birds like.

5.   Be sure your landscaping allows you to see the birds, perhaps from a window, patio, or terrace.

RULES FOR APPROACHING AND HANDLING A HORSE.

1.   Always speak to a horse as you are approaching it. A horse's vision is restricted directly in front and to the rear but its hearing is acute. If you startle the horse it may kick you.

2.   Always approach at an angle, never directly from the front or rear.

3.   Pet a horse by first placing a hand on its neck or shoulder. Touch with a rubbing action and do not "dab" at the end of a horse's nose.

4.   Always walk around a horse out of kicking range. You may want to keep a light hand on his back as you move around him.

5.   While working around horses stay close to the horse so that if it kicks, you will not receive the full impact.

6.   Work about a horse from a position as near the shoulder as possible.

7. Never stand directly behind a horse to work with its tail. Stand off to either side, facing to the rear and draw the tail toward you.

8. Be calm, confident, and collected around a horse. Nervous handlers cause nervous and unsafe horses.

9. If you must punish a horse, do it only at the instant of disobedience. If you wait, even for a minute, it will not understand why it is being punished. Learn and use simple methods of firm restraint. Never strike a horse in the head.

10. Wear footgear that will protect you from being stepped on. Never wear sneakers or go barefooted.

11. Make the horse walk beside you when you lead it. A position even with the horse's head is considered safest.

12. Always turn the horse to the right and walk around it. Use a long lead strap, folded in your left hand, with the right hand positioned to hold the lead up near the halter. Lead from the left or "near" side.

13. When leading a horse through a doorway or into a stall, be certain you have control, then walk through first. Step through quickly and then move to one side.

14. When releasing a horse into a field, it is safest to lead completely through the gate and turn the horse around, facing the direction from which you came. Slowly release the horse and stand quietly.

RULES OF THE FUTURE: TRANSIT IN AMERICA
(OCCURRING BEFORE 1990)

1. The 55-mph speed limit will continue and people will be encouraged to carpool and use mass transit systems through widespread educational programs urging energy conservation.

2. All fossil fuels will be deregulated.

3. There will be periodic rationing of fuels.

4. Tax incentives will be provided to increase research efforts in developing alternative travel methods.

5. Taxes will be levied on automobiles by weight and horsepower.

6. Public transit costs will remain fairly steady for the next ten years (but will then increase by 20 percent by 1995).

7. Driving automobiles will be discouraged and tolls for entering downtown areas will be imposed in some cities; cars will be banned from downtown areas altogether.

8. Lack of adequate highway maintenance will raise insurance rates and cause more accidents.

9. There will be rigid enforcement of land use controls to prevent urban sprawl.

RULES FOR SMART SHOPPING

1. Weigh distance against savings. Don't drive twenty-five miles out of your way to save a few pennies on a can of something or other. Same goes for walking. A small savings probably isn't worth spending all day trudging around for. Your time is money, too.

2. Get to know the stores where you shop. And get to know the people who work there. The best strategy is to shop the sales of three or four nearby stores and shop them regularly. Once the produce man gets to know you, he's much more likely to tip you off that the beans are lousy today but the melons are really worth a second look. You'll also find out about characters like the overeager stock clerk who gets busy stamping Monday's higher prices on everything when it's still only Saturday afternoon.

3. Find out what time of the day fresh supplies are delivered, usually mid-morning, and shop then. Avoid rush hours, especially just before dinnertime. Always eat something before going to the grocery store. How come? Because impulse buying and excess spending are often triggered by the bizarre promptings of an empty stomach. Did you ever wonder why big supermarkets don't have little coffee bars or restaurants? That's why. They know it, too, and the hungry shopper is their all-time favorite.

4. Don't take the children shopping with you if you can possibly avoid it. Having the kid yelling, "I want a cookie," at the top of her lungs is every bit as brain-rattling as being hungry. If you must take them, make sure the kids are calm and well disciplined. Shopping only once a week, by the way, increases the likelihood that you'll be able to get a baby-sitter for the little dears at grocery time.

5. Read the labels. Not the part that tells you how yummy the stuff is, but the little print, where it says how much you're getting for your money. In some places "unit pricing" is required. This means that the store has to put up signs below each product telling you how many ounces per dollar or pounds per cent or whatever. In practice, the little signs are usually too dirty to read, and somebody shelved the peanuts over the sign that tells you about a brand of orange juice that the store is out of anyway. If you're serious about systematic shopping, a pocket calculator might be a good investment. In contrast to almost everything else, electronic gadgets are actually getting cheaper, and this one can help you quite a bit.

6. Ask for a raincheck if sale merchandise is sold out. Some places, the law requires stores to issue such promissory notes. Even if they're not bound to do it, big chains often will give you a raincheck just to maintain good will.

7. Use free product and cent-off coupons. These might show up to be clipped out of the newspaper, or may be mailed to you by the manufacturers. Sometimes you find them inside the boxes. Sometimes you have to invest a stamp and mail in your request. Whatever you have to do, do it. If you use the product involved and would buy it anyway, you're foolish not to get and use all the coupons you can. By the same token, though, if you wouldn't normally buy the product, don't let the promise of a few cents off seduce you into getting something you don't need.

RULES TO HELP YOU GUARD AGAINST LOSING YOUR PET PERMANENTLY

1. Be sure he has an ID tag attached to his collar, bearing his and your name and address.

2. Have your animal tattooed with a mark on a part of his body where it can't be removed.

3. Keep a record of your pet's height, weight, breed, sex, color, special marks, and traits.

4. Always have on hand a color photograph of your pet, no more than a year old.

5. Seach the neighborhood, if you are home when you discover your pet is missing.

6. When looking for your pet, move in increasingly large circles. Wandering dogs stray in circles or in a straight line until meeting an obstacle, when they change direction and again follow a straight line.

7. Check alleys and driveways.

8. Ask people on the street if they have seen him.

9. Place ads in local newspapers and post notices in nearby police stations, post offices, supermarkets, shops, pet stores, and veterinary hospitals, if you do not find your pet the day he strays.

10. Contact local postmen, sanitation men, delivery boys, and neighbors.

11. Check animal shelters.

12. Offer a reward for your pet's return. Some animals are stolen and held for reward or ransom.

RULES FOR BUYING A HORSE

1. One white foot—try him,

2. Two white feet—buy him,

3. Three white feet—look well about him;

4. Four white feet—go without him.

RULES FOR CONSERVING ENERGY IN HOME OR OFFICE

1. Check your attic to see if your home needs insulation.
2. Insulate floors over unheated spaces, such as garages and crawl spaces.
3. Calk and weather-strip doors and windows to reduce fuel use.
4. Install storm windows: combination screen and storm, single-pane storm, or clear plastic film taped or stapled to the window frame.
5. Add storm doors to your house if you live in a very hot or very cold climate.
6. Lower thermostat settings to 65° F during the day and 55° F at night. Dress warmly if you're cold.
7. Let the sun shine in during the day to warm the house; close draperies and shades at night to hold heat in.
8. Have your furnace checked once a year to make sure the unit is as efficient as possible.
9. If you're buying a gas furnace, look for one that has an automatic flue gas damper to reduce heat loss when the furnace is off.
10. Don't set the thermostat at a warmer setting than normal when you first turn up the heat; the house will not warm up faster.
11. Clean or replace the filter in your forced-air heating system about once a month for better system efficiency.
12. Don't heat rooms that you're not using; close them off and save energy.
13. Install glass doors on your fireplace to reduce heat loss up the chimney. You can still enjoy the warmth of the fire.
14. Don't waste hot water by letting faucets drip or by running water needlessly.
15. Do as much household cleaning as possible with cold water.
16. Make sure the temperature in your gas waterheater is no more than 120° F (140° F if you have a dishwasher).
17. Be sure your dishwasher and washing machine are full but not overloaded when you turn them on.
18. Don't use the "rinse/hold" feature if you have one on your dishwasher.
19. Let the dishes in your dishwasher air dry by turning it off and by opening the doors at the beginning of the drying cycle.
20. Keep your refrigerator at 38° to 40° F for the fresh food compartment, 5° F for the freezer compartment.
21. Turn off decorative gaslights or replace them with electric ones.
22, If you're buying a new gas oven or range, look for one that has an electronic igniter instead of a pilot light.
23. Use lids on pots and pans for faster cooking time and therefore less energy.

RULES FOR TREATING SHOCK

1. Recognize these signs/symptoms:
    - a) Shallow breathing.
    - b) Rapid and weak pulse.
    - c) Nausea, collapse, vomiting.
    - d) Shivering.
    - e) Pale, moist skin.
    - f) Mental confusion.
    - g) Drooping eyelids, dilated pupils.
2. Provide this first aid treatment:
    - a) Establish and maintain an open airway.
    - b) Control bleeding.
    - c) Keep victim lying down.

    Exceptions: Head and chest injuries, heart attack, stroke, sunstroke. If no spine injury, victim may be more comfortable and breathe better in a semireclining position. If in doubt, keep the victim flat.
    - d) Elevate the feet unless injury would be aggravated by this position.
    - e) Maintain normal body temperature. Place blankets under and over victim.
    - f) Give nothing by mouth, especially stimulants or alcoholic beverages.
    - g) Always treat for shock in all serious injuries and watch for it in minor injuries.

RULES FOR CONDUCT OF A KNIGHT (MIDDLE AGES)

A knight must display:
1. Unswerving belief in the Church and obedience to her teachings.
2. Willingness to defend the Church.
3. Respect and pity for all weakness and steadfastness in defending them.
4. Love of country.
5. Refusal to retreat before the enemy.
6. Unceasing and merciless war against the infidel.
7. Strict obedience to the feudal overlord, so long as those duties did not conflict with duty to God.
8. Loyalty to truth and to the pledged word.
9. Generosity in giving.
10. Championship of the right and the good, in every place at all times, against the forces of evil.

MATH RULES FOR WORKING WITH PERCENTS

1. The percent symbol, %, indicates a denominator of 100.

2. To write a percent as a decimal fraction, move the decimal point 2 places to the left and drop the percent symbol.

3. To write a decimal fraction as a percent, move the decimal point 2 places to the right and add the percent symbol.

4. To find a percent of a number, change the percent to a decimal fraction and multiply.

RULES FOR READING YOUR ELECTRIC AND GAS METERS

Your Electric Meter—An electric meter records your use of kilowatt-hours of electricity. The interpret it:

1. Read dials from the left to right. (Note that numbers run clockwise on some dials and counterclockwise on others.)

2. The figures above each dial show how many kilowatt-hours are recorded each time the pointer makes a complete revolution.

3. If the pointer is between numbers, read the smaller one. (The 0 stands for 10.) If the pointer is pointed directly at a number, look at the dial to the right. If that pointer has not yet passed 0, record the smaller number; if it has passed 0, record the number the pointer is on.

4. This reading is based on a cumulative total—that is, since the meter was last set at zero, 9,449 kilowatt-hours of electricity have been used. To find your monthly use, take two readings one month apart, and subtract the earlier one from the later one.

5. Some electric meters have a constant, or multiplier, indicated on the meter. You follow the same steps as outlined above, and then multiply the usage reading by this number. This type of meter is primary for high-usage customers.

Your Gas Meter—Read it as you would an electric meter.

1. A gas meter tallies the number of cubic feet of natural gas that you have used.

2. Some gas meters have more than four dials. If yours does, and you cannot decide by what number to multiply the reading, call your gas company for directions.

3. The figures above each dial show how many cubic feet of natural gas are recorded each time the pointer makes a complete revolution.

MATH RULES FOR WORKING WITH DECIMALS

1. To add or subtract decimals, align the decimal points, keep the decimal and add or subtract the numbers.

2. To multiply decimals, multiply the factors and give the product as many decimal places as there are in the sum of the decimal places in the factors, counting from right to left; add as many zeroes as are needed on the left.

3. To divide decimals, move the decimal point in the divisor as many places as needed to make it a whole number, and move the decimal point in the dividend the same number of places adding zeroes as needed. Place the decimal point in the quotient above the new position of the decimal point in the dividend, and divide the numbers.

4. To change a common fraction to a decimal fraction, divide the numerator of the fraction by its denominator.

5. To change a decimal fraction to a common fraction, write the decimal fraction as a common fraction whose denominator is 10, 100, etc., according to the place value chart, and reduce the fraction to lowest terms.

MATH RULES FOR WORKING WITH FRACTIONS

1. To change an improper fraction to a mixed number, divide the denominator into the numerator.

2. To change a mixed number to an improper fraction, multiply the whole number by the denominator of the fraction and add the numerator, and use the result as the new numerator, keeping the original denominator.

3. To add or subtract fractions with the same denominator, keep the denominator and add or subtract the numerators: $a/b + c/b = \frac{a+c}{b}$; $a/b - c/b = \frac{a-c}{b}$.

4. To add or subtract fractions with different denominators, express each fraction in terms of a common denominator, then keep the denominator and add or subtract the numerators.

5. To reduce fractions to lower terms, divide the numerator and denominator by the same amount: $a/b = \frac{a \div c}{b \div c}$.

6. To raise fractions to higher terms, multiply the numerator and denominator by the same amount: $a/b = \frac{a \times c}{b \times c}$.

7. To multiply fractions, multiply the numerator and multiply the denominators: $\frac{a}{b} \times \frac{c}{d} = \frac{ac}{bd}$.

8. To divide fractions, invert the divisor and multiply the resulting fractions: $a/b \div c/d = a/b \times d/c = ad/bc$.

RULES FOR AN EFFECTIVE JOB INTERVIEW

A. *Preparing for the interview*

1. Assemble in easily available order all the papers you need to take with you. The principal one is your resume—unless you have submitted it before the interview. If you have not prepared a resume, take your school records, social security card, and work records, with the names of your employers and dates of employment. (Prepare your own list if you have no formal records.) You may also need any licenses, union card, or military records you have. If your work is the sort that you can show at an interview, you may want to take a few samples (such as art or design work or published writings).

2. Learn all you can about the company where you are going for an interview—its product or service, standing in the industry, number and kinds of jobs available, and hiring policies and practices.

3. Know what you have to offer—what education and training you have had, what work you have done, and what you can do. If you have not prepared a resume, review your inventory chart before you go.

4. Know what kind of job you want and why you want to work for the firm where you are applying.

5. If you do not have a resume that includes references, be prepared to furnish the names, addresses, and business affiliations of three persons (not relatives) who are familiar with your work and character. If you are a recent graduate, you can list your teachers. When possible, ask your references for permission to use their names.

6. Lean the area salary scale for the type of job you are seeking.

7. Never take anyone with you to the interview.

8. Allow as much uninterrupted time for the interview as it may require. (For example, do not park your car in a limited time space.)

9. Dress conservatively. Avoid either too formal or too casual attire.

B. *During the interview*

1. Be pleasant and friendly but businesslike.

2. Let the employer control the interview. Your answers should be frank and brief but complete, without rambling. Avoid dogmatic statements.

3. Be flexible and willing but give the employer a clear idea of your job preferences.

4. Stress your qualifications without exaggeration. The employer's questions or statements will indicate the type of person wanted. Use these clues in presenting your qualifications. For example, if you are being interviewed for an engineering position and the employer mentions that the job will require some customer contact work, use this clue to emphasize any work, experience, or courses you

have had in this type of work.

5. If you have not sent your resume in advance, present it or your work records, references, personal data, work samples, or other materials to support your statements when the employer requests them.

6. In discussing your previous jobs and work situations, avoid criticizing former employers or fellow workers.

7. Don't discuss your personal, domestic, or financial problems unless you are specifically asked about them.

8. Don't be in a hurry to ask questions unless the employer invites them. But don't be afraid to ask what you need to know. If the employer offers you a job, be sure you understand exactly what your duties will be. You should also find out what opportunities for advancement will be open to you. A definite understanding about the nature of your job will avoid future disappointment for either you or your employer.

9. Be prepared to state the salary you want, but not until the employer has introduced the subject. Be realistic in discussing salary.

10. If the employer does not definitely offer you a job or indicate when you will hear about it, ask when you may call to learn the decision.

11. If the employer asks you to call or return for another interview, make a written note of the time, date, and place.

12. Thank the employer for the interview. If the firm cannot use you, ask about other employers who may need a person with your qualifications.

RULES FOR WRITING THE ACCOMPANYING LETTER OF APPLICATION

1. Type neatly, using care in sentence structure, spelling, and punctuation.

2. Use a good grade of letter-sized white bond paper.

3. Address your letter to a specific person, if possible (use city directories or other sources).

4. State exactly the kind of position you are seeking and why you are applying to the particular firm.

5. Be clear, brief, and businesslike.

6. Enclose a resume.

RULES FOR PREPARING YOUR RESUME

1. Begin with your name, address, and telephone number. Other personal data, such as your date of birth (optional) and your marital status and dependents, may follow or appear at the end of your resume.

2. Indicate the kind of job you are seeking. If you are qualified for several jobs and are preparing one all-purpose resume, list them in order of your preference.

3. Organize work history information in two ways. Choose the one that presents your work experience better.

a) *By job* List job separately (even if the jobs were within the same firm), starting with the most recent one and working backward. For each job, list:

Dates of employment.

Name and address of employer and nature of the business.

Position you held.

Then describe your job showing:

Specific job duties—The tasks you performed, including any special assignments and use of special equipment or instruments.

Scope of responsibility—Your place in the organization, how many people you supervised, and, in turn, the degree of supervision you received.

Accomplishments—If possible, give concrete facts and figures.

b) *By function* List the functions (fields of specialization or types of work, such as engineering, sales promotion, or personnel management) you performed that are related to your present job objectives.

Then describe briefly the work you have done in each of these fields, without breaking it down by jobs.

4. List your formal education, giving:

High school (can be omitted if you have a higher degree), college, graduate school, and other courses or training.

Dates of graduation or leaving school.

Degrees or certificates received.

Major and minor subjects and other courses related to your job goal.

Scholarships and honors.

Extracurricular activities (if you are a recent graduate and your activities pertain to your job goal).

5. List your military service if it is recent or pertinent to your job goal, indicating:

306

Branch and length of service.

Major duties, including details of assignments related to the job you seek.

(Indicate any pertinent military training here or under your education.)

6. Provide miscellaneous information. If appropriate to your field of work, give such information as:

Knowledge of foreign languages.

Volunteer or leisure time activities.

Special skills, such as typing, shorthand, or ability to operate special equipment.

Membership in professional organizations.

Articles published, inventions, or patents.

7. As references, give the names, positions, and addresses of three persons who have direct knowledge of your work competence. If you are a recent graduate, you can list teachers who are familiar with your schoolwork. When possible, you should obtain the permission of the persons you use as references.

RULES FOR DETERMINING GENETIC CHARACTERISTICS IN FUTURE CHILDREN

1. If dark eyes dominate any one side of a family, almost all offspring will be born with dark eyes regardless of eye color in the other parent.

2. If both parents have light eyes, most of their offspring will have light eyes.

3. If both parents have straight hair, most of their children will be straight-haired.

4. If one side of the family has curly hair as a dominant characteristic, most children will be born with curly hair, even if the other parent has straight hair.

5. If both parents are curly-haired but each has some straight-haired relatives, the odds are near three to one that their offspring will have curly hair.

6. If one parent has curly hair and straight-haired relatives while the other parent has straight hair, the offspring has an equal chance of being either straight haired or curly.

7. If both parents are dark-haired or both parents blond, children will follow suit in most cases.

8. If both parents are dark-haired with blond-haired members in their families, there is a three to one probability of giving birth to dark-haired offspring.

9. If one parent has dark hair and some blond relatives and the other parent is blond, there is a fifty-fifty chance of producing offspring with dark or blond hair.

10. If both parents have red hair, they will almost always have red-haired children.

ANCIENT ALCHEMISTS' RULES FOR MAKING GOLD

1. Melt the following ingredients in separate crucibles:
   - 20 parts platinum
   - 20 parts silver
   - 240 parts brass
   - 120 parts nickel
2. Combine them and you have gold!

RULES OF SPELLING

1. I before E, except after C is the likely pattern. If the letter C is pronounced S, in long E syllables, it is followed by EI. When C is pronounced SH, it is followed by IE (efficient).
2. Only use "ise" after the letter V, never "ize".
3. For words ending in "ce" or "ge", keep final E before adding "able".
4. Drop the final E before adding "ble" when the E is preceded by a consonant other than C or G.
5. Words of one syllable, ending in a single consonant preceded by a single vowel, double the final consonant before a suffix beginning with a vowel.
6. "Able" is added to a complete word. "Ible" is added to a root that is not a complete word.
7. Usually, final y changes to i before a suffix is added. When final Y is preceded by a vowel, S or ed is added directly. Y remains unchanged.

WINSTON CHURCHILL'S RULES FOR WHAT TO DO WITH YOUR BOOKS

1. Read them.
2. If you cannot read them, at any rate handle them and, as it were, fondle them.
3. Peer into them.
4. Let them fall open where they will.
5. Read on from the first sentence that arrests the eye.
6. Then turn to another.
7. Make a voyage of discovery, taking soundings of uncharted seas.
8. Set them back on their shelves with your own hands.
9. Arrange them on your own plan, so that if you do not know what is in them, you at least know where they are.
10. If they cannot be your friends, let them at any rate be your acquaintances.
11. If they cannot enter the circle of your life, do not deny them at least a nod of recognition.

RULES FOR KEEPING YOUR YARD FREE OF MOSQUITOES

1. Eliminate all standing fresh water.
2. Flatten all tin cans or puncture both ends.
3. Completely seal cesspools and screen all vents.
4. Clean regularly clogged roof gutters and drain flat roofs, so no water stays.
5. Cover all standing receptacles, such as rain barrels in rural areas, with netting.
6. Empty and refill outdoor birdbaths daily.
7. Stock garden pools with goldfish.
8. Tilt wheelbarrows and other machines with containers to prevent holding water.
9. Empty water can after using around the garden.
10. Dispose of old tires, or anything which holds water.

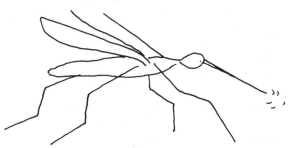

RULES FOR AVOIDING INSECTS DURING OUTDOOR RECREATION

1. Do not overlook mechanical methods of protecting yourself from insects. When camping, make sure all windows in your tent are screened.
2. Make sure the floor is tightly fastened to the sides, to keep scorpions or spiders out of your tent.
3. Wear slacks or long trousers and tuck them into the tops of your socks or boots, to avoid ticks.
4. Cover open food dishes with a small fine-mesh net, to keep insects from landing on food.
5. Practice sanitation. A clean campsite or picnic area is less likely to attract most kinds of insects than a littered area.
6. Before pitching a tent, clear the area of dead leaves, twigs, and loose stones.
7. If possible, do not camp near rockpiles or fallen trees; scorpions and spiders often hide in such places.

RHYMING RULES FOR WEATHER FORECASTING

1. Red sky at night,
   Sailors delight;
   Red sky in the morning,
   Sailors take warning.
2. Evening red and morning gray
   Sets the traveler on his way;
   Evening gray and morning red
   Brings down rain upon his head.
3. When the dew is on the grass,
   Rain will never come to pass.
4. Sound traveling far and wide
   A stormy day will betide.
5. Mackerel sky, mackerel sky,
   Never long wet, never long dry.
6. Mackerel scales and mare's tails
   Make lofty ships carry low sails.

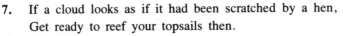

7. If a cloud looks as if it had been scratched by a hen,
   Get ready to reef your topsails then.
8. Ants that move their eggs and climb,
   Rain is coming anytime.
9. When charged with stormy matter lower the skies,
   The busy bee at home her labor plies . . .
10. When the glowworm lights her lamp,
    The air is always damp.
11. When eager bites the thirsty flea,
    Clouds and rain you sure shall see.
12. A fly on your nose you slap and it goes,
    If it comes back again, it will bring a good rain.
13. When spiders' web in air do fly
    The spell will soon be very dry.

14. When trout refuse bait or fly,
    There ever is a storm a-nigh.

15. Before the storm the crab his briny home
    Sidelong forsakes, and strives on land to roam.

16. When black snails on the road you see,
    Then on the morrow rain will be.

17. If fowls roll in the sand,
    Rain is at hand.

18. When numerous birds their island home forsake,
    And to firm land their airy voyage make,
    The ploughman, watching their ill-omened flight,
    Fears for his golden fields a withering blight.

19. Seagull, seagull, sit on the sand,
    It's never good weather while you're on the land.

20. When the barnyard goose walks south to north,
    Rain will surely soon break forth.

21. When cocks crow and then drink,
    Rain and thunder are on the brink.

22. When the rooster crows on the ground,
    The rain will fall down:
    When he crows on the fence,
    The rain will depart hence.

23. Swallows fly high: clear blue sky;
    Swallows fly low: rain we shall know.

24. When pigs carry sticks,
    The clouds will play tricks;
    When they lie in the mud,
    No fears of a flood.

25. When sheep do huddle by tree and bush,
    Bad weather is coming with wind and slush.

26. When the donkey blows his horn
    'Tis time to house your hay and corn.

RULES FOR COMBATING MALE CHAUVINIST ATTITUDES TOWARD WOMEN EXECUTIVES IN BUSINESS

To change the pattern you've got to break the pattern. Here are six rules which, if followed, will drive the inveterate MCP nuts and cause the rest of the male staff to think at least once:

1. *Be careful taking notes at a meeting.*

If you take notes, make sure there are others in the meeting doing likewise. Don't be the only person taking notes. If notes should be taken, call a secretary in. Behave like an executive.

2. *Never admit that you know stenography.*

If you take notes in a meeting, use a yellow ruled letter tablet, preferably enclosed in a leather holder. Never use a steno pad. Never use shorthand for taking notes in front of others. Always take notes in longhand. A San Francisco advertising executive agrees with that advice: "I used to be good at shorthand, but now the only time I use it is when nobody's looking. At a client meeting, I write everything down in longhand, even though it will take longer. I don't want people to know that I can take it."

3. *Never type your own letters.*

The fact that you can type is acceptable, but never type your own letters. Only type interoffice memos if others on your level do. Your method of correspondence indicates your status within the organization.

4. *Rarely get the coffee.*

Rarely, because sometimes you should get it out of common courtesy, like it's your turn, that kind of thing. If you notice coffee is absent from a meeting, the best thing to do is ask one of the secretaries to bring it in. (It's degrading for a secretary to bring your coffee when you are alone in your office, but it's acceptable for her to bring coffee in to a group, especially if there are outsider visitors.)

5. *Never clean up after everybody's left.*

Even if you have an overwhelming compunction to do so, don't. The only exception is if very special circumstances dictate otherwise, or everyone else is helping. Even if you're itching to get your hands on those dirty coffee cups, keep your hands in your pockets.

6. *Never pose as a model.*

If someone wants to take your picture because you're you, such as for the company newspaper or annual report, then go ahead. But refuse to pose in any pictures as a model demonstrating a product, no matter how flattering the offer is to your ego. The use of you as a sex object is demeaning to you as an executive.

RULES FOR QUIETING YOUR HOME

1. Use noise-absorbing materials on floor, especially in areas where there is a lot of traffic.

2. Hang heavy drapes over the windows closest to outside noise sources.

3. Put rubber or plastic treads on uncarpeted stairs. (They're safer, too.)

4. Use upholstered rather than hard-surfaced furniture to deaden noise.

5. Install sound-absorbing ceiling tile in the kitchen. Wooden cabinets will vibrate less than metal ones.

6. Use a foam pad under blenders and mixers.

7. Use insulation and vibration mounts when installing dishwashers.

8. Install washing machines in the same room with heating and cooling equipment, preferably in an enclosed space.

9. Remember that a hand-powered lawn mower does the job and gives you excercise, too. If you use a power mower, operate it at reasonable hours.

10. Use a headset when you are the only one interested in listening to the hi-fi. Also, keep the volume down.

11. Place window air-conditioners where their hum can help mask objectionable noises. However, try to avoid locating them facing your neighbor's bedrooms.

12. Beware that children's toys need not make intensive or explosive sounds. (Some can cause permanent ear injury, in addition to getting on your nerves.)

13. Compare the noise outputs of different makes of an appliance before making your selection.

RULES OF BASIC LANDSCAPING

1. Count on it—if you plant little trees next to your house, they will grow into giant sequoias in four years, rot out the siding, and eventually fall on your roof.

2. And—if you plant little trees out on the lawn away from the house, they will get no taller than your knee, and you will spend the rest of your life tripping over them and moving around them.

3. Finally—if you plant little trees at the edge of your property, they will grow to medium height and die after your neighbor saws off half the limbs.

313

RULES FOR FINDING A QUIET PLACE TO LIVE

1. Stay away from major noise sources such as airport flight paths, heavy truck routes, high-speed freeways. When buying a home, check the area zoning master plan for projected changes. (In some places, you can't get FHA loans for housing in noisy locations.)

2. Look for wall-to-wall carpeting, especially in the apartment above you and in the corridors.

3. Find out about the wall construction (staggered-stud interior walls are among the quietest). Can you hear a portable radio at normal volume in the adjoining apartment?

4. Check the electrical outlet boxes. If they are back-to-back, they will act as noise transmitters.

5. Ask about the door construction. Solid or core-filled doors with gaskets or weather stripping are quieter.

6. Make sure sleeping areas are well away from rooms with noise-making equipment.

7. Check the heating and air-conditioning ducts. Inside insulation makes them quieter.

RULES FOR ORGANIZED HOUSE CLEANING

Organize your work into these four groups:
1. *Daily Tasks:* Preparation, serving and cleaning up after meals
   Straightening up and routine housecleaning
   Care of children, if any
   Period of relaxation
   Personal grooming
2. *Weekly Tasks:* Thorough housecleaning
   Washing and ironing
   Menu planning and marketing
   Baking and special food preparation
3. *Special Tasks:* Entertaining and trips outside the house
   Mending, sewing, clothes care
   Accounts, correspondence, records
4. *Seasonal Tasks:* Special cleaning
   Annual conversion of house to winter
   Annual conversion of house to summer
   Annual conversion of clothes to winter
   Annual conversion of clothes to summer
   Holiday preparations
   Canning
   Gardening

RULES FOR PREDICTING RAIN

Expect rain:
1. Within three days if the horns of the moon point down.
2. If leaves show their backs.
3. If cows are lying down in the pasture.
4. If there is a ring around the moon. Count all stars in the ring and it will rain within that many days.
5. If the sun sets with clouds.
6. If an ant covers the hole to his anthill.
7. If earthworms come to the surface of the ground.
8. If birds fly low.
9. If it rains on Easter Sunday, it will rain every Sunday for seven weeks.
10. If it begins raining on the day the moon becomes full, it will continue raining until the moon quarters.

RULES FOR HANDLING PET BIRDS

1.   Catch the bird.

2.   Keep him in your hands without suffocating him but without letting him fly away. Before anything else, you have to learn how to take hold of him. To do so:

> a) Close all the windows and doors, because if he gets away from you . . .
> b) Get rid of everything on which he could perch beyond your reach: curtain rods, etc. If you don't, you can spend all day chasing him,
> c) If your bird is in his cage, stick your hand inside and gently but firmly grasp the bird and gather him in. You must hold his wings; if not, one may break. Leave only the two feet and the head free.

3.   If you have to deal with a biting parrakeet, hold his neck between your index and middle fingers. This will allow him to turn his head but not to pinch you with his beak.

4.   For very large birds—macaws, cockatoos, Great Amazons—it is best to have leather gloves. For even if they are tame and like their owner, they will rebel if he tries to meddle in some matter which, in their opinion, doesn't concern him.

5.   Large parrots are very strong, so they have to be held securely. To do so, two people are needed. Your helper grasps the bird the way you hold hens out in the country: after placing its body under his left arm and pressing it between his arm and his side, he takes its neck in his right hand. The bird is thus totally immobilized—which puts him in a very bad humor. But this is the only way that he can be cared for.

6.   In order to administer a pill, you need two people. While one person holds the bird in the manner suggested in Rule 5, the other teases its beak with the handle of a spoon. Already furious, the parrot at once takes out his anger by seizing the handle. All that remains is to turn the handle so it is vertical. The bird finds itself with its beak wedged open and all you have to do is to slip the pill into the corner of its beak; the bird will be forced to swallow it.

7. If by chance you find a diurnal or nocturnal bird or prey that is injured and you want to save it, you will have to grab it as you would a parrot. But be careful: its talons are more formidable than the powerful claws of a cockatoo!
8. There is a very simple way to handle screech owls, and you can also use it on turtledoves even though they are a very different bird. Turn the bird over on its back and it won't budge.

RULES FOR RAISING FROGS

1. Choose marshy land, fence it in, and either let nature take its course or stock the place with a species that is suitable for marketing as well as easily grown in your locale.
2. Be aware that, in the spring of her third year, the female frog begins to lay eggs at the rate of from twenty thousand to thirty thousand a year. In seventy-two to a hundred hours, the eggs, or spawn, which are gathered in galvanized tubs, hatch into tiny tadpoles and are then transferred to troughs supplied with running water. A diet of ground beef and rolled oats is supplied, and, in due course, the tadpoles develop into frogs salable the next year.
3. Hang electric lights around your pond. This will attract millions of insects, since after attaining adulthood the frog diet is of insects, minnows, crawfish, and animalcules found upon the submerged foliage.
4. Beware . . . frogs have many enemies. The giant water beetle preys on the tadpoles and young frogs, and raccoons, cranes, herons, turtles, snakes, and large fish enjoy their delicate flesh. Moreover, frogs are cannibals and have a great fondness for kinfolk. Segregation is necessary to keep down the mortality rate, which is very high, at best.
5. Capture your frogs for market by walking around the special pool reserved for adult frogs and herd them from the banks into the water. Then the water is drained off until it concentrates in a shallow, central pool from which are lifted enough frogs to fill the orders on hand. The pool is then reflooded pending the next haul.

PIONEER RULES FOR WASHING CLOTHES

1. Build a fire in back yard to heat kettle of rainwater.
2. Set tubs so smoke won't blow in eyes if wind is present.
3. Shave cake of lye soap in boiling water.
4. Sort things, making three piles—one of white, one of colored, and one of rags and britches.
5. Still flour in cold water to smooth for starch and then thin down with boiling water.
6. Rub dirty spots on board, then boil. Rub colored but don't boil. Take white things out of kettle with broom handle. Then rinse, blue, and starch.
7. Spread tea towels on grass. Hang old rags on fence.
8. Pour rinse water in flower bed.
9. Scrub privy seat and floor with the soapy water.
10. Turn tubs upside down. Put on clean dress. Comb hair. Sit and rest a spell and count your blessings.

RULES FOR BUYING A NEWLY BUILT HOME

1. Test the reliability of the builder. Arrange to talk with people who are living in houses constructed by him.
2. Don't be overwhelmed by the appearance of a model home. Pin down exactly which features are provided with the new house and which are "extras."
3. If the community is to have new street paving, water and sewer lines and sidewalks, make sure you know whether you or the builder will assume the costs. Find out about charges for water and trash collection.
4. If you buy from a model, check the lot site in advance. Is it the size and setting you want? After the bulldozer arrives, it may be too late.
5. Don't take just anyone's word about the zoning uses permitted for the area in which you plan to buy a home. This information could affect future property values. Check yourself with the city, county, or township clerk's office for zoning information.
6. Remember, the contract with the builder should set forth the total sales price. If possible, try to locate a lender who will allow you to take advantage of lower interest rates which may apply at the time of closing. Avoid an arrangement which would allow the lender to increase the mortgage interest rate if market conditions change between the date of mortgage commitment and the closing date.
7. Be sure your contract with the builder definitely stipulates the completion date of your new home.

8. Don't be afraid to check construction progress regularly while the house is being built.

9. Be sure the contract is complete and that there is agreement on all the details of the transactions. Any extra features that are to be included in the finished house should be described in writing.

10. The day before you take title to the house, make a thorough inspection. Check all equipment, windows, and doors. This is your last chance to request changes.

11. Insist on these papers when you take possession: (a) warranties from all manufacturers for equipment in the house, (b) certificate of occupancy, and (c) certificates from the Health Department clearing plumbing and sewer installations and all applicable certificates of code compliance.

RULES FOR FORECASTING THE WEATHER BY ANIMALS

Expect a bad winter if:

1. Squirrels begin gathering nuts early (middle or late September).

2. The north side of a beaver dam is more covered with sticks than the south.

3. Squirrels' tails grow bushier.

4. Fur or hair on animals such as horses, sheep, mules, cows, and dogs is thicker than usual.

5. The fur on the bottom of rabbits' feet is thicker.

6. Birds huddle on the ground.

7. Birds eat up all the berries early.

8. Worms are bending up and going into people's houses and abandoned buildings in October.

9. There are a lot of spiders, frost worms, and black bugs about in the fall.

10. Crickets are in the chimney.

11. The black band on the woolly caterpillar's back is wide. (The more black than brown he is, and/or the wider the black stripe, the worse the winter.)

RULES FOR BUYING CLOTHES THAT FIT

1.   Always try it on, even if you know your size and it's been the same since high school. Unfortunately, and alas, the size may have changed even if you haven't. And you may have, even if you don't want to admit it. Try it on. Make sure you can see the fit in a full-length mirror, and, better yet, two mirrors. If it looks like you need the next size, try one on. The sizes really do vary from brand to brand and store to store. And just in case the growth has been yours, you'll look thinner in a size that fits.

2.   Read the tag. There may be some important information on the tag. If there's a size chart giving measurements, follow it instead of buying your normal size. This is especially true when buying clothes for infants and small children. Sizes in this range vary so widely as to be virtually meaningless.

3.   Know a good fit when you see it. The most painstaking session in the fitting room is no good unless you know what to look for.

Shirts should button confortably across the chest and not gap when you move. The collar should be close without being snug. Sleeves should be long enough to cover the wristbone when you bend your elbows, and shirttails should stay tucked in when you bend and stretch. Men's shirts are sold by collar size and arm length, and are fairly standard.

Women's shirts and blouses may be sold by size (e.g., 12) or bust size (36), and tend to be less uniform.

Slacks for women are usually sized like dresses. Men's pants have a waist size (e.g., 36) and an inseam length (e.g., 30). All pants should fit comfortably loose in the crotch, with the legs hanging straight to the tops of the shoes. They should never be so long that they touch the floor at any point.

(Pants with cuffs can be difficult to shorten, so be sure they fit before you buy.) Here again, men's sizes are more reliable than women's. Women, by the way, can wear men's jeans as hip huggers. Once you find the size that fits, you can walk into a men's store and buy them off the table. Often men's pants are better made than women's, so give it a try.

320

Dresses, suits, shirts, and jackets for women are usually all sold according to the same size.

Misses sizes are for the woman of "average" height (5'5" to 5'8") and proportions. For a size 12, these proportions are: bust 34", waist 25 ½", hips 36". If one of your measurements exceeds these, you'll have to buy the next larger size.

Junior sizes are for the typical "youthful" figure, shorter in the waist, with a small, high bust. Some women can wear both misses and junior sizes, some junior and junior petite, which is proportioned for even shorter smaller figures.

Petite sizes are for the short (5'5" and under) women with the same proportions as misses. Tall sizes are for the tall women with about the same proportions, except for longer waist, as misses.

Women's sizes are for women of average height with slightly fuller figures than misses size.

Infants' and children's clothing sizes are, if anything, screwier than women's sizes. The best advice is to try it on the child, but not at the store. Buy only from stores where you can return, at least until you determine what the right size is. Take the garment home and let the child put it on, move around, voice any complaints. Buy children's clothes roomy, but not so big as to be uncomfortable. A few pointers:

The most important thing about shoes, for anyone, is that they shouldn't be too tight. This goes double for children, whose growing feet can be deformed by tight shoes. Even if you think you know what size you wear, always try on a new pair of shoes. Take your time, walk around. Never buy a pair that you hope will stretch. Never buy a pair that hurts or pinches in any way. They probably won't stretch, and any pair of shoes you can't wear is a really expensive pair of shoes. With children, recheck their shoes every couple of months. They may not complain until their feet literally can't be crammed into the shoes. By then, some damage may already have beed done.

Infants' sizes are for babies. This means large in the bottom (to accommodate diapers) and short in the legs. If your child is walking, infants's sizes won't work for him, even though his height and weight may indicate he could fit. Toddlers's sizes are made with the big seat but longer legs to fit the walking baby. These sizes run up to 4T, but if your child is out of diapers and has begun to slim down, 4T pants may fall right off. Then he's ready for children's sizes. These run up to 12, and are made to fit the child (boy or girl) whose body has not yet begun to develop adolescent characteristics. Once they do, it's on into teen and subteen sizes, which also go under other names, such as "student." These older boys' sizes, by the way, are made to fit a person of up to thirty-six-inch chest and about six feet in height. Student clothes are cheaper than women's and the teenage boy's department is a good place for women to buy (for themselves) things like sweat shirts, ponchos, jeans, and denim shirts. Small women may do well in the girl's department.

RULES FOR BUYING FURNITURE

1. Remember, form follows function. A good maxim for art, and a good one for interior design as well. If you know what a piece of furniture is supposed to do in your life, you won't have nearly as much trouble choosing what it should look like. Does the kitchen table have to double as a work space? Then it should be made of sturdy, no-stain material such as Formica or butcher block. Is the new sofa supposed to be the focus of a formal living room or the extra bed in the playroom downstairs? In short, how do you and your family live, and what job(s) do you want this new piece of furniture to do for you?
2. Be prepared when you shop. Take along lists, descriptions, etc., that you've written down at home. Bring any relevant measurements (e.g., how big is the door the sofa has to fit through to get into your house?), color charts, swatches, paint chips, or whatever.
3. If you buy new, make sure you know what you're buying. Is there a guarantee? How long does it last? Will the store deliver, install, replace? Read all tags and labels telling how to use and care for the piece. Does that kind of care fit in with your life-style?
4. Shop around. Different stores may have drastically different prices on the same brand-name merchandise. Look for big-name sales. Furniture sales, like clothing sales, seem to occur on a seasonal basis. Big furniture sale months are usually February (post-Christmas) and August (post-move). Watch for bargains on seconds, irregulars, or floor samples. But be particularly careful to check out such bargains before you buy.
5. Consider unfinished funiture. It's not only cheaper, but allows you to personalize it with just the right finish to suit your decor.
6. Whatever you buy, examine it thoroughly. Never mind what the people in the store think, lie down on the sofa, open drawers, and take the cushions off the chair to look at the construction.

7. Take your time. Talk over any major purchase with the whole family and the bank that's giving you the loan to buy it. Don't let yourself be high-pressured into making a snap decision you may regret.

8. What about secondhand furniture? There was a time when nobody wanted anything but the newest. But these days there's status as well as saving in turning as auction of thrift shop purchase into a beautiful conversation piece. Secondhand shopping, like unfinished furniture, presupposes that you're willing to do some work. It also assumes that you know a little something about furniture construction, so you can tell a deal from a rip-off.

9. Do it yourself. If you like woodworking or painting or paperhanging, or whatever, you can cut furnishing costs down to the bone. There are furniture kits available from everybody, from Sears to the fanciest specialty stores. Plans, which come a lot cheaper than kits, can be had from magazines catering to home owners and hobbyists.

10. Get it for free. There are two ways of obtaining furnishings for absolutely nothing. (a) Get it from someone you know. Be on hand when Aunt Ethel moves to a smaller place (you might offer her a little help). Never refuse a piece of furniture being given away by a friend or relative unless you're absolutely positive you can't use it or store it. You'll regret it next winter when you have to buy one. (b) Get it from people you don't know. These unknown folks may be throwing it away. If you know the days that large garbage (like old chest and mattresses) is collected, you'll know when to look. As to where, look where rich people live, naturally. Who else ever throws out a piece of furniture before it falls apart? In this same category is the dump. Big city dumps are usually less yielding than ones in little towns. The latter sometimes offer real antiques along with the (perfectly serviceable) aluminum kitchen chairs. You don't have to tell people where these goodies came from once you get them home and give them a coat of paint.

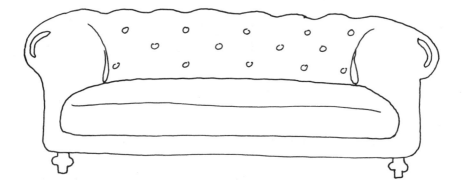

RULES FOR SURVIVING A HEAT WAVE

1. Slow down. High temperatures and humidity sap your energy, and put a strain on your heart. Listen to your body. If it says, "Go loll in the shade, friend," go loll.

2. Don't dry out. Excessive perspiration will make you thirsty. Obey your body—drink up. Take a salt tablet: sweating drains your normal supply, and you need it. If you are on a salt-restricted diet, of course, ask the advice of your doctor. Overuse of tablets may cause stomach upset.

3. Dress in lightweight, light-colored clothes. Light colors throw back the sun's rays. Take a tip from the Tuaregs, the dwellers of western and central Sahara. When the sun sears, they wear white cotton undergarments, and envelop themselves in white cotton or woolen cloaks, covering their heads and lower faces.

4. Remember, in a real heat wave, the best defense is to be where the heat is not. Find an air-conditioner, take in a cool movie, go shopping where they have chilled air. If you can't find air conditioning, get out of the sun. Even a slightly stuffy room is better than stinging rays. The effects of heat exhaustion mount up. You are more likely to be in a worse way on Thursday of a heat wave than you were on Monday.

5. Don't overeat. You probably won't feel like it anyway, but stay away from heavy foods. Light salads, fruits, cottage cheese, and lots of liquids are good for you and don't take unnecessary energy to digest.

6. Make it easy on yourself. Even on moderately hot days, ration your sun-worshipping: five or ten minutes the first day, and add to it slowly. Sunburn is very painful. You probably won't die from it, but it may make you want to.

7. Pray for rain. Or snow.

RULES FOR SURVIVING TORNADOES

1. In open country, move away from a tornado's path at right angles. If there is no time to escape, lie flat in the nearest ditch or ravine.

2. Keep in mind, structures with wide, freespan roofs like auditoriums, gymnasiums, and schools which don't have reinforced construction are unsafe. Go to a nearby building of reinforced construction instead, or take cover outside on low, protected ground.

3. Remember, in homes the basement is the safest place. Seek shelter under sturdy furniture if possible. If the nearest house has no basement, take cover in the center of the house, on the lowest floor, in a small room like a closet or bathroom, under sturdy furniture. Keep some windows open to help equalize pressure, but stay away from them because they may shatter.

4. Go to a designated shelter area in shopping centers; a car is an unsafe place to be.

5. Go to an interior hallway on the lowest floor or to a designated shelter area in office buildings.

6. Be aware, mobile homes are especially dangerous during strong winds, and should be evacuated when strong winds are forecast. You can minimize destruction by securing them with cables or tie-down straps anchored in concrete footing, or with screw anchors in the soil. Mobile home parks should have a community storm shelter, and someone to monitor broadcasts during a severe storm. If there is no shelter nearby, leave the trailer park and take cover elsewhere.

RULES FOR USING THE BEAUFORT SCALE (0–12) TO DETERMINE WIND SPEED

Scale

(0) If smoke rises vertically and winds feel calm, estimate 0–1 mph.

(1) If smoke drifts slowly and light air movement is felt, estimate 1–3 mph.

(2) If there's a slight breeze and leaves rustle, estimate 4–7 mph.

(3) If leaves and twigs are set in motion by gentle breeze, estimate 8–12 mph.

(4) If small branches move and moderate breezes are felt, estimate 13–18 mph.

(5) If fresh breezes cause small trees to sway, estimate 19–24 mph.

(6) If strong breezes cause large branches to sway, estimate 25–31 mph.

(7) If whole trees are set in motion by moderate gale winds, estimate 32–38 mph.

(8) If fresh gale winds cause twigs to break off, estimate 47–54 mph.

(9) If strong gale winds break branches off, estimate 47–54 mph.

(10) If trees snap and are blown down from strong gale winds, estimate 55–63 mph.

(11) If stormy winds cause widespread damage, estimate 64–72 mph.

(12) If a hurricane strikes inflicting extreme property damage, estimate 73–82 mph.

RULES FOR OUTDOOR LIVING

1. Be clean in your outdoor manners—rubbish has no place in the American landscape. Make "Leave No Trace" your slogan and dispose of rubbish properly.

2. Keep candy wrappers, cigarette packages, and similar "pocket trash" in your pocket until you can throw them into a waste container or your home wastepaper basket. Trash along roadsides is a national problem requiring the expenditure of millions of dollars a year in cleanups. Help solve the problem by keeping a trash bag in your car in which to accumulate trash that collects during a ride.

3. Deposit garbage in a waste container. If none is available, dispose of burnable garbage by burning and carry unburnable garbage out with you.

4. Never break bottles and jars and never throw them in a fire—hundreds of first aid cases are caused annually in our parks by broken glass. Never throw cans about and never bury them—at best it will take several years for cans to rust to powder and, if buried, animals dig them up in short order. Instead, deposit bottles, jars, and cans in a waste container. If none is at hand, take them with you—if you had room to pack in the full containers, you have room to pack out the empty ones for proper disposal.

5. Be careful with fire. Nine out of ten fires in our outdoors areas are caused by thoughtless and careless smokers and campers.

6. After using a match, break it in two before disposing of it. This is an old-timer's trick. The breaking is not the point—the point is that you can't break a match without touching the burned part, and you will then know quickly enough whether or not the match is out.

7. Never, never, never flip a glowing cigarette or cigar out of a car window—use the ashtray. Never smoke in areas where a fire danger exists. Carefully follow smoking rules of the outdoor area you are visiting.

Extinguish a cigarette by crushing out the burning ember completely against mineral dirt or rock; then fieldstrip the butt: tear open the paper, scatter the tobacco, roll up the paper in a tiny ball. Crush out the ember of a cigar in the manner; then break the butt apart. Knock out pipe heels on mineral dirt protected from the wind, so that the wind will not carry away sparks; then crush out embers.

8. Follow the park rules for the lighting of campfires. In many parks open fires may be used only in certain areas, or in permanent stone or metal fireplaces.

Where no fireplaces are available, clean a fire spot down to mineral ground—sand, gravel, clay, or rock—and remove all flammable materials for a safe distance. Never build a fire on duff—dry, decaying vegetable matter, leaves and grass: the fire may spread underground. Have a container of water on hand for extinguishing.

9. Keep your fire small—just big enough for the job. Keep it attended at all times. "Chaperone your fire"—never let a fire go out alone.

10. Extinguish your fire until it is not just out, but *DEAD OUT!* Drown the fire with water, then stir up and turn over ashes and half-burned twigs with a stick and drown again. Where water is scarce, work mineral dirt into the ashes, then stir and stir again until the last ember is out. Cover the extinguished remains with mineral dirt and do some "gardening" in the soil to help heal the fire scar.

11. Be considerate in the outdoors. Treat property and other people the way you would want to have your own property treated and the way you would like to be treated by other people. Be considerate, in your behavior, of other people's feelings and desire for privacy.

12. Never trespass private property—get permission. Don't cross planted fields—crops are valuable. Don't climb fences—use gates; close them after you if you had to open them; leave them open if that was the way you found them. Leave animals undisturbed. Don't destroy private property—whether stone fences or windowpanes in an empty building.

13. Heed the advice of "the man with the badge"—the park ranger, forest ranger, or game warden. Follow rules for the use of the picnic spot or camping area you are using. Refrain from damaging park furniture and fixtures. The innocent-sounding "souvenir hunting" spells T-H-E-F-T in plain English and should be pronounced that way! Spare the wild flowers. Do not deface living trees. Use available toilet facilities, or bury human wastes. Clean up after you so that the place looks the way you would like to have found it yourself—even though it wasn't that clean when you arrived. If you make use of firewood already cut and stored, replace it, with interest, for the party that follows you. Keep trails open and in good condition.

14. Be conservation-minded. The more you travel in the outdoors, the more will grow your desire to protect our natural resources for your own use and for the future, and to do your part in their conservation.

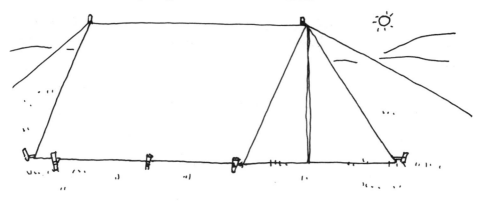

RULES FOR SURVIVAL IN THE CITY

1.   Be alert. If a potentially dangerous situation can be avoided, that is the best self-defense.
2.   Have keys ready well before arriving at the front door.
3.   Keep a shrill whistle attached to your key chain.
4.   Change all locks when you move into a new home.
5.   Lock your doors during the day even if you are at home and even if you only leave it for a few minutes.
6.   Leave lights on at night when you're away from home, changing location of lights from time to time.
7.   When you go away, do it quietly.
8.   Be suspicious of unnecessary shoving when in crowds.
9.   If you are afraid of a particular block, walk in the middle of the street.
10.   Know your neighborhood. Know where police boxes are, all-night cafes, and buildings with doormen.
11.   If you walk quickly and with confidence, a suspicious character is inclined to avoid you.
12.   If you think you are being followed, cross the street, if necessary crisscross.
13.   If you are being followed, start to run. Throw your purse or wallet in a mailbox.
14.   In an elevator always stand near the control panel. If attacked, hit the alarm button and press as many other buttons as you can reach with your arm.
15.   When leaving car keys with a doorman, garage or parking attendant, leave only the ignition key.
16.   Females traveling by car alone should lock all doors and have windows opened only slightly.
17.   If your door locks simply by "slamming" it, you are depending on an ineffectual security device known as a spring latch. This can be opened in seconds by a burglar.
18.   Doors should be equipped with double-cylinder dead-bolt devices. For added security, your locks should have "pick-resistant" cylinders and should be professionally installed.

19. Chain locks in addition to the dead-bolt offer added security. They should be used whenever it is necessary to open the door to strangers.

20. Peepholes allow you to see strangers before opening the door to them.

21. Doors with solid cores are preferable to panel doors or doors with glass panels. Thin-paneled or hollow-cored doors should be lined with metal sheets. Glass-paneled doors should be covered with closely spaced steel bars or with strong mesh on the inside of the door.

22. Windows which are easily accessible should be equipped with security devices. Windows leading to fire escapes should be secured with key-controlled inside locks. All other windows should be secured by ferry gates, bars, mesh, or by key-controlled inside locks.

23. Don't open your door to a stranger unless he identifies himself satisfactorily.

24. Don't carry a purse loosely or swinging behind the body.

25. Don't lay the purse in a shopping cart.

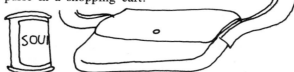

26. Don't leave your purse on the seat when you are driving. Put it out of view.

27. Don't pick up hitchhikers.

28. Don't carry identification on your key chain.

29. Don't place keys under mats or other receptacles outside the door.

30. Don't daydream while traveling.

31. Don't walk too near a building line or automobiles.

32. Don't enter an apartment if the door was forced or broken while you were out. Call the police emergency and wait outside until they arrive.

33. Always lock your door with a key.

34. Change the lock cylinder whenever a key-holding employee is discharged, a key is lost, or you move into a new home or office.

35. Use a chain bolt when it is necessary to open your door to strangers.

36. Carry your purse with one end in the palm of your hand and the other in the bend of the elbow and draw it close to your body.

37. Place your wallet, valuables, keys in your pocket and carry your handbag.

28. Hang up quickly if you receive obscene or nuisance calls. (See Rules for Handling an Obscene Phone Call.)

39. Turn street corners in a wide arc.

40. If attacked, make as much noise as possible.

41. If threatened by a robber, do as you are told. Observe as much as possible, and then call the police.

42. Cancel deliveries before going on vacation.

RULES FOR BUILDING A FIRE IN YOUR HOME FIREPLACE

1. Make sure the room is well ventilated, the damper open, and the flue unobstructed before lighting your fire.
2. Avoid burning wet or green wood.
3. Place a screen in front of your grate to catch any sparks that fly.
4. Keep a fire extinguisher handy and keep other combustibles at a distance.
5. Never use flammable liquids indoors to light your fire.
6. Place two logs on the iron grate or fire basket and lay the tinder between them.
7. Place above this a small handful of dry twigs or split softwood kindling.
8. Next, place small, dry logs over this base.
9. Create a teepee formation of kindling and small branch wood to ease your fire through early combustion stages until the logs are aglow. Place these logs close.
10. Remember, generally no more than four logs are needed to make a good fire.
11. Adjust the logs and maintain the flames by pushing the ends into the flame from time to time.
12. Add kindling and new logs as needed to rekindle a dying glow.
13. Rake coals toward the front of the grate before adding new logs.
14. Add new logs at the rear of the fireplace; there they will reflect light and heat into the room.

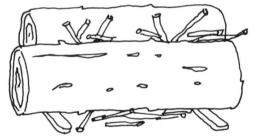

RULES FOR ESCAPING FROM FIRES

1. Plan an escape route from your room and home.
2. Practice using it.
3. Work out an alternate route—just in case.
4. Close your bedroom door before going to sleep. If fire should break out elsewhere in the house, the closed door may keep flames, gases, or smoke away

long enough for rescue to reach you. Flames terrify, but gas is the greatest danger in a fire.

5.   Never open a hot door. If you smell smoke or think there is fire in the house, touch-test the inside of your door. If it is hot, don't open it. Go to the window and wait for rescue there.

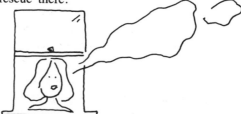

RULES FOR RIGHT OF WAY OF SAILING VESSELS

1.   A vessel which is running free shall keep out of the way of a vessel which is close-hauled.

2.   A vessel which is close-hauled on the port tack shall keep out of the way of a vessel which is close-hauled on the starboard tack.

3.   When both are running free, with the wind on different sides, the vessel which has the wind on the port side shall keep out of the way of the other.

4.   When both are running free, with the wind on the same side, the vessel which is to the windward shall keep out of the way of the vessel which is to the leeward.

5.   A vessel which has the wind aft shall keep out of the way of the other vessel.

Definitions for the above rule:

Close-hauled (beating)—Wind from direction within five points (approximately) of dead ahead. When the average boat sails with the wind broad on her bow, she is beating.

Wind Aft (running before the wind)—Wind from direction within two points of dead astern.

Running Free (includes close reach, beam reach, and broad reach)— wind from direction between five points aft the bow to two points forward of the stern.

RULES FOR AVOIDING "CON" ARTISTS AND RACKETS

1. Don't be fooled by the "money pitch." This is a clever scheme to get you to buy something—with the implication that you can get your money back by referring the salesman to some friends and neighbors.

The game is to lure you into signing an installment contract. But instead of getting paid, you wind up paying out money you hadn't meant to spend, perhaps every month for a long period of time.

2. Watch out for the "pigeon drop" racket. Some fine day a nice-looking man or woman may show you a large bundle of money and tell you he or she found it and will divide it with you if you'll show "good faith" by putting up some money. This trick has taken millions of dollars away from unsuspecting people, usually older men and women. Walk away from anyone who offers you a quick profit if you'll just show "good faith" by putting up some money. And notify the police.

3. Don't fall for the bank examiner racket. If you ever get a call from a person who claims to be a bank examiner and needs your help in trapping a dishonest teller, call the police. The racket is to get you to withdraw money from your account, which of course is to be refunded to you immediately. Once the money is withdrawn, the con man is long gone. Professional gypsters put on a very convincing act and fool many people with this one.

4. Be wary of accepting C.O.D. packages for a neighbor. Unless your neighbor has arranged this with you, you may be the victim of a very common swindle. A person dressed as a deliveryman says you can save your neighbor a long wait at the post office by paying for a package for him. The contents turn out to be unordered and unwanted "junk."

5. Be on guard against financing with a final "balloon payment." This calls for small monthly payments, on some purchase, with a final unlooked-for big payment at the end, called a "balloon payment." When you buy anything on the installment plan, read the contract carefully before you sign.

6. Look out for home improvement frauds. Offers to replace or repair furnaces, roofs, driveways, chimneys, etc.—or to make a free inspection—are often "gyp" deals by a traveling crew that gives you a fast sales talk, does an inferior job, collects, and then is long gone. The number and variety of home improvement rackets is so great we can't describe here. But these rules should help:

a) Know the people you deal with—or find out about them—before you sign anything or even give a verbal go-ahead.

b) Get references and check them carefully.

c) Check with your local Better Business Bureau or Chamber of Commerce.

d) Make sure all of the salesman's promises are written into the agreement.

e) Get competitive bids from contractors or dealers you know, either from past experience or by reputation.

f) Never sign a completion certificate before the work is completed to your satisfaction.

RULES FOR INVESTORS

1. Before buying . . . think!

2. Don't deal with strange securities firms. Consult your broker, banker, or other experienced person you know and trust.

3. Beware of securities offered over the telephone by strangers.

4. Don't listen to high-pressure sales talk.

5. Beware of promises of spectacular profits.

6. Be sure you understand the risks of loss.

7. Don't buy on tips and rumors. Get all the facts!

8. Tell the salesman to put all the information and advice in writing and mail it to you. Save it!

9. If you don't understand all the written information, consult someone who does.

10. Give at least as much consideration to buying securities as you would to buying other valuable property.

SOME BASIC RULES FOR NIGHT DRIVING

1. Drive slower at night. Even if you are driving a familiar road you have no guarantee that you may not run into an emergency around the corner. Or tonight may be the night the glare of headlights hits you at the wrong time.

2. You should not drive at night when you are just learning to drive. You have to be sure of your car and know a lot about day traffic before you even attempt night driving. You must not try it until you already have some experience as a daytime driver.

3. Watch your general fatigue and your eye fatigue with special care when driving at night. Approaching headlights are dim at first and then go by with a bright flash. Your eye can adapt to the bright flash but then it has a hard time adapting to the darkness which comes afterward. Doing this adaptation over and over again literally tires the muscles of the eye. The human eye was never meant to adapt to such conditions and it cannot do it endlessly. Watch out for eye fatigue.

4. Calculate the range of your headlights and how well you can see by them. Don't make the mistake of driving faster than your headlights and vision will permit you to see—and to stop.

5. Never use sunglasses. Do not buy windshields that are completely tinted. Even windshields that are tinted only at the top can be dangerous, particularly when you are driving into a valley between two hills. As you do this you are watching the road through the dark portion of the tinted windshield. This is especially dangerous at twilight.

6. Reduce speed when glaring headlights approach and look to the right-hand side of the road. Keep your speed low until your eyes have recovered.

7. Remember to depress your headlights when you are approaching other cars. If the other man is not depressing his headlights, do not flash your lights at him. It may cause him to lose control and crash his car and yours too.

8. Depress your lights when following another driver.

9. Have your headlights adjusted between annual inspections.

10. Allow for the fact that your night vision will get somewhat worse as you get older.

11. Keep your eyes dark-adapted as much as you are able. Do not turn on the overhead light inside the car to try to look at a map while night driving. Remember that if you strike a match to light a cigarette you will momentarily blind yourself.

RULES FOR PREVENTING ACCIDENTS IN THE HOME

1. Keep traffic lanes through all rooms free from hazards to stumble over.

2. Always light the way ahead when entering a room or going up and down stairs.

3. Never have small rugs at top or bottom of stairs.

4. Don't smoke in bed or ANYWHERE when you are sleepy.

5. Don't use matches to hunt in closets.

6. Be sure all burners and appliances are turned off after use—especially a heating pad when you get sleepy.

7. Handle electrical appliances with care. Never touch electrical connections with wet hands or when standing on damp ground. Replace damaged electrical cords.

8. Do not give or take medicine in the dark. Never put two kinds of medicine together on your bedside table—confused by sleep, you might take the wrong one. Keep only enough medicine there for one night. Never mix two kinds of pills in one box.

9. Keep sharp knives separate from other utensils—a hanging rack is safest. If you do store them in a drawer, never reach in without looking first—a bad cut could result. And remember, when washing or drying knives, always keep their sharp edge away from your hand.

10. In your hobby shop, be careful with all cutting, jabbing tools, and particularly with power-driven ones. When using a tool that might slip, always use it pointing away from your body.

RULES FOR SELECTING FIREPLACE WOOD

1. Remember, softwoods, like pine, spruce, and fir, are easy to ignite because they are resinous. They burn rapidly with a hot flame.

2. Since softwoods alone burn out quickly, use them when you want a quick warming fire or a short fire that will burn out before you go to bed or before you step out for the evening.

3. For a longer lasting fire, add the heavier hardwoods, such as ash, beech, birch, maple, and oak.

4. For aroma choose woods of fruit trees, such as apple and cherry, and from nut trees, such as beech, hickory, and pecan.

RULES FOR REDUCING YOUR POTENTIAL LOSSES IN A MOVE

1. Buy all the insurance you can. The standard amount of coverage that comes with a moving contract is minuscule. For local moves, there may be no insurance. When moving long distance, ask the company how much extra insurance you can buy from them, and buy it. In the case of local moves, plan to stay with the van, following it in your car to the destination. Make sure you have the amount of coverage in writing before the van pulls away with your Chippendale chairs inside. Otherwise you might end up with a pile of Chippendale chips (plus reimbursement at the rate of sixty cents a pound). If you have anything, like antiques, that is of great value, you might try to get outside insurance for full value of the objects. Brokers are often reluctant to do this, however, because they can't be on hand to inspect the damage when the move is complete.

2. Stick with the movers while they load. This is equally important whether the move is short or long. On a big job, the driver will make an inventory of every piece of furniture and its condition. Go along with him to be sure that his assessment of condition as well as his count are accurate. You'll be asked to sign a statement, so you'd better know what you're signing. Watch the packing to make sure that they get everything and that everything is properly protected.
3. Be nice. It can't hurt. Remember that these same guys will be unloading and setting up your things at the other end. Supervise, yes, but do it tactfully. Offer coffee or soda (no beer!). Prepare whatever you can ahead of time so as not to waste their time and yours.
4. Don't assume that they know best. The driver may be experienced but his helpers could easily have been hired the previous morning with no training at all. Tell them anything you can think of about those tricky back stairs or how to get the truck parked closer to the door.

RULES FOR SURVIVING FLASH FLOODS

1. Know what a forecast river height means in terms of your own property.
2. Know how far your property is above or below anticipated flood levels. If bad weather is expected, or it is annual flood season where you live, you should

know before you camp out how far your campsite is above or below waterways near you.

3. Know, in order to make and sense of 2, above, how this elevation relates to river gauges for which forecasts are prepared.

4. Know the location of safe areas in case of flooding.

5. Always seek higher ground, staying out of known water paths such as dry creek or river beds.

6. Get the above information on flood levels and land elevation relative to rivers and creeks from your local city government or from the state ranger.

RULES AFTER THE FLOOD

1. Don't use water or foods which have come in contact with floodwaters. They could be contaminated.

2. Boil water until the supply has been tested unless officially advised that water supplies are safe. To be safe, bring water to a rolling boil for ten to fifteen minutes.

3. Go to the nearest Red Cross station if you need medical aid, food, shelter, or clothes.

4. Don't go to disaster areas unless you have some real help to offer. Sightseers are like the rest of the debris—they're in the way and have to be moved.

5. Use your head in unfamiliar situations. Don't look for gas leaks with a lighted match; gas explodes. Don't handle wet electrical equipment; you could get electrocuted. Don't use the telephone unless you have a genuine emergency to report; the lines will be needed for emergency traffic.

6. Try to clear away mud and wreckage around your home and areas close to you. Maybe you can offer some shelter, comfort, or food to those in worse shape than you are.

RULES FOR KEEPING PERSONAL FINANCIAL RECORDS

1. Make sure that you keep all your records for at least three years (from the date you file your return)—just in case you happen to be audited. There's a Statute of Limitations that says "the IRS can't touch you after three years—except in special situations."
2. Be sure that the records you keep will hold up—in case there's an investigation. The best kind of records are canceled checks and bills that are marked "Paid." The IRS has also been known to accept written diaries of your activities—along with bus and toll receipts—as well as other records.
3. Keep in mind, your records should have the following information: the date on which the expense was incurred, the amount that you paid, the fact that you actually did pay the person (or company)—and, of course, the business purpose of the payment.
4. Remember, just in case you don't have all the facts, if all the information that you need is simply not available, the IRS may accept—in some situations—information that is incomplete but corroborated. For example, if you claim a medical deduction based on a seven-week hospital stay, and you are unable to come up with the actual receipt of your hospital bill, then a copy of your diary combined with a letter from your doctor may be accepted by an IRS investigator.
5. Keep your records divided according to the type of deduction that you'll be claiming. Keep all charity deductions in one file folder. Keep all household expenses in another folder. Keep all medical and dental expenses in another. Each individual must determine exactly how many different "folders" he will need for his records. Some families require only a few; others may need as many as twenty different folders, depending on the number or types of tax forms that you file and the extent and nature of your financial operations.

RULES FOR PLUMBING EMERGENCIES

1. The name, address, and phone number of a plumber who offers twenty-four-hour service should be posted in a conspicuous place.
2. For a burst pipe or tank, immediately cut off the flow of water by closing the shutoff valve nearest the break. Then arrange for repair.
3. In case of water-closet overflow, do not use water closet until back in working order. Check for and remove stoppage in closet bowl outlet, drain line from closet to sewer, or sewer to septic tank. If stoppage is due to root entry into pipe, repair of pipe at that point is recommended.
4. If there is a rumbling noise in the hot-water tank, cut off the burner

immediately. This is likely a sign of overheating which could lead to the development of explosive pressure. (Another indication of overheating is hot water backing up in the cold-water supply pipe.) Be sure that the pressure-relief valve is operative. Then check (with a thermometer) the temperature of the water at the nearest outlet. If above that for which the gauge is set, check the thermostat that controls burner cutoff. If you cannot correct the trouble, call a plumber.

5. If the heating system fails in your house (or if you close the house and turn off the heat) when there is a chance of subfreezing weather, completely drain the plumbing system. A drain valve is usually provided at the low point of the water-supply piping for this purpose. A pump, storage tank, hot-water tank, water-closet tank, water-treatment apparatus, and other water-system appliances or accessories should also be drained. Put antifreeze in all fixture and drain traps. Hot-water and steam heating systems should also be drained when the house temperature may drop below freezing.

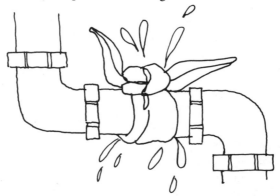

RULES FOR WALKING AS A PEDESTRIAN

1. Don't rely too much on traffic signals and stop signs. Signals and signs DON'T physically stop the cars. It is possible for a car to go through a stoplight or a stop sign. They do it every day. So wait until the cars themselves actually stop before you move across a street in front of them.

2. Be a defensive pedestrian and watch out for the other fellow.

3. Start to cross at the moment the light says "Walk," not when it is about to change back to "DON'T."

Use your eyes—then your feet.

4. Cross at intersections. Preferably where there is a traffic light or traffic officer.

5. Never walk into the street from between parked cars.

6. Wear light-colored clothing when walking at night, and carry a flashlight.

FOLK RULES OF MARRIAGE

1. When to marry:
    > Monday for health,
    > Tuesday for wealth,
    > Wednesday the best day of all,
    > Thursday for losses,
    > Friday for crosses,
    > And Saturday no luck at all.

2. What should the weather be?
    > Happy the bride the sun shines on,
    > Tears for the bride the rain falls on.

3. What to wear:
    > Something old,
    > Something new,
    > Something borrowed,
    > Something blue,
    > And a new dime in the shoe.

4. What color gown?
    > Married in blue, love ever true,
    > Married in white, you've chosen right,
    > Married in red, you'll wish yourself dead,
    > Married in black, you'll wish yourself back,
    > Married in gray, you'll go far away,
    > Married in brown, you'll live out of town,
    > Married in green, ashamed to be seen,
    > Married in pink, of you only he'll think,
    > Married in pearl, you'll live in a whirl,
    > Married in yellow, jealous of your fellow.

SAFETY RULES FOR WOMEN DRIVING ALONE

1. Make sure all doors are locked before you drive away and before you walk away after parking.
2. Fasten your seat belts and make your kids and other passengers do likewise.
3. When you leave your car unattended, put the transmission in Reverse or First Gear (standard) or put it in Park (automatic). Remove the key and lock up.
4. Always use the hazard switch when you stop for any reason on the highway or in any unusual place.
5. Always park in well-lighted areas.
6. Don't leave packages on the seats.

7. Carry a whistle on your key chain, or wherever convenient, to scare away an attacker and a signal for help.

8. Think in terms of your own safety (without becoming paranoid) and avoid potentially unsafe places and situations such as dark parking lots late at night.

9. If stranded in a lonesome spot, wait for help *inside* the car.

GENERAL RULES FOR SAFE DRIVING

1. Always wear safety belts, and make sure all members of your family do—including the children, who for maximum safety should be in the back seat whenever possible. Make it a habit to use safety belts and special belts for children.

2. Don't drive and drink.

3. Don't exhaust yourself on long trips. Plan your trips to include stops. Use highway rest areas.

4. Keep yourself in safe driving condition with regular health checkups. Ask your physician if your physical or mental condition or the medicines you use will impair your driving. Follow his advice, and if you have any doubts about your ability to drive safely—don't drive.

5. If you need glasses for driving, wear them.

6. Keep your car in good shape. Keep your tires properly inflated and replace damaged or badly worn tires.

7. Slow your driving speed in poor weather or road conditions.

8. Be especially alert for walkers or cycle riders along the road, particularly youngsters in residential areas.

9. Never leave small children unattended in cars with power windows with the key in the ignition. Make sure your windows will not operate with the ignition switch in the "off" position. If they do, have the wiring modified to prevent window operation unless the ignition is "on."

10. Make certain to fully close and lock your doors.

11. Keep vent or window open to minimize carbon monoxide, especially if smoking.

12. Use four-way flasher when stopped on or next to roadway.

13. Know the correct emergency procedure in the event your vehicle's accelerator control malfunctions. One countermeasure is to turn the ignition to "off" and apply the brakes. Be sure you turn the key to "off" position; *do not turn to the "lock" position*. On some vehicles the steering wheel can't be turned when the ignition is locked.

FIRST AID RULES FOR HEART ATTACK

1. Recognize these signs/symptoms:
    a) Shortness of breath.
    b) Anxiety.
    c) Crushing pain in chest, under breastbone, or radiating down left arm.
    d) Ashen color.
    e) Possible perspiration and vomiting.
2. Provide this first aid treatment:
    a) Place victim in a semireclining or sitting position.
    b) Give oxygen if available.
    c) Loosen tight clothing at the neck and waist.
    d) Administer nitroglycerine pill if victim is carrying them and asks you to get them (they are administered by putting one under the tongue).
    e) Keep onlookers away.
    f) Comfort and reassure him.
    g) Do not allow him to move around.
    h) Give no stimulants.

BASIC RULES FOR ALL FIRST AID

1. Remember, when a person is injured or ill, someone must take charge, send for a doctor, and apply first aid. The person taking charge must make a rapid but effective examination to determine the nature of the injuries.
2. Do not move the injured person until you have a clear idea of the injury and have applied first aid, unless the victim is exposed to further danger at the accident site. If the injury is serious, if it occurred in an area where the victim can remain safely, and if medical aid is readily obtainable, it is sometimes best not to attempt to move the person, but to employ such emergency care as is possible at the place until more highly qualified emergency personnel arrive.
3. Be aware the first-aider must not assume that the obvious injuries are the only ones present because less noticeable injuries may also have occurred. Look for the causes of the injury; this may provide a clue as to the extent of physical damage.
4. Keep in mind, while there are several conditions that can be considered life-threatening, respiratory arrest and severe bleeding requre attention first.
5. Consider, in all actions taken during the initial period, the first-aider should be especially careful not to move the victim any more than necessary to support

life. Any unnecessary movement or rough handling should be avoided because it might aggravate undetected fractures or spinal injuries.

6. Remember, once respiratory arrest and severe bleeding have been alleviated, attention should be focused on other obvious injuries—open chest or abdominal wounds should be sealed, open fractures immobilized, burns covered, and less serious bleeding wounds dressed. Again, remember to handle the victim carefully.

7. Be sure once the obvious injuries have been treated, you make a secondary survey to detect less easily noticed injuries that can be aggravated by mishandling. A closed fracture can become an open fracture if not immobilized. The secondary survey is a head-to-toe examination. Start by examining the victim's head, then neck, trunk, and extremities looking for any type of abnormalities such as swelling, discoloration, lumps, and tenderness that might indicate an unseen injury.

RULES FOR SELECTING A BED

1. Pick the size that's best for you.

> a) *Standard double (53 by 75 inches):* Although it's a popular choice for newlyweds, the double bed actually offers minimum sleeping comfort for two people.
>
> b) *King (76 by 80 inches):* Almost two feet wider and half a foot longer than the double, the king size has 50 percent more sleeping room.
>
> c) *Queen (60 by 80 inches):* About half a foot longer and wider than the standard double, the queen-size has 20 percent more space to roll around in!
>
> d) *California king (72 by 84 inches):* The longest bed of all, the California king is mainly found west of the Rockies.

2. Look for firmness, confortable support for hips and shoulders, stronger support for your sides and back.

3. Test for firmness, and don't be shy! Lie down, turn around, and stretch out so you can move comfortably.

4. Check, who's taller, you or your spouse? Your mattress should be six inches longer than the tallest sleeper.

5. Look for innersprings with reinforced support at the center. The coiled springs support each part of the body.

6. Remember, the box-spring foundation gives the best overall support. Flat springs can sag, and metal coils may rust.

RULES FOR SELECTING THE RIGHT PAINT COLOR

1.   Use light colors in a small room to make it seem larger.
2.   Aim for a continuing color flow through your home—from room to room—using harmonious colors in adjoining areas.
3.   Paint the ceiling of a room in a deeper color than walls, if you want it to appear lower; paint it a lighter shade for the opposite effect.
4.   Study color swatches in both daylight and nightlight. Colors often change under artifical lighting.
5.   Never paint woodwork and trim of a small room in a color which is different from the background color, or the room will appear cluttered and smaller.
6.   Do not paint radiators, pipes, and similar projections in a color which contrasts with walls or they will be emphasized.
7.   Avoid use of glossy paints on walls or ceilings of living areas since the shiny surface creates glare.

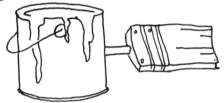

RANGNEKAR'S RULES FOR DECISION AVOIDANCE

1.   If you can avoid a decision, do so.
2.   If you can avoid a decision, don't delay it.
3.   If you can get somebody else to avoid a decision, don't do it yourself.
4.   If you cannot get one person to avoid the decison, appoint a committee.
5.   If you must, use these techniques to avoid the decisions:

   a) *Tantrum Method*—When the initiator offers a proposal, throw a tantrum.

   b) *Hush-Hush Method*—Warn the initiator that he is rushing in where angels fear to read.

   c) *More-Details-Please Method*—Keep asking for more and more details; the initiator will sooner or later abandon his proposal.

   d) *Doubletalk*—Use management jargon to confuse the initiator.

   e) *No-Problem-Exists Method*—Deny the very existence of the problem.

   f) *That's-Your-Problem Method*—Throw it back at the initiator.

RULES FOR A FEMALE SECRETARY TRAVELING WITH HER BOSS

1. When the executive and his secretary travel together, hotel accomodations should be on different floors. The secretary shouldn't overdo it, however, by going to another hotel. That would make it much too inconvenient to take dictation and might defeat her employer's reason for bringing her along.

2. The executive may want a suite for himself, but the secretary's accommodations should be a little more modest.

3. The executive usually signs the register, but the secretary may do it. Whoever does sign should do so for both. The register should read as below:

John Doe, Lux Corporation, Englewood Cliffs, N.J.

Miss Mary Jones, Secretay to Mr. Doe, Englewood Cliffs, N.J.

The secretary's business relation to her employer should always be included. This insures that the room clerk will give you rooms on separate floors, unless you otherwise specify. Also, the address should be the same for both executive and secretary—the address of your business.

4. If the hotel has mistakenly given you rooms on the same floor, there is no reason to become overly upset. If, however, the hotel should give you adjoining rooms, you are right to voice your objections. Simply tell the clerk in a quiet manner that your accomodations are not what you resquested.

5. The executive who has a sitting room adjoing his room may ask his secretary to take dictations from him there. If he has only one room, the hotel lounge or sitting room might better be used for that purpose. Sometimes, however, it is necessary that the secretary work in her employer's room. But under no circumstances may the secretary's room be used.

6. If the secretary is to take dictation in her employer's room, the following rules of etiquette should be observed:

  a) The room should be made up. If this is not possible, the bed-covers should be pulled up and the bed put in order.

  b) The door may be closed but it should not be locked.

  c) Both the executive and his secretary should be dressed the way they are always dressed for the home office.

7. The executive and his secretary may dine together while traveling or in the hotel dining room, if their normal business relationship involved the occasional lunch or dinner together. But since a business trip is merely a continuation of regular business dealings, it would be unnatural to expect an executive and his secretary, who meet only during business hours, to dine together at all times during the trip.

8. Whenever the executive and his secretary dine together, they should avoid having cocktails or drinks together.

RULES OF GEOMETRY

1. To find the area of a triangle, multiply one half its height times the length of its base.

2. To find the area of a square, multiply the length of one side by itself.

3. To find the diameter of a circle, multiply two times its radius.

4. To find the circumference of a circle take two, times pi, times the radius— or pi times the diameter.

5. To find the area of a circle, take pi, times the radius squared; or pi, times the diameter squared, the total divided by four.

6. One circle equals four quadrants. One quadrant equals 90°, so a circle equals 360°.

7. The volume of a sphere equals four, divided by three, times pi, times the radius squared.

8. The surface area of a sphere equals four times pi, times the radius squared.

9. The volume of a cone equals one third times pi, times the radius squared, times the height of the cone.

10. To find the surface area of a cone, take pi times the radius, times the slant height of the cone.

11. To find the volume of a cylinder, take pi, times the radius squared, times the height.

12. The curved surface area of a cylinder equals two times pi, times the radius, times the height.

13. The total surface area of a cylinder equals two times pi, times the radius, times the height, plus two times pi, times the radius squared.

14. To find the area of an ellipse, take pi times one half the length of the minor axis, times one half the length of the major axis.

15. To find the volume of a pyramid, take the length of a side, squared, times the height, times one third.

16. To find the surface area of a pyramid, take two times the slant height, times the length of a side, plus the length of a side squared.

17. To find the area of a trapezoid, take the sum of the lengths of the two parallel sides, times one half, times the height.

18. To find the area of a pentagon, take the length of one side squared, times 1,720,477.

19. To find the area of a hexagon, take the length of one side squared, times 2,598,076.

20. To find the area of a heptagon, take the length of one side squared, times 3,633,912.

21. To find the area of an octagon, take the length of one side squared, times 4,828,427.

346

22. To find the area of a nonagon, take the length of one side squared, times 6,181,824.

23. To find the area of a decagon, take the length of one side squared, times 7,694,209.

24. To find the speed per second acquired by falling body, multiply the time in seconds by 32.

25. To find the distance (in feet) traveled by a falling body, take the time in seconds, squared, and multiply your answer by 16.

26. To find the speed of sound (in feet per second) through any given temperature of air, take the temperature in degrees Centigrade, multiply by 1,087, and divide the total by 16.52.

RULES FOR MAKING YOUR HOUSE SMELL RIGHT

1. Air every room every day, summer and winter. Air mattresses, pillows, blankets, and clothes. Perspiration, according to recent studies, is rated as the most annoying odor in the catalog.

2. Clean everything thoroughly. Clean blankets and pillows, clean cloths and rugs, clean upholstery, curtains, draperies. Clean water in flower vases and clean ashtrays have no odor.

3. Watch cooking operations. Keep the kitchen windows open or the ventilating fan going while baking, broiling, or cooking smelly foods. Don't burn toast or bacon—or anything else. Cook cabbage, cauliflower, and other strong-smelling vegetables by the short process—in a pressure cooker. Wash utensils and plates that have been used for fish at once, using first a salt-water solution as a deodorizer before soap and water. Remove every trace of burned fat from the oven and broiler after each use and do not tolerate partially decayed apples, onions, and potatoes in kitchen bins.

4. Install an electric ventilator in the kitchen and use it. Be scrupulous in the care of the bathroom and the kitchen. Use antiseptics for washing floors, walls, fixtures. Use drain cleaners. Keep range, refrigerator, and garbage can immaculately clean.

5. Don't overlook the attic and basement. They should be clean, dry, and well ventilated.

RULES FOR PRESENTING YOUR HOUSE FOR SALE

1. Don't do any major remodeling.
2. Don't keep apologizing for the appearance of the house or grounds.
3. Don't trail around after the broker and his customer listening to what they say.
4. Don't have the radio or television blaring when the house is being shown.
5. Don't go around turning off lights and cleaning ashtrays until after the broker and potential buyer have left.
6. Don't try to sell a potential buyer draperies, carpets, or other furnishings until the deal on the house is made.
7. Do clean the grounds, paint the exterior, keep the grass mowed, and create an orderly look.
8. Do clean rubbish out of garage, basements, and attics. Repair walks and steps and remove clutter.
9. Do wash windows and make rooms look light and bright.
10. Do keep the house smelling sweet and clean; unaired houses can be very unpleasant.
11. Do see that all lamps and ceiling fixtures have bulbs in them which will give the rooms brilliance when they are turned on. Put extension cords and bulbs in basement and attic if no lights are there.

RULES FOR CLEANING A LIVING ROOM

1. Remember, like all work tasks, a room cleaning can be done more efficiently and more quickly if a system is used.
2. Gather all your equipment first.
3. Keep in mind, dust and dirt fall down, so start at the top and work to the floor.
4. Save time by learning to work with both hands at the same time.
5. Clean ashes out of fireplace with doors and windows closed.
6. Remove all faded flowers and leaves. Groom plants.

7. Open a window but avoid strong cross drafts. Dust windowsills inside and out. A vacuum cleaner does this nicely.

8. Dust ceilings and moldings, walls, doors, and screens, bookshelves, books, and radiators. In old houses inspect corners and under cornices for spider webs. To dust use (a) the wand of the vacuum cleaner, (b) a hand vacuum, (c) a long-handled brush, or (d) a broom with a clean cloth tied around it, or a bag made for the purpose with a drawstring top which ties around the broom handle.

9. Brush all fabrics—draperies, curtains, pillows, upholstery, and lampshades. Use a whisk broom or vacuum cleaner. If there are any grease spots on rug or upholstery, remove with cleaning fluid. Likely locations are under dining table, or upholstered dining-room chairs, in front of sofa or fireplace if food has been served there.

10. Wipe off or polish all vases, ashtrays, ornaments, lamp bulbs, and reflectors. Even a trace of dust on a light bulb or the reflecting surfaces of a lamp reduces the light in the room. Use a damp cloth or a processed cloth or processed tissue paper for polishing and cleaning metals.

11. Dust and polish all furniture and baseboards. Wipe finger marks off doors and doorknobs.

12. Now, if you are using a vacuum cleaner, do the carpet or wood floor. But if you are using a carpet sweeper do the rug next, then last dust the floor, using a dry mop.

13. Vacuum the rug thoroughly. Turn back the corners and sides of the rug and clean the back. Finish by rolling back the rug pad and clean under it. Once a week allow twenty minutes to vacuum thoroughly a nine-by-twelve area.

14. Return the room to order. Replace all chairs, tables, and accessories.

15. Clean equipment and put it away. Remove the vacuum-clean bag if it is full, clean out brushes, shake mops, shake and/or wash dustcloths and sponges, depending on their nature. Put stoppers on bottles or cans of cleaning agents.

16. Put out fresh flowers and leaves.

BASIC RULES FOR HORSE SAFETY

1. Buy or ride a safe horse.
2. Don't be overmounted (too spirited or too large a horse).
3. Know your horse.
4. Don't surprise your horse.
5. Check your tack.
6. Watch small children around horses.
7. Tie your horse with care.
8. Know trailer safety.
9. Don't crowd others.

RULES FOR HANDLING WATER EMERGENCIES

1.   If you have muscle cramps it is usually the ensuing panic and exhaustion that gets the victim into trouble, and not the restricted movement caused by a cramp. If you feel the warning that usually precedes a cramp, stretch the muscle and knead it till the cramp subsides.

2.   If you're in heavy surf, swim only in guarded areas and discuss with a lifeguard particular surf conditions and what precautions to take.

3.   If you are trapped in a rip current (sea pusses or riptides), this phenomenon looks like a long, narrow seaward-moving streak of water. If you get caught in the "neck" where the current rushes through the breakers, don't try to swim straight back to the beach. Either swim parallel to the shoreline and thus out of the rip, or let it carry you out past the breakers. Once out of the current, you should be able to swim to shore.

4.   In river currents swimming across diagonally puts the current's force in your favor. You may wind up farther downriver, but on dry land.

5.   If lightning strikes, the worst place to be during a lightning storm is in the water or in an open boat, because water conducts electricity well. If you can, get into a house, car, or under a steel bridge. Or lie flat on the ground.

RULES FOR ELIMINATING WATER POLLUTION

1.   Don't flush unnecessarily (cigarettes, facial tissues, etc.).

2.   Don't put heavy paper, cloths, rags, disposable diapers, grease, solvents, into water disposal systems.

3.   Use white toilet tissue (also paper towels, napkins, etc.). Dyes pollute.

4.   Wash dishes and/or run your dishwasher only once a day.

5.   Use detergents low on phosphates and not containing enzymes. Phosphates help algae and weeds grow, thus reducing oxygen level. Do check your own shopping area for stores that post phosphate content.

6.   Don't use full amounts listed on detergent boxes in your dishwasher or clotheswasher.

7.   Promote regional sewage disposal systems. Eliminate cesspools.

8.   Organize groups to haul junk out of rivers, streams, and important marshlands. High-school kids are demons at this.

9.   Exert pressure on high factory officials to clean up. Take snapshots of visible pollution sources and date them. Take later snapshots at the same place if your complaints are ignored.

10.   Write to your state and local officials about evidence of pollution in your area. Make your snapshots available to your local paper.

RULES OF POWER TOOL SAFETY

1.   Keep work area clean. Cluttered areas and benches invite accidents.
2.   Avoid dangerous environment. Don't expose power tools to rain. Don't use power tool in damp or wet locations. And keep work area well lit.
3.   Keep children away. All visitors should be kept safe distance from work area.
4.   Store idle tools. When not in use, tools should be stored in dry, high or locked-up place—out of reach of children.
5.   Don't force tool. It will do the job better and safer at the rate for which it was designed.
6.   Use right tool. Don't force small tool or attachment to do the job of a heavy duty tool.
7.   Wear proper apparel. No loose clothing or jewelry to get caught in moving parts. Rubber gloves and footwear are recommended when working outdoors.
8.   Use safety glasses. Use safety glasses with most tools. Also face or dust mask if cutting operation is dusty.
9.   Don't abuse cord. Never carry tool by cord or yank it to disconnect from receptacle. Keep cord from heat, oil, and sharp edges.
10.   Secure work. Use clamps or a vise to hold work; it's safer than using your hand and it frees both hands to operate tool.
11.   Don't overreach. Keep proper footing and balance at all times.
12.   Maintain tools with care. Keep tool sharp at all times, and clean for best and safest performance. Follow instructions for lubricating and changing accessories.
13.   Disconnect tools when not in use, before servicing, when changing accessories such as blades, bits, cutters, etc.
14.   Remove adjusting keys and wrenches. Form the habit of checking to see that keys and adjusting wrenches are removed from tool before turning it on.
15.   Avoid accidental starting. Don't carry plugged-in tool with finger on switch. Be sure switch is off when plugging in.

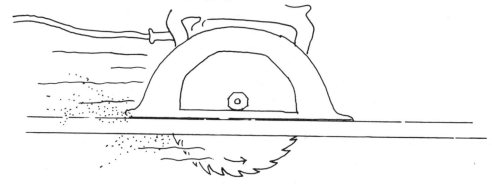

RULES FOR CARE OF PHOTOGRAPHIC FILMS, NEGATIVES, AND PRINTS

Motion Picture Film:

1. Give motion picture films the same care given to other films, but keep in mind that, in addition, they can be seriously damaged by improper threading of the projector, dirt on the rollers or on the face plate of the film gate, or by bending or creasing through careless handling.

2. Do not stop the projector for more than a few seconds to view a particular scene, as a buildup of heat may cause warping, buckling, or burn-through of the film.

3. If you purchase film but do not or cannot use it for some time, store it in the refrigerator. Before it is used, however, it should be allowed to stand for at least two or three hours, or until it reaches room temperature. Most films can be safely stored this way without harm because they are usually sealed in aluminum foil. Storage in a refrigerator should be avoided after the package has been opened.

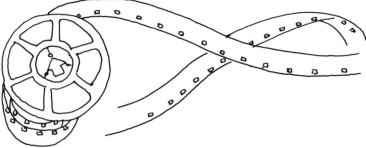

Negatives:

1. Never pick up negatives between the thumb and forefinger. This leaves fingerprints on the film which often cannot be removed from the emulsion. Handle negatives with clean white cotton or plastic gloves, or hold the film lightly with the outer edges between the thumb and forefinger.

2. When negatives are received from the processor, place them in separate envelopes; or if several are stored in one envelope, they should be separated by sheets of thin paper. This will help prevent scratches.

3. Be certain envelopes for negatives are of good-quality paper.

4. Insert the negative in the envelope so that the emulsion side (dull finish) is away from the glued seam, because adhesives can stain and damage the emulsion. The glued seam should preferably be at one side of the envelope. Glassine and brown paper envelopes should be avoided.

5. Keep negatives free from dust. Even if they are carefully stored in envelopes, dust can filter in unless the storage area is kept clean and dust-free.

6. Never store processed films in hot attics or damp basements. The ideal

conditions for storage of negatives include a darkroom, a temperature of 70° Fahrenheit, and a relative humidity of not less than 25 percent or more than 40 percent.

7.   Remember, color negatives are especially fragile. Ideally, these should be stored at a temperature of about 40° Fahrenheit and at a relative humidity of 30 to 40 percent.

Prints:

1.   Be aware chemical contamination, unsuitable storage condition, or poor choice of mounting materials can cause staining or discoloration.

2.   If you do your own developing and printing, follow the manufacturer's instructions, and wash prints with extreme care. Inadequate fixing and washing are major causes of deterioration. Chemical contamination is more likely to be present with photographs than with negatives.

3.   If possible, use photographic dry-mount tissue or photographic mounting corners made of paper to mount photos. Prints are often stained and discolored by the material used in mounting. Many glues and adhesives yellow or turn brown with age. Rubber cement also discolors and leaves stains which cannot be removed.

4.   Store photographs in a dry, cool place, and the emulsion side of one photograph should never be placed against the emulsion side of another.

RULES FOR PRUNING TREES AND SHRUBS

1.   Try to eliminate undesirable branches or shoots while they are young. Drastic, difficult, or expensive pruning may be avoided by early correcting pruning.

2.   Remove dead, dying, or unsightly part of trees and sprouts growing at or near the base of the tree trunk.

3.   Remove branches if they cross and rub together. Disease and decay fungi can enter the tree through the abraded parts.

4.   Remove one of the members forming a V crotch if it is possible to do so without ruining the appearance of the tree. V crotches split easily; their removal helps to prevent storm damage to the tree.

5.   If several leaders develop on a tree that normally has only a single stem and you wish the tree to develop its typical shape, cut out all but one leader. This restores dominance to the remaining stem.

6.   Cut out branches that are likely to interfere with electric or telephone wires. Remove branches that shade streetlights or block the view in streets so as to constitute a traffic hazard. Prune out branches that shut off breezes. Cut off lower limbs that shade the lawn excessively.

RULES FOR WINTER SURVIVAL IN YOUR HOUSE WITHOUT HEAT

When your hose is without heat because of malfunctioning equipment, lack of fuel, or any other reason, there are ways to preserve some of the home's heat and stay relatively comfortable.

1. Dress warmly. Wool clothing, worn in direct contact with the skin, is the warmest. Do not put a layer of cotton underneath. If wool clothing is not available, heavily layered cotton or synthetics will do. Layers of protective clothing are more effective protection against cold than a single layer of thick clothing—entrapped, insulating air is warmed by body heat. The layers can be removed as needed to prevent perspiring and subsequent chill.

2. Eat well-balanced, nutritional meals to allow the body to produce its own heat efficiently, especially quick-energy foods (raisins, other dried fruit, other such foods).

3. Wear a wool hat, especially when sleeping under these emergency conditions. The body loses between half and three quarters of its heat through the head.

4. Use several lightweight blankets rather than one very heavy blanket for the most warmth while sleeping.

5. Close off those rooms which are not absolutely needed.

6. Hang blankets over windows at night (let the sun shine in during the day). Stuff cracks around doors with rugs, newspapers, towels, or other such materials.

7. Prevent water pipes from bursting by wrapping them with newspaper or plastic. Collect water for drinking and store in covered containers. Close the water inlet valve on the toilet and then flush to prevent freezing damage.

8. Don't hesitate to ask for help if the situation starts to get out of control. Call a neighbor or a local social or emergency service agency. Write those phone numbers down in advance and keep them handy.

RULES FOR IDENTIFYING COUNTERFEIT MONEY

1. Look for differences, not similarities.
2. Look for red and blue fibers embedded in the paper.
3. Look for the three-dimensional quality of the printing.
4. Look for clarity in the portrait and distinct edges on the Treasury seal.
5. If you suspect you have received a counterfeit note, contact the police or the United States Secret Service.

RULES FOR CHARITABLE GIVING

1. Don't give to an organization that sends you unordered merchandise. This approach is used to make you feel guilty if you don't send money. Throw the stuff in the wastebasket or give it to a thrift shop if anyone else could use it.

The sending of unordered goods is a high-cost method of raising money, ranging up to ninety cents, or even ninety-nine cents, to bring in a dollar. You can make this unprofitable, and perhaps turn the group toward more ethical money-raising methods, by not paying for the name stickers, license tags, dolls, handkerchiefs, or ties that come in the mail. And don't send them back to the charity; they'll just be mailed to someone else.

2. Don't contribute in response to a phone call from a stranger. This approach is excessively expensive. Sometimes a "boiler room" is set up, where fast-buck artists sell tickets over the phone for, say, a circus. Some of the money goes to charity; most doesn't. Though some legitimate charities solicit by phone, it's best to ask them to write to you.

3. Don't be impressed by a letterhead filled with big names. You can't judge a charity's quality by the number of big-name board members.

4. Don't be swayed by dramatic fund-raising appeals. A socko photograph of, say, a tiny child crying tell nothing about the charity's efficiency or quality.

5. Figure out what charities you really want to support, and devise a budget for your giving. A good time to do this is while you're listing income tax deductions for donations you made last year.

RULES FOR USING JUMPER CABLES TO START YOUR CAR

1. Find the positive and negative terminals on your battery and on the battery you are jumping from. Stamped near the terminals will be the "−" and "+" signs. If you cannot find such marks, follow both cables to their other ends. The negative cable will just be attached by a bolt to the engine or frame. The positive cable will attach to the starter and usually will be longer than the negative cable. Keep in mind that with anything electric, if you touch the positive and negative terminals at the same time, your body is completing the circuit.

2. Always attach a positive terminal to a positive terminal with one cable, and always attach a negative terminal to a negative terminal with the other cable.

If you reverse this connection rule, you can blow up the battery, hurt yourself, and damage the alternator and regulator. One spark is all that is necessary because a lot of gas is emitted from the battery.

3. When the cables are attached correctly and the car you are jumping from is running, try to start the dead car.

What you are actually doing is using the other car's battery to start your car; you are not really recharging your battery.

4. Disconnect the cables, as soon as your dead car starts and you can keep it going. (Remove them from the dead car first.)

Because getting a jump only started your car but did not recharge the battery, you will either have to drive your car until the alternator recharges the battery or you will have to have the battery recharged on a slow charging machine (found at most gas stations).

MILKING A GOAT

1. Carefully wash the goat's udder before milking her.

2. Milk the first stream or two from each teat into a small cup. The openings in each teat may contain foreign matter that will affect the taste of your milk so you should throw this first milk away.

3. Be sure your hands are clean and dry. Do not let them come in contact with the milk.

4. Clip the hair on the goat's udder and flanks to prevent it from falling into the milk.

5. Use a clean, seamless, tin pail for milking and strain milk through a clean, finely woven cloth which has been boiled or is sanitary. A sterilized metal strainer will also do fine.

RULES FOR DETERMINING A GOOD HORSE—1496

1. A good horse sholde have three propyrtees of a man, three of a woman, three of a foxe, three of a haare, and three of an asse.
2. Of a man, bolde, prowde, and hardy.
3. Of a woman, fayre-breasted, faire of heere, and easy to move.
4. Of a foxe, a fair taylle, short eers, with a good trottle.
5. Of a haare, a grate eye, a dry head, and well rennynge.
6. Of an asse a bygee chynn, a flat legge, and a good hoof.

RULES FOR EQUIPPING YOUR CAR FOR WINTER DRIVING

1. Put the following items into your glove box so that they'll be readily available when you need them in inclement winter weather.
    a) A flashlight.
    b) An ice scraper.
    c) A brush to remove snow from the vehicle (depending on size, you may have to store this under the seat).
    d) Extra fuses for vehicle systems (see your owner's manual for type).
    e) A rag to clean lights and to clean windshield on long trips over slushy roads, when you may run out of washer fluid. (May also be stored under the seat.)
2. Don't wait until the last minute to load your trunk with these items you'll need to fight snow and ice.
    a) Chains (if you use them). You'll also need some extra chain links to repair those that may break while driving.
    b) A spare container of washer fluid.
    c) A pair of work gloves.
    d) A small shovel to help you get out of deep snow, when necessary.
    e) A small bag of sand or road salt to be thrown under your wheels for traction if you become stuck. (Traction mats may also be used for this purpose.)
    f) If you expect to be doing long-distance driving in relatively remote areas (e.g., wide open country with a lot of distance between towns), also consider adding a blanket and some extra-heavy winter clothing in the event you become stranded or stuck in a snowstorm.
    g) Booster cables to enable you to get your car started in the event of battery failure.

RULES FOR SELECTING REPLACEMENT TIRES

1.   Never choose a smaller size than those which came with the car. Tires should always be replaced with the same size designation, or approved options as recommended by the automobile or tire manufacturer.

2.   When radial tires are used with bias or belted bias constructions on the same vehicle, the radials must always be placed on the rear axle. If selecting only a pair of replacement tires in the same size and construction as on the car, they should be put on the rear wheels for better traction, handling, and extra protection against flats.

3.   Pair a single new tire on the rear axle with the tire having the most tread depth of the other tires.

4.   Be aware that a "break-in" period is also recommended for all new or previously unused tires—the tires on a new car, the spare put on after a flat, and all replacements. Limiting speed to 55 mph for the first 50 miles of driving enables the many complex elements in a tire to adjust gradually to each other and function as an integral unit.

stand tire size designations. In numerical designations, e.g., 7.75-14, the first number (7.75) refers to the approximate cross section width of an inflated tire in inches and the second number (14) is the rim diameter. "78", "70", "60", and "50 Series" tires use alphabetical letters, F, G, H, etc., to identify size. The lower the letter, the smaller the tire size.

RULES FOR KEEPING AND PREPARING MANURE—
THIRTEENTH CENTURY

1.   Do not sell your stubble or take it from the ground if you do not want it for thatching; if you take away the least you will lose much.

2.   Good son, cause manure to be gathered in heaps and mixed with earth, and cause your sheepfold to be marled every fortnight with clay land or with good earth, as the cleansing out of ditches, and then strew it over.

3.   And if fodder be left beyond that estimated to keep your cattle cause it to be strewed within the court and without in wet places.

4.   And your sheephouse and folds also cause to be strewed.

5.   And before the drought of March comes let your manure, which has been scattered within the court and without, be gathered together.

6.   And when you must cart marl or manure have a man in whom you trust to be over the carters the first day, that he may see that they do their work well without cheating, and at the end of the day's work see how much they have done, and for so much must they answer daily unless they are able to show a definite hindrance.

7. Put your manure which has been mixed with earth on sandy ground if you have it. The weather in summer is hot, and the sand hot and the manure hot; and when these three heats are united after St. John's Day the barley that grows in the sand is withered, as you can see in several places as you go through the country. In the evening the earth mixed with manure cools the sand and keeps the dew, and thereby is the corn much spared.

8. Manure your lands, and do not plow them too deeply, because manure wastes in descending.

9. If the manure was quite by itself it would last two or three years, according as the ground is cold or hot; manure mixed with earth will last twice as long, but it will not be so sharp. Know for certain that in descending and marl in ascending.

10. And why will manure mixed last longer than pure manure? I will tell you. Of manure and the earth which are harrowed together the earth shall keep the manure, so that it cannot waste by descending as much as it would naturally. I tell you why, that you may gather manure according to your power.

11. And when your manure has been spread and watered a little, then it is time that it should be turned over; then the earth and the manure will profit much together.

12. And if you spread your manure at following it shall be all the more turned over at a second plowing, and at sowing shall come up again and be mixed with earth.

13. And if it is spread at second plowing at sowing it is all the more under the earth and little mixed with it, and that is not profitable. And the nearer the fold is to the sowing the more shall it be worth.

RULES FOR ADMINISTERING MOUTH-TO-MUZZLE RESPIRATION TO DOGS

1. Immediately carry the dog into another room and place him before a wide-open window. If he doesn't come around at once, you must:

2. Give "mouth-to-muzzle" respiration. Here's how:

> a) If it bothers you to have your mouth in contact with the animal's muzzle, place a very fine handkerchief or gauze bandage—something that air can pass through—over the muzzle.

> b) Inhale and exhale in accordance with your own respiratory rate— about sixteen times per minute.

> c) Massage the dog's chest to the same rhythm. This will help prompt the resumption of breathing and will also facilitate the heart's beating, or help it resume beating if it has stopped.

RULES FOR SELECTING A NEW PUPPY

1. Examine the puppy yourself. He should be cheerful and lively, with cold nose and a shiny coat.
2. If his nose is runny, he may have just a cold. But you can eliminate the risk of a viral ailment if you wait several days before buying him. If he has crusty deposits around his nostrils, beware: he is sick.
3. If an eye is teary, it is simply because his teeth are coming in: no danger.
4. If his belly is swollen and stretched like a drum, he has worms: it will be necessary to deworm him as soon as you have bought him.
5. If he is prostrate, lying hunched together in a corner unresponsively, he is a sick little animal.
6. You should not take a puppy:
    > a) Whose cage is soiled by diarrhea.
    > b) If there is any dried discharge at the edge of the nose, if the eyes run, or if the nose is dry.
    > c) If when you pet him under the throat he begins to cough (he has a throat infection).
7. Have him examined by a vet within forty-eight hours after the purchase.
8. A puppy must be vaccinated against certain diseases. Therefore ask to see the vaccination certificate when buying.
9. When buying a purebred dog, inquire about his pedigree or "papers."

RULES FOR RAISING WORMS FOR PROFIT

1. Do not grow garden worms. They reproduce too slowly to be commercially feasible. Red worms are generally the most financially rewarding.
2. Remember, the ideal size for a commercial worm bed is $1' \times 4' \times 8'$.
3. Do not use redwood boards to build a worm bed frame, as they contain an acid harmful to worms.
4. Use only thoroughly decomposed organic matter for worm bedding (not redwood sawdust or chips). Organic matter that is still decomposing can cause tremendous heat buildup, driving your worms from the beds.

360

5. Use ground limestone in your bedding to control odor and reduce bedding acidity.

6. Feed your worms rabbit, steer, cow, or horse manure, about 4 cubic feet per feeding. (Make sure the horse manure is not contaminated with a deworming agent—some agents kill the worms, others tranquilize them temporarily.)

7. Provide a dark environment for your worms by covering the bed with carpet, newspaper, burlap bags, or an old blanket—anything that allows good air circulation.

8. Keep out rain by covering your worm bed frame with a wooden lid. Worms like moisture, but they will leave a flooded bed.

9. Add more feed to your bed when pulverized worm castings are visible on the soil surface in patches 8 to 12 inches in diameter.

10. Do not harvest more than a third of your worms every thirty days, to keep a bed continually productive. The standard $4' \times 8'$ bed will produce about ten pounds of worms per month.

11. Remember, worms are generally sold by the pound. An acceptable rule of thumb is that 1,000 mature worms, 2,000 medium-sized worms, or 2,500 mixed-size worms make one pound.

RULES FOR BUYING MEAT FOR YOUR FREEZER

1. Before buying, consider the amount of meat you can store in your freezer.

2. Consider the amount of meat your family can use within a reasonable time.

3. Be aware of the kinds of cuts and quality your family prefers.

4. Remember, a carcass, side, or quarter is normally sold by its "hanging" or gross weight, the weight before cutting or trimming. Therefore, the amount of usable meat you take home will be considerably less.

5. Remember too, a rule of thumb for carcass beef is: 25 percent waste, 25 percent ground beef and stew meat, 25 percent steaks, and 25 percent roasts.

6. Be aware that a hindquarter of beef will yield more steaks and roasts than a forequarter but will cost more per pound.

7. Look for meat that has passed federal inspection for *wholesomeness*. It is stamped with a round purple mark, "U.S. INSP'D and P'S'D'." This mark is put on carcasses and major cuts, so may not appear on such cuts as roasts and steaks.

8. Remember, the shield-shaped USDA grade mark is a guide to the *quality* of meat—its tenderness, juiciness, and flavor.

9. Don't forget, inspection (as in rule 7) is required under federal law for meat to be sold in interstate commerce. Grading (rule 8) is a voluntary service offered to packers, and others, who pay a fee for the service.

RULES FOR HOUSEBREAKING YOUR DOG

1. Confine the puppy to a room or fenced-off area near an outside door and cover the floor with newspaper.

2. Remember, after a few days the puppy should be using one corner, usually the farthest away from the feeding dish. Praise the dog when this place is used.

3. Observe the puppy's schedule, and begin taking it out after each meal and sleep, always to the same area. Praise the dog for using it.

4. Remove the newspaper. Dogs never foul their own area, and when mistakes happen the dog has usually selected an area of the house it considers to be "outside."

5. Do not punish the dog. It is useless to discipline after the event: The dog will not understand.

6. Never rub a dog's nose in its own excrement. The dog will not understand what is meant by this, and may even develop an undesirable appetite.

7. Clean and disinfect the area, and continue to praise for successes.

RULES FOR TRAINING YOUR DOG

1. *Sit.* Before dinner, take the dog on a leash to a quiet room. Firmly say "sit" and press down on the hindquarters, forcing the dog to sit. Reward and praise.

2. *Down.* With the dog sitting, press its shoulders, say "down," and pull the forelegs forward. Reward and praise.

3. *Stay.* With the dog on a leash and sitting down, move back away from it while saying "stay." Continue training until the dog will stay without the leash.

4. *Come.* All dogs should be taught to come when called by name. Reward and praise when the dog responds to calling

5. *Heel.* Take the leash in the right hand, keeping the dog on your left side. The leash should be held slack. Say "heel" and move forward, correcting with the right hand and patting with the left when the dog responds.

6. *Fetch.* Many dogs will retrieve naturally. Before being trained to fetch, a dog should respond to commands to sit, stay, and come.

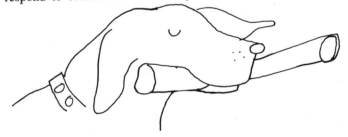

RULES ON BRINGING FOOD, PLANT, AND ANIMAL PRODUCTS INTO THE UNITED STATES

1.   Declaration must be made on items brought into the United States. A U.S. customs declaration form must be completed on all food, plant, and animal products you acquired abroad before your arrival in the United States. Undeclared items subject you to a fine. Declaration forms are given to travelers on airplanes, ships, and trains.

2.   You should not smuggle food, plant, and animal products in the United States. It is a federal offense and persons found guilty of such smuggling are subject to a fine and/or imprisonment.

3.   Declare if you visited a farm or ranch in a foreign country. Unknowingly, a livestock disease may be picked up on your shoes or clothes that could debilitate or kill animals. These precautions help keep foreign livestock diseases from infecting animals here.

4.   Get written permission before bringing restricted items into the United States. Only residents of the United States may apply for permits, but they may do so on behalf of foreign visitors who intend to bring in restricted items

5.   Restrictions are placed on the entry of pet birds and many other live animals, poultry, and other birds (and hatching eggs). Some animals are prohibited; other must be held in USDA animal import centers or by the owner for thirty to sixty days after entry.

6.   Animals and birds must be inspected by the Animal and Plant Health Inspection Service (APHIS) veterinarians before they may enter the country. Make advance arrangements because this inspection service is available only at certain ports. The U.S. Public Health Service restricts imports of dogs, cats, monkeys, and birds.

7.   Restrictions are placed on imports of meat, game carcases and hunting trophies, hides, dairy products, and other animal products. Fresh meat is generally prohibited from many countries.

8.   Canned meat is permitted if commercially canned, hermetically sealed, and storable without refrigeration. Other canned, cured, and dried meat is severely restricted from most countries.

9.   A USDA permit is required before certain plant materials can be brought into the United States. These include fruits, vegetables, and plants or plant parts intended for growing.

10.   Mail plants home. Mail restricted materials are sent directly to one of the plant inspection stations. Ask the Permit Unit (USDA-APHIS-PPQ, Federal Building, Hyattsville, Maryland 20782) for mailing labels when you apply for a permit.

RULES FOR INDICATING DISTRESS AT SEA

1. Fire a gun or other explosive signal at intervals of about a minute.
2. Make a continuous sounding with any fog-signaling apparatus.
3. Launch rockets or shells, throwing red stars fired one at a time at short intervals.
4. Signal by radiotelegraphy or by any other signaling method consisting of the group . . . — — — . . . (SOS) in the Morse Code; or the spoken word "Mayday."
5. Use the International Code Signal of distress indicated by N.C.
6. Raise a signal consisting of a square flag having above or below it a ball or anything resembling a ball.
7. If there is a fire, flames on the vessel (as from a burning tar barrel, oil barrel, etc.) will indicate distress.
8. Display a rocket parachute flare or a hand flare showing a red light.
9. Send a smoke signal giving off orange-colored smoke.
10. Slowly and repeatedly raise and lower arms outstretched to each side.
11. Use the radiotelegraph alarm signals.
12. Use the radiotelephone alarm signal.

Editor's Note: The use or exhibition of any of the foregoing signals except for the purpose of indicating distress and need of assistance and the use of other signals which may be confused with any of the above signals is prohibited.

Attention is drawn to the relevant sections of the International Code of Signals, the Merchant Ship Search and Rescue Manual, and the following signals:

1. A piece of orange-colored canvas with either a black square and circle or other appropriate symbol (for identification from the air).
2. A dye marker.

RULES OF RIGHT OF WAY ON THE WATER

1. A power vessel must keep out of the way of a sailing vessel.
2. A sailing vessel must keep out of the way of a vessel engaged in fishing.
3. A powered vessel less than sixty-five feet in length and sailing vessel must keep out of the way of a large powered vessel restricted to a channel.
4. A vessel engaged in fishing must not obstruct fairway.

Editor's Note: Not withstanding the right of way between the above categories, an overtaking vessel must keep out of the way of vessel overtaken.

RULES FOR GETTING THE BEST GAS MILEAGE FOR YOUR CAR

1. Check your tire pressure and treadwear pattern periodically. Too low tire pressure increases rolling resistance, causes increased tread wear, and reduces gasoline mileage. If your tires wear unevenly, your gasoline mileage will also drop.

2. Consider using radial tires. They can improve gasoline mileage about 3 percent over conventional belted or bias ply tires.

3. Avoid pressing you accelerator all the way down when climbing hills and long grades. It wastes gasoline.

4. Avoid excessive high speed or jerky driving; learn to drive as smoothly and steadily as traffic and road conditions allow.

5. Turn off your engine if you stop more than a minute. Restarting uses less gasoline than a minute's idling.

6. Use the brake rather than the accelerator to hold your car in place on a hill.

7. Avoid jumpy starts and fast getaways. They can burn over 50 percent more gasoline than normal acceleration.

8. Avoid weaving, spurting, and lane changing in heavy traffic. Such practices waste fuel.

9. Look ahead and pace yourself to minimize stops at traffic lights and jam-ups.

10. Slow down. Excessive speed is the greatest waster of gasoline. For best mileage do not exceed fifty miles per hour.

11. Limit the use of auto air conditioners and other fuel-consuming accessories.

12. If you get a sudden drop in gasoline mileage, check with your mechanic. Trouble is brewing, and the sooner you have it fixed the less it is likely to cost you.

13. Make fuel economy a consideration in any new car purchase.

14. Reduce the number of unessential auto trips through careful trip planning.

15. Use mass transit, car pools, or bicycles when feasible.

RULES FOR SELLING YOUR CAR PRIVATELY

1. Realize that spring is generally the best time to sell.

It's after the Christmas crunch and tax time, and people are thinking about cars to get them out in the country. A late-model car in good condition is usually easy to sell at almost any time of the year.

2. Check safety features, especially brakes. Be sure they are in good shape, and if inspection is required in you state, the car should be in condition to pass. Appearance counts heavily, so give the car a thorough clean-up inside and out.

3. Know that options like air conditioning, radial tires, and a stereo or tape deck can up the value of a car a bit. Options like a fancy paint job, carpeting, or plush upholstery, while good selling points, don't really increase the car's book value. If you've kept receipts on repairs or record of oil changes, show these to prospective buyers as evidence that the car has been well maintained.

4. Watch the classified ads in your local newspaper for a few weeks to see the price range of your model and year. It's a good idea to look at some of the cars advertised to see how their condition compares with your car's. Both new-car dealers who sell used cars, and used-cars dealers will probably offer you about the same amount for your car. The price they quote isn't arbitrary; it's based on auction reports which all dealers use. You might pick up a copy of *Edmund's Used Car Prices* to get an idea of the car's approximate "book" value.

5. If you sell you car to a private party, don't expect to get as high a price as a dealer would get—you can't provide the warranty he offers. However, by selling privately, you're almost sure to get a higher price than a dealer would pay you. A good rule of thumb is to set a price halfway between the wholesale book value (which a dealer would pay you) and the resale value (which a dealer would sell it for). For example, if the wholesale book value of your car is $1,600 and you've seen the same model in similar condition on a lot for $2,000, aim for a selling price of $1,800. This way, you'll make $200 more than if you sell it to a dealer, and the buyer will save $200. You might consider, though, whether what you save will be worth the work of selling your car privately.

Editor's Note: Every potential buyer will want to take the car for a road test. (Always accompany anyone taking your car anywhere!) A shopper may bring a mechanic along or want to take the car to a shop (go along). If the mechanic discovers that the car needs work, the buyer may want you to subtract the cost of the repair from the selling price. You may want to negotiate here; your mechanic might do the job for less.

6. Realize that if you trade in the car for a newer model, a dealer will adjust the price of the new car based on the wholesale value of your old one. This may save you money because in some states you pay taxes on the discounted price of the new car instead of on its full value. Because of the two transactions

involved—selling and buying—there's more room for bargaining here, so do some extra shopping around to find the best deal.

7.   Before the actual sale transaction, call your local Department of Motor Vehicles to find out how to transfer ownership—regulations vary from state to state. Ask the buyer for a certified check or cash payment, and make sure you receive it *before* you sign the transfer documents. Remove your license plates from the car before turning it over to its new owner. Otherwise, in case of an accident, your insurance policy will be affected. Notify your insurance company that you've sold your car.

RULES FOR AVOIDING COLLISION ON WATER

1.   Any action taken to avoid collision shall, if the circumstances of the case admit, be positive, made in ample time and with due regard to the observance of good seamanship.

2.   Any alteration of course and/or speed to avoid collision shall, if the circumstances of the case admit, be large enough to be readily apparent to another vessel observing visually or by radar; a succession of small alterations of course and/or speed should be avoided.

3.   If there is sufficient sea room, alteration of course alone may be the most effective action to avoid a close-quarters situation provided that it is made in good time, is substantial, and does not result in another close-quarters situation.

4.   Action taken to avoid collision with another vessel shall be such as to result in passing at a safe distance. The effectiveness of the action shall be carefully checked until the other vessel is finally past and clear.

5.   If necessary to avoid collision or allow more time to assess the situation, a vessel shall slacken her speed or take all way off by stopping or reversing her means of propulsion.

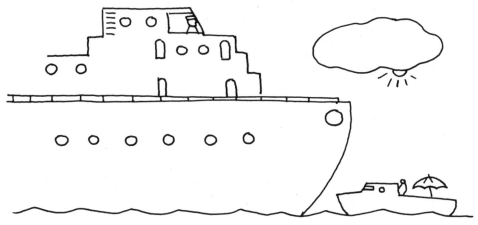

RULES FOR BUYING A USED CAR

1.   Study the highlights and reflections along the body surfaces of the car. Areas that show ripples, bumps, or a mismatch of color indicate repaired sheet-metal damage.

2.   Examine the lower edges of body, areas behind the bumpers, and rocker panels for rusted-out spots. Surface pimples, pitting, or blemishes indicate rusting under paint and lead to extensive rust areas in no time.

3.   Operate all windows, doors, doorlocks, and seat adjustments.

4.   Look inside the car for badly worn (or brand-new) pedal pads or floor mats. This indicates "hard" driving. Check tires for uneven tread. This signifies the possibility of front end problems.

5.   Start the engine and listen carefully for loud noises while the starter is operating. Be sure all gauges (oil, generator, etc.) go on when the ingnition is turned on and go out after the car has started.

6.   Push down on each corner of the car in succession to get it bouncing. If shock absorbers are good the car should move up, then stop at an equilibrium position.

7.   Accelerate briskly from 15 or 20 mph up to 55 mph in high gear so that the engine labors. If the car picks up speed smoothly without bucking, you can assume that the engine is in good condition.

8.   Free play at the steering wheel rim should not exceed two inches, when the wheels point straight ahead. Negotiate several sharp turns at low speeds in both directions. If the steering is in good condition, it should not stiffen and bind.

9.   Decelerate from 50 to 15 mph on a flat area without using the brake. Then, step hard on the accelerator and watch closely for a puff of bluish exhaust smoke. This is a reliable warning that new piston rings will soon be needed or that the engine will need overhauling.

10. Take a short ride over a really bumpy road. This will show you every little rattle and squeak that could need attention as well as the condition of the car's front end, shocks, and steering.

RULES FOR THE GAME OF LIFE

1.   There is one player per game.
2.   No player may play another's game.
3.   All limits are self-impressed.
4.   Moves are simultaneous in four dimensions.
5.   It is possible to lose. It is not possible to win.
6.   Play is continuous. There are no time-outs.
7.   The game is over when the plug is pulled.

HIPPOCRATES' RULES OF SCIENCE

1. There is no authority except facts.
2. Facts are obtained by accurate observation.
3. Deductions are to be made only from facts.

STORING POULTRY AND MEAT

1. Store these foods at 0° C or lower, no longer than the time shown.

Chicken (whole) ....6 to 12 months
Chicken (cut up) ....6 months
Turkey ....6 months
Duck, goose (whole) ....6 months
Chicken (fried) ....3 months
Sliced meat with gravy ....3 to 6 months
Fresh veal, lamb ....6 to 9 months
Ground beef, veal and lamb ....3 to 4 months
Ground pork ....1 to 3 months
Variety meats ....3 to 4 months

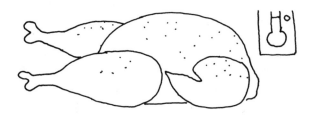

BUYING AND USING EGGS

1. Buy eggs from a refrigerated case.
2. Refrigerate eggs promptly at home, large end up, to help maintain quality. Variations in temperature while the eggs are stored cause egg whites to become thin.
3. Use only high-quality, clean eggs with sound shells when making eggnogs, milk shakes, or lightly cooked dishes.
4. Cook at low to moderate temperatures—high temperatures and overcooking toughens eggs.
5. Remember, shell color is determined by breed of the hen and does not affect the grade, nutritive value, flavor, or cooking performance of the egg.

RULES FOR DIETING—THE DO'S

1. Do it yourself. Nobody can do it for you.
2. Do seek the assistance and encouragement of family and friends in changing your lifetime eating habits.
3. Do, if you are a man, wear suspenders or an elastic belt, so you won't be constantly pushing out your tummy to keep your pants up.
4. Do, if you are a woman, buy a new dress—a dress more expensive than you can afford and one size too small. That'll make you reduce.
5. Do weigh yourself on the same scale, under the same conditions, every week at the same time.
6. Do have a good breakfast, rich in protein food, every morning for a consistent sense of well-being.
7. Do eat as though your life depended on it, for frequently it does.
8. Do take the edge off your appetite by starting lunch or dinner with your soup or salad.
9. Cook thinner if your pants fit too snugly around the hips.
10. Do avoid fat meat and fish, fried foods, gravies, rich sauces, mayonnaise, oily salad dressings, nuts, whipped cream, candy, jelly, pastries, too much bread, cereal, or potatoes.
11. Do get as satisfactory an amount of bulk as you can for the calories eaten.
12. Do have dinner an hour earlier and avoid the cocktail hour.
13. Do remember that you are what you eat. The more you eat, the more you are.
14. Do consider, when you are tempted by a beautiful but fattening dessert, how it will look in a bathing suit.
15. Do remember there is no law that makes you finish everything on your plate. Stop when you're still a little hungry.
16. Do recall the ancient Roman proverb "Plures crapula quam gladius," or "Gluttony kills more than the sword."
17. Do keep in mind, when giving a party, those who are dieting, and have some nonfattening foods.
18. Do remember, a full belly makes a dull brain.

RULES FOR DIETING—THE DON'TS

1. Don't bore everyone with continual news bulletins on your dieting.

2. Don't be discouraged if it takes time to lose those first few pounds. Water frequently displaces fat temporarily.

3. Don't worry if your weight fluctuates up and down during the week. It's that once-a-week result that tells the story.

4. Don't let your blood sugar get so low that you become irritable and snappish.

5. Don't let up. Eternal vigilance is the price of a good figure.

6. Don't skip meals. You're bound to overload your digestive system later.

7. Don't forget that, as we grow older, our lean tissue turns to fat.

8. Don't neglect green salads, lean meat and fish, cranberries, melons, cucumbers, skim milk, tomato juice, unsugared gelatines, and slim soups.

9. Don't play doctor by giving your diet to your friends. It may not fit them any better than your shoes.

10. Don't take any drugs or medicine for reducing without your physician's advice.

11. Don't eat a heavy meal when overly tired or emotionally upset. Rest first.

12. Don't serve diet portions in large plates or cups. Cutting down the size of the dishes makes the eye help the mind adjust the stomach.

13. Don't keep getting in the way of temptation. If those french fries are not on your plate you can't eat them.

14. Don't load your system with "empty calories," the cooking oils and sugar devoid of protein, vitamin, or mineral values.

15. Don't bolt it and beat it. Eat slowly and eat less for better digestion.

16. Don't forget that one of the finest reducing exercises is turning your head from side to side when offered a second portion and another is simply pushing yourself away from the dining-room table.

17. Don't start unless you've made up your mind to keep holding down your weight all of your days.

18. Don't forget that Rome wasn't built in a day. Habits of years cannot be broken by magic overnight.

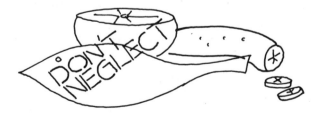

RULES FOR BUYING CHEESE

1. *Check the label.* The labels of natural cheese, pasteurized process cheese, and related products carry important descriptive information. The name of a natural cheese will appear as the variety such as "Cheddar cheese," "Swiss cheese," or "Blue cheese." Pasteurized process cheese labels will always include the words "pasteurized process," together with the name of the variety or varieties of cheese used, for instance, "pasteurized process American cheese" or "pasteurized process Swiss and American cheese."

2. *Check the cure.* A very important bit of information on the label of certain varieties of natural cheese pertains to the age or degree of curing.

3. *Check the name.* Look for the name of the article. Do not confuse the name brand with the name of the cheese. For some purposes you may want natural cheese, for others, process cheese or cheese foods, and for still others, pasteurized process cheese spread or coldpack cheese may best serve your needs.

4. *Check for quality.* To assure you a quality product look for the USDA grade shield. This shows that the cheese has been inspected and graded by an experienced and highly trained government grader. And it means the cheese was produced in a USDA inspected and approved plant, under sanitary conditions. It is your guarantee of consistent and dependable quality.

RULES FOR BLEEDING WITH LEECHES—1876

1. Before applying a leech, it is best to let it crawl for a short time on a clean dry napkin or towel; and if, after that, there is any difficulty in getting it to fix, smear the part with a little milk and sugar mixed, and make rather warm.

2. If, in consequence of cold, the creature appears sluggish and inactive, put it in water at a temperature of about seventy degrees, with a couple of tablespoonfuls of porter in it.

3. Should it be desirable to detach the leech before it has done sucking, do not pull it off forcibly, but sprinkle a few grains of salt on its head. The old practice, of putting the creature when gorged into a plate of salt, is not a good one; the better plan is to immerse it in a solution, not very strong, of this substance, and, when it has thrown up as much blood as it will, to "strip" it thoroughly, by holding the tail end firmly between the finger and thumb of the left hand, and drawing it steadily between those of the right, nearly effectual for cleansing the animal, so that it may be preserved for future use.

4. It should be put into clean fresh water, which, for the first three or four days, should be changed twice a day; afterward, every four or five days will do. The temperature of the water should not be lower than fifty degrees Farenheit, and the place in which it is kept should be airy, and free from strong odors—the vessel, a wide-mouthed jar or bottle, about half-filled, with a little clean sand at the bottom; the top covered with a piece of muslin or gauze.

5.   When leeches are applied, it should be over a bone, against which pressure can be made, if necessary, to stop the bleeding, and never on a soft part, such as the neck or abdomen, especially with children, who have sometimes died from loss of blood, the flow of which it has been found impossible to stop, in consequence of there being no basis for the application of pressure.

6.   The best and simplest way of applying leeches is to confine them to the desired spot within an inverted wineglass, through the sides of which it can be seen when they have bitten; a large pillbox, which is sometimes used, has not this advantage, and must be frequently lifted, by which the animals are disturbed, and bites sometimes prevented. Putting them on individually, holding the leech by the larger end in a towel or napkin, is a very tedious process, and letting them crawl at will over the surface, a very uncertain one, as to the exact spot on which they will fasten.

7.   If it is to such a part as the interior of the mouth from which the blood is to be extracted, a leech-glass must be used in this manner:

> a) Put the leech, head-foremost, into the broader end of the glass.
> b) It will naturally slide to the smaller end, which must be applied to the gum or other diseased spot, so that the creature cannot escape, and if at all inclined to bite will soon do so.
> c) The glass must be kept in its position until the sucking is over, and the hold of the leech is loosened, when it can be removed without any unpleasant contact with the mouth.

This mode can also be adopted with the vagina, or other part near the surface of the body whence it is desirable to abstract blood.

RULES ON DRINKING ETIQUETTE

1.   Know your limit.
2.   Eat while you drink.
3.   Don't drink fast. Sip for enjoyment; don't gulp for effect.
4.   Accept a drink only when you really want it.
5.   Cultivate taste. Choose quality rather than quantity.
6.   Skip a drink now and then.
7.   When dining out, if you must drive home, have your drinks with your dinner, not afterward.
8.   Beware of unfamiliar drinks.
9.   Remember that the purpose of a party is togetherness, not tipsiness.

RULES OF TOY SAFETY

1. Remove these banned toys from children if purchased before banning or if unlawfully sold!

    a) Toy rattles containing rigid wires, sharp points, or loose small objects that could become exposed and cause cuts, punctures, or other injuries.

    b) Any toy with noisemaking parts that could be removed by a child or swallowed or inhaled.

    c) Any doll, stuffed animal, or similar toy having parts that could become exposed and cause cuts, punctures, or other similar injuries.

    d) Lawn darts and other sharp-pointed items for outdoor use that could cause puncture wounds, unless they have included appropriate cautionary language, adequate directions, and warnings for safe use and are not sold by toy stores dealing primarily in toys and other children's articles.

    e) Caps intended for use with toy guns or toy guns that cause noise above a certain level.

    f)"Baby Bouncers" and similar articles that support very young children while sitting, walking, or bouncing, which could cause injury to the child such as pinching, cutting, or bruising.

    g) Toys known as clacker balls which could break off or fracture and thereby cause injury.

2. Be sure toys suit the skills and abilities of the child. Avoid toys that are too complex for young children.

3. Look for labels that give age recommendations or safety information such as "Not Recommended for Children Under Three" or "Non-Toxic" on toys likely to end up in little mouths.

4. Watch out for toys that have sharp edges, small parts, or sharp points. Avoid toys that produce extremely loud noises that can damage hearing and propelled objects that can injure eyes.

5. Explain to the child how to use toys properly and safely.

6. Always try to supervise young children while they play.

7. Insist that children put their toys away so they do not get broken and so that no one else trips or falls on them.

RULES FOR CALCULATING WITH AN ABACUS

1. Place the abacus as pictured and be sure you are familiar with the place values of each vertical place rod. (Each bead below the center counts as a single unit and each bead above counts as 5 times the place value.)

2. To add, for example, 71 + 127 set the 71 by moving up one single on the 1's rod, 2 singles on the 10's rod, and then move down the five on the 10's rod (1 + 20 + 50 = 71).

3. To set the 127, move down the five bead on the 1's rod, and move up two singles on the same rod. Then move up two singles on the 10's rod and one single on the 100's rod (7 + 20 + 100 = 127).

4. To get the total, read all the correct values on the rods from left to right at the center bar, it should read:100 + 90 + 8 = 198.

RULES FOR FINDING THE DAY OF THE WEEK FOR ANY DATE

---

1. Take the last two figures of the given year and add one fourth of itself to it.

2. Add also to this the day of the month and the ratio of the month (shown below).

Ratio:

> 6 for February, March, and November; 1 for September and December;
>
> 2 for April and July; 4 for May; 3 for January and October;
>
> 5 for August; June is 0.

3. Subtract 2 and divide the sum by 7. The remainder will be the day of the week. (1 denotes Sunday, 2 denotes Monday, 3 Tuesday, etc. No remainder . . . Saturday.)

Example: December 7, 1941

a) Last two figures of year:	41
b) Divide 41 by 4 (add to total):	10
c) Add day of the month:	7
d) Add ratio of the month:	1
	Total: 59

e) Subtract 2 and divide by 7.

59 − 2 =57; 57 divided by 7 =8, with remainder of 1.

f) Answer: 1, the first day of the week, or Sunday.

Editor's Note: This formula is for the twentieth century. To find dates in the nineteenth century, do not subtract 2 before dividing by 7 (in Rule 3). To find dates in the eighteenth century, add 2 before dividing by 7. In leap years, subtract 1 from the ratio of January and February.

RULES FOR IDENTIFYING WHAT "-ITIS" YOU HAVE

1. If you have inflamed lymphatic glands, you have adenitis.
2. If you have an inflamed vermiform appendix, you have appendicitis.
3. If you have inflamed joints, you have arthritis.
4. If you have an inflamed eyelid, you have blepharitis.
5. If you have inflamed bronchial tubes, you have bronchitis.
6. If you have inflamed bursa, you have bursitis.
7. If you have an inflamed heart, you have carditis.
8. If you have an inflamed brain, you have cephalitis or cerebritis or encephalitis.
9. If you have an inflamed neck of the uterus, you have cervicitis.
10. If you have an inflamed lip, you have cheilitis.
11. If you have an inflamed gall bladder, you have cholecystitis.
12. If you have an inflamed ureter, you have ureteritis.
13. If you have an inflamed colon, you have colitis.
14. If you have an inflamed bladder, you have cystitis.
15. If you have inflamed skin, you have dermatitis.
16. If you have an inflamed diaphragm, you have diaphragmatitis.
17. If you have an inflamed diverticulae of the colon, you have diverticulitis.
18. If you have an inflamed duodenum, you have duodenitis.
20. If you have inflammation of "an encysted tumor," you have encystitis.
21. If you have an inflamed endocardium, you have endocarditis.
22. If you have inflamed bowels, you have enteritis.
23. If you have an inflamed colon and small intestine, you have enterocolitis.
24. If you have an inflamed esophagus, you have esophagitis.
25. If you have inflamed fibrous tissues, you have fibrositis.
26. If you have an inflamed stomach, you have gastritis.
27. If you have inflamed gums, you have gingivitis.
28. If you have an inflamed tongue, you have glossitis.
29. If you have an inflamed upper jaw or cheek, you have gnathitis.
30. If you have an inflamed liver, you have hepatitis.
31. If you have an inflamed vitreous humor of the eye, you have hyalitis.
32. If you have an inflamed uterus, you have hysteritis.
33. If you have an inflamed iris, you have iritis.
34. If you have an inflamed cornea, you have keratitis.
35. If you have an inflamed larynx, you have laryngitis.
36. If you have an inflamed breast (female), you have mastitis.
37. If you have inflamed meninges, you have meningitis.
38. If you have an inflamed myocardium, you have myocarditis.
39. If you have inflamed muscle, you have myositis.

40. If you have inflamed kidneys, you have nephritis.

41. If you have inflamed nerves, you have neuritis.

42. If you have an inflamed navel, you have omphalitis.

43. If you have an inflamed ovary, you have oophoritis.

44. If you whole eye is inflamed, you have ophthalmitis.

45. If you have inflamed testes, you have orchitis.

46. If you have an inflamed urethra, you have urethritis.

47. If you have an inflamed ear, you have otitis.

58. If you have inflamed ovaries, you have ovaritis.

49. If you have an inflamed pancreas, you have pancreatitis.

50. If you have inflamed parotid glands (e.g., mumps), you have parotitis.

51. If you have an inflamed jaw (part around the tooth), you have periodontitis.

52. If you have an inflamed pharynx, you have pharyngitis.

53. If you have an inflamed vein, you have phlebitis.

54. If you have an inflamed vulva, you have vulvitis.

55. If you have inflamed lungs, you have pneumonitis.

56. If you have inflammation of gray matter of spinal cord (or paralysis due to this), you have poliomyelitis.

57. If you have an inflamed pelvis of the kidney, you have pyelitis.

58. If you have inflamed gums, you have ulitis.

59. If you have an inflamed rectum, you have rectitis.

60. If you have an inflamed retina, you have retinitis.

61. If you have an inflamed womb, you have uteritis.

62. If you have an inflamed scrotum, you have scrotitis.

63. If you have an inflamed sinus, you have sinusitis.

64. If you have an inflamed air cavity in the sphenoid bone, you have sphenoiditis.

65. If you have an inflamed vagina, you have vaginitis.

66. If you have inflamed vertebrae, you have spondylitis.

67. If you have an inflamed mouth, you have stomatitis.

68. If you have inflamed tonsils, you have tonsillitis.

69. If you have an inflamed trachea, you have tracheitis.

70. If you have an inflamed eardrum, you have tympanitis.

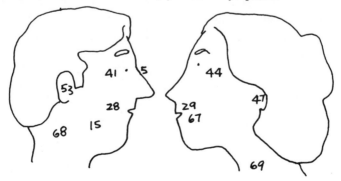

RULES FOR GOOD HORSEMANSHIP

1. Approach a horse from his left. Never walk or stand behind a horse unannounced; let him know that you are there by speaking to and placing your hand on him. Otherwise, you may get kicked.

2. Pet a horse by first placing your hand on his shoulder or neck. Do not dab at the end of his nose.

3. Grasp the reins close to the bit on the left side when leading a horse.

4. Walk the horse to and from the stable; this prevents him from running home and from refusing to leave the stable.

5. See that the saddle blanket or pad is clean and free of dried sweat, hair, caked dirt, or any rough places; any of which will cause a sore back.

6. Check the saddle and bridle before mounting. The saddle should fit and be placed just back of the withers; it should not bear down on or rub the withers, nor should it be placed too far back. The girth should be fastened snugly and should not be too close to the forelegs. Be sure that the bridle (or hackamore) fits comfortably and that the curb chain or strap is flat in the chin groove and fastened correctly.

7. Mount and dismount from the left side. Make the horse stand until the rider is properly seated in the saddle or has dismounted.

8. Assume the correct seat for the style of riding intended.

9. Retain the proper tension on the reins; avoid either tight or dangling reins.

10. Keep the hands and voice quiet when handling your horse. Avoid "clucking" to the horse, loud laughing, or screaming (never scream—no matter how excited or frightened you may be; it will only make matters worse), and slapping him with the ends of the reins; such things are unnecessary and in poor taste.

11. Warm up the horse gradually; walk him first, then jog him slowly.

12. Keep to the right side of the road except when passing, and never allow you horse to wander all over the road. Give right-of-way courteously.

13. Walk the horse across bridges, through underpasses, and over pavements and slippery roads.

14. Slow down when making a sharp turn.

15. Walk the horse when going up or down hill; running may injure his legs and wind. Do not race horses; when so handled, they form bad habits and may get out of control.

16. Keep the horse moving when car passes. If you stop, he may act up or back into the passing vehicle.

17. Anticipate such distractions as cars, stones, paper, trees, bridges, noises, dogs, children, etc.; in other words, think ahead of your horse.

18. Vary gaits; and do not force the horse to take a rapid gait—canter, rack, or trot—for more than half mile at a time without allowing a breathing spell in the interim.

19. Keep the horse under control at all times. If you are riding a runaway horse, try to stop him by sawing the bit back and forth in his mouth so as to break

a) his hold on the bit and

b) his stride; if in an open space, pull one rein hard enough to force him to circle.

RULES FOR THE HOME ELECTRICAL SYSTEM

1. Do not put 30-amp fuses in 115-volt circuits.

2. A burned fuse should be replaced with a fuse whose ampere rating matches its predecessor's.

3. If you find that you are frequently blowing fuses due to appliance overloading, an electrician can save you money in the long run by putting heavily used outlets onto new circuits with separate fuses.

4. To find a short circuit, go through the checklist below:

    a) Undo the last thing you did before blowing the fuse.

    b) Locate in the fuse box the fuse whose glass reveals a blackened interior. Replace it with a new fuse of equal amperage rating. You will find either that the lights have been restored or that you simply sacrificed another fuse and the lights are still out.

5. If lights are not restored:

a) Unplug everything in sight and turn off every fixture that depends on the affected fuse. Examine each wall outlet for foreign objects (e.g., a bobby pin) or for a smudge of smoke. If you find a bobby pin, the cure is obvious; if you find evidence of smoke or heat at one of the sockets, the trouble could be either in the outlet or in the plug that you removed. You'll know which it is after you take the next step.

b) Install a new fuse. If it blows with nothing going, it's the wall socket. Get advice from your electrician. If you don't see a suspicious wall socket, and the new fuse blew, it's time to call an electrician.

c) If you get through step (b) with a healthy fuse, start plugging things in and turning lights on. You'll finally come to the culprit. The fuse will blow once more, and you're ready to move to (d) below.

6. If lights are restored:

d) Make sure the defective unit is unplugged.

e) Sniff for the smell of burned insulation; feel for a warm spot (caused by arcing—electricity jumping from wire to wire). The hot spot or smell spot is it.

f) If your act that blew the fuse was to employ a switch on an appliance, suspect the switch, or a more serious defect within the unit. Unfortunately, it's usually the latter.

g) If your fuse-blowing act was to insert a plug into an outlet, suspect the plug, the appliance wire, and the switch. It's wise (and fairly cheap) to replace all three if the problem isn't obvious.

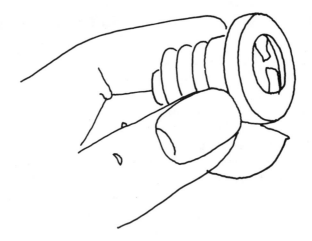

RULES FOR CARING FOR CLOTHES

1. Keep clothes clean. Never put away an outfit that's stained or soiled. Wash it promptly or, if necessary, have it dry-cleaned. Don't leave soiled clothes in a pile or hamper for any longer than you have to, since it inflicts extra wear on the garments.

2. Store clothes properly. Carefully fold them in drawers or hang in a spacious closet on the right kind of hanger. Woolens must be protected from moths during summer or in tropical climates. Furs should be in cold storage.

3. Rotate clothing use. Garments will last longer if given a rest between wearings and, more important, washings. Don't overlaunder. There is nothing antisocial about wearing a shirt a second day if it isn't dirty. Suits and jackets can be given a spot cleaning instead of sending them to the dry cleaners. Use the gentle cycle on your washing machine for lightly soiled clothes and never (almost never) wash longer than ten minutes. You'll save water and power, too.

4. Return clothing that wears out too soon. Some garments are guaranteed for some period, usually a year. Most should last longer than that, especially cotton and wool. Children's clothes are almost always outgrown before they're worn out. Save them for smaller children, your own or others. In fact, a clothing exchange with relatives or close friends could give refreshment to the whole family without buying a single new thing.

5. Mend and repair clothes promptly. A small hole becomes a big one if you let it go.

6. Buy the highest quality you can afford. A forty-dollar snowsuit may seem like a big investment, but if it lasts four years it will turn out to be a better buy than the $29.95 snowsuit that's worn out after two years.

RULES FOR PREVENTING HEATING EQUIPMENT FIRES

1. Follow the manufacturer's maintenance instructions. Kerosene and oil burning appliances usually need cleaning and adjusting annually. Motors, blowers, and pumps need periodic oiling.

2. Where inspection is possible, check chimneys annually for cracks, loose bricks and mortar, and excessive soot accumulation (especially if you burn coal or wood). Check the connectors between appliance and chimney for tightness, rusted-out spots, and proper operation of adjustable dampers.

3. Carefully follow the instructions provided for lighting of gas, oil, or gasoline burning devices. Never bypass any of the safety controls.

4. Use only the fuel for which the appliance was designed.

5. Keep boxes, trash, and other combustibles at least three feet away from any heating appliance.

6. Place portable heaters where they won't tip over, and where curtains and bedding won't fall on them. Make sure there is a guard over electric heating coils to prevent contact of the coils with things that burn.

7. Never use gasoline, gasoline lantern fuel, kerosene, naphtha, or any other flammable or combustible liquid to start or freshen a fire in a coal or wood burning stove.

8. Give burners the fresh air they need for most efficient combustion, by adjusting as recommended in the manufacturer's specifications. "Dirty," yellow flames produce soot accumulations which can ignite or cause a burner to malfunction.

9. If a heating appliance isn't working properly, repair immediately.

10. Keep a good-quality metal screen in front of the fireplace. The area in front of the fireplace should be clear of anything that burns.

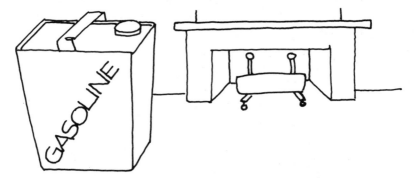

RULES FOR THE CARE AND FEEDING OF TOOLS

1. Save and file any instruction sheets.

2. Keep tools clean and dry.

3. Inspect electrical cords, before and after each use, for cuts, abrasions, or breaks in insulation—and repair them if necessary.

4. Lubricate regularly if there are moving parts, but *don't* soak your tools in oil (follow that instruction sheet).

5. Don't wear clothes with long loose sleeves, jewelry, or anything that can get caught in the moving parts of a tool.

6. Don't let long hair fall forward into a moving tool; tie it back, wrap it, put it up—even cut it—but keep it out of the way.

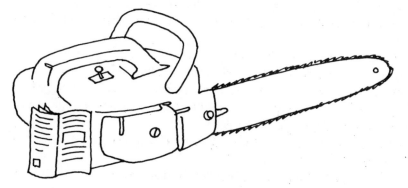

GENERAL RULES FOR HANDLING PETS

1. Avoid most adult wild animals. They do not tame readily or tame not at all.

2. Use patience and slow and gentle movements at all times when working with a pet.

3. Talk to a pet in soft, low tones.

4. When picking up a pet, be sure to give it support for its feet.

5. Be careful handling small rodents; heat and moisture from human hands are not good for them.

6. Avoid:

    a) Sudden jerky movements when working with pet.

    b) Sudden loud and unusual noises.

    c) Placing hands on or over back of pet.

    d) Unnecessary fright.

    e) Handling smaller animals, such as mice, rats, and chipmunks. Allow them to run over you, but they do not feel safe when confined by your hands.

    f) Picking up pets by ears, tails, or legs.

    g) Teasing, since it produces an irritable and bad-tempered animal.

8. Realize the most animals will bite or try to bite when frightened. It is a wise precaution to wear heavy gloves when picking up animals that are of uncertain temper or unused to being handled. There is no point at all in handling venomous animals, such as black-widow spiders, centipedes, or scorpions. Even nonpoisonous snakes can inflict an unpleasant bite. Many species become quite docile after getting accustomed to a home terrarium. Still, anybody who handles a wild animal does so at his own risk.

RULES FOR CAGING ANIMALS

1. Be sure the cage is large enough to give the animal abundant freedom of movement. Exercise is essential if the pet is to remain healthy.

2. Provide enough to make it possible to reproduce the natural habitat of the pet.

3. Choose a cage that allows adequate space for sleeping or nesting quarters when such are required. Space must also be allowed for playthings such as wheels for chipmunks, spinners for mice, ladders for rats, and so on.

4. Be sure doors are placed so as to allow ease in feeding while at the same time preventing the escape of the pet.

5. The cage must be constructed so that cleaning can be performed quickly and easily.

6. Larger cages should have good rollers so that they can be moved with ease.

Editor's Note: Commercial cages with wire bottoms are not desirable for small animals that need a sawdust-shaving mixture, sand, or soil on the cage bottom. The wire floor is uncomfortable. Moreover, variously sized animal cages are manufactured which have removable trays for litter and bedding and no wire bottom. (To clean the cage, simply hold the animal up off the tray and slide it out.) If necessary, a guinea pig can be made comfortable in a wire-floored cage if the wire is covered with plenty of bedding material.

RULES OF HUSBANDRY—THIRTEENTH CENTURY

1. You must keep you plow beasts so that they have enough food to do their work, and that they be not too much overwrought when they come from the plow, for you shall be put to too great an expense to replace them; besides, your tillage shall be behindhand.

2. Do not put them in houses in wet weather, for inflammation arises between the skin and the hair and between the skin and the wool, which will turn to the harm of the beasts.

3. And if your cattle are accustomed to have food, let it be given at midday by one of the messers or the provost, and mixed with little barley, because it is too bearded and hurts the horses' mouths.

4. And why shall you give it them before oxherds and horses? I will tell you. Because it often happens that the oxherds steal the provender, and horses will eat more chaff for food and grow fat and drink more.

5. And do not let the fodder for oxen be given them in a great quantity at a time, but little and often, and then they will eat and waste little.

6. And when there is a great quantity before them they eat their fill and then lie down and ruminate, and by the blowing of their breaths they begin to dislike the fodder and it is wasted.

7. And let the cattle be bathed, and when they are dry curry them, for that will do them much good.

8. And let your cows have enough food, that the milk may not be lessened.

9. And when the male calf is calved let it have all the milk for a month; at the end of the month take away a teat, and from week to week a teat, and then it will have sucked eight weeks, and put food before it, that it may learn to eat.

10. And the female calf shall have all the milk for three weeks, and take from it the teats as with the male.

11. And let them have water in dry weather within the houses and without, for many die on the ground of a disease of the lungs for lack of water.

12. Futher, if there be any beast which begins to fall ill, lay out money to better it, for it is said in the proverb, "Blessed is the penny that saves two."

RULES FOR ADDRESSING LETTERS TO ENGLISH NOBILITY

1. To the King or the Queen.
To the King's (or Queen's) Most Excellent Majesty. Sire, or Sir (or Madam): —Most Gracious Sovereign: —May it please Your Majesty: —

2. Sons and Daughters, Brothers and Sisters of Sovereigns.
To His Highness the Prince of Wales. To Her Royal Highness the Duchess of York. Sir or Madam: —May it please Your Royal Highness: —

3. Other branches of the Royal Family.
To His Highness the Duke of Cambridge. Or, To Her Highness the Princess Mary of Teck. Sir or Madame: —May it please Your Highness: —

4. A Duke or Duchess:
To His Grace the Duke of Montrose. Or, To Her Grace the Duchess of Montrose. My Lord or My Lady: —May it please Your Grace: —

5. A Marquis or Marchioness.
   To the Most Noble the Marquis (or Marchioness) of Lansdowne. My Lord (or My Lady): —May it please Your Lordship (or Ladyship): —

6. An Earl or Countess.
   To the Right Honorable the Earl or (Countess) Russell. My Lord (or My Lady: —, etc.)

7. A Viscount and a Baron.
   A Viscount (or Viscountess) and a Baron (or Baroness) are also addressed as Right Honorable, with the salutation, My Lord (or My Lady): —etc.

8. A Member of His Majesty's Most Honorable Privy Council.
   To the Right Hon. Earl Granville, Her Majesty's Principal Secretary of State for Foreign Affairs. Sir: —Right Hon. Sir: —or My Lord (as the case may require).

9. An Ambassador.
   To His Excellency the American (or other) Ambassador. Sir, or My Lord, or Your Excellency: —

10. An Archbishop.
    To His Grace the Archbishop of C. Or, To the Most Reverend Father in God, Archbishop, Lord Archbishop of C. My Lord: —May it please Your Grace: —

11. Military.
    To the Field-Marshal His Grace the Duke of W. My Lord, etc.

    In the Navy, Admirals are styled Right Honorable, and the rank of the flag follows their names and titles, thus:
       To the Right Honorable the Earl of Eglinton, G.C.B., Admiral of the Blue.

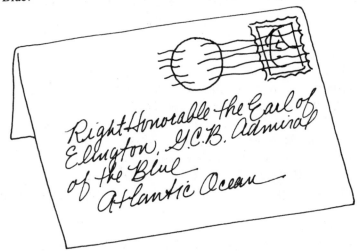

RULES FOR PUTTING OUT SMALL HOUSEHOLD FIRES

1. *Fire from grease*: Smother flames with soda—cover pan with lid. For grease fire in the oven, close oven door and turn off oven.

2. *Fire from electricity*: Unplug or shut off electricity. Use dry chemicals or carbon dioxide extinguisher. If plug is pulled, it is safe to use water.

3. *Fire from coal or wood*: Cover with water.

4. *Fire from kerosene or gasoline*: If it is a small fire, smother with soda, sand, or dirt. For a larger one, get away from it, and call the fire department.

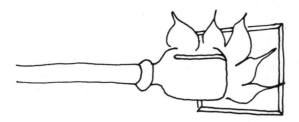

THE NAVY'S RULES FOR DEALING WITH A COLLISION AT SEA

The Calls

1. Signal the emergency by the following:

a) General alarm.

b) One long blast of the siren.

c) The warning howlers.

d) Word passed by boatswain's mate as to location of injury.

e) Assembly on the bugle.

2. Report to officers' stations and commence duties:

a) Executive in general charge.

b) Gunnery officer shall take charge of placing of collision mats.

c) Navigating officer shall inform himself of the course and distance to the nearest shore; be prepared to serve out charts, navigating outfits, and to relieve the deck.

d) Engineer officer shall see that the pumps are put on flooded compartments or on drainage systems; and shall keep the executive informed as to the condition of all compartments in his department.

e) First lieutenant and damage control officer exercises supervision over the divers. He assures himself that the arrangements outside the engineers' department permit pumping of damaged compartments.

f) Assistant to the damage control officer takes station in central station, receives reports from the various divisions, and makes reports to executive officer over the general announcing system.

g) Medical officer, at the sick bay, shall make preliminary provision for removal of sick; and shall be prepared to receive injured and to dispatch a first aid party.

h) Supply officer shall be prepared to supply storeroom keys, and shall make preliminary provision for saving public money and records.

VICTORIAN RULES OF CONVERSATION

1. Let your conversation be adapted as skillfully as may be to your company. Some men make a point of talking commonplaces to all ladies alike, as if a woman could only be a trifler. Others, on the contrary, seem to forget in what respects the education of a lady differs from that of a gentleman, and commit the opposite error of conversing on topics with which ladies are seldom acquainted. A woman of sense has as much right to be annoyed by one, as a lady of ordinary education by the other. You cannot pay a finer compliment to a woman of refinement and esprit than by leading the conversation into such a channel as may mark your appreciation of her superior attainments.

2. In talking with ladies of ordinary education, avoid political, scientific, or commercial topics, and choose only such subjects as are likely to be of interest to them.

3. Remember that people take more interest in their own affairs than in anything else which you can name. If you wish your conversation to be thoroughly agreeable, lead a mother to talk of her children, a young lady of her last ball, an author of his forthcoming book, or an artist of his exhibition picture. Having furnished the topic, you need only listen; and you are sure to be thought not only agreeable, but thoroughly sensible and well informed.

4. Be careful, however, on the other hand, not always to make a point of talking to persons upon general matters relating to their professions. To show an interest in their immediate concerns is flattering; but to converse with them too much about their own arts looks as if you thought them ignorant of other topics.

5. Do not use a classical quotation in the presence of ladies without apologizing for or translating it. Even this should only be done when no other phrase would so aptly express your meaning. Whether in the presence of ladies or gentlemen, much display of learning is pedantic and out of place.

6. Remember, there is a certain distinct but subdued tone of voice which is peculiar to only well-bred persons. A loud voice is both disagreeable and vulgar. It is better to err by the use of too low than too loud a tone.

7. Remember, too, that all "slang" is vulgar. It has become of late unfortunately prevalent, and we have known even ladies pride themselves on the saucy chic with which they adopt certain cant phrases of the day. Such habits cannot be too severely reprehended. They lower the tone of society and the standard of thought. It is a great mistake to suppose that slang is in any way a substitute for wit.

8. The use of proverbs is equally vulgar in conversation; and puns, unless they rise to the rank of witticisms, are to be scrupulously avoided. There is no greater nuisance in society than a dull and persevering punster.

9. It is considered extremely ill-bred when two persons whisper in society, or converse in a language with which all present are not familiar. If you have private matters to discuss, you should appoint a proper time and place to do so, without paying others the ill compliment of excluding them from your conversation.

10. A well-bred lady of the present day is expected to know something of music besides merely playing a difficult piece. She should be able to discuss the merits of different styles of music, modestly and intelligently; a little reading on the subject, and some attention to the intellectual character of music, will enable her to do so; and as music is becoming quite a national passion, she will find the subject brought forward very frequently by gentlemen.

11. You should endeavor to have the habit of talking well about trifles. Be careful never to make personal remarks to a stranger on any of the guests present; it is possible, nay probable, that they may be relatives, or at least friends.

12. A well-bred person always refuses to understand a phrase of doubtful meaning. If the phrase may be interpreted decently, and with such interpretation would provoke a smile, then smile, to just the degree called for by such interpretation, and no more. The prudery which sits in solemn and severe rebuke at a *double entendre* is only second in indelicacy to the indecency which grows hilarious over it, since both must recognize the evil intent. It is sufficient to let it pass unrecognized.

13. Not so when one hears an indelicate word or expression, which allows of no possible harmless interpretation. Then not the shadow of a smile should flit across the lips. Either complete silence should be preserved in return or the words "I do not understand you" be spoken. A lady will always fail to hear that which she should not hear, or having unmistakably heard, she will not understand.

14. A gentleman should never permit any phrase that approaches to an oath to escape his lips in the presence of a lady. If any man employs a profane expression in the drawing room, his pretensions to good breeding are gone forever. The same reason extends to the society of men advanced in life; and he would be singularly defective in good taste, who should swear before old persons, however irreligious their habits might be. The cause of profanity being offensive in these cases is that it denotes an entire absence of reverence and respect from the spirit of him who uses it.

RULES FOR SAFE EXPRESSWAY DRIVING

1. When entering the expressway, forget the standard procedure of stopping to yield the right-of-way. Instead, steadily but cautiously increase speed so that by the time your car leaves the entrance ramp, approaching traffic can let you in without inconvenience. The emphasis should be on teamwork between drivers already on and those merging onto the expressway. Be ready, though, for the driver on the expressway who refuses to cooperate.

2. When changing lanes, anticipate your move and maintain about a two-to three-second interval between cars in front and behind you. Signal every intention to change lanes well in advance of your move.

3. When exiting, chart your course in advance so you'll have plenty of time to find the proper exit and move accordingly. If you still miss your turnoff, don't panic. Simply drive to the next exit and backtrack to the correct destination. Don't swerve across traffic at the last second or back up to reach an exit; police accident reports are full of accounts of motorists who have lost their lives trying to save a few minutes.

4. When you do exit, remember to use the entire exit ramp to gradually slow down; braking heavily before the exit or at the last moment invites collisions.

5. Be careful when braking. If sudden rain or fog reduces your visibility, don't stomp the brakes in panic. Remember that the driver behind you is having an equally difficult time seeing the road, and his car's front end could easily wind up in your trunk. The key is to slow down gradually; never slam on the brakes unless you absolutely have to.

6. Remain alert! This is important to safe expressway travel, especially at night. "Highway hypnosis" can easily set in when you stare too long at the taillights of a preceding car. There are cases of drivers following a car in front off an expressway into a gas station where a rear-end collision occurred when the first driver stopped at the pumps.

The best ways to avoid this driving trance are frequent stops for refreshments and stretching, plus constant eye scanning of the road ahead. Another effective, if less conventional, fatigue fighter is dialing the radio to the loudest rock station you can find and singing as long as your passengers will tolerate it.

7. The first precaution in handling expressway emergencies is to make sure your car is in good mechanical condition before you drive. But if a breakdown should occur, pull off as far as possible onto the right-hand shoulder and raise the car's hood, tying a handkerchief on the antenna, flashing warning lights or using some method to indicate that your car is disabled. Try to flag down a policeman for assistance; don't leave your car unless you cannot obtain help in a reasonable amount of time.

TURN-OF-THE-CENTURY RULES OF GENTLEMANLY ETIQUETTE

1. Etiquette requires of a man that he shall attend to his social duties promptly; that he shall be as polite to the lady whose advancing years have robbed her of her physical charms as to the budding beauty of girlhood; that the aged of both sexes shall be the objects of his attention.

2. Remove the hat on entering the church doors, and do not replace it until you have reached the outer vestibule in passing out.

In passing a lady upon the hotel stairs, or riding in the elevator with one, a gentleman should lift his hat. Acquaintanceship is not required.

3. Do not leave a lady alone in the theater while you go out to "see Tom Cook," or to speak to a man on business. It is very bad manners, as well as showing great selfishness. If she would like to leave her seat between the acts for a promenade in the lobbies, accompany her.

4. Do not whisper or converse with her during the performance. Some people act as though the theater or opera was a visiting place, where they can detail all their private affairs, to the disgust of those who paid for the privilege of hearing the play.

5. In giving up his seat in the car to a lady, he should raise his hat. In this connection, it may be well to say that she should never omit to thank him.

6. In the streetcars, when a seat is vacated, a gentleman looks around to see if there are any ladies standing before he drops into it. Neither does he remain seated while an old or lame person, or a woman with a baby, is standing.

7. When a gentleman is walking with two ladies he should offer his arm to but one, and the other lady should walk at her side.

8. When leaving a lady at her own house, he should wait on the steps until he sees that she is admitted before he takes his departure.

9. He must carry a lady's parcels, especially if they are heavy.

10. He can take either side of the pavement, but it is usual for him to walk on the side where the greatest number pass, so as to protect his companion from being jostled. He should not offer his arm save in the evening, or where her safety demands its protection.

11. If a gentleman invites a lady to a place of amusement, he should send her flowers. They are but tokens of purest friendship. A card should be sent bearing the lady's name, and over it the name of the sender, with the words: "With the compliments of _____ "

12. A gentleman who by chance meets a lady friend in a car or on a ferryboat, or any other public conveyance, is not expected to pay her fare. The assurance with a "Two, please" is deeply offensive to most women. It places them under an obligation which they cannot repay, as men can. It is wiser to allow the lady to pay her own fare rather than take the liberty of doing so. If she is accompanying by invitation, it is to be presumed that you will pay the fare, as well as all other expenses.

13. There may be a case where she has unknowingly spent all her money, or has left her purse at home. Then it is right that you should come to her assistance, and allow her to pay it back, trifling as the sum seems to you.

14. Never borrow money of a lady, and have as few dealings with acquaintances of the opposite sex in financial matters as possible.

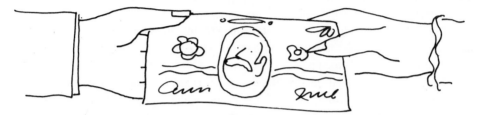

RULES OF TENNIS ETIQUETTE

1. Wear sneakers—a must to protect the court, give you more secure footing.

2. On a busy day, play doubles rather than singles and vacate the court after one or two sets (or whatever the court or club rule is).

3. Change courts—usually on odd games—so the sun doesn't beat continually in the same eyes.

4. Make sure your opponent is ready before you serve (you can always ask, "Ready?"). If it's the first game and you want to take a few practice serves, ask first if you may. If you're used to serving FBI (first ball in), ask your opponent if that's his practice too.

5. If the third ball is lost, keep the game going with the two you have instead of holding up the game while you scuffle through the pachysandra.

6. The server is responsible for keeping and announcing the score.

7. Always replay a doubtful point—especially if you think you've won it!

8. If you hit someone with a ball, run into your partner, flub a crucial point, say distinctly, "I'm awfully sorry," but don't moan on and on about it.

9. Many courts require a white tennis outfit, white sneakers.

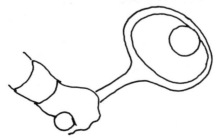

RULES FOR BUYING TOP-QUALITY CLOTHES

1. Check seams—Look inside the garment to see how it's made. Seams should be at least an inch wide and should be bound with stitching so they don't pull apart. Outside seams should be perfectly matched if the fabric has any pattern such as plaid, stripe, or check.

2. Check hems—They should be deep enough so that the garment can be let down at least an inch. Permanent press garments often cannot be lengthened satisfactorily, because the hemline is permanent too.

3. Check stitching—It should be uniform and the garment should be free of tangled or loose threads. Clothes with careful topstitching and similar details are more likely to be well made.

4. Check buttons—High-quality buttons are perhaps the quickest tip-off about the quality of clothes. Good buttons are bone, leather, pearl, or metal. Plastic buttons are usually lesser quality. Look at how the button is sewn, too. The best coats, for example, have buttons held on by smaller buttons on the wrong side. They also usually have an extra button or two attached somewhere. While you're looking at the buttons, check the buttonholes. Handmade are stronger than machine-made. If they're made by a machine, check to see if the holes are double-stitched or given the quick once-over.

5. Check zippers—Metal zippers may be uglier, but they're a lot more reliable than the plastic ones. Especially on garments where the zipper is hard to replace, like coats, better stick to the old-fashioned kind. Check to see if the stitching is straight around the zippers and whether the teeth are hidden when the zipper is closed. Of course, you should work the zipper a few times to be sure the teeth mesh properly.

6. Check linings—These are a surefire mark of good workmanship in coats, men's jackets, slacks, dresses, and skirts. Jackets should have lining everywhere. (Check the sleeves.) Make sure the lining is well secured so it won't droop after a few trips to the cleaners. Be sure the seams and construction of the lining are as good as the garment itself.

7. Check pockets—They are a sign of quality in women's and children's clothing. The cheaper pants for women and girls will have no pockets or one patch pocket in front. Turn pockets inside out to check for holes and fraying. Good pockets are reinforced or even lined.

8. Check reinforcing—In general this makes the garment a better buy. Children's jeans should have reinforcing at the knees. Shirts should have a folded, placket front. Waistbands and collars should be backed with a stiffening material such as Pellon. Children's clothing that snaps in the crotch should have a double seam to prevent the snaps from pulling holes in the fabric. Two-piece garments—like pajamas—that snap together should have an extra row of snaps for grow room.

RULES FOR LAYING AN EGG

1. Make Sure You Are a Hen.

2. Really Want to Lay an Egg. More Than Anything in the World, You Must Want to Lay an Egg.

3. Wake Up at Dawn. You Will Know It Is Dawn Because the Sun Will Be Just Behind the Trees.

4. Hunt for a Good Place to Lay Your Egg.

5. Once You Have Decided, Gather Bits of Soft Straw and Alfalfa Leaf for Your Nest.

6. Bring Along Books, Puzzles, and Games to While the Time Away.

7. Surround Yourself with Words of Wisdom, e.g., "Patience is a virtue," to Help Guide You Toward Your Goal.

8. Now That You Are Ready to Lay the Egg, Concentrate Carefully.

RULES FOR SENTENCING CONVICTED CRIMINALS TO THE DEATH PENALTY

1. In sixteen states (Alaska, Hawaii, Iowa, Kansas, Maine, Maryland, Massachusetts, Michigan, Minnesota, New Jersey, New Mexico, North Dakota, Oregon, South Dakota, West Virginia, and Wisconsin) no one may be sentenced to death.

2. In many states, aggravating and mitigating circumstances must be considered by the jury before the death penalty can be imposed.

3. In Florida, persons convicted of rape of a minor may be sentenced to death.

MARK TWAIN'S RULES FOR TELLING A HUMOROUS STORY

1. The humorous story may be spun out to great length, and may wander around as much as it pleases, and arrive nowhere in particular; but the comic and witty stories must be brief and end with a point. The humorous story bubbles gently along, the others burst.

2. The humorous story is told gravely; the teller does his best to conceal the fact that he even dimly suspects that there is anything funny about it; but the teller of the comic story tells you beforehand that it is one of the funniest things he has ever heard, then tells it with eager delight, and is the first person to laugh when he gets through. And sometimes, if he has had good success, he is so glad and happy that he will repeat the "nub" of it and glance around from face to face, collecting applause, and then repeat it again. It is a pathetic thing to see.

3. Very often, of course, the rambling and disjointed humorous story finishes with a nub, point, snapper, or whatever you like to call it. Then the listener must be alert, for in many cases the teller will divert attention from that nub by dropping it in a carefully casual and indifferent way, with the pretense that he does not know it is a nub. But the teller of the comic story does not slur the nub; he shouts it at you—every time. And when he prints it, in England, France, Germany, and Italy, he italicizes it, puts some whooping exclamation points after it, and sometimes explains it in a parenthesis. All of, which is very depressing, and makes one want to renounce joking and lead a better life.

4. To string incongruities and absurdities together in a wandering and sometimes purposeless way, and seem innocently unaware that they are absurdities, is the basis of the American art, if my position is correct. Another feature is the slurring of the point. A third is the dropping of a studied remark apparently without knowing it, as if one were thinking aloud. The fourth and last is the pause.

5.   Artemus Ward dealt in numbers three and four a good deal. He would begin to tell with great animation something which he seemed to think was wonderful; then lose confidence, and after an apparently absentminded pause, add an incongruous remark in a soliloquizing way; and that was the remark intended to explode the mine—and it did.

6.   The pause is an exceedingly important feature in any kind of story, and a frequently recurring feature, too. It is a dainty thing and delicate, and also uncertain and treacherous; for it must be exactly the right length—no more and no less—or it fails of its purpose and makes trouble. If the pause is too short the impressive point is passed, and the audience have had time to divine that a surprise is intended—and then you can't surprise them, of course.

RULES FOR SAVING MONEY ON TELEPHONE CALLS

1.   Make long distance calls on weekdays after 5:00 P.M., when the rates are lower.

2.   Make long distance calls on weekends between 8 A.M. on Saturday and 5:00 P.M. on Sunday, when rates are at their lowest.

3.   Take advantage of the special one-minute bargain rate between 11:00 P.M. and 8:00 A.M. every day, when you may call anywhere in the continental United States for 21 cents or less for the first minute. Additional minutes cost even less.

4.   Use Toll Free "800" numbers for your business calls whenever possible. To see if there is such a number for the business you are calling, check the phone book or dial (800) 555-1212 for information.

5.   Tell the operator immediately if you reach a wrong number or get a poor connection when calling long distance. The charge will be removed from your bill.

6.   Prearrange long distance calls whenever possible so that you're sure the person you're calling will be there. You'll be able to take advantage of lower rates for station-to-station, direct dial calls, rather than phoning person to person.

7.   Be sure to order all extensions needed when your phone service is first installed, so that you won't have to pay extra installation charges at a later date.

8.   Do not give anyone your credit card billing number—you may find calls you haven't made billed to your account.

NOTES

PAGE

1   *The Star*, October 10, 1978.

2   Walter Perschke, "Six Rules for Successful Auction Buying," in *Barron's National Business & Financial Weekly,* October 2, 1978.

3   Norbert Elias, *The Civilizing Process*, Vol. I (New York: Urizen Books, 1978).

4   *The Civilizing Process.*

12   *1978 Catholic Almanac.*

13   *Folklore in America.*

16   Lady Stearn Robinson and Tom Corbett, *The Dreamer's Dictionary: The Complete Guide to Interpreting Your Dreams* (New York: Taplinger Publishing Co., 1974).

19   Carl Selmer, *An Unrecorded Old German Augustinian Rule* (New York: Columbia University Press, 1937).

20   Raymond T. McNally and Radu Florescu, *In Search of Dracula, A True History of Dracula and Vampire Legends* (New York: Warner Books, 1973).

22   Tristam P. Coffin and Hennig Cohen, eds., *Folklore in America* (Garden City, N.Y.: Doubleday & Company, 1966).

23   George Lyman Kittredge, *Witchcraft in Old and New England* (New York: Russell & Russell, 1958).

23   Jeanne Rose, *Herbs & Things* (New York: Grosset & Dunlap, 1972).

27   Robert W. Pelton, *Voodoo Signs and Omens* (Cranbury, N.J.: A. S. Barnes & Co., 1974).

28   *Voodoo Signs and Omens.*

28   *Voodoo Signs and Omens.*

29   Maggie MacKenzie, a Scottish witch, cited in *Herbs & Things.*

32   *Amy Vanderbilt's Etiquette.*

34   H. P. Stone, *Tonight's the Night: The Fireplace Entertainment Book* (New York: Manor Books, 1976).

36   Amy Vanderbilt, *Amy Vanderbilt's Etiquette* (Garden City, N.Y.: Doubleday & Company, 1972).

38   *Amy Vanderbilt's Etiquette.*

44   *The Seventeen Book of Etiquette and Entertaining.*

49   *The Seventeen Book of Etiquette and Entertaining.*

50   *The Seventeen Book of Etiquette and Entertaining.*

50   *The Seventeen Book of Etiquette and Entertaining.*

50   *The Seventeen Book of Etiquette and Entertaining.*

51   *The Seventeen Book of Etiquette and Entertaining.*

52   *The Seventeen Book of Etiquette and Entertaining.*

53   *The Seventeen Book of Etiquette and Entertaining.*

54   Updated by Lawrence P. Crocker, *The Officer's Guide*, 40th ed. (Harrisburg, Pa.: Stackpole Books, 1973).

57   *Amy Vanderbilt's Etiquette.*

57   Felician A. Foy, ed., *1978 Catholic Almanac* (Huntington, Ind.: Our Sunday Visitor, 1978).

58   Dick Hyman, *The Trenton Pickle Ordinance and Other Bonehead Legislation* (Brattleboro, Vt.: The Stephen Greene Press, 1976).

58   *Herbs & Things.*

59   Peg Bracken, *I Try to Behave Myself* (New York: Harcourt, Brace and World, 1960).

60 *I Try to Behave Myself.*

62 *The Star,* October 10, 1978.

63 *The Star*, October 10, 1978.

64 The National Institute of Mental Health.

66 Jack Last, *Everyday Law Made Simple* (Garden City, N.Y.: Doubleday & Company, 1954).

68 *Everyday Law Made Simple.*

68 *Everyday Law Made Simple.*

69 *Everyday Law Made Simple.*

71 *Everyday Law Made Simple.*

72 Clement G. Martin, *How to Live to Be 100; Actively, Healthily, Vigorously* (New York: Frederick Fell Publishers, 1963), p. 54.

72 Roger J. Williams, *Nutrition in a Nutshell* (Garden City, N.Y.: Dolphin Books, Doubleday & Company, 1962).

73 *Who's Who in America*, 40th edition (Chicago: Marquis Who's Who, 1977–79).

74 The editors of Time-Life Books, *How Things Work in Your Home* (New York: Time-Life Books, 1975).

74 *The Wise Encyclopedia of Cookery.*

75 Courtesy of New Jersey State Bar Association, Trenton, N.J.

80 Irma Kurtz, "Deciding ... " in *Cosmopolitan*, November 1977.

80 *English Grammar and Usage for Test-takers.*

81 David R. Turner, *English Grammar and Usage for Test-takers.* (New York: Arco Publishing Co., 1976).

84 Jeffrey Feinman, *How to Stop Being Shy* (New York: Zebra Books, 1977).

85 Rudolf Flesch, *How to Write, Speak, and Think More Effectively* (New York: Harper & Brothers, 1960).

86 Jean Key Gates, *Introduction to Librarianship* (New York: McGraw-Hill Book Company, 1976).

86 "The Real Value Guide," in *The Star*, March 5, 1975.

88 Henry Blake, *Talking with Horses* (New York: E. P. Dutton & Co., 1976).

92 *Introduction to Librarianship.*

94 Royal L. Garff, *You Can Learn to Speak!* (Portland, Me.: The Bond Wheelwright Co., 1966).

95 John Mack Carter and Lois Wyse, *How to Be Outrageously Successful with Women* (New York: William Morrow & Co., 1975).

99 Mary Gillies, *The New How to Keep House* (New York: Harper & Row, 1968).

106 "The Arboretum at Harvard University," in *Arnoldia*, Vol. 34, No. 2, March–April 1974, Arnold Arboretum, Jamaica Plains, Mass., pp. 42-43.

106 Clement G. Martin, *How to Live to Be 100; Actively, Healthily, Vigorously* (New York: Frederick Fell Publishers, 1963), pp. 33–35.

107 Lester Barlow and Anne R. Sommers, "Lifetime Health-Monitoring Program," *New England of Medicine*, March 17, 1977, as published in *Review Magazine* (Eastern Airlines).

107 *How to Be Outrageously Successful with Women.*

108 Harry F. Swartz, *Allergy; What It Is and What to Do About It* (New York: Frederick Ungar Publishing Co., 1966).

109 *How to Be Outrageously Successful with Women.*

114 Dan Greenburg, *How to Be a Jewish Mother* (Los Angeles: Price, Stern, Sloan, 1965).

115 Duncan Emrich, *Folklore on the American Land* (Boston: Little, Brown & Company, 1972).

119 Genevieve Painter, *Teach Your Baby* (New York: Simon & Schuster, 1971).

121 *The Officer's Guide.*

122   Dan Golenpaul, ed., *Information Please Almanac* (New York: Theodore Dolmatch, 1978).

124   *The Seventeen Book of Etiquette and Entertaining.*

130   William H. Tate, *A Mariner's Guide to the Rules of the Road* (Annapolis, Md.: Naval Institute Press, 1976).

131   Mary Clanfield and Cecil Hanna, *Teach Spelling by All Means* (San Francisco, Fearon Publishers, 1961).

133   Eric Sloane, ed., *Eric Sloane's Don't: A Little Book of Early American Gentility* (New York: 1968).

135   *A Parents' Guide to Child Safety.*

140   D. X. Fenten, *Clear and Simple Gardening Guide* (abridged from *Greenhorn's Guide to Gardening*) (New York: Grosset & Dunlap, 1971).

142   *A Parents' Guide to Child Safety.*

144   *Clear and Simple Gardening Guide.*

146   *The Wise Encyclopedia of Cookery.*

148   *Clear and Simple Gardening Guide.*

152   Jack G. Shiller, *Childhood Illness* (New York: Stein & Day Publishers, 1972).

152   Jessie Conrad, *A Handbook of Cookery for a Small House* (Garden City, N.Y.: Doubleday, Page & Co., 1923).

153   National Shooting Sports Foundation.

156   *The Wise Encyclopedia of Cookery.*

157   *The Everyday Reference Library.*

162   *Staying Slilm the Natural Way.*

162   David B. Wise, *The Wise Encyclopedia of Cookery* (New York: Wm. H. Wise & Co., 1949).

164   *A Parents' Guide to Child Safety.*

164   *Clear and Simple Gardening Guide.*

169   Eliot Wigginton, ed., *The Foxfire Book* (Garden City, N.Y.: Doubleday & Company, 1972), p. 246.

170   *Design for Flowers*, publication 138 of the Extension Division of Virginia Polytechnic Institute and State University, reprint of December 1977.

175   Vincent J. Fontana, *A Parents' Guide to Child Safety* (New York: Thomas Y. Crowell Company, 1973), p. 31.

176   *The Wise Encyclopedia of Cookery.*

184   Untitled research, 1971, courtesy of John Hopkins University Hospital, Baltimore, Md.

186   *A Parents' Guide to Child Safety.*

187   Arthur S. Freese, *Headaches: The Kinds and Cures* (Garden City, N.Y.: Doubleday and Co., 1973).

188   Leonard Haimes and Richard Tyson, *How to Triple Your Energy* (New York: Signet Books, New American Library, 1978).

189   *The Everyday Reference Library.*

190   Marcille Gary Williams, *The New Executive Woman* (Radnor, Pa.: Chilton Book Company, 1977).

192   *New Woman,* September–October, 1978.

194   Desmond Morris, *Intimate Behaviour* (New York: Random House, 1972).

198   *The Wise Encyclopedia of Cookery.*

200   *Travel & Leisure Magazine,* July 1978, p. 34.

200   *Travel & Leisure Magazine,* July 1978, p. 34.

204   The Administration of Aging.

206   Bob Gilsvik, *The Complete Book of Trapping* (Radnor, Pa.: Chilton Book Company, 1976).

209 *Allergy; What It Is and What to Do About It.*

217 The American National Red Cross.

219 Sherman A: Minton, Jr. and Madge Rutherford Minton, *Venomous Reptiles* (New York: Charles Scribner's Sons, 1969).

219 U. S. Department of Transportation, Transportation Guides, 1972.

221 *A Parents' Guide to Child Safety,* p. 14.

225 *The Seventeen Book of Etiquette and Entertaining,* p. 38.

226 U. S. Food and Drug Administration, *Guide to Foods, 1967.*

226 *The Everyday Reference Library.*

228 Peter Quimme, *The Signet Book of Coffee and Tea* (New York: Signet Books, New American Library, 1976).

228 *The Wise Encyclopedia of Cookery.*

230 Virginia Livingston, *Staying Slim the Natural Way* (New York: Western Publishing Co., 1972).

232 *Corporate Etiquette.*

234 National Selected Morticians Code of Ethics, 1971.

239 J. S. Bright, *The Dictionary of Palmistry* (Thompson, Conn.: Interculture Associates, 1959).

252 Lewis Copeland and Lawrence W. Lamm, eds., *The Everyday Reference Library* (Chicago: J. G. Ferguson and Associates, 1951).

256 *The New Executive Woman.*

259 *The Wise Encyclopedia of Cookery.*

262 Jeffrey Feinman, *How to Win! Sweepstakes, Contests, Lotteries, and Bingo* (Chicago: Playboy Press, 1976).

266 U. S. Department of Health, Education, and Welfare, Public Health Services, *Special Report,* 1975.

270 *The Everyday Reference Encyclopedia.*

273 Whitehall Harcourt, *Structural Essentials of English* (New York: Harcourt, Brace & World, 1965).

281 Enid Haupt, *The Seventeen Book of Etiquette and Entertaining* (New York: David McKay Co., 1963).

282 Dereck Williamson, *The Complete Book of Pitfalls* (New York: McCall Publishing Co., 1971), p. 19.

283 *Teach Spelling by All Means.*

284 "Mario Puzo's Godfatherly Rules for Writing a Novel," in *Time,* August 28, 1978.

284 Laurence Perrine, *Sound and Sense: An Introduction to Poetry* (New York: Harcourt, Brace & Company, 1956). (NOTE: in original source, these items were given as suggestions, not as hard and fast rules.)

285 *Mademoiselle,* November 1975.

286 Milla Alihan, *Corporate Etiquette* (New York: Weybright & Talley, 1970).

288 Courtesy of New Jersey State Bar Association, Trenton, N.J.

288 *Mademoiselle,* November 1975.

289 Arnold Lazarus and Allen Fay, *I Can If I Want To* (New York: William Morrow & Co., 1975).

291 *How to Be Outrageously Successful with Women.*

291 *How to Be Outrageously Successful with Women.*

297 "Transit in America," in *The Futurist,* June 1978.

298 *Inflation Fighter's Handbook.*

299 "Gossip Is True," in *The Star,* October 10, 1978.

308   Sir Winston Churchill, "Painting as a Pastime," in *Amid These Storms* (New York: Charles Scribner's and Sons, 1932).

309   New Jersey Mosquito Extermination Association, *Ten Commandments of Mosquito Control,* 1971.

310   Albert Lee, *Weather Wisdom* (Garden City, N.Y.: Doubleday & Company, 1976).

313   *The Complete Book of Pitfalls.*

315   *The New How to Keep House.*

315   *The Foxfire Book.*

316   *What to Do Till the Veterinarian Comes.*

317   *The Wise Encyclopedia of Cookery.*

319   Eliot Wigginton, ed., *The Foxfire Book* (Garden City, N.Y.: Doubleday & Company, 1972).

320   Jeffrey Feinman, *Inflation Fighter's Handbook* (New York: Award Books, Universal-Award House, 1976).

322   *Inflation Fighter's Handbook.*

326   William Hillcourt, *Field Book of Nature Activities and Conservation* (New York: G. P. Putnam's Sons, 1961).

334   Aerospace Education Foundation, *The Safe Driving Handbook* (New York: Grosset & Dunlap, 1970).

336   *Inflation Fighter's Handbook.*

337   *A Mariner's Guide to the Rules of the Road,* pp. 31–32.

338   George Landsman and Jay R. Walter, *Tax Guide and Financial Planning Book* (New York: Ventura Associates, 1978).

340   *What Every Woman (and Most Men) Should Know About Her Car.*

343   "Bedding Down," in *Seventeen,* February 1977.

347   *The New How to Keep House.*

348   *The New How to Keep House.*

348   *The New How to Keep House.*

350   *Travel & Leisure Magazine,* July 1978, p. 34.

355   James G. Driscoll, *Survival Tactics* (Princeton, N.J.: Dow Jones Books, 1973).

356   *What Every Woman (and Most Men) Should Know About Her Car.*

357   Dorothy Jacson, *What Every Woman (and Most Men) Should Know About Her Car* (Radnor, Pa.: Chilton Book Company, 1974).

359   *What to Do Till the Veterinarian Comes.*

360   Jean Pommery, *What to Do Till the Veterinarian Comes* (Radnor, Pa.: Chilton Book Company, 1976).

360   Hank Haynes, *There's a Fortune in Worms* (Chatsworth, Calif.: Brooke House, Crown Publishers, 1976).

362   Robert Walsh, *Pets: Every Owner's Encyclopedia* (New York: Paddington Press, 1978).

362   *Pets.*

364   *A Mariner's Guide to the Rules of the Road.*

364   *A Mariner's Guide to the Rules of the Road.*

366   "What You Need to Know Before You Sell Your Car," in *Glamour,* April 1978.

367   *A Mariner's Guide to the Rules of the Road.*

368   Consumers Union of United States, *The 1978 Buying Guide Issue of Consumer Reports* (Mount Vernon, N.Y.: Consumers Union of United States, 1977.)

368   "The Door in the Wall, Part I: An Experiment in Autohypnosis," in *Human Behavior,* June 1978.

370   Leonard Louis Levinson, *The Complete Book of Low Calorie Cooking* (New York: Hawthorn Books, 1964).

371   *The Complete Book of Low Calorie Cooking.*

374   Max S. Shapiro, ed., *Mathematics Encyclopedia* (Garden City, N.Y.: Doubleday & Company, 1977).

374   U.S. Consumer Product Safety Commission, *Your Safety,* 1975.

378   Keith Walters, *Horses* (Shawnee Mission, Kans.: Carnation Company, Milling Division, 1978).

379   *The You-Don't-Need-a-Man-to-Fix-It Book.*

381   *Inflation Fighter's Handbook.*

382   Jim Webb and Bart Houseman, *The You-Don't-Need-a-Man-to-Fix-It Book* (Garden City, N.Y.: Doubleday & Company, 1973).

383   Esther L. Guthrie, *Home Book of Animal Care* (New York: Harper & Row, 1966).

384   *Home Book of Animal Care.*

391   John Duggleby, "An Inside Lane to Expressway Safety," in *Discovery Magazine,* Autumn 1977.

393   *The Seventeen Book of Etiquette and Entertaining.*

393   *The Seventeen Book of Etiquette and Entertaining.*

394   *Inflation Fighter's Handbook.*

395   Bernard Waber, *How to Go About Laying an Egg* (Boston: Houghton Mifflin Company, 1963).

All rules, including this one, are meant to be broken.

ABOUT THE AUTHORS

Steve Kirschner is Vice President/Creative Director for Gillespie & Pavelec, a New Jersey advertising agency. His diversified background includes television production work with ABC Sports, advertising and creative direction with Edmund Scientific Company and science teaching. While away from the typewriter, he enjoys nature photography, wild birds, thoroughbred race horses and body building. Mr. Kirschner and his family enjoy the outdoor solitude of their country home in Medford, New Jersey.

Barry J. Pavelec, currently spends 3 days a week in New York City as Marketing Director of the Advertising Research Foundation. The balance of the week is occupied as President of the Publications Division of The Delta Group, a management information and consulting firm which produces newsletters. His past activities include serving as an advertising agency's Creative Director and Circulation Sales Manager for Barron's. He, his wife, Cathy, and 4 children live in South Brunswick, New Jersey.

Jeff Feinman is President of Ventura Associates, a New York marketing consulting firm. In addition, he has been involved in the publishing business on many levels; as a writer, agent and creator of book concepts. He also teaches at the New School for Social Research. Mr. Feinman is always involved in at least a dozen projects and lives by one abiding rule, which is not to live by the rules.

Ivor Parry (Illustrator) is a graduate of Pratt Institute and a former advertising art director. He has his own design firm in New York City. He was selected to illustrate this book because he understands the publisher's rule, "There're only ten days to do this three month job."

"It is more trouble to make a maxim than it is to do right."—
Mark Twain